Here is a new Lincoln story of the parallel lives of Horace Greeley, founder and editor of the *New York Tribune*, and Abraham Lincoln, lawyer and president. It covers, in richly documented detail, the points at which the lives of these famous contemporaries touched. The encounters were always dramatic; they usually led to friction; they sometimes set off sparks of fury and invective in the impulsive editor, and they often revealed irritation held in check only by the deep-seated patience of the cautious lawyer.

Lincoln and Greeley were not friends. In fact, they were never far from becoming enemies. Even so, their backgrounds, careers, ideals, and unswerving devotion to their country were amazingly similar. Both came from poor families; each had similarly haphazard schooling and upbringing, the one in Kentucky, Indiana, and ·Illinois, the other in New England and New York; both were guided by great, almost impossible, ambitions; both succeeded spectacularly. And when they first met in their early thirties, it was on the common ground of corresponding political beliefs.

The apex of their careers came at a time to try men's souls—the Civil War years. It was during these years that the man in the White House and the man in the most powerful editorial chair in the country, each in his own way and sometimes openly at cross purposes with the other, fought for the principles they both believed in—

rvation of the Union.
worship in this study.
editorials, and the
for the reader to
The book is not in-
of either Lincoln's or
rilliant study limited
It is a portrait of
nding, ruggedly in-
another, and to the
try in one of its most

Harlan Hoyt Horner,
arly years in Lincoln
llinois, and is a well
nd Greeley material.
of Illinois, Harvard,
ge for Teachers, and the University of Chicago. Later he was secretary to President Andrew Sloan Draper of the University of Illinois, and became Associate Commissioner of Higher Education of the State of New York. Among his previous publications are *The Life and Work of Andrew Sloan Draper*, and *The Growth of Lincoln's Faith*.

LINCOLN AND GREELEY

by **HARLAN HOYT HORNER**

THE UNIVERSITY OF ILLINOIS PRESS 1953

To the unfading memory of

Eugene Brandon Horner 1845–1890 and
Susan Cordelia (Sears) Horner 1852–1936

My special interest in Lincoln and Greeley dates from the centennial celebration of Lincoln's birth on February 12, 1909, and a like celebration of Greeley's birth on February 3, 1911. On the occasion of the Lincoln Centenary I was called upon, as Chief of the Administration Division of the University of the State of New York, to prepare a brochure for use in the schools of the state. My chief, Dr. Andrew Sloan Draper, State Commissioner of Education, wrote the preface for the brochure. I was impressed then, and still am, by the words with which Dr. Draper closed his brief message to the schools:

His life was the best expression we have ever had of the humanity, the industry, the sense, the conscience, the freedom, the justice, the progress, the unity, and the destiny of the Nation. His memory is our best human inspiration. So we may well honor ourselves by studying about him and by holding special exercises in the schools in memory of him upon the one hundredth anniversary of his birth.

Two years later came the hundredth anniversary of the birth of Horace Greeley. Subsequently, by special legislative action, the Division of Archives and History of the University of the State of New York was authorized to prepare a Memorial to Horace Greeley. My colleague, James Austin Holden, State Historian, edited the volume and wrote the introduction. I was impressed then, and still am, by the closing words Mr. Holden employed:

Taken all in all, Horace Greeley was one of those rare characters which appear once in an age and, like the comet flashing athwart the sky, make a brilliant path across human events and then disappear, their exact like possibly never to be seen again.

In commemoration of this great life, therefore, the Division of History of the University of the State of New York submits this publication, in the hope that another and younger generation to whom he is all but unknown may learn from it somewhat of the man who in the days of newspaper giants, towered above them all.

In the intervening forty years my principal avocation, shared fully for the second half of that period by my wife, Henrietta Calhoun

Horner, has been the vain but challenging effort to accumulate a private library which should contain all that has been printed, in our own and in other tongues, about Abraham Lincoln and Horace Greeley.

When my interest in these two great Americans was first aroused, I was moved by the prevailing literature. Lincoln had become a hero, a myth, a legend, a superman. I so regarded him. Greeley, so far as I knew anything about him, was always a crotchety old man with a fringe of white whiskers around his chin, a broad-brimmed slouch hat, and a wrinkled linen duster.

The years have given me a kinship with Lincoln and Greeley. They seem, by reason of my long association with them, to belong to me. So far as I permit myself hero-worship, it is bestowed upon Lincoln. He is no longer, however, above the clouds. His legs were always long enough to reach the ground, as he said any man's ought to be. The evidence of his uncommon, common sense now for me destroys all the myths. And my affection for Greeley has grown with the years. He was erratic, uncertain, impulsive, extraordinarily anxious to be noticed and to impress his convictions upon others, but he was above the crowd.

This book is not intended in any sense to be a history of Lincoln's and Greeley's time or a full account of their careers. It is an attempt to present their common experiences and especially to portray their relations and interactions upon the "great and durable element of popular action" to which they devoted their lives.

Albany, New York   HARLAN HOYT HORNER

contents

I was with the old-line Whigs from the origin to the end of that party.

Lincoln[1]

I clung fondly to the Whig party.

Greeley[2]

1 Fellow Whigs

Just when Abraham Lincoln and Horace Greeley first became aware of each other is not known, but that they saw each other in action for the first time at the great River and Harbor Convention, held in Chicago in 1847, is certain. Lincoln was then thirty-eight years old, a small-town lawyer, and one of the Illinois delegates from Sangamon County on his first overland journey to Chicago. His appearance was described by Elihu B. Washburne, convention delegate from Jo Daviess County, Illinois:

One afternoon, several of us sat on the sidewalk under the balcony in front of the Sherman House, and among the number the accomplished scholar and unrivaled orator, Lisle Smith. He suddenly interrupted the conversation by exclaiming, "There is Lincoln on the other side of the street. Just look at 'Old Abe,' " and from that time we called him "Old Abe." No one who saw him can forget his personal appearance at that time. Tall, angular and awkward, he had on a short-waisted, thin swallow-tail coat, a short vest of same material, thin pantaloons, scarcely coming down to his ankles, a straw hat and a pair of brogans with woolen socks.[3]

It is not surprising that Lincoln made little stir in the convention. The proceedings indicate merely that "Abraham Lincoln of Illinois, being called upon addressed the Convention briefly."[4] His remarks

---

[1] John G. Nicolay and John Hay, eds., *Complete Works of Abraham Lincoln*, V, 38.
[2] Horace Greeley, *Recollections of a Busy Life*, p. 285.
[3] Allen Thorndike Rice, *Reminiscences of Abraham Lincoln by Distinguished Men of His Time*, p. 16.
[4] Robert Fergus, comp., *Chicago River-and-Harbor Convention*, Fergus' Historical Series, Number Eighteen, p. 81.

were prompted by an address of David Dudley Field, the noted New York lawyer, who appeared in the convention as a "Strict Constructionist" and as a defender of President Polk. From his earliest political efforts Lincoln had been interested in the navigation of rivers and in internal improvements generally. He no doubt sprang to the defense of Whig principles, although the managers of the convention were at some pains to keep politics out of the meeting.

What is surprising is that Greeley, a big-city editor and a delegate from New York, took notice of Lincoln in reporting the proceedings for the *New York Tribune* which he had founded in 1841. In his report of July 6, he gave an account of the meeting for that day and noted that, "In the afternoon, Hon. Abraham Lincoln, a tall specimen of an Illinoian, just elected to Congress from the only Whig district in the State, was called out, and spoke briefly and happily in reply to Mr. Field."[5]

Thurlow Weed of Albany, New York, who reported the proceedings to his paper, the *Albany Evening Journal*, was apparently not impressed enough by Lincoln's speech to make any note of it, but at least one Chicago newspaper discovered his presence in the city.

Abraham Lincoln, the only Whig representative to Congress from this State, we are happy to see in attendance upon the Convention. This is his first visit to the commercial emporium of the State, and we have no doubt his visit will impress him more deeply, if possible, with the importance, and inspire a higher zeal for the great interest of River-and-Harbor improvements. We expect much from him as a representative in Congress, and we have no doubt our expectations will be more than realized, for never was reliance placed in a nobler heart and a sounder judgment. We know the banner he bears will never be soiled.[6]

While Greeley, who was then thirty-six years old, may not have presented as grotesque an appearance as Lincoln, he was nevertheless sufficiently peculiar to attract notice. A subsequent account of him may be regarded as indicating the way he appeared in 1847.

He was the most public character in the country. The oddities of his appearance and manner, the patriarchal head and face, the old hat and old white coat, the cravat awry, the shapeless trousers, the shambling gait, celebrated and exaggerated in print and caricature, made him one of the

---

[5] Rice, *op. cit.*, p. 141.
[6] *Chicago Journal*, July 6, 1847; Fergus, *op. cit.*, p. 138.

sights of New York, and would have been recognized at any crossroads in the United States.[7]

Greeley took a prominent part in the convention and was honored by being called upon to preside at a meeting of the Committee of the Whole which was held immediately after the adjournment of the regular sessions. He spoke during the convention and stepped down from the chair to speak at the meeting over which he presided.

In reporting the first day's proceedings of the convention, Thurlow Weed had this to say of an address by Greeley:

When Mr. Corwin closed there was a general call for "Greeley," whom Mr. Wentworth introduced to the Convention. Mr. Greeley remarked that he had hoped that his reputation as a bad speaker would have saved him from the embarrassment of addressing so large an assemblage. Mr. Greeley then spoke for half an hour with much effect in favor of the objects of the meeting. He was listened to with great attention and warmly cheered in concluding. Every word that Mr. Greeley uttered was full of truth and wisdom.[8]

The River and Harbor Convention in Chicago had been called at the suggestion of William Mosley Hall of Buffalo, New York, to voice a widespread protest against the veto by President Polk of a river and harbor bill. Although Chicago in 1847 was a city of sixteen thousand, and without a single railroad leading into it, twenty-five thousand delegates and visitors arrived, mostly by steamboat and stage, and were somehow accommodated. They came from Connecticut, Florida, Georgia, Indiana, Illinois, Iowa, Kentucky, Maine, Massachusetts, Michigan, Missouri, New Hampshire, New Jersey, New York, Ohio, Pennsylvania, Rhode Island, South Carolina, and Wisconsin. Among the distinguished delegates were Schuyler Colfax of Indiana; Justin Butterfield, Isaac N. Arnold, Norman B. Judd, John Wentworth, and Elihu B. Washburne of Illinois; Anson Burlingame of Massachusetts; Edward Bates of Missouri, chairman of the convention; David Dudley Field, John C. Spencer, and Thurlow Weed of New York; and Thomas Corwin of Ohio. Regrets were received from Daniel Webster, Henry Clay, Lewis Cass, and Martin Van Buren. It was perhaps the most significant, and certainly the largest, meeting that had ever been held

---

[7] Albert E. Pillsbury, "Memorial to Horace Greeley," *Proceedings and Commemorative Observances of 1911*, the University of the State of New York, p. 69.

[8] Fergus, *op. cit.*, p. 152.

in the country. Not until thirty-five years after adjournment were the full proceedings finally published.

The fifteen resolutions adopted by the convention, with almost complete unanimity, expressed the judgment of the delegates that the improvement of rivers and harbors throughout the country was highly desirable and was a proper and constitutional function of the Federal government. A committee of representatives from each of the states sending delegates was constituted to transmit the proceedings of the convention to President Polk and to the House and the Senate. The committee was also requested "to collect accurate information of the nature and extent of the trade and commerce of the Lakes and navigable Rivers, and the amount of the losses of lives, property, and vessels by storm, for want of adequate harbors, or in consequence of obstructions in the navigable Rivers of the United States and the condition of our harbors."[9]

Greeley and Weed both gave glowing accounts to their papers of the principal addresses at the convention, notably those of Thomas Corwin of Ohio, Thomas Butler King of Georgia, Andrew Stewart of Pennsylvania, and Governor William Bebb of Ohio. But they were agreed that the most forceful, constructive, and inspiring address was made quite unexpectedly by Edward Bates of St. Louis, the presiding officer, just before the adjournment of the regular sessions. Weed regarded Mr. Bates's speech as "most appropriate" and declared that "The speech, if ever published as delivered, will be pronounced one of the richest specimens of American eloquence. He was interrupted continually by cheer upon cheer; and at its close, the air rung with shout after shout, from the thousands in attendance."[10] Greeley reported Mr. Bates's speech as able and forceful "and replete with the soul of eloquence. I will not attempt to give an account of this wonderful speech. . . . No account that can now be given will do it justice. . . . His speech was greeted at its close by the whole convention rising and cheering long and fervently."[11] These views of Greeley and Weed are especially noteworthy in the light of subsequent events; at the Wigwam Convention at Chicago, which nominated Lincoln for the presidency thirteen years later, Weed championed William H. Seward, and Greeley was the earnest advocate of Edward Bates. Seward became Lincoln's Secretary of State; and Bates, his Attorney-General.

[9] *Ibid.*, p. 85.
[10] *Ibid.*, p. 160.
[11] *Ibid.*, p. 142.

For his time and environment Lincoln became a remarkably success-ful lawyer; Greeley became the greatest editor and publicist of America; and politics was their meat and drink throughout their lives. Greeley professed to be able to recall that at nine years of age he had sympa-thized with the uprising in New England against the admission of Mis-souri as a slave state and that he had known "disappointment and cha-grin" at the enactment of the Missouri Compromise. He was thirteen years of age at the time of the presidential campaign of 1824 and eagerly endorsed the electoral vote of New England which "was cast solid for John Quincy Adams." At seventeen, well into his printer's apprenticeship at East Poultney, Vermont, he recalled, "we were badly beaten," when in 1828 Adams went down to defeat before Andrew Jackson.[12]

Lincoln was hardly as precocious as Greeley, even in politics, and suffered the handicap of having to extricate himself from the political beliefs of his family and of the region in which he lived in Indiana. Thomas Lincoln and his tribe and, indeed, nearly all people in poor circumstances in southern Indiana in Lincoln's youth were Jackson Democrats. At fifteen years of age, Lincoln no doubt joined with his father and the neighbors in shouting for Andrew Jackson in 1824. But by the time of the next presidential campaign, through the influence of William Jones, the storekeeper for whom he worked at Gentryville, Lincoln had become a regular reader of the *Louisville Journal* which "was violently opposed to Jackson and fervently supported Clay." At nineteen, the young Jackson Democrat by inheritance had quietly be-come a National Republican by personal conviction. He did not say much about his changed attitude at the time; he was already giving unmistakable signs of the political cunning of which he was later to be master.[13]

By 1832, the year of the first presidential election in which Lincoln and Greeley were old enough to vote, they had come to the same broad political platform and both cast their votes for Henry Clay. They were already worshiping at the shrine of that great statesman, and he was almost literally to be their political idol for the next twenty years. Clay was nominated unanimously in a convention held by the National Re-publicans at Baltimore on December 12, 1831. The principles of the National Republicans became the nucleus of the Whig party, founded

---

[12] Greeley, *op. cit.*, pp. 106–08.
[13] Albert J. Beveridge, *Abraham Lincoln*, I, 96–99.

in 1834.[14] Lincoln and Greeley lived through the rise and fall of the Whig party and were closely identified with it throughout its active history. But Lincoln was careful in the beginning not to mix state and national politics. While "he was an avowed Clay man" in 1832, he did not mention Clay or refer to national issues in the circular he addressed to "The People of Sangamon County" on March 9 announcing his candidacy "for the honorable office" of representative in the General Assembly of Illinois.[15] In the fall of 1832 Greeley paid a visit to his beloved New England and returned to New York just in time to "vote right heartily for the anti-Jackson ticket, but without avail."[16]

In 1836 Henry Clay was not a candidate for the presidency. The Democrats were strongly united for Martin Van Buren of New York on whom President Jackson had let his mantle fall. The Whigs were hopelessly divided, having three tickets in the field, headed by General William Henry Harrison of Ohio, Daniel Webster of Massachusetts, and Hugh L. White of Tennessee. White was an anti-Jackson Democrat affiliated with the Whig party and was supported by the Whigs of the West and Southwest. Lincoln was now a candidate for a second term in the General Assembly of Illinois. A suggestion signed "Many Voters," appearing in the *Sangamo Journal*, that all the candidates "show their hands," brought from Lincoln under date of June 3, 1836, the response: "If alive on the first Monday in November, I shall vote for Hugh L. White for President."[17]

Greeley was strong for General Harrison and in later years recalled: "I was among the very few in the Eastern States who had taken any interest in bringing forward General Harrison as a candidate, believing that there was the raw material for a good run in his history and character; but this was not generally credited."[18] At election time, Lincoln—who had been a clerk, mill roustabout, postmaster, surveyor, and bankrupt storekeeper—had been admitted to the bar and was thinking of starting practice in Springfield. Greeley, a former typesetter, was editing his own paper in New York and staving off his creditors. They stuck to Whig standard bearers while differing in their choice of presidential candidates. Their votes were for a second time without avail, and they were never reconciled to the election of Van Buren.

[14] James Albert Woodburn, *American Politics. Political Parties and Party Problems in the United States*, pp. 43–55.
[15] Nicolay and Hay, *op. cit.*, VI, 31; I, 1–9.
[16] Greeley, *op. cit.*, p. 90.
[17] Nicolay and Hay, *op. cit.*, I, 14–15.
[18] Greeley, *op. cit.*, p. 112.

The Whigs made early preparation for the presidential campaign of 1840. The first Whig National Convention was held at Harrisburg, Pennsylvania, beginning on December 4, 1839. "Of its doings," Greeley "was a deeply interested observer." At the opening of the convention there was a plurality for Henry Clay but not a majority. Harrison emerged as the successful candidate, again to be pitted against Van Buren. Greeley was well pleased at Harrison's nomination and labored unceasingly for the success of the ticket. After the election he recorded his satisfaction vigorously:

The Verdict of the People has been rendered, and its thunderous tones are now pealing through the land! It is the knell of Loco-Focoism; it is the funeral dirge of Van Burenism; it is the death-note, we will fondly hope, of Official Insolence and unblushing Corruption! Parties must ever exist, and party struggles—often fierce and vehement—must from time to time convulse the country, but we hope never again to see the day when One Hundred Thousand Office-Holders and other direct dependents on the bounty of the Federal Government shall openly marshal, drill, animate and lead on a party having for its chief end the perpetuation of power in the hands of their leader and chief and of the honors and emoluments of public station in their group. Never before in the country was so gross and sweeping a violation of the vital principles of Freedom exhibited as in this contest.[19]

In Illinois Lincoln worked with equal zeal for the election of Harrison. Shortly after the Harrisburg Convention, as a member of a state Whig committee, he prepared a circular addressed to local county committees throughout the state in which he rallied the Whigs to the support of their candidate:

Our Whig brethren throughout the Union have met in convention, and after due deliberation and mutual concessions have elected candidates for the presidency and the vice-presidency not only worthy of our cause, but worthy of the support of every true patriot who would have our country redeemed, and her institutions honestly and faithfully administered. . . . Our intention is to organize the whole State, so that every Whig can be brought to the polls in the coming presidential contest. . . . Inclosed is a prospectus for a newspaper to be continued until after the presidential election. It will be superintended by ourselves and every Whig must take it. . . . We have the numbers, and if properly organized and exerted, with the gallant Harrison at our head, we shall meet our foes and conquer them in all parts of the Union.[20]

---

[19] *Log Cabin*, November 9, 1840.
[20] Nicolay and Hay, *op. cit.*, I, 142–45.

Lincoln was made an Illinois elector. He stumped the state and aided in the preparation of the Whig campaign paper, the *Old Soldier*. Although the electoral vote of Illinois was cast solidly for Van Buren, Harrison won; Lincoln and Greeley had at last voted for a candidate who was elected. But Harrison's triumph was short-lived; barely a month after his inauguration he was in his grave. Vice-President Tyler, who succeeded Harrison, was a disappointment to both Lincoln and Greeley, for he promptly abandoned the Whig platform and policy.

In the campaign of 1844, Henry Clay made another fruitless bid for the presidency. Lincoln was again made an elector and spoke throughout Illinois for the Whig ticket. He also made some speeches in Indiana, including a visit to his old home at Gentryville. He was now earnestly anxious to go to Congress, as the following letter to Joshua F. Speed testifies:

Springfield, March 24, 1843.

Dear Speed: . . . We had a meeting of the Whigs of the county here on last Monday to appoint delegates to a district convention; and Baker beat me, and got the delegation instructed to go for him. The meeting, in spite of my attempt to decline it, appointed me one of the delegates; so that in getting Baker the nomination I shall be fixed a good deal like a fellow who is made a groomsman to a man that has cut him out and is marrying his own dear "gal." About the prospects of your having a namesake in our town, can't say exactly yet.

A. *Lincoln.*[21]

Greeley was at his best in promoting Clay. Indeed, he placed Clay's name at the masthead of the *Tribune's* editorial page in 1842, two years ahead of time, as he then said, "there to remain until he has been elected to the high status which he has so richly deserved, and which he is so eminently qualified to adorn."[22] In addition to the regular issues of his paper he published a weekly, the *Clay Tribune*, throughout the campaign. He was never more determined in his whole tumultuous career. Reviewing this campaign later he said, "from the day of his nomination in May to that of his defeat in November, I gave every hour, every thought to his election. . . . I travelled and spoke much; I wrote, I think, an average of three columns of the *Tribune* each secular day, and I gave the residue of the hours I could save from sleep to watching the canvass and doing whatever I could to render our side of it more

---

[21] *Ibid.*, p. 261.
[22] *New York Tribune*, September 7, 1842. All references, unless otherwise indicated, are to the daily issue. (Cited hereafter as the *Tribune*.)

effective."[23] Greeley took Clay's defeat well. The day James K. Polk was inaugurated as President, Greeley said that Tyler had been retired to a "fitting obscurity" and that the nation would rejoice at "this consummation." He held that Mr. Polk was not a man of genius nor of commanding talent but he had considerable shrewdness and great tact and that he was not likely to cause his friends "to blush for him" and to "feel ashamed" that they had aided in electing him. He said that Polk might do far better than Tyler and that he could "hardly by possibility do worse."[24]

Again Lincoln and Greeley had cast their votes for losing candidates. Lincoln saw the entire electoral vote of Illinois go for James K. Polk, the Democratic candidate. Their disheartenment at an election was perhaps never greater.

The presidential campaign of 1848 found Lincoln immersed in politics between the long and short sessions of the Thirtieth Congress to which he had been elected a member in 1847. The Democratic National Convention began its sessions at Baltimore on May 22, and on May 25, on the fourth ballot, nominated Lewis Cass of Michigan for President.[25] The Whig National Convention for 1848 held its first session in Philadelphia on June 7, and on June 9, on the fourth ballot, nominated General Zachary Taylor for President.[26]

Lincoln and Greeley were in attendance at the Whig Convention and among the active participants in the log-rolling which took place.[27] Their differing views at this time illustrate their life-long habits in politics: Lincoln was a political realist, Greeley was a political idealist. For several months, as shown by his letters, Lincoln had believed that Taylor was the only man who could be elected on the Whig ticket; he therefore took the position that Taylor was the man to be nominated. He did not presume to compare Clay, who was again a candidate, with Taylor, nor to abandon his fealty to the fundamental principles advocated by Clay. He merely held that "Mr. Clay's chance for election is just no chance at all" and worked hard for Taylor, the man he thought could be elected.[28] Greeley who observed "that the shrewd, influential, managing politicians were generally for Taylor" labored heroically and

---

[23] Greeley, *op. cit.*, pp. 166–67.

[24] *Tribune*, March 4, 1845.

[25] Horace Greeley and John F. Cleveland, eds., A *Political Text-book for 1860*, pp. 16–17.

[26] *Ibid.*, p. 15.

[27] Benjamin P. Thomas, *Lincoln, 1847–1853*, pp. 76–77; Greeley, *op. cit.*, pp. 210–12.

[28] Nicolay and Hay, *op. cit.*, II, 16–17.

uncompromisingly for Clay.[29] The final electoral vote stood: Taylor, 171; Scott, 60; Clay, 35; Webster, 14. The Taylor managers, because of the great dissatisfaction among the Clayites, finally gave up their own slate and consented to the nomination of Millard Fillmore of New York for Vice-President.

Greeley took Clay's defeat very hard. He admitted that Clay had committed errors and that the imputations of faults of temper or mistakes in judgment hurled against him had some foundation in truth. He insisted, however, that Clay of all living men had earliest and most fully comprehended the true genius of the American government and that he was "among the first who elaborated that comprehensive policy of Internal Improvement and Industrial Protection justly termed THE AMERICAN SYSTEM."[30] Greeley ultimately supported Taylor and voted for him, but recalled "I did not hurry myself to secure his election."[31] The *Tribune* did not come out for Taylor and Fillmore until September 29, 1848.

Lincoln returned to Congress from the Philadelphia Convention predicting "a most over-whelming, glorious triumph,"[32] and at once began to devise ways of aiding the Whig ticket, as this letter to Richard S. Thomas will indicate:

Washington, June 19, 1848

Friend Thomas: Do you know any democrats who will vote for Taylor? and if so, what are their names? Do you know any Whigs who will not vote for him? and if so, what are their names? and for whom will they vote? Please answer this just as soon as it is received.

Yours as ever,
A. Lincoln.[33]

"All is high hope and confidence," Lincoln wrote Herndon, his law partner in Springfield, and urged him to rally the young men of Springfield for the election of "Old Zach" in a "Rough and Ready Club," insisting that everyone could do his part, some could speak, some could sing, and all could "holler."[34] Although he had planned to stay only two weeks in Washington after the adjournment of Congress in August

---

[29] Greeley, *op. cit.*, p. 212.
[30] *Tribune*, June 13, 1848.
[31] Greeley, *op. cit.*, p. 215.
[32] Nicolay and Hay, *op. cit.*, II, 27.
[33] Gilbert A. Tracy, *Uncollected Letters of Abraham Lincoln*, p. 33.
[34] Nicolay and Hay, *op. cit.*, II, 49–53.

"to frank documents,"[35] he stayed more than three weeks and, in addition to franking documents, spoke at Whig meetings in Washington and in Maryland. In September before heading for Illinois he invaded New England and got himself invited to speak at several Whig meetings.

Both the Democrats and the Whigs were having troubles. The Barnburners, a discontented faction of the Democratic party, not satisfied with the nomination of General Cass and resolved "to be anti-slavery men first and party men afterwards,"[36] held a convention of their own at Utica, New York, in the summer of 1848 and nominated Martin Van Buren for President. The National Free-Soil party, organized in 1847–48 to oppose the extension of slavery into the territories, held a convention at Buffalo in August and also accepted Van Buren as their presidential candidate. Van Buren's running mate for Vice-President was, strangely enough, his life-long political opponent, Charles Francis Adams, the son of John Quincy Adams. John P. Hale, who had been nominated for President by the Liberty party, also withdrew in Van Buren's favor, and many Whigs in Massachusetts, led by Adams and Charles Sumner, were going over to the Free-Soilers.

Lincoln apparently saw an opportunity to put in an oar. He appeared at Worcester, Massachusetts, on September 12, the day before the assembling of the Whig State Convention, without notice and without invitation. As it turned out the local Rough and Ready Club had arranged a mass meeting at the city hall on the eve of the convention and was embarrassed because none of the invited speakers would accept. The strange Whig congressman from Illinois readily consented to save the day. A newspaper in Boston said: "Mr. Lincoln has a very tall and thin figure, with an intellectual face, showing a searching mind, and a cool judgment. He spoke in a clear and cool, and a very eloquent manner, for an hour and a half, carrying the audience with him in his able arguments and brilliant illustrations—only interrupted by warm and frequent applause."[37]

It would seem that Lincoln had anticipated that he would be called upon. The local Whig managers warmed up to him at once. He spoke briefly the following day at an open-air meeting, attended the Whig State Convention during the day, and was a guest at an elaborate dinner

---

[35] Tracy, *op. cit.*, p. 34.
[36] Woodburn, *op. cit.*, p. 79.
[37] *Boston Daily Advertiser*, September 14, 1848.

in the evening given by Levi Lincoln, a former governor of Massachusetts, a distant relative, and a presidential elector. Thereafter he spoke at New Bedford, Lowell, Dorchester, Chelsea, Dedham, Cambridge, and Taunton, and returned to Boston on Friday, September 22, to attend a huge mass meeting held in Tremont Temple.[38] At this meeting the principal speaker was William H. Seward of New York who had been four years governor of the state and was then slated for the United States Senate. Lincoln followed Seward, "spoke about an hour, and made a powerful and convincing speech."[39]

Starting for Illinois, Lincoln did not overlook an opportunity to call on Thurlow Weed at Albany, New York. Mr. Weed took him to see Millard Fillmore, Taylor's running mate, who was state comptroller at Albany. The Illinois congressman apparently did not make a deep impression on Weed. His paper, the *Albany Evening Journal*, failed to record Lincoln's presence in the city. The rival paper, the *Albany Atlas and Argus*, a Democratic organ, also overlooked Lincoln's visit. Thirteen years later Lincoln was to be welcomed in Albany by thousands and escorted to the Old Capitol to address the joint Houses of the New York Legislature, and four years thereafter a procession was to move continually all night long and half the day following through the Old Capitol where his body lay in state. Shortly after Lincoln was nominated for President at the Wigwam Convention in Chicago in May, 1860, Mr. Weed, at the invitation and suggestion of Judge David Davis and Leonard Swett, chief among Lincoln's managers and advisers, called upon Lincoln at Springfield and was surprised to discover that the presidential candidate was the Illinois congressman who had once visited him in Albany. "I had supposed," Weed said, "until we now met, that I had never seen Mr. Lincoln, having forgotten that in the fall of 1848, when he took the stump in New England, he called upon me at Albany, and that we went to see Mr. Fillmore, who was then the Whig candidate for Vice-President."[40]

En route to Springfield, Lincoln addressed a large Whig meeting at Chicago on October 6, and another at Peoria on October 9, reaching home on October 10. Before the election in November he canvassed "quite fully his own district in Illinois."[41] On November 7 Lincoln cast

---

[38] Thomas, *op. cit.*, pp. 90–91; Percy C. Eggleston, *Lincoln in New England.*
[39] *Boston Atlas*, September 23, 1848. See also F. Lauriston Bullard, "Lincoln's 'Conquest' of New England," *The Abraham Lincoln Quarterly*, II, 49–79.
[40] Harriet A. Weed and Thurlow Weed Barnes, eds., *The Life of Thurlow Weed*, I, 602–03.
[41] Nicolay and Hay, *op. cit.*, VI, 37.

his vote at Springfield for the Whig presidential electors as did Greeley in New York. This time they had picked the winning candidate. "Old Zach" was elected with 163 electoral votes against 127 for General Cass. But again their victory was brief, for President Taylor served only a year and four months before he died on June 9, 1850.

Shortly after the inauguration in 1849 Lincoln employed every means at his command to secure an appointment from President Taylor as commissioner of the General Land Office. Lincoln's letters reveal how earnestly he sought the position.[42] "It will now mortify me deeply," he wrote on April 25, "if General Taylor's administration shall trample all my wishes in the dust." His humiliation was complete, for his wishes were wholly disregarded. He did not nourish resentment, however, and promptly accepted the invitation of a committee of citizens of Chicago to deliver a eulogy on Zachary Taylor at a public meeting in the city hall, which was held on July 25, 1850. Lincoln said that the American people in electing General Taylor to the presidency had shown their appreciation of his "sterling but unobtrusive qualities" and had done their country a service and themselves "an imperishable honor."[43]

Greeley also came through handsomely. He was in Syracuse, New York, when word of Taylor's death reached him, and he dispatched a characteristic message to the *Tribune:*

I never spoke nor wrote to Gen. Taylor, nor sought his acquaintance in any way. To the extent of my ability and industry, I opposed to the last his selection as the Whig candidate for President. I believed that his education and political knowledge were not such as that office required, and that one serious consequence of his selection would be an inflammation of the youthful passion for Military achievement and renown which is one of the chief perils of our Republic. That he was patriotic, brave, upright and naturally sagacious, I did not doubt; that his heart was generous, kind and true, who ever doubted? That he has done better as President than was anticipated is, I think, a very general conviction. Peace to the ashes, honor to the memory of the just and good man![44]

The presidential campaign of 1852 lacked the spirit of violent controversy best calculated to stir both Lincoln and Greeley to action, and witnessed the virtual dissolution of the Whig party to which they had been faithful throughout its existence. The Democratic National Con-

---

[42] Paul M. Angle, *New Letters and Papers of Lincoln*, pp. 55–60. See also Nicolay and Hay, *op. cit.*, II, 104–27.
[43] Angle, *op. cit.*, pp. 67–76.
[44] *Tribune*, July 17, 1850.

vention, assembling at Baltimore on June 1, nominated Franklin Pierce of New Hampshire for President on the forty-ninth ballot, rejecting Douglas, Buchanan, Marcy, and Cass. William R. King of Alabama was named for Vice-President. The Whig National Convention was also held at Baltimore, convening on June 16. On the fifty-third ballot General Winfield Scott, hero of the Mexican War, was nominated for President in preference to Millard Fillmore and Daniel Webster. William A. Graham of North Carolina was named for Vice-President. The Whigs took the same position as the Democrats on the vital issue of the day, the Compromise of 1850, both pledging themselves to adhere to a faithful execution of the acts embodied in the Compromise and deprecating any further agitation of the slavery question.[45] The platforms of the two parties, almost identical, left little ammunition for Lincoln, the campaign orator and stump speaker, or for Greeley, the newspaper editor and pamphleteer.

This period is almost the leanest in Lincoln's political career. According to the official record he did not exercise his customary bent for letter writing or speech making. He was on the Scott electoral ticket and he served as the Illinois member of the National Whig Committee. On his own testimony he "did something in the way of canvassing, but owing to the hopelessness of the cause in Illinois he did less than in previous presidential canvasses." His apathy in the campaign may have been due in part to the fact that "upon his return from Congress he went to the practice of law with greater earnestness than ever before."[46]

Greeley vigorously opposed the nomination of Fillmore because he held that Fillmore could not be elected. He urged the nomination of Scott because he thought Scott could be elected. In this view he was following the position Lincoln had taken in 1848 when he preferred Taylor to Clay. The *Tribune* published and advertised widely a campaign life of General Scott. Not satisfied with the platform adopted by the Whigs, Greeley wrote and published his own platform, which was a bit more faithful to traditional Whig doctrine than the official document.[47] He then addressed himself throughout the campaign to expounding almost daily in his paper the relatively greater virtues of Scott over Pierce. "Admitting that Mr. Pierce is a good citizen and a respectable man," he said, "there is nothing about him to be named beside the lofty character, the eminent abilities displayed in important civil, as

---

[45] Horace Greeley, *The American Conflict*, I, 222–23.
[46] Nicolay and Hay, *op. cit.*, VI, 37.
[47] *Tribune*, June 24, 1852.

well as military affairs, and the illustrious services of Winfield Scott. The name of the one is indelibly identified with his country's fame, but were the other to be removed from life tomorrow, the history of America might be written without the slightest need for recording that he had ever lived."[48]

The Free-Soil party at a convention held at Pittsburgh on August 11, 1852, nominated John P. Hale of New Hampshire for President and George W. Julian of Indiana for Vice-President. The Free-Soilers did not carry a single state, and such gains as they made were at the expense of General Scott. Again Lincoln and Greeley cast their votes for a losing candidate. Scott carried only Massachusetts, Vermont, Kentucky, and Tennessee. "Never before," said Greeley, "was there such an overwhelming defeat of a party that had hoped for success."[49]

In the midst of the campaign Lincoln and Greeley were called upon to mourn the passing of the great Whig leader whose political philosophy had been their guide. Henry Clay died on June 29, 1852, and was spared the dissolution of the party he had nurtured for twenty years. On July 16 the citizens of Springfield, Illinois, gathered in the Statehouse to listen to a eulogy by Abraham Lincoln, who pictured Henry Clay as "the most loved and most implicitly followed by friends, and the most dreaded by opponents, of all living American politicians" and declared "there has never been a moment since 1824 till after 1848 when a very large portion of the American people did not cling to him with an enthusiastic hope and purpose of still elevating him to the Presidency." Lincoln went on to voice a universal judgment when he said:

Mr. Clay's predominant sentiment, from first to last, was a deep devotion to the cause of human liberty—a strong sympathy with the oppressed everywhere, and an ardent wish for their elevation. With him this was a primary and all-controlling passion. Subsidiary to this was the conduct of his whole life. He loved his country partly because it was his own country, and mostly because it was a free country; and he burned with a zeal for its advancement, prosperity, and glory, because he saw in such the advancement, prosperity, and glory of human liberty, human right, and human nature.[50]

Greeley had been more devoted to Henry Clay than to any other public figure. The day after Clay's death the entire editorial page of the *Tribune* was given to his eulogy and to accounts of his life and public

---

[48] *Ibid.*, October 7, 1852.
[49] Greeley, *American Conflict*, I, 224.
[50] Nicolay and Hay, *op. cit.*, II, 155–77.

service. The columns of the editorial page were encased in heavy black borders. Greeley wrote,

> *For this man had a large, warm, gallant human heart, a true, lofty, generous, manly soul. By nature frank, brave and cordial, he drew kindred souls to him by the power of an electric sympathy, and kindled noble impulses in breasts of common mold. . . . He sought National greatness and glory through the facilitation and cheapening of internal intercourse, the creation of new branches of Industry, the improvement of National resources, rather than through the devastation of foreign territories and the dismemberment of foreign countries. Of that wise and beneficent system of policy justly known as the American System, he was one of the founders and the foremost among its untiring and efficient champions.*[51]

On October 24 of that same year Daniel Webster also died. The Whig party, shorn of its two great long-time leaders in less than six months, defeated that November in the presidential election, and without a unified national policy, was rapidly coming to an end. It yet remained for the repeal of the Missouri Compromise by the Kansas–Nebraska Act to bring on its demise. By the time of the next presidential election in 1856, a new party had come into existence in which Lincoln and Greeley were to be deeply concerned for the rest of their lives.[52]

---

[51] *Tribune*, June 30, 1852.
[52] For full discussion of Lincoln's experiences as a Whig, see Beveridge, *op. cit.*, Vol. I; and Don C. Seitz, *Lincoln the Politician*. For accounts of Greeley as a Whig, see Henry Luther Stoddard, *Horace Greeley, Printer, Editor, Crusader*; William Harlan Hale, *Horace Greeley, Voice of the People*; and Jeter A. Isely, *Horace Greeley and the Republican Party*.

I was born, and have ever remained, in the most humble walks of life.

Lincoln[1]

All were measurably poor—yet seldom were any hungry.

Greeley[2]

2 Common grounds

There was reason enough why Lincoln and Greeley became stalwart Whigs and devoted disciples of Henry Clay. Their paternal ancestors, six generations back, came to America from England in the time of Charles I and Cromwell. Lincoln's ancestor, Samuel Lincoln, was a weaver from Hingham; and Greeley's ancestor, Andrew Greele, was a miller from near Nottingham. Samuel Lincoln settled at Hingham, Massachusetts, and died there on May 26, 1690.[3] Andrew Greele—the surname was not spelled Greeley until the third generation in America —settled at Salisbury, Massachusetts, and died there on June 30, 1697.[4]

The Lincolns were restless. They migrated from Massachusetts to New Jersey, to Pennsylvania, to Virginia, to Kentucky, to Indiana, and finally to Illinois. The Greeleys were less adventurous, moving from Massachusetts to New Hampshire, to Vermont, to Pennsylvania, and finally to New York. The early generations of both the Lincolns and the Greeleys were prolific, with families ranging from five to eighteen. Until Abraham Lincoln and Horace Greeley appeared, there were no especially distinguished men in either direct line. They were weavers, millers, blacksmiths, ironmongers, carpenters, and farmers, mainly plain, honest, respectable citizens. With the exception of Ezekiel Greeley, a great-grandfather of Horace, who was a lawyer as well as a

---

[1] John G. Nicolay and John Hay, eds., *Complete Works of Abraham Lincoln*, I, 8.
[2] Horace Greeley, *Recollections of a Busy Life*, pp. 23–24.
[3] Waldo Lincoln, *History of the Lincoln Family*, pp. 1–7; Henry Lea and J. R. Hutchinson, *The Ancestry of Abraham Lincoln*, pp. 1–32.
[4] George Hiram Greeley, *Genealogy of the Greely-Greeley Family*.

farmer, not one of the Greeleys and Lincolns in the direct lines practiced a profession. There was not a college graduate among them.

Of Lincoln's father, Thomas, the best than can be said is that the record shows him to have been an honest, law-abiding citizen who never harmed anyone. He was always looking for a bend in the road to bring him fortune, but he never prospered in his several moves from one farm to another in Kentucky, Indiana, and Illinois. At sixty-eight years of age he begged his son, then a congressman, for twenty dollars to save his land in southern Illinois from sale.[5] Improvident and shiftless—it is hard to make out any other case for him—he died at Goose Nest Prairie, near Farmington, Illinois, on January 17, 1851. Thousands of pilgrims now visit his grave every year because of the one great distinction of his less than ordinary life—he was the father of Abraham Lincoln.[6]

Zaccheus Greeley, the father of Horace, was not unlike Thomas Lincoln. He was honest and inoffensive, and, it would seem, more disposed to hard work than Thomas Lincoln. Reverses came to him early, and he sought to improve his lot by changing locations. Losing his land in New Hampshire, he struggled for a time against great odds in Vermont and finally ventured into the wilds of Erie County, Pennsylvania. He eventually acquired some land in Pennsylvania but never realized the quiet, peaceful contentment and sense of success which had characterized the lives of his New England ancestors. Like Thomas Lincoln, looking for the golden bend in the road, he went farther afield than any of his American forebears and on the whole accomplished less than any of them. The end of the road for this hardy but ineffectual pioneer came at Wayne, New York, on December 18, 1867.[7]

In tracing the ancestry of great men to discover inherited qualities of character and personality, biographers and genealogists persist in sticking mainly to the paternal side. Thus inheritances which may have come from the maternal line are often undervalued or overlooked. It is not possible to go back with assurance for six generations in America in tracing the maternal ancestors of Lincoln and Greeley.

Fruitless but perhaps praiseworthy efforts have been exerted to pro-

[5] Nicolay and Hay, *op. cit.*, II, 96.

[6] William E. Barton, *The Lineage of Lincoln*, pp. 82–83; Albert J. Beveridge, *Abraham Lincoln*, I, 1–99; Harry E. Pratt, *The Personal Finances of Abraham Lincoln*, pp. 3–5, 60–61; Raymond Warren, *The Prairie President*, pp. 1–18.

[7] Greeley, *op. cit.*, pp. 55–59, 78–79, 426; William Harlan Hale, *Horace Greeley, Voice of the People*, pp. 1–14; James Parton, *The Life of Horace Greeley*, pp. 52–56, 108.

vide an honorable lineage for Lincoln's mother, Nancy Hanks.[8] Distinguished authorities have frankly acknowledged that she was born out of wedlock.[9] The record of the Hanks family in America is a chain with many weak, broken, and even missing links. There was a Thomas Hanks in Virginia as early as 1653. Whether he was the father of William Hanks, married to one Sarah ——— about June, 1678, in Rappahannock County, Virginia, is not known. It is believed that William and Sarah Hanks had a son John, who was married about June, 1714, to one Katherine ———. They had a son Joseph, born in North Farnham Parish, Virginia, on December 20, 1725. Joseph married Ann Lee. It is claimed that they had a daughter Lucy, born about 1765, who came with the family to Kentucky about 1786. Lucy Hanks brought with her a daughter Nancy, then about two years old, whose father is not known. Nancy married Thomas Lincoln and became the mother of Abraham. According to research by Oliver R. Barrett, the famous Lincoln collector, Lincoln entered the record in his stepmother's Bible that "Thos. Lincoln was born Jan. the 6th A.D. 1778 and was married June 12th 1806 to Nancy Hanks who was born Feb. 5th 1784."[10] This is all the known ancestral record of Nancy Hanks.

The maternal ancestry of Horace Greeley presents a clearer picture. His mother's maiden name was Mary Woodburn. The founder of her branch of the Woodburn family in America was John Woodburn who came from Londonderry, Ireland, to Londonderry, New Hampshire, about 1720 and took up an allotment of one hundred and twenty acres which was "by his industry" transformed into a farm. This farm remained in the possession of his descendants for many years. John Woodburn flourished at Londonderry, was married twice, and died in 1780. David Woodburn, oldest son of John, carried on the Woodburn tradition at Londonderry. He married Margaret Clark, and they had a daughter Mary, who became the wife of Zaccheus Greeley and the mother of Horace.[11]

Mary Woodburn's early environment was quite different from that of Nancy Hanks. Her mother died when she was five years old, and she received her early education from her aged grandmother. Greeley left

---

[8] Caroline Hanks Hitchcock, *Nancy Hanks, The Story of Abraham Lincoln's Mother;* Louis A. Warren, *Lincoln's Parentage and Childhood;* Lea and Hutchinson, *op. cit.*

[9] Barton, *op. cit.,* p. 214; Beveridge, *op. cit.,* I, 14; Carl Sandburg, *Abraham Lincoln: The Prairie Years,* I, 11–12.

[10] Carl Sandburg, *Lincoln Collector: The Story of Oliver R. Barrett's Great Private Collection,* pp. 106–08.

[11] Parton, *op. cit.,* pp. 31–33.

the record that his mother "was a glad, easy learner, whose schooling was better than that of most farmers' daughters in her day, and who naturally became a most omnivorous and retentive reader. There were many, doubtless, whose literary acquisitions were more accurate and more profound than hers; but few can have been better qualified to interest or to stimulate the unfolding mind in its earliest stages of development. . . . I was her companion and confidant about as early as I could talk; and her abundant store of ballads, stories, anecdotes and traditions were daily poured into my willing ears."[12]

The formal schooling of Lincoln and Greeley was over before they were fifteen. Their own testimony has left a clear picture of the extent and character of their schooling.

Lincoln was born in the crude pioneering days of Kentucky. His parents were wholly without education, and his father had no respect for learning of any kind. Schools were few, unorganized, and ill sustained by a people who were mainly uneducated and hard pressed to keep body and soul together. Teaching was an accidental, catch-as-catch-can calling. With his sister Sarah he trudged to ABC schools for short periods in Kentucky before the family moved to Indiana. He also went to ABC schools "by littles" in Indiana. Referring to these schools in a sketch of his life, prepared in 1859, Lincoln said: "There were some schools, so called, but no qualification was ever required of a teacher beyond readin', writin', and cipherin' to the rule of three. If a straggler supposed to understand Latin happen to sojourn in the neighborhood, he was looked upon as a wizard. There was absolutely nothing to excite ambition for education. Of course, when I came of age I did not know much. Still, somehow, I could read, write, and cipher to the rule of three, but that was all. I have not been to school since."[13] In his famous autobiography prepared for campaign purposes in June, 1860, which was written in the third person, Lincoln again referred to his meager education:

"Abraham now thinks that the aggregate of all his schooling did not amount to one year. He was never in a college or academy as a student, and never inside of a college or academy building 'till since he had a law license. What he has in the way of education he has picked up. After he was twenty-three and had separated from his father, he studied English grammar—imperfectly, of course, but so as to speak and write as well as he now does. He studied and nearly mastered the six books

---

[12] Greeley, *op. cit.*, p. 41.
[13] Nicolay and Hay, *op. cit.*, V, 287.

of Euclid since he was a member of Congress. He regrets his want of education and does what he can to supply the want."[14]

Greeley had superior advantages. He was born in a well-established New England community. His parents, especially his mother, were educated even beyond their surroundings. Education was valued by the countryside, orderly schools were close at hand, and teachers were already being chosen, to some extent, for their fitness. In addition, Greeley had the good fortune of being able to learn to read at his mother's knee. Often while his mother worked at her spinning wheel he read from a book in her lap and early acquired the knack of reading from a book sidewise or upside down as readily as in the usual way. By the time he was five he had, with his mother's help, read through the Bible. His first schoolmaster was a college graduate "who did his very best, which included liberal application of birch and ferule." His next teacher, to whom he was greatly devoted, "governed by moral force." When he was ten years old, the leading men of the neighborhood in New Hampshire offered to send Horace to Phillips Academy at Exeter and thence to college. His parents declined the offer, saying that they would give their children the best education they could afford—and there stop. In later years Greeley recorded this incident: "I do not remember that I then had any decided opinion or wish in the premises; but I now have; and, from the bottom of my heart, I thank my parents for their wise and manly decision. Much as I have needed a fuller, better education, I rejoice that I am indebted for schooling to none but those of whom I had a right to ask and expect it."[15]

The family moved, the summer of Greeley's tenth year, from New Hampshire to Vermont, and he found the schools in Vermont "rather better," if for no other reason than that the "terms were longer." Thereafter he went to school with some regularity until he was about fifteen. There was not much offered, even in the schools of Vermont, beyond reading, writing, spelling, arithmetic, grammar, and geography. Greeley later became aware of the limited range of his education, felt the need of instruction in science, and paid his respects in strange fashion to algebra: "I deeply regret that such homely sciences as Chemistry, Geology, and Botany were never taught,—were not even named therein. Had our range of studies included these, I had ample time to learn something of them; and this would have proved of inestimable value to me evermore. Yet, I am thankful that Algebra had not yet

---

[14] *Ibid.*, VI, 27–28.
[15] Greeley, *op. cit.*, pp. 41–47, 56.

been thrust into our rural common schools, to knot the brains and squander the time of those who should be learning something of positive and practical utility."[16]

The full education of these two distinguished Americans was largely, to use Lincoln's phrase, "picked up," and the self-educating process continued throughout their lives. The few conventional textbooks which fell into their hands undoubtedly helped to give them the simple rudiments of knowledge, but life itself molded them and was their academy, college, and university. They were both exposed in their early days to Dilworth's *Spelling Book*, Webster's *American Spelling Book*, Murray's *English Reader*, Pike's *Arithmetic*, and Lowe's *Columbian Class Book*. Both had a genuine hunger for learning, and they were omnivorous readers.

Lincoln also encountered Scott's *Lessons in Elocution* and the *Kentucky Preceptor*. After he came of age he studied assiduously, at New Salem, Kirkham's *Grammar* and Gibson's and Flint's *Surveying*; and, as has been indicated, he "nearly mastered" Simson's *Euclid* after his return from Congress. Leonard Swett, a fellow lawyer, who rode the Eighth Judicial Circuit with Lincoln for eleven years in Illinois, recorded an interesting account of a long drive on the circuit with Lincoln when they exchanged confidences about their early years. Lincoln told Swett of his life as a boy and a young man in Indiana and said that "he had got hold of and read through every book he ever heard of in that country for a circuit of about fifty miles."[17] Among the books Lincoln almost devoured and literally made a part of himself were Ramsey's *Life of Washington*, Weems's *Life of Washington*, Grimshaw's *History of the United States*, *Aesop's Fables*, Bunyan's *Pilgrim's Progress*, and Defoe's *Robinson Crusoe*. There is evidence also that he became thoroughly familiar with the Bible during this period, but details are lacking as to when his life-long interest in Shakespeare began.[18]

Greeley also recalled, among his early textbooks, the *American Preceptor*, the *Art of Reading*, Morse's *Geography*, and a grammar by Caleb Bingham, "as poor an affair as its name would indicate," known as *The Ladies Accidence*.[19] Greeley had an even greater zeal than Lincoln for learning through books, and he cherished the memory of the

---

[16] *Ibid.*, p. 56.

[17] Allen Thorndike Rice, *Reminiscences of Abraham Lincoln by Distinguished Men of His Time*, p. 459.

[18] William E. Barton, *The Life of Abraham Lincoln*, I, 121–22; Roy P. Basler, ed., *Abraham Lincoln, His Speeches and Writings*, p. 5.

[19] Greeley, *op. cit.*, p. 45; Basler, *op. cit.*, pp. 1–4; M. L. Houser, *Abraham Lincoln, Student—His Books*; Nicolay and Hay, *op. cit.*, VI, 30.

first book he ever owned, *The Columbian Orator*, which was his "prized text-book for years."[20] He undoubtedly had access to all the books which came Lincoln's way as a boy and a young man, and perhaps many more. It is known that he read *Pilgrim's Progress*, *The Arabian Nights*, and *Robinson Crusoe*, and he could hardly have escaped Weems's *Life of Washington*.[21] The Bible was the foundation of his learning to read. An enthusiastic biographer, James A. Parton, who may have been guilty of overstatement but who certainly had some warrant for his claims, said of Greeley: "Horace scoured the country for books. Books were books in that remote and secluded region; and when he had exhausted the collections of the neighbors, he carried the search into the neighboring towns. I am assured that there was not one readable book within seven miles of his father's home which Horace did not borrow and read during his residence at Amherst. He was never without a book."[22]

It is not surprising that these eager youths, pursuing their self-education, should have turned also to such newspapers as came within their reach for intellectual nourishment. So far as is known there were no newspapers in Lincoln's home in Indiana. Lincoln's appetite was whetted, as we have seen, by the *Louisville Journal* which William Jones put into his hands. William Wood, a neighbor, also took newspapers which Lincoln could borrow. There is ample evidence that he got the newspaper habit pretty thoroughly during the last five or six years of his life in Indiana.[23] The Greeley household had one newspaper during Horace's boyhood and youth, the *Farmer's Cabinet*. The story has come down that this weekly paper did more than anything else to open his mind to the outside world. It is said that he often went to meet the post-rider on newspaper day to be sure that he would have the first *read*.[24]

Beyond the education they got from schooling, books, and newspapers, Lincoln and Greeley developed their intellectual powers through yet another avenue. Dennis Hanks, Lincoln's cousin, who lived with the Lincoln family for a time in Indiana, in answering a question Herndon asked as to how Dennis and Abraham had learned so much in Indiana in spite of the disadvantages under which they lived, replied: "We learned by sight, scent and hearing. We heard all that was said and talked over and over the questions heard, wore them slick, greasy

---

[20] Greeley, *op. cit.*, pp. 45–46.
[21] Don C. Seitz, *Horace Greeley*, p. 21.
[22] Parton, *op. cit.*, p. 48.
[23] Beveridge, *op. cit.*, I, 97.
[24] Henry Luther Stoddard, *Horace Greeley, Printer, Editor, Crusader*, p. 9.

and thread-bare."[25] Lincoln and Greeley were as anxious to express themselves in speech and in writing as they were to discover the secrets within the covers of books.

Lincoln began very early to embellish and to pass on to his associates the stories he picked up in the neighborhood. He soon had an audience at the Gentryville store, at the grist mill, and at the ferry landing. Then, whenever he could find listeners, he began to make speeches, an old stump or a rail fence serving for a platform. And soon he was putting his thoughts down in writing. His declaration that "there was absolutely nothing to excite ambition for education" in his Indiana environment was quite wrong, for the excitement and the ambition came from within him and led him constantly to use the opportunities of his humble surroundings to test himself. His passion for understanding what he heard and for putting it into language anyone could understand was a forecast of the lucid style he became master of in later years.[26]

Greeley was quite like Lincoln in his desire to express his thoughts in speech and writing in plain language. He often asked awkward questions of his teachers. We are told that "he was not to be put off with common-place solutions of serious difficulties. He wanted things to hang together, and liked to know, if *this* was true, *that* could be true also." It was therefore perfectly natural, when he became a printer's apprentice, for him to bring his own ideas together for publication, and he soon experienced the stimulus, which stirred him all his life, of seeing his own ideas in print. A lyceum in East Poultney, Vermont, gave him the opportunity of matching his wits with others before a critical audience. It is said that he stuck to his views against all opposition when he felt that he was right.[27]

Thus the self-imposed training of these ambitious youths proceeded along similar lines. They succeeded well throughout their careers in expressing their ideas on the platform and in print. A distinguished English critic, Earl Curzon, of Kedleston, chancellor of the University of Oxford, in an address before the University of Cambridge on November 6, 1913, on "Modern Parliamentary Eloquence" designated as the three "supreme masterpieces" of English eloquence: the toast of William Pitt after the victory of Trafalgar, Lincoln's Gettysburg Address, and Lincoln's Second Inaugural.[28] In the celebration of the one-

---

[25] Beveridge, *op. cit.*, I, 91.

[26] Ida M. Tarbell, *The Life of Abraham Lincoln*, I, 43–44.

[27] Parton, *op. cit.*, pp. 61, 92.

[28] Barton, *Life of Abraham Lincoln*, II, 224–25.

hundredth anniversary of the birth of Horace Greeley, it was said by distinguished fellow countrymen: "The real power of the press in this country began with Greeley, and if it did not end with him, it has gained nothing since." "He was a master of what has been called the art of putting things."[29]

There were, finally, disciplines in the early lives of Lincoln and Greeley wholly beyond school, independent reading, and social contacts. Born on the soil in humble circumstances, they were early put to work; and the dire necessity of persevering "until the job was done" which confronted them in their boyhood and youth may have had something to do with the formation of the courage and character which held them to more difficult and more momentous undertakings in later years. Work, hard grinding work, mental or physical, even though it be done without enthusiasm or unwillingly, is still held in some quarters to have virtue in the character-building process. It appears that neither Lincoln nor Greeley had any relish for the farm work in which they were obliged to persevere. Indeed, Lincoln was characterized as downright lazy and had to be spurred to labor. John Romine, a neighbor of the Lincolns in Indiana, is reported to have said that Lincoln told him "his father taught him to work but never learned him to love it."[30] Although Greeley in later years owned a farm and sought relaxation on it, he did not have a pleasant memory of his youthful experience. "I know I had the stuff in me for an efficient and successful farmer, but such training as I received at home would never have brought it out. And the moral I would deduce from my experience is simply this: Our farmers' sons escape from their fathers' calling whenever they can, because it is made a mindless, monotonous drudgery, instead of an ennobling, liberalizing, intellectual pursuit."[31]

Speculation upon what influence orderly, systematic secondary school and college education might have had on Lincoln and Greeley is idle. They were born with that intangible quality out of which character and manhood are built. They had the blessed inner urge to know and the intellectual curiosity which are the basis of true learning. They took to learning naturally and easily. And although they had no formal education to guide them, they employed every means that came to hand to discover what men have done and said in all ages past, which, it is

---

[29] Albert E. Pillsbury, "Memorial to Horace Greeley," *Proceedings and Commemorative Observances of 1911*, University of the State of New York, pp. 76, 110.

[30] Beveridge, *op. cit.*, I, 68.

[31] Greeley, *op. cit.*, pp. 59–60.

widely believed, supply the chief materials of the educative process. Coupled with their hunger for learning was their deep-seated social instinct. They wanted the good opinion of their fellows. They early sought the exercise of their own powers of influence to bring others to their way of thinking. The fact that they had no taste for the physical labor that was forced upon them seems not to have lessened its usefulness as a discipline in their training. Possibly Lincoln, as President, might have acted more wisely when his great trial came if he had been educated in the ritualistic grooves of high school and college. Possibly Greeley, as editor, might have influenced his public more effectively if he had gone to Exeter and Harvard. Who knows?

Getting on in the world constituted a continuing process in the adult education of Lincoln and Greeley. They each sought a "sphere and vocation" quite different from what their forebears had known. Lincoln was uncertain as to the choice of a career. At twenty-three, he studied what he should do—"thought of learning the blacksmith trade —thought of trying to study law—rather thought he could not succeed at that without a better education."[32] Not so with Greeley. When "but eleven years old" he trudged nine miles from his home in Vermont "and tried hard to find favor in the printer's eyes" at Whitehall, New York. He went home "downcast and sorrowful" because he was rejected as too young. More successful at fifteen, he left home to become a printer's apprentice at East Poultney, Vermont. He stayed there four years, received only his board and lodgings for the first six months, and thereafter earned, in addition, forty dollars a year for clothing. No wonder he was able to say in his mature years: "Having loved and devoured newspapers—indeed every form of periodical—from childhood, I early resolved to be a printer if I could."[33]

Lean years characterized Lincoln's progress toward a competence and a profession. He earned his first dollar rowing two men out to a passing steamboat on the Ohio River in a scow he had built himself. Many years afterward he told his Cabinet in Washington of this incident. "I could scarcely credit," he said, "that I, a poor boy, had earned a dollar in less than a day—that by honest work I had earned a dollar. The world seemed fairer and wider before me. I was a more hopeful and confident being from that time."[34] His biggest job while still a youth in Indiana was to help pilot a flatboat of produce to New Orleans for which he

[32] Nicolay and Hay, *op. cit.*, VI, 32.
[33] Greeley, *op. cit.*, p. 61.
[34] Francis B. Carpenter, *Inner Life of Abraham Lincoln*, pp. 96–97.

was paid eight dollars a month and expenses.[35] When the family moved
to Illinois in 1830, Lincoln drove one of the ox teams and peddled notions along the way, doubling his investment of his total savings of
about thirty dollars.[36]

Lincoln helped the family to build a cabin on the bank of the Sangamon River, ten miles from Decatur, Illinois, and to fence ten acres for
cultivation. The story persists that he split rails at this time for enough
brown jean, dyed with white walnut bark, to make him a pair of trousers.[37] After a second flatboat trip to New Orleans, this time from
Beardstown, Illinois, at twelve dollars a month, he "stopped indefinitely
and for the first time, as it were, by himself at New Salem," where one
Denton Offut employed him as a clerk in charge of a store and mill.
This enterprise failed in a few months, and Lincoln then volunteered
as a private in the Black Hawk War of 1832. He was elected captain
and served nearly three months. Many years later, after he had been
nominated for the presidency, he recalled that he had "not since had
any success in life which gave him so much satisfaction." Back in New
Salem after the war, Lincoln ran for election to the House of Representatives of the General Assembly of Illinois and was defeated, "his
own precinct, however, casting its votes 277 for and 7 against him."
Being now without means and work, and wishing to stay in New Salem,
he purchased with Berry as a partner "an old stock of goods, upon
credit." They got "deeper and deeper in debt," and the store finally
"winked out," leaving Lincoln with personal obligations of $1,100
which he was years in paying and which he referred to as the "National
Debt."[38]

Lincoln then "procured bread, and kept soul and body together" by
a small income as postmaster of New Salem and by service as deputy
surveyor of Sangamon County. Again he ran for public office, and this
time fortune smiled on him. He was elected to the Illinois House of
Representatives and re-elected for three additional terms, serving from
December, 1, 1834, to March 1, 1841. With the prospect of a salary of
$3 a day as a legislator and $3 for each twenty miles of travel to and
from the capital, then at Vandalia, Lincoln borrowed $200 to get a new
suit, to pay off some of his most pressing debts, and to meet immediate

---

[35] Nicolay and Hay, *op. cit.*, VI, 28.
[36] Tarbell, *op. cit.*, I, 48.
[37] Fred L. Holmes, *Abraham Lincoln Traveled This Way*, pp. 47–48.
[38] Nicolay and Hay, *op. cit.*, VI, 31–32; Benjamin P. Thomas, *Lincoln's New Salem*,
pp. 70–74; Pratt, *op. cit.*; Zarel C. Spears and Robert S. Barton, *Berry and Lincoln—
The Store That "Winked Out."*

traveling expenses. After his first election, encouraged by Major John T. Stuart, a Springfield lawyer, Lincoln decided finally to study law. He "borrowed books of Stuart, took them home with him, and went at it in good earnest. He studied with nobody."[39]

On March 1, 1837, the Supreme Court of Illinois granted Lincoln a certificate of admission to the bar. Major Stuart had expressed willingness to enter into partnership with him. On April 15 Lincoln rode into Springfield on a borrowed horse, his license to practice law and all his possessions, beyond the clothes on his back, in his saddlebags. He was even then without the $17 necessary to buy "the furniture for a single bed." Joshua F. Speed, who told the story of Lincoln's arrival in Springfield, saved the day for the young lawyer by sharing his own bed with him in a room over his store. And shortly after, William Butler, clerk of the Sangamon Circuit Court, took him in for meals without mention of payment.[40] On the day of his arrival the *Sangamo Journal* announced the beginning of the conjoint practice of "J. T. Stuart and A. Lincoln, Attorneys and Counsellors of law." The new firm had plenty of work at once, but the cases were mainly trifling and the fees were small. It was fortunate for the junior partner that indulgent friends provided him with bed and board, for both Stuart and Lincoln were more interested in politics at this time than in the practice of law. Stuart wanted to go to Congress. He realized his ambition in 1838 and was re-elected in 1840. When he took his seat in Congress for his second term, the partnership was dissolved.

Troubles of another character greatly distressed Lincoln during these years. The untimely death of his New Salem sweetheart, Ann Rutledge, on August 25, 1835, according to legend, had left him prostrated with grief. Another affair in which his heart was not greatly enlisted, served to humiliate him and to make him uncertain of himself. His engagement to Mary Todd, broken off in January, 1841, left him, as he revealed in a letter to Stuart, "the most miserable man living."[41]

But two fortunate events followed soon after. The first was a new law partnership with Judge Stephen T. Logan, which began on April 14, 1841. Logan was about ten years older than Lincoln, had served two years as judge of the Circuit Court, and already stood at the head of the Illinois bar. Lincoln needed and profited by the discipline he got from contact with Logan. He was compelled to give up the disorderly

---

[39] Beveridge, *op. cit.*, I, 162; Nicolay and Hay, *op. cit.*, VI, 33.

[40] Tarbell, *op. cit.*, I, 147–48.

[41] Nicolay and Hay, *op. cit.*, I, 157–59.

ways he had picked up with Stuart for the systematic, methodical procedures of Logan. Logan and Lincoln soon became known as one of the leading law firms in Illinois. For the first time in his life Lincoln's earnings furnished him with more than the bare necessities. The second fortunate event, notwithstanding the never-ending complexities her fiery and unstable temperament eventually brought him, was his marriage on November 4, 1842, to Mary Todd. He was anchored at last. Henceforth, earning a competence through the force of the new necessity of establishing a home and rearing a family left him no time for being "the most miserable man living."[42] Approaching his thirty-fourth birthday, Lincoln was established in his private life and in his profession.

When Greeley finished his four-year apprenticeship with the *Northern Spectator* at East Poultney, Vermont, in June, 1830, he was nineteen. He cherished "fervid and grateful recollections" of his life in East Poultney and remarked many years later that he had "never since known a community so generally moral, intelligent, industrious, and friendly." The young printer then set out to join his family in western Pennsylvania. He traveled twelve miles by wagon to Comstock's Landing on the Champlain Canal where he took a line-boat to Troy, and thence to Buffalo on the Erie Canal. He took a steamboat from Buffalo to Dunkirk on Lake Erie, and then walked overland to his father's "cabin" in Erie County, Pennsylvania, just across the state line from Clymer, New York. After some weeks at home he found work as a journeyman printer at Jamestown and later at Lodi (now Gowanda), New York, where he received $11 a month. Later he found work for nearly a year with the *Erie Gazette* at $15 a month. The work at Erie finally gave out, and he could find no opening in that region for labor "at case and press . . . for $15. per month and board, or even less."

Greeley then divided his Erie earnings with his father, and with $25 in his pocket and his extra clothing in a bundle, he set out for "the Commercial Emporium" of New York. He left no record of how he got from Erie County to Lockport, New York, but he probably traveled on Lake Erie and the Erie Canal. It is known that he walked from Lockport to Gaines, a distance of perhaps twenty miles on the "ridge road," where he stopped overnight with a friend, and that he walked from Gaines to Brockport, "some fifteen miles," where he got a line-boat on the Erie Canal to Schenectady. He "took the turnpike" from Schenec-

---

[42] Albert A. Woldman, *Lawyer Lincoln*, pp. 16–44; Frederick Trevor Hill, *Lincoln, the Lawyer*, pp. 70–95, 112–33.

tady to Albany, and thence made the last lap of the journey on a tow-boat on the Hudson River. He reached New York City at six o'clock on the morning of August 17, 1831. "I was twenty years old the preceding February," Greeley said years later, "tall, slender, pale, and plain, with ten dollars in my pocket, Summer clothing worth perhaps as much more, nearly all on my back, and a decent knowledge of so much of the art of printing as a boy will usually learn in the office of a country newspaper."

Greeley soon found work setting type and was employed intermittently by several printing shops during the next eighteen months. About the first of January, 1833, he formed a partnership in the establishment of a "printery." The total resources of the partners were about $200. Greeley had sent home a good part of his savings to aid his father "in his struggle with the wilderness." The printery had its ups and downs, and after a year and a half the first partner was drowned while bathing, and a new one taken in. "A moderate but steady prosperity ensued." On March 22, 1834, "without premonitory sound of trumpet" the firm issued the *New Yorker*, "a large, fair, and cheap weekly folio, devoted mainly to current literature, but giving regularly a digest of all important news, including a careful exhibit and summary of election returns and other political intelligence." Greeley edited and made up the paper, and his partner took charge of the jobbing business. The paper subsisted for the first two years on the profits of the job work. Then the partnership was dissolved, the partner taking the jobbing business and Greeley, the *New Yorker*.

Deeming himself on the way to a competence, Greeley was married on July 5, 1836, to Mary Y. Cheney, a schoolteacher from Connecticut who taught for a time in a private school in New York City. The marriage was never a success. Mary Cheney was even more eccentric than Mary Todd, and Greeley never had a home which attracted or held him. At the time of his marriage he estimated that he was worth perhaps $5,000 with a yearly income of $1,000. What he called the "Commercial Revulsion of 1837" brought on hard times. The *New Yorker* went from bad to worse, but Greeley held on to its publication until September 20, 1841. He then had barely enough money to reimburse the subscribers who had paid in advance, and he was left with $10,000 in bad debts on his books. "My only requital," he said, "was a sorely achieved but wholesome lesson."

During his struggles with the *New Yorker*, Greeley engaged in two pot-boiling editorial adventures. At the behest of Thurlow Weed, editor and publisher of the *Albany Evening Journal,* he undertook the editorship of a Whig campaign paper to be issued at Albany for one year under the title of the *Jeffersonian.* He was paid $1,000 for this service and was obliged to spend half of each week in Albany during the summer and nearly all of his time in winter during the legislative session. The *Jeffersonian* was issued weekly, the first issue appearing on February 17, 1838, and the last on February 9, 1839. It was an able and dignified campaign document, and Thurlow Weed's immediate object was accomplished in the triumphant election of William Henry Seward as governor of the state of New York.

The other venture was also a campaign document which Greeley undertook on his own account in support of the candidacy of General William Henry Harrison for the presidency in 1840. The first issue of the *Log Cabin,* as the new paper was known, came out on May 2, 1840, and was continued for a year after its original purpose had been accomplished. As a campaign sheet it was a marked success, its circulation running up to 80,000. It made "very little money" but apparently paid for itself. Its editor was able to announce in its columns the victory of General Harrison at the polls and was obliged to record Harrison's untimely death one month after inauguration.

Indeed, it fell to Greeley's lot to announce the passing of President Harrison in three papers. While still nursing the expiring *New Yorker* and getting satisfaction if not income from the *Log Cabin,* "incited to this enterprise by several Whig friends," Greeley determined to issue a cheap daily with Whig leanings. The first issue of the *New York Tribune* came out on April 10, 1841, on the very day New York City witnessed a great funeral parade and pageant in honor of President Harrison who had died six days before. Financially, it was hard going for the *Tribune* at first. Greeley's net worth at this time was about $2,000, half of it in printing materials. Five hundred subscribers had been secured in advance, two thousand copies were being issued by the end of the first week, and the circulation soon reached ten thousand. Unfortunately, expenses rose with circulation. The expenses for the first week were about $525 and the receipts $92. In spite of all the persistent editor could do, week by week his expenses exceeded his income, and he faced a repetition of his experience with the *New Yorker.* Unexpected good fortune came his way when Thomas McElrath, a New York lawyer who had had experience in printing, offered to invest $2,000 in the undertaking on a partnership basis and to take over the business management of the paper. The harassed editor, who held that no man was qualified at once to edit and to manage a daily paper, gladly accepted. From that hour his "load was palpably lightened" and he entered on a "long era of all but unclouded prosperity."[43]

Times have changed in the century that has passed since Lincoln and Greeley were young men, but the spirit and fiber of young men who mean to make their mark in the world today remain much the same. Lincoln and Greeley had native capacity; they had ambition, persistence, vision, and goals; they took defeat and disappointment as hard as any, but they took it. The young man today, whatever his background, who becomes a member of his state legislature at twenty-five, attracts notice; the young lawyer today, whatever his training, who finds himself well established in his profession in his early thirties, is regarded as doing well. Today any young man who, by his own energy and industry, is editing and publishing his own newspaper at thirty-one, is a distinct success.

They did a good job of getting on, these ambitious youths of the nineteenth century. At thirty-three, Lincoln had served four terms in the Illinois Legislature and was practicing law in the capital city of his state in partnership with one of the distinguished lawyers of the Middle West. At thirty-one, already widely known as an editor, Greeley had founded one of the great metropolitan newspapers which still survives today.

---

[43] Greeley, *op. cit.*, pp. 75–97, 129–43.

Being elected to Congress, though I am very grateful to our friends for having done it, has not pleased me as much as I expected.

Lincoln[1]

I look back upon those three months I spent in Congress as among the most profitably employed of any in the course of my life.

Greeley[2]

3   Congressmen

Lincoln and Greeley did not become personally acquainted until they met as fellow congressmen in the second session of the Thirtieth Congress in December, 1848. Lincoln served throughout that Congress, and Greeley was elected to fill a vacancy for the second or short session. At least it was Greeley's recollection that he "first met Mr. Lincoln late in 1848 at Washington, as a representative in the xxxth Congress—the only one to which he was ever elected," and that he was "a genial, cheerful, rather comely man, noticeably tall, and the only Whig from Illinois, not remarkable otherwise, to the best of my recollection."[3] The hesitant congressman-elect from Illinois had apparently not pushed himself forward to meet the distinguished editor at the River

[1] John G. Nicolay and John Hay, eds., *Complete Works of Abraham Lincoln*, I, 298, Lincoln to Joshua F. Speed.

[2] Horace Greeley, *Recollections of a Busy Life*, p. 233.

[3] MS, Greeley's lecture on "Abraham Lincoln," p. 13. Henry E. Huntington Library, San Marino, California. There is some uncertainty as to whether or not the lecture was ever delivered. It was edited by Joel Benton and first published in the *Century Magazine*, July, 1891. It was later brought out in book form by Benton under the title, *Greeley on Lincoln and Mr. Greeley's Letters*. Benton took unwarranted liberty with Greeley's punctuation and capitalization, and deciphered certain words from Greeley's atrocious handwriting incorrectly. See facsimile of the original manuscript and annotated copy with notes on Benton's changes by Harlan Hoyt Horner and Henrietta Calhoun Horner, Lincoln Room, University of Illinois Library, Urbana, Illinois.

and Harbor Convention which they had both attended at Chicago in July, 1847. In another connection Greeley said: "I knew him more than sixteen years, met him often, talked with him familiarly."[4] In the absence of any other record we must conclude that the lawyer and the editor first took each other's measure face to face as congressmen in Washington in December, 1848.

There were then six rows of seats in semicircular form in the House. Lincoln's seat was number 191 in the last row to the left of the Speaker on the Whig side. To the right sat Harmon S. Conger of New York and to the left, John Gayle of Alabama. Greeley's seat was number 25 in the front row to the left of the Speaker on the Whig side. To the right sat Hugh L. White and to the left, David Romney, Jr., both of New York.[5]

James K. Polk of Tennessee was then President and George M. Dallas of Pennsylvania was Vice-President. There were then twenty-eight states in the Union, and the Democrats held the balance of power. At the opening of the first session in December, 1847, there were thirty-two Democrats and twenty-two Whigs in the Senate, with two vacancies in Democratic states, one in Alabama and one in Texas. In the House the Whigs outnumbered the Democrats 117 to 110; and there was one Native-American party member.[6]

Prominent among the senators were Daniel Webster of Massachusetts, with whom Lincoln became well acquainted; John P. Hale of New Hampshire, one of the organizers of the Republican party and a staunch supporter of the Union throughout the Civil War; Simon Cameron of Pennsylvania, an early leader in the Republican party, a candidate for the presidency at the Wigwam Convention in 1860, and Lincoln's first Secretary of War; Reverdy Johnson of Maryland, who supported Douglas for the presidency in 1860 and who was commissioned by President Lincoln after the capture of New Orleans in the Civil War to revise the decisions of the military commandant, General B. F. Butler, in regard to foreign governments; John Bell of Tennessee, Southern Whig leader, who was the candidate of the Constitutional Union party for the presidency in 1860; Lewis Cass of Michigan, whom Lincoln *vigorously* and Greeley *mildly* helped to defeat in his race for the presidency against Zachary Taylor; John J. Crittenden of Kentucky,

---

[4] Greeley, *op. cit.*, p. 405.

[5] Letter to author from William Tyler Page, Washington, D. C.

[6] *Cong. Globe*, 30th Cong., 1st sess., p. 1.

who helped to keep his state in the Union; and finally Thomas Corwin of Ohio, Stephen A. Douglas of Illinois, Jefferson Davis of Mississippi, and the veteran John C. Calhoun of South Carolina.

Among the outstanding members in the House were George Ashmun of Massachusetts, who presided at the Wigwam Convention in 1860; Joshua R. Giddings of Ohio, vigorous opponent of slavery and one of Lincoln's messmates at Mrs. Spriggs's boarding house; Alexander H. Stephens of Georgia, who became Vice-President of the Confederacy; Robert Toombs, also of Georgia, who became Secretary of State of the Confederacy and a Brigadier General in the Confederate Army; Caleb B. Smith of Indiana, who became Lincoln's first Secretary of the Interior; Robert C. Winthrop of Massachusetts, Speaker of the House; David Wilmot of Pennsylvania, author of the Wilmot Proviso, who was appointed by Lincoln as a member of the United States Court of Claims; Robert Barnwell Rhett of South Carolina, who was a leader in the promotion of secession; the veteran John Quincy Adams of Massachusetts; and finally Andrew Johnson of Tennessee, destined to become President of the United States under the most tragic circumstances in the history of the country.

Greeley went to Washington in February, early in the session, to look the new Congress over, before he had any notion that he would himself be a member before its expiration. He reported to his newspaper that it was a decided improvement over its immediate predecessor "in intellect, in character and in manners" and that among the new members on the Whig side who would in due time "make themselves heard" was Abraham Lincoln of Illinois.[7] Greeley kept a close eye on this Congress, but it did not come up to his expectations. In the latter part of April, 1848, he went to Washington again and found everything substantially as he had left it in February with nothing of consequence being done.[8]

Lincoln's presence in this Congress, while it did not please him as much as he had expected, was the result of a long-nourished ambition. He was scarcely out of the Illinois Legislature in 1841 when he began to think seriously of going to Congress. He was not hesitant about acquainting his friends with his aspirations as the following letters testify. They were written on the same day; the first to Richard S.

---

[7] *Tribune*, December 11, 1847.
[8] *Ibid.*, April 29, 1848.

Thomas, a lawyer and old-time Whig of Virginia, Illinois; and the second to Alden Hull of Pekin, another staunch Whig whom Lincoln had known in the legislature.

Springfield, Ills., Feb. 14, 1843

Friend Richard. . . . Now if you should hear anyone say that Lincoln don't want to go to Congress, I wish you as a personal friend of mine, would tell him you have reason to believe he is mistaken. The truth is, I would like to go very much. Still, circumstances may happen which may prevent my being a candidate.

If there are any who be my friends in such an enterprise, what I now want is that they shall not throw me away just yet.

Yours as ever,
A. Lincoln[9]

Springfield, Feby. 14, 1843

Friend Hull:

Your county and ours are almost sure to be placed in the same Congressional district. I would like to be its Representative, still circumstances may happen to prevent my even being a candidate. If, however, there are any whigs in Tazewell who would as soon I should represent them as any other person, I would be glad they would not cast me aside until they see and hear farther what turn things take.

Do not suppose, Esqr., that in addressing this letter to you, I assume that you will be for me against all other whigs; I only mean, that I know you to be my personal friend, a good whig, and an honorable man, to whom I may, without fear, communicate a fact which I wish my particular friends (if I have any) to know.

There is nothing new here now worth telling.

Your friend as ever,
A. Lincoln[10]

"Circumstances" did "happen" shortly thereafter in rapid succession to prevent his "being a candidate." Under the national census of 1840 Illinois was given seven representatives in Congress. The election which would ordinarily have been held in 1842 was carried over to 1843 because the state did not define its congressional districts until

---

[9] Gilbert A. Tracy, *Uncollected Letters of Abraham Lincoln*, pp. 9–10. See also Donald W. Riddle, *Lincoln Runs for Congress*.

[10] Paul M. Angle, *New Letters and Papers of Lincoln*, p. 16. Facsimile of this letter, Carl Sandburg, *Abraham Lincoln: The Prairie Years*, I, 295.

March 1 of that year.[11] In March the Whigs of Sangamon County instructed their delgates to the district convention to vote for Edward D. Baker in preference to Lincoln. At the district convention held at Pekin, Tazewell County, in April, John J. Hardin nosed out both Lincoln and Baker, and was nominated by the Whigs. He was elected in August and took his seat in Congress in December. Under the new arrangement the next election occurred in August, 1844. This time Lincoln gave way to Baker, but promptly made plans to succeed Baker.

His letters, during this period, to friendly newspaper editors and to local political managers contained adroit appeals for support.

If your feelings toward me are the same as when I saw you (which I have no reason to doubt), I wish you would let nothing appear in your paper which may operate against me.[12]

I now wish to say to you that if it be consistent with your feelings, you would set a few stakes for me.[13]

My reliance for a fair shake (and I want nothing more) in your county is chiefly on you, because of your position and standing, and because I am acquainted with so few others.[14]

I should be pleased if I could concur with you in the hope that my name would be the only one presented to the convention; but I cannot.[15]

Don't fail to write me instantly on receiving telling me all—particularly the names of those who are going strong against me.[16]

I have not time to give particulars now; but I want you to let nothing prevent your getting an article in your paper of this week, taking strong ground for the old system under which Hardin and Baker were nominated, without seeming to know or suspect that anyone desires to change it.[17]

Lincoln had long urged that Hardin, Baker, and himself "should take a turn apiece" in Congress and he made much of his insistence that his "turn" would come in 1846. Hardin and Baker both wanted the nomination. Lincoln managed to induce Baker to withdraw from the contest, but he had a struggle with Hardin. The climax of his efforts came in a letter to Hardin on February 7, 1846, in which he reviewed at great length their previous correspondence and understandings and pleaded

---

[11] *Laws of Illinois*, 1843, Chap. 71.
[12] Nicolay and Hay, *op. cit.*, I, 278, Lincoln to B. F. James, November 17, 1845.
[13] Tracy, *op. cit.*, pp. 14–15, Lincoln to Henry E. Dummer, November 18, 1845.
[14] Nicolay and Hay, *op. cit.*, I, 280–81, Lincoln to Dr. Robert Boal, January 7, 1846.
[15] *Ibid.*, pp. 282–84, Lincoln to B. F. James, January 14, 1846.
[16] *Ibid.*, pp. 284–85, Lincoln to John Bennett, January 15, 1846.
[17] *Ibid.*, pp. 285–86, Lincoln to B. F. James, January 16, 1846.

with Hardin to withdraw, ending his letter with the words, "I believe you do not mean to be unjust, or ungenerous; and I, therefore am slow to believe that you will not yet think *better* and think *differently* of this matter."[18]

Hardin finally capitulated and Lincoln was nominated by acclamation at a Whig Convention held at Petersburg on May 1, 1846. His opponent was the famous Methodist revivalist, Peter Cartwright, who had defeated Lincoln when he first ran for the Illinois Legislature in 1832. The Whigs in the Seventh Congressional District were better organized than the Democrats; and the Democrats early gave up the contest, polling only forty-two per cent of their total vote. Lincoln was elected on August 3, 1846, with a majority of 1,511 votes.[19] It is true that the Whigs were in the majority in the district, and that Lincoln was personally more popular than the acidulous Cartwright. It cannot be said, however, that Abraham Lincoln went to Congress because of any spontaneous uprising in his behalf. He was nominated and elected primarily because he wanted to go to Congress and because he had worked for four or five years, early and late, to that end.

Much as Greeley secretly craved office throughout his life, and more than once publicly sought it, his presence in the short session of the Thirtieth Congress was a political accident. In the election of 1846 David S. Jackson, a Democrat, had triumphed over Colonel James Monroe, the Whig candidate, for election to Congress from the Sixth Congressional District of New York, comprising the upper portion of New York City, "by importing the adult male paupers from the almshouse on Blackwell's Island."[20] On the opening day of the new Congress, December 6, 1847, Monroe gave notice that he would contest the right of Jackson to a seat in the House.[21] Testimony was taken by depositions and referred to the Committee on Elections unopened. The testimony was later printed for the use of the House. The majority of the committee reported in favor of Monroe and a minority in favor of Jackson. Monroe was given permission to be heard in person at the bar of the House. Parliamentary maneuvering ensued and final action was taken by the House on April 19, 1848, to the effect that Jackson was not entitled to the seat he held and that Monroe was not entitled to it

---

[18] Angle, *op. cit.*, pp. 22–28.
[19] Albert J. Beveridge, *Abraham Lincoln*, I, 383; Riddle, *op. cit.*, pp. 176–85.
[20] L. D. Ingersoll, *Life and Times of Horace Greeley*, p. 205.
[21] *House Journal*, 30th Cong., 1st sess., p. 15.

either.[22] Lincoln had taken this position in all the votes he cast in the contest. This action made a new election necessary.

Colonel Monroe planned to be a candidate for the remaining short term and for the Thirty-first Congress as well, but another candidate had been promised the nomination for the new Congress, and Monroe indignantly declined the nomination for the short session only. It was tendered to Greeley. "I at first resolved to decline also," he later recorded, "not seeing how to leave my business so abruptly for a three months' sojourn at Washington; but the nomination was so kindly pressed upon me, with such apparently cogent reasons therefor, that I accepted it."[23] As it turned out, Greeley was on the Whig ticket with Zachary Taylor in the election of 1848. Greeley got 1,425 more votes than his two competitors on the split Democratic tickets, and took his seat at the opening of the short session on December 4, 1848.

The sole Whig member from Illinois was reasonably obedient to the will of the slight Whig majority in the Thirtieth Congress, and was on hand at twelve noon on Monday, December 6, 1847, when the House opened. The Whigs organized the House and named the principal officers. Robert C. Winthrop of Massachusetts was chosen Speaker; Thomas J. Campbell of Tennessee, Clerk; Nathan Sargent, Sergeant-at-Arms; Robert E. Horner, Doorkeeper; John M. Johnson, Postmaster; and the Rev. R. R. Gurley, a Presbyterian, Chaplain. Lincoln voted for Winthrop, Campbell, Sargent, and Horner. He preferred William J. McCormick for Postmaster and a Baptist minister, the Rev. R. W. Cushman, for Chaplain. Lincoln, the ex-postmaster of New Salem, Illinois, was appropriately appointed on the Committee on the Post Office and Post Roads, being eighth in the list of nine members. He was also appointed on the Committee on Expenditures in the War Department, being fifth and last member on this committee. The fourth member was David S. Jackson of New York whose seat was declared vacant and whose place in Congress was taken by Greeley in the short session. This recognition was perhaps as much as a new and unknown member could expect. He was reappointed on the first committee for the second session, and his appointment on the second stood for the entire Congress.[24]

Lincoln was a dutiful congressman. The record for the entire first

---

[22] *Ibid.*, p. 709.
[23] Greeley, *op. cit.*, p. 216.
[24] *Cong. Globe*, 30th Cong., 1st sess., pp. 1–24.

session from December 6, 1847, to August 14, 1848, shows him absent from Washington only once. He attended the National Whig Convention at Philadelphia, leaving Washington on Tuesday, June 6, and returning on Sunday, June 11.[25] After reading the *Journal* the House adjourned on Tuesday until Friday, and perfunctory sessions were held on Friday and Saturday, since many other members were also at Philadelphia.[26] The record shows that he was regular in attendance upon the sessions of the House. The yeas and nays were called for three hundred and nine times during the session. Lincoln missed none of these votes from the beginning of the session until May 11, 1848, and missed only nine such votes in the entire session.[27] Upon the occasion of these nine calls for the yeas and nays the record shows that Lincoln was actually present in the House and voting on other questions on six of the given days. Thus on Monday, June 12, the day after his return from Philadelphia, he missed the first vote, participated in the second, and missed the third. No doubt he was busy writing letters in a committee room when the roll was called, for he wrote to Herndon that day saying, "Excuse this short letter—I have so many to write, that I cannot devote much time to anyone." He also wrote to Mrs. Lincoln, beginning his letter to her, "On my return from Philadelphia yesterday, where in my anxiety I have been led to attend the Whig Convention, I found your last letter. I was so tired and sleepy, having ridden all night, that I could not answer it till today; and now I have to do so in the H. R." Later in the same letter he wrote: "Since I began this letter, the H. R. has passed a resolution for adjourning on the 17th of July, which will probably pass the Senate."[28]

He had an uncanny way of lining up with the majority even when the issue was not strictly political. In the 309 calls for the yeas and nays Lincoln found himself with the majority 218 times, with the minority 79 times, and in a tie 3 times. He took the floor throughout the session perhaps 25 times, speaking briefly 10 or 12 times on relatively unimportant matters and taking little space in the record. He reported three bills and one Joint Resolution for the Committee on the Post Office and Post Roads. One of the bills did not pass the House, and of the two passed one became a law. The Joint Resolution passed the House but was not approved. He introduced one bill on his own account which did

[25] Benjamin P. Thomas, *Lincoln, 1847–1853*, pp. 76–77.

[26] *House Journal*, 30th Cong., 1st sess., pp. 879–82.

[27] *Ibid.*, pp. 787–88, 836–37, 844–45, 880–81, 882–85, 990–91, 1181–82, 1191–93.

[28] Emanuel Hertz, *Abraham Lincoln—A New Portrait*, II, 573–74.

not pass the House.[29] He made three rather extended speeches, no one of which was addressed to a specific issue before the House, which got into the Appendix of the *Congressional Globe*. He did not go to Congress with a burning desire to institute any universal reforms or with any specific legislation in mind for the benefit of his constituents. The unadulterated truth is that his primary concern was to distinguish himself in some way and thus to promote his own advancement. "As you are all so anxious for me to distinguish myself," he wrote Herndon on December 13, one week after the session opened, "I have concluded to do so before long."[30]

The annual message of President Polk presented to the Congress the second day of the session afforded Lincoln the opportunity for which he was looking. President Polk reiterated the position he had taken in messages to the Twenty-ninth Congress that the Mexican government "under wholly unjustifiable pretexts, involved the two countries in war, by invading the territory of the state of Texas, striking the first blow and shedding the blood of our citizens on our own soil."[31] The Whigs in Congress made a concerted attack upon President Polk, in part because they believed that the war with Mexico had been unconstitutionally begun, and in part because they were looking forward to possible success in the next presidential election.

On December 22, as a preliminary step toward distinguishing himself, Lincoln presented a preamble and a series of resolutions in the House calling rather bluntly and pre-emptorily upon the President to inform the House whether the "spot" on which American blood was first shed in the Mexican War was not within the territory claimed by Mexico.[32] The preamble and resolutions were read, laid on the table, and never acted upon. President Polk took no notice of the incident, and it apparently made no stir in Congress. Brief mention was made of the resolutions by Greeley's Washington correspondent in his regular report to the *Tribune*.[33] The resolutions promptly got back home to Springfield, however, where the war had been immensely popular in the beginning and was still supported, and served as the initial step in the undoing of Lincoln's congressional career. On January 3 on a vote

---

[29] *House Journal*, 30th Cong., 1st sess., bills 89, 92, p. 1326; bill 301, p. 1336; bill 599, p. 1350; Joint Resolution 18, p. 1450.
[30] Nicolay and Hay, *op. cit.*, I, 317.
[31] *Cong. Globe*, 30th Cong., 1st sess., Appendix, pp. 1–8.
[32] *Cong. Globe*, 30th Cong., 1st sess., p. 64.
[33] *Tribune*, December 23, 1847.

of 82 to 81 the House inserted, in a resolution of thanks to Major General Taylor, the words "in a war unnecessarily and unconstitutionally begun by the President of the United States." Lincoln voted for the amendment.[34] On January 8 Lincoln wrote Herndon, "As to speech-making, by way of getting the hang of the House I made a little speech two or three days ago on a post-office question of no general interest. I find speaking here and elsewhere about the same thing. I was about as badly scared, and no worse, as I am when I speak in court. I expect to make one within a week or two, in which I hope to succeed well enough to wish you to see it."[35]

He had apparently been quietly and carefully at work on a speech on the Mexican War designed to follow the preamble and "spot" resolutions which he had introduced in the House on December 22. At the close of the session on January 11 he obtained the floor and gave notice of his intention to speak. The next day in the course of its business the House resolved itself into a Committee of the Whole House with Representative Joseph R. Ingersoll of Pennsylvania in the chair. Lincoln made his contemplated speech at this time. He reiterated his position that the war with Mexico had been "unnecessarily and unconstitutionally commenced by the President" and again called upon him to name the "spot" on American soil where blood was first shed by act of Mexico. The speech was closely patterned after the Whig program of criticism of President Polk and was not greatly different from other speeches made in like vein.[36]

Lincoln's speech did not break into the *Tribune*, but there is abundant evidence that Greeley subscribed wholeheartedly to the Whig position voiced by Lincoln.

Greeley was vigorously outspoken in his condemnation of the war. In a hot editorial headed "What Means This War," shortly after the war began, he declared, "the laws of Heaven are suspended and those of Hell established in their stead. It means that the Commandments are to be read and obeyed by our People thus—Thou *shalt* kill Mexicans; Thou *shalt* steal from them, hate them, burn their houses, ravage their fields, and fire red-hot cannon balls into towns swarming with their wives and children."[37] Commenting on the boundary question a few days later, he said that the shifts and tricks by which "Wrong seeks

---

[34] *House Journal*, 30th Cong., 1st sess., p. 184.
[35] Nicolay and Hay, *op. cit.*, I, 325.
[36] *Cong. Globe*, 30th Cong., 1st sess., Appendix, pp. 93–95.
[37] *Tribune*, May 13, 1846.

to pass itself off for Right" would often be ludicrous if it were not for "their fearful tendencies and consequences." He went on with the thrust, "And in all our experience of powerful Knavery impudently adventuring into the arena of Logic, this pretence of extending Texas to the Rio Grande has never been paralleled."[38] Under date of January 13, 1848, the day after Lincoln's speech in Congress, one of Greeley's Washington correspondents, signing himself Richelieu, wired his paper that "This is the anniversary of the day on which James K. Polk unnecessarily and unconstitutionally commenced the war with Mexico."[39]

Back home in Illinois where the war sentiment was still keen, news of Lincoln's speech was rapidly spread and it was promptly condemned.[40] It clearly portrayed the attitude of the Whig leaders in Congress but it was untimely and impolitic and sealed Lincoln's undoing as a congressman. A treaty of peace was signed with Mexico at Guadalupe Hidalgo on February 2, 1848, transmitted by President Polk to the Senate on February 22, and with slight changes ratified on May 30.[41] General John J. Hardin, Lincoln's predecessor from the Seventh Congressional District in the Twenty-eighth Congress, had fallen in battle at Buena Vista; General James Shields, an Illinois legislator, had been severely wounded at Cerro Gordo; and Colonel E. D. Baker, Lincoln's immediate predecessor from the Seventh Congressional District, who had organized a regiment in Illinois without resigning from Congress, had taken command of Shields's brigade and had distinguished himself in battle. The people of Illinois were in no mood to tolerate what seemed to be a failure on Lincoln's part to support the army. Always desiring the good opinion of his fellows, Lincoln was sorely hurt at the reception of his speech and was at some pains for the remainder of his life to explain his position.

He was on the lookout to correct what he conceived to be mistaken views of the Whig position. An innocent little paragraph relating to the Texas boundary question dated June 24, 1848, which appeared in the *Tribune*, excited his attention.[42] Apparently assuming that this obscure item, hidden away on the editorial page of the *Tribune* under correspondence from Washington, had been written by Greeley, Lincoln promptly dispatched a letter setting him straight. He must by this

---

[38] *Ibid.*, May 21, 1846.
[39] *Ibid.*, January 15, 1848.
[40] Beveridge, *op. cit.*, I, 429.
[41] *House Journal*, 30th Cong., 1st sess., pp. 991–97.
[42] *Tribune*, June 26, 1848.

time have become a very thorough and painstaking reader of the *Tribune* to have noticed the article at all; and he must have been watching very alertly for anything that might undermine his "course in Congress" on the Mexican situation. Greeley must have been greatly surprised at the letter. There is no record that he replied to it directly, but he did print it without comment in the *Tribune* on June 29 under the heading:

The Boundary of Texas—Letter from Hon. Abraham Lincoln of Ill.

[*June 27, 1848*]

Friend Greeley: In the "Tribune" of yesterday I discovered a little editorial paragraph in relation to Colonel Wentworth of Illinois, in which, in relation to the boundary of Texas, you say: "All Whigs and many Democrats having ever contended it stopped at the Neuces." Now this is a mistake which I dislike to see go uncorrected in a leading Whig paper. Since I have been here, I know a large majority of such Whigs of the House of Representatives as have spoken on the question have not taken that position. Their position, and in my opinion the true position, is that the boundary of Texas extended just so far as American settlements taking part in her revolution extended; and that as a matter of fact those settlements did extend, at one or two points, beyond the Neuces, but not anywhere near the Rio Grande at any point. The "stupendous desert" between the valleys of those two rivers, and not either river, has been insisted on by the Whigs as the true boundary.

Will you look at this? By putting us in the position of insisting on the line of the Neuces, you put us in a position which, in my opinion, we cannot maintain, and which therefore gives the Democrats an advantage of us. If the degree of arrogance is not too great, may I ask you to examine what I said on this very point in the printed speech I send you.

Yours truly,

A. Lincoln[43]

Peace had then been established. Lincoln's war speech had been largely forgotten except by the outraged voters in the Seventh Congressional District of Illinois who were then getting ready to defeat Judge Stephen T. Logan who was ambitious to succeed Lincoln in Congress. Largely because of dissatisfaction with Lincoln's record, the district did defeat Logan on August 7, 1848, and by a majority of 106 sent a Democrat to the next Congress. Even as late as 1860, in his autobiographical sketch written for campaign purposes, Lincoln was still explaining his "course in Congress."[44]

---

[43] Nicolay and Hay, *op. cit.*, II, 53–54.
[44] *Ibid.*, VI, 35–36.

Discouraged by the Illinois reception of his first attempt to "distinguish" himself, Lincoln nevertheless sought another opportunity. This time he deliberately chose an issue more likely to have favorable reception. The Whigs were still critical of President Polk for his veto of the River and Harbor bill in the previous Congress, and Lincoln recalled the enthusiasm of the whole Northwest for internal improvements exhibited at the convention he had attended at Chicago. On June 20, 1848, in the course of its business the House resolved itself into a Committee of the Whole on the state of the Union, Joseph M. Root of Ohio in the chair, and proceeded to a consideration of the Civil and Diplomatic Appropriations bill. Lincoln knew he was out of order but decided it was an opportune time to get his effort into the record. Securing the floor he announced his intention of making a speech on internal improvements and said he would take his seat if the chair ruled him out of order. The chairman replied that he would not undertake to rule upon the speech in advance and said that he would pass upon any question of order that might arise. Thus Lincoln proceeded to make his speech without interruption.[45]

Two days later Lincoln closed a letter to Herndon with the remark, "I made an internal-improvement speech day before yesterday, which I shall send home as soon as I can get it written out and printed,—and which I suppose nobody will read."[46] It was sound Whig doctrine but the setting for the speech was not such as to give it special notice. Herndon thought that it deserved "only passing mention."[47] But the Washington correspondent of the *Tribune* thought better of it and reported under date of June 20:

> *The Civil and Diplomatic bill being before the House in the Committee of the Whole, sundry speeches were let off, having of course no relation to the subject. Mr. Lincoln of Ill. made a very sensible speech upon the question of Internal Improvements. He evidently understood the subject, and, better still, succeeded in making the House understand it. Tall men come from Illinois. John Wentworth and Lincoln are both men of mighty stature, and their intellectual endowments correspond with their physical. Mr. Lincoln was succeeded by Mr. Wick of Ind.—a wick without oil.*[48]

Lincoln sought a third time to "distinguish" himself from the floor of the House on July 27, 1848. On July 24 he "obtained the floor

---

[45] *Cong. Globe*, 30th Cong., 1st sess., Appendix, pp. 709–11.
[46] Nicolay and Hay, *op. cit.*, VI, 53.
[47] William H. Herndon and Jesse William Weik, *The Life of Lincoln*, II, 286.
[48] *Tribune*, June 22, 1848.

amongst many competitors" and gave notice that he "desired to make a general speech."[49] He gave way at that time for a member who wished to speak directly on the question then before the House. On July 27 a special order for the day was the consideration of messages from the President, under date of July 6, relative to the ratification of the treaty of peace with Mexico, and, under date of July 24, in answer to a resolution of the House requesting information concerning New Mexico and California.[50] Lincoln got the floor toward the end of the consideration of the special order. With rare and surely unintentional humor the *Congressional Globe* records that "Mr. Lincoln spoke on politics in general and on the merits of the candidates for the Presidential office."[51]

The speech is to be found in full in the Appendix.[52] It is wholly innocent of any reference to the treaty of peace with Mexico or to New Mexico and California. It was clearly a practice stump speech in which Lincoln was getting ready for the part he was to take in the campaign between "Old Zach" Taylor and General Cass for the presidency, and was largely devoted to demonstrating that Taylor was a safer risk than Cass. In this campaign speech he not only was distinctly out of order from a parliamentary point of view, as he had also been in his speech on internal improvements, but even descended into pure billingsgate and left on the record a political harangue which sheds no luster on his career.

Lincoln's campaign speech for Taylor in Congress was not reported and received no editorial comment in the *Tribune*. There is no record that the speech came to Greeley's notice; but, on occasion, he had a way of ignoring what he had no taste for. As early as May 1, 1847, he wrote to Schuyler Colfax: "I don't like to support Taylor for next President on many grounds—especially the slavery aspect and the War aspect." Again on April 13, 1848, he wrote Colfax: "I have just two points clear with regard to the Presidential canvass: 1st. Clay is the man who *ought* to be President; 2nd. We *cannot* with any decency support Gen. Taylor." Again on September 15: "You needn't ask me to do any more than I *am* doing for Taylor. I do all I have any stomach for. Let him whose digestion is ranker do more."[53]

The slavery issue in one form or another came to the front at frequent

[49] *Cong. Globe*, 30th Cong., 1st sess., p. 990.
[50] *House Journal*, 30th Cong., 1st sess., p. 1122.
[51] *Cong. Globe*, 30th Cong., 1st sess., p. 1006.
[52] *Cong. Globe*, 30th Cong., 1st sess., Appendix, pp. 1041–43.
[53] Greeley Papers, New York Public Library, New York City.

intervals throughout the session. Lincoln took no aggressive action, offered no bills or petitions, but on the whole voted consistently against the suppression of full discussion and consideration of the specific questions on slavery which arose in Congress.

On December 21, 1847, Joshua R. Giddings of Ohio presented a memorial of certain citizens of the District of Columbia with reference to the slave trade asking "that all laws authorizing or sanctioning such trade within such District may be repealed." On a motion to lay the memorial on the table, which was lost after a tie by the Speaker's vote in the negative, Lincoln voted nay.[54]

On December 28 Caleb B. Smith of Indiana presented a petition of 211 persons of Jay County, Indiana, "praying for the abolition of slavery and the slave trade in the District of Columbia." On a motion to lay the petition on the table, which prevailed 76 to 70, Lincoln voted nay.[55]

On December 30 Amos Tuck of New Hampshire presented a petition of 71 citizens of Philadelphia, "praying Congress to appropriate the proceeds of the public lands for the extinction of slavery in the United States." On a motion to lay the petition on the table, which prevailed 87 to 70, Lincoln voted nay.[56]

On January 17, 1848, Joshua R. Giddings moved a preamble and resolution and asked for the previous question thereon. The situation came about as the result of the violent seizure of a Negro by armed persons engaged in the slave trade; the Negro was employed as a waiter in a boarding house patronized by members of Congress. The resolution provided, "That a select committee of five members be appointed to inquire into and report upon the facts aforesaid; also as to the propriety of repealing such acts of Congress as sustain or authorize the slave trade in this District, or to remove the seat of Government to some free State." On a motion to lay the resolution on the table which was lost, 85 to 87, Lincoln voted nay. Giddings then modified his preamble and resolution slightly, and on a second motion to lay the resolution on the table, which prevailed 94 to 88, Lincoln again voted nay.[57]

On January 31 Joshua R. Giddings moved "That a select committee of five members be appointed to inquire into and report to this House whether the slave trade is carried on within the District of Columbia; if so, by what legal authority it is sustained; and whether any modifica-

---

[54] *House Journal*, 30th Cong., 1st sess., pp. 139–40.
[55] *Ibid.*, pp. 160–61.
[56] *Ibid.*, pp. 167–68.
[57] *Ibid.*, pp. 250–52.

tion of the existing acts of Congress on that subject is expedient at this time." On a motion to lay the resolution on the table, which was lost 87 to 91, Lincoln voted nay.[58]

On February 28 Harvey Putnam of New York moved a preamble and resolution with reference to slavery in territory which might be acquired from Mexico. The resolution provided "That in any territory which may be acquired from Mexico, over which shall be established Territorial Governments, slavery or involuntary servitude, except as a punishment for crime, whereof the party shall have been duly convicted, should be forever prohibited; and that, in any act or resolution establishing such Governments, a fundamental provision ought to be inserted to that effect." On a motion to lay the resolution on the table, which prevailed 105 to 93, Lincoln voted nay.[59]

On April 10 the House concurred in a Joint Resolution from the Senate tendering the congratulations of the American people to the French people "upon the success of their recent efforts to consolidate the principles of liberty in a republican form of government." The vote of the House was overwhelmingly for the resolution, 173 to 2, and Lincoln voted yea.[60] The next day John G. Palfrey of Massachusetts moved a reconsideration of the vote by which the Joint Resolution was passed, his purpose being to propose an amendment as a prefix to the resolution, "That no despotism is more effective than that which exists under the semblance of popular institutions; and that a great nation emancipated from the control of an oligarchy of two hundred thousand voting citizens is entitled to the congratulations of every friend of freedom." A heated debate on slavery ensued in which Lincoln took no part. On a motion to lay the motion to reconsider on the table, which prevailed 123 to 46, Lincoln voted yea. Lincoln evidently took the view voiced in the debate that the amendment which had been contemplated was not relevant to the resolution of congratulations to France.[61]

On April 19 John G. Palfrey provoked a long debate by the presentation of a preamble and resolution calling for an inquiry into acts of violence on the two nights previous in the District of Columbia, the basis of the resolution being the imprisonment of eighty slaves who had tried to escape on a steamer that docked at Georgetown.[62] The

---

[58] *Ibid.*, pp. 324–25.
[59] *Ibid.*, pp. 453–54.
[60] *Ibid.*, pp. 669–70.
[61] *Ibid.*, pp. 671–72.
[62] *Cong. Globe*, 30th Cong., 1st sess., p. 649.

debate raged for five days, Lincoln remaining silent. On April 25, on a motion to lay the whole subject on the table, which prevailed 130 to 42, Lincoln voted yea.[63] He doubtless took the view which was frequently expressed in the debate that there was no relevancy between the question of privilege under which the preamble and resolution were offered and the basic issues of slavery which were dragged into the discussion.

On May 19 the House passed a bill "providing for the payment to the legal representatives of Cornelius Manning, deceased, of Maryland, of two hundred and eighty dollars, the value of a slave conveyed from the United States by the British fleet in 1814." The bill passed by a vote of 125 to 28, the Abolitionists opposing it. Lincoln voted yea.[64]

On May 29 Amos Tuck offered a preamble and resolution with reference to the many memorials and petitions received by the House on the subject of abolishing slavery and the slave trade in the District of Columbia. The resolution provided, "That the several committees of the House to whom have been referred petitions or memorials for the abolition of slavery and the slave trade in the District of Columbia be directed to take the same into consideration, and to report thereon at the earliest practicable period." Objection being made, on a motion to suspend the rules to enable Tuck to get his resolution before the House, which was lost 54 to 90, Lincoln voted nay.[65] The anti-slavery group voted for suspension of the rules. Lincoln voted with the Southern group. His vote in this case was quite out of line with his regular procedure, and is difficult to explain.

On July 28 the bill from the Senate to establish territorial governments in Oregon, California, and New Mexico was taken from the Speaker's table. This bill provided that the anti-slavery laws of Oregon should continue in effect, but forbade the legislatures of California and New Mexico to pass any law relating to slavery. The status of slavery in those territories was to be decided by appeal to the Supreme Court. On a motion to lay the bill on the table, which prevailed 112 to 97, Lincoln voted yea.[66]

On August 2 the House considered a bill of its own reported by the Committee of the Whole to establish the Territorial Government of Oregon. On a proposed amendment, striking out the heart of the bill,

---

[63] *House Journal*, 30th Cong., 1st sess., pp. 720–21.
[64] *Ibid.*, pp. 824–25.
[65] *Ibid.*, pp. 840–41.
[66] *Ibid.*, pp. 1124–25.

the provision extending the Ordinance of 1787 over the territory, which was lost 88 to 114, Lincoln voted nay. The bill was then passed, 128 to 71, Lincoln voting yea.[67] On August 11 the House again had the Oregon bill under consideration, as amended by the Senate to extend the Missouri Compromise line to the Pacific. The House rejected the amendment, 82 to 121, Lincoln voting nay.[68]

By Joint Resolution the Senate and the House of Representatives adjourned sine die at twelve noon on Monday, August 14, 1848, and the first session of the Thirtieth Congress came to an end. Lincoln's successor for the Thirty-first Congress from the Seventh Congressional District of Illinois had already been chosen. The election had been held on August 7 and his one-time law partner, Judge Logan, went down to defeat before Major Thomas L. Harris, the Democratic candidate, who was a hero of the Mexican War. It was commonly understood that Logan's defeat was due to the reaction against Lincoln. Fortunately he did not go to Logan's assistance; Lincoln's ear was to the ground, and he knew very well that he could not help Logan. He was in no hurry to get home and stayed on "to frank documents"[69] and to size up the prospects of General Taylor in New England in the coming presidential election. "I would rather not be put upon explaining how Logan was defeated in my district,"[70] he wrote William Schouler on August 28. What with one thing and another, Lincoln did not reach home until October 10, and by that time the people of the Seventh Congressional District of Illinois were thinking more about the approaching presidential election than about the shortcomings of their congressman.

The "fag-end" congressman from the Sixth Congressional District of New York took his seat in the House promptly at the convening of the second session of the Thirtieth Congress on Monday, December 4, 1848, and was appointed ninth and last member of the Committee on Public Lands.[71] Lincoln, somewhat subdued, did not arrive until Thursday, December 7. Greeley, the New Yorker, came to Congress expecting to "kick up some dust" concerning the mileage allowance of members, and very soon his "expectations were far outrun."[72] Lincoln, "the tall specimen from Illinois,"[73] was soon more interested in being ap-

---

[67] *Ibid.*, pp. 1153–56.

[68] *Ibid.*, pp. 1245–46.

[69] Tracy, *op. cit.*, p. 34, Lincoln to William Schouler, August 8, 1848.

[70] *Ibid.*, p. 35, August 29, 1848.

[71] *Cong. Globe*, 30th Cong., 2d sess., pp. 2, 22.

[72] Greeley, *op. cit.*, p. 220.

[73] Robert Fergus, comp., Fergus' Historical Series, Number Eighteen, p. 141.

pointed Commissioner of the Land Office by "Old Zach" Taylor, whom he had helped to elect, than in instituting any reforms in Congress.[74]

Greeley buzzed with activity and frequently took part in the debates; Lincoln kept quietly in the background. The index to the *Congressional Globe* for the short session makes 71 references to Greeley and only 11 to Lincoln. Greeley had one brief speech on the bill to provide a territorial government for California, reported in the Appendix; Lincoln had none. Lincoln spoke only once throughout the session, his remarks on that occasion appearing in the *Globe* and opening with the statement that "he had not risen for the purpose of making a speech."[75] The bill under consideration at the time originated in the Senate and had to do with the disposal of public lands for the building of railroads and canals.

Both Lincoln and Greeley were in very regular if not constant attendance upon the sessions of the House. During the session the yeas and nays were called for 154 times. Lincoln missed 7 such calls, namely, on December 22, 1848, January 15, January 22, February 23, February 24, February 26, and March 1, 1849, and in all but two of these occasions he was present and voting on other issues. He was recorded as among the absentees on December 22; on February 26 his name does not appear on the only roll call.[76] Greeley missed four calls for the yeas and nays (one on December 29, 1848, two on February 10, and one on February 23, 1849).[77] On this last date he was recorded as present and voting on other issues. He was not recorded as absent at any time. On the 154 calls for the yeas and nays, Lincoln voted 111 times with a majority, 36 times with a minority, and missed seven votes; Greeley voted 100 times with a majority, 50 times with a minority, and missed four votes. Lincoln and Greeley voted the same way 95 times, 79 times with a majority, and 16 times with a minority. They disagreed in 49 votes, Lincoln going with a majority 31 times and Greeley 18 times.

Slavery was a paramount issue in the debates, and the abolition of the slave trade in the District of Columbia was again urged early in the session. On December 13, 1848, on a motion to permit the introduction of a bill "to repeal all acts of Congress establishing or maintaining slavery and the slave trade within the District of Columbia," which was defeated 70 to 82, Greeley voted yea and Lincoln nay.[78] On the

[74] Beveridge, *op. cit.*, I, 489.
[75] *Cong. Globe*, 30th Cong., 2d sess., p. 533.
[76] *House Journal*, 30th Cong., 2d sess., pp. 142, 531.
[77] *Ibid.*, pp. 165–68, 416, 521.
[78] *Ibid.*, p. 97.

same day a resolution was offered instructing the Committee on Territories to report "a bill or bills providing a territorial government for each of the territories of New Mexico and California, and excluding slavery therefrom." After the defeat of a motion to lay the resolution on the table, 80 to 106, upon which Lincoln and Greeley voted nay, the resolution was adopted, 108 to 80, with Lincoln and Greeley voting for it.[79] Five days later they joined again in defeating a motion to reconsider the vote by which the resolution was adopted, 105 to 83.[80]

On December 18 Joshua R. Giddings obtained leave and introduced a bill "to authorize the people of the District of Columbia to express their wishes as to the continuance of slavery and the slave trade within said district." On a motion that the bill be laid on the table, which prevailed 106 to 79, Lincoln voted yea and Greeley nay.[81]

On December 21 Daniel Gott of New York offered a preamble and resolution providing "That the Committee for the District of Columbia be instructed to report a bill as soon as practicable prohibiting the slave trade in said district." On a motion to lay the resolution on the table, which was defeated 81 to 85, Lincoln voted yea and Greeley nay. On the question "Shall the main question be now put?" which was carried 113 to 63, Greeley voted yea and Lincoln nay. The resolution was then adopted, 98 to 87, Greeley voting yea and Lincoln nay.[82] On January 31, 1849, the committee, without following its instructions implicitly, reported a bill "to prohibit the introduction of slaves into the District of Columbia as merchandise or for sale or hire." On a motion to lay the bill on the table, which was defeated 72 to 117, Lincoln and Greeley both voted nay.[83]

On January 6 a bill reported by the Committee of the Whole House, granting $1,000 to the legal representatives of a slave owner—whose slave had joined the Seminole Indians in 1835, was captured by United States troops, and then sent West with the Indians—came to vote. The bill was lost, after some confusion as to the final vote, 89 to 90, with Lincoln and Greeley voting against it.[84] On January 19 on a motion to reconsider, which prevailed 98 to 93, Lincoln and Greeley both voted

[79] *Ibid.*, pp. 98–100.
[80] *Ibid.*, p. 105.
[81] *Ibid.*, pp. 106–07.
[82] *Ibid.*, pp. 132–35.
[83] *Ibid.*, pp. 347–48.
[84] *Ibid.*, pp. 207, 211.

nay. The bill was then passed, 101 to 95, with Lincoln and Greeley voting against it.[85]

On January 8 Richard K. Meade of Virginia moved that the rules be suspended to enable him to offer a preamble and resolution concerning the apprehension of fugitive slaves providing, "That the Committee on Judiciary is hereby instructed to report a bill to this House, providing effectually for the apprehension and delivery of fugitives from labor, who have escaped, or may hereafter escape from one State into another." The House declined to suspend the rules, 79 to 100; Greeley voted yea and Lincoln, nay.[86]

On February 27 the Committee of the Whole House reported a bill "to establish the territorial government of Upper California" including the provision "That there shall be neither slavery nor involuntary servitude in the said State otherwise than in the punishment of crimes whereof the party shall have been duly convicted." The bill was passed, 126 to 87, with Lincoln and Greeley both voting yea.[87]

On March 2 the House rejected an amendment of the Senate to the Civil and Diplomatic Appropriations bill providing for the extension of the laws and Constitution of the United States over the new territories west of the Rio Grande. The vote on the amendment was 101 to 115, with Lincoln and Greeley both voting nay.[88] The next day the House receded from this action, 111 to 106; Lincoln and Greeley both voted nay.[89] The House then amended the amendment in certain particulars and finally agreed to it as amended, 110 to 103, with Lincoln and Greeley both voting yea.[90]

Singularly enough, hating slavery as they both did and absorbed as they were in its issues in later years, they took no aggressive part in the discussion of these questions on the floor of the House. Indeed, Lincoln scarcely lifted his voice, except in one instance; and Greeley was mainly content to express his views on slavery questions by his vote. He did participate mildly in the debates on the bills to establish territorial governments in California and in New Mexico.[91]

Lincoln sent up one trial balloon. On January 10 in the midst of the

---

[85] *Ibid.*, pp. 276–77.
[86] *Ibid.*, pp. 213–14.
[87] *Ibid.*, p. 539.
[88] *Ibid.*, pp. 600–01.
[89] *Ibid.*, p. 637.
[90] *Ibid.*, pp. 645–46.
[91] *Cong. Globe*, 30th Cong., 2d sess., pp. 608–11.

discussion of Daniel Gott's resolution calling upon the Committee on the District of Columbia to report a bill prohibiting the slave trade in the District, Lincoln spoke. The immediate question was the proposal to reconsider the vote by which the resolution had been adopted. Securing the floor, Lincoln said that if the vote on the resolution was reconsidered he should make an effort to introduce an amendment. He then proceeded without interruption to read the amendment he proposed to offer. It struck out all after the word "resolved" in Gott's resolution and provided that the Committee on the District of Columbia be instructed to report a bill which he then proposed in exact terms. Slavery in the District was to be confined to slaves then living in the District except that government officials might bring in and take out the "necessary servants of themselves and their families." Children born of slave mothers after January 1, 1850, were to be free. Slaves in the District were to continue as such "at the will of their owners," but provision was made to compensate an owner from the national treasury for any slave he wished to make free. Municipal authorities of Washington and Georgetown were empowered to provide "active and efficient means to arrest and deliver up to their owners all fugitive slaves escaping into said District." Finally, provision was made for an election in the District in which white male citizens would vote for or against the project.[92]

Lincoln then said that of about fifteen of the leading citizens of the District of Columbia to whom his proposal had been submitted there was not one but who approved of its adoption. He could not say that they would vote for the bill, but he was authorized to say that every one of them favored some such action. There were immediate cries for the names of the persons, but Lincoln remained silent, and the business of the House went on as if nothing had happened. On January 13 Lincoln "gave notice of a motion for leave to introduce a bill to abolish slavery in the District of Columbia, by consent of the free white people of said District, and with compensation to owners."[93] He did not follow up this notice with the introduction of a bill and took no part in the subsequent and fruitless debates on the issue.

On the second day of the session, December 5, 1848, before Lincoln had arrived, Greeley had sent up his first trial balloon, through notice of a motion for leave to introduce a bill "To discourage speculation in public lands, and to secure homes thereon to actual settlers and culti-

---

[92] *Ibid.*, p. 212.
[93] *House Journal*, 30th Cong., 2d sess., p. 242.

vators."[94] He promptly followed up this notice on December 13 with the introduction of such a bill, which was read a first and second time and referred to the Committee on Public Lands of which he was a member.[95] Greeley was apparently unable to win the support of his fellow committeemen, and the bill quietly reposed in committee until February 27 when the chairman reported it back to the House without amendment. Greeley explained the terms of the bill and said that it was "the only bill which had been before the Committee on Public Lands this winter, proposing to recognize in any form, the principle that a man is entitled to live *somewhere*, although he has no money wherewith to buy land to live on." He charged the committee with having reported the bill to be "summarily dismissed" and asked for the yeas and nays in the rejection of the bill. Thereupon a motion was made that the bill be laid upon the table. Greeley then asked for the yeas and nays on that motion. Since only about twenty members came to his aid by rising to second the call for the yeas and nays, they were not ordered; and the bill, by a *viva voce* vote, was laid on the table, and that ended his effort on this issue.[96]

Greeley's most sensational undertaking in Congress, which he expected "would kick up some dust," began with what he called the "mileage exposé" in the *Tribune*. As soon as he reached Washington and found that he had access to the records, he set a clerk at work upon the mileage paid each member of Congress for the previous session. The law provided that each member should receive $8 for every twenty miles traveled in coming to and returning from Congress by the usually traveled route. Greeley held that the changed mode of travel from horseback, stage, and canal to steamboats and railroads, shortening the distance and lessening the time, had outlawed the statute and made the mileage charge a scandal. On December 22 he published in the *Tribune* a tabular statement showing: (a) the name of each member of Congress; (b) the number of miles from his home to Washington by the shortest post-route; (c) the number of miles charged; (d) the amount of mileage charged; (e) the excess of mileage charged over what would have been charged if it had been computed on the basis of the shortest post-route. This statement showed that the shortest post-route from Springfield, Illinois, the home of Congressman Abraham

[94] *Ibid.*, p. 9.
[95] *Ibid.*, p. 95.
[96] *Cong. Globe*, 30th Cong., 2d sess., p. 605.

Lincoln, was 780 miles, that he had charged for a distance of 1,626 miles, that he had collected $1,300.80 for the roundtrip to the first session of the Thirtieth Congress, and that this was an excess charge of $676.80.

Greeley was careful to point out that he did not accuse any member of Congress of dishonesty or misconduct. His purpose, he insisted, was to bring about an amendment to the law, and thus to reform an iniquitous practice. The dust the exposé kicked up far exceeded his expectations and promptly made him the most unpopular man in the House.

The exposé came up in the House on December 27 and a bitter debate ensued, the chief protagonist being Lincoln's colleague, Thomas J. Turner from Illinois. He declared that "the whole article abounded in gross errors and wilfully false statements, and was evidently prompted by motives as base, unprincipled and corrupt as ever actuated an individual in wielding his pen for the public press." Continuing, he characterized the editor of the *Tribune* as "the thing that penned that article" and concluded his sharp castigation by offering a resolution calling for an inquiry into the mileage situation and for questioning whether the publication in the *Tribune* constituted an allegation of fraud against most of the members of the House.[97]

On a motion to lay the resolution on the table, which was lost 28 to 129, Greeley and Lincoln both voted nay.[98]

Greeley stood his ground, freely acknowledged authorship of the article, admitted that there might be clerical errors in the computations, and insisted that his purpose was the reform of an abuse. In the course of the discussion, the question being on the adoption of the resolution, Lincoln called for a division of the question so that it could be taken on the resolutions separately. It was so ordered. The first resolution was adopted without the yeas and nays being called for. The second resolution was adopted, 100 to 43, with Greeley voting yea and Lincoln voting nay.[99] The question was then taken on the third resolution and it was rejected. On January 12 the Committee on Mileage made its report which was promptly laid on the table.[100]

In the meantime on January 9, the Civil and Diplomatic Appropriations bill being under consideration, a motion was made by Elisha Embree of Indiana to amend the item for compensation and mileage of

---

[97] *Ibid.*, p. 109.
[98] *House Journal*, 30th Cong., 2d sess., p. 155.
[99] *Ibid.*, pp. 156–57.
[100] *Cong. Globe*, 30th Cong., 2d sess., p. 238.

members of Congress by adding the following phrase: *"Provided,* That the mileage of members of both Houses of Congress shall hereafter be estimated and charged upon the shortest mail route from their places of residence, respectively, to the city of Washington."[101]

Debate ensued in which Amos Tuck was about the only member who stood by Greeley. Albert Gallatin Brown of Mississippi took this fling at Greeley: "If gentlemen were so anxious to correct abuses, let them correct their own first; let this thing of editing papers by gentlemen who were paid from the public treasury for public service cease." The committee rose without action and resumed its consideration of Elisha Embree's amendment on January 11.[102] A long debate took place in which Greeley was again hard pressed. The committee again rose without action, and the House voted to terminate debate after one hour when the question should next be considered. The same procedure and a like debate took place on January 16 without action.[103] The debate was renewed the next day, various amendments to the amendment were proposed, and out of the muddle the matter was settled by the Committee of the Whole "by providing that in lieu of the mileage and per diem at present allowed to members of Congress, there should be allowed ten cents per mile on the usual mail routes between the respective residences of members of Congress and the seat of Government, and a compensation of $2,000 per annum."[104]

This proposal in substance came to a vote in the House on January 23, and was rejected, 36 to 150, Greeley and Lincoln both voting nay. Two days later under date of January 23 the Washington correspondence in the *Tribune* contained this item: "The coppers were placed decently on the eyes of the Mileage Reform today, and the old and annually aggravated abuse is to go on until the People shall see fit to stop it. While they remain passive nothing will be done here. This voting money out of its own pocket is rather a severe strain on modern patriotism."[105]

Thus the dust Greeley had kicked up settled down. In the entire discussion, as lively and spirited as any in the entire session, Lincoln raised his voice only to propose action on the resolution which started the fuss. "But," as Greeley wrote about Lincoln many years later, "as

---

[101] *Ibid.*, pp. 200–03.
[102] *Ibid.*, pp. 224–31.
[103] *Ibid.*, pp. 271–74.
[104] *Ibid.*, p. 284.
[105] *Tribune*, January 25, 1849.

I had made most of the members my enemies, at an early stage of that short session, by printing an elucidated exposé of the iniquities of Congressional mileage; and as he did not join the active cabal against me, though *his* mileage figured conspicuously and by no means flatteringly in that exposé, I parted from him at the close of the Congress with none but grateful recollections."[106]

The deliberations of the House in the short session of the Thirtieth Congress came to an end at 7 A.M. on Sunday, March 4, 1849, with Lincoln and Greeley in their places. In the midst of the evening session which had begun at 6 P.M. on March 3—while the Senate "was chewing" on the territorial clause in the appropriations bill, which was finally expunged, "leaving the question of Slavery in the new Territories as a legacy of trouble to the incoming Administration"—Horace Greeley drew from his drawer "a resolve, which had lain there for weeks," and solemnly offered it as a Joint Resolution for the consideration of the House. It was read twice and laid on the table, but it got into the *Congressional Globe*. Its import was that the United States should "hereafter be known and officially designated by the name or appellation Columbia."[107]

Lincoln and Greeley attended the inauguration of Zachary Taylor as President on March 5, as well as the grand inaugural ball in the evening. Lincoln went to the ball with a party of friends including Elihu B. Washburne. When it came time to go home at three or four o'clock in the morning, he could not find his hat.[108] Greeley wrote to Schuyler Colfax: "I was in Washington at the inauguration and the hideously vulgar ball."[109]

Lincoln left little record of his experience in Congress beyond his fruitless effort to explain his position on the Mexican War. He was not anxious to go home and hoped that Zachary Taylor would make him commissioner of the General Land Office. He made no report to his constituents, left little intimation of his impression of his associates, and no record of the activities in Congress. Greeley, on the other hand, never failed to get his experiences and observations into writing. On February 16 he wrote Schuyler Colfax: "We are going to do nothing this session, and a great deal of it."[110] He confirmed this view in a three-

---

[106] MS, Greeley's lecture on "Abraham Lincoln," *op. cit.*, p. 14.

[107] *Cong. Globe,* 30th Cong., 2d sess., p. 694.

[108] Allen Thorndike Rice, *Reminiscences of Abraham Lincoln by Distinguished Men of His Time,* pp. 19–20.

[109] Greeley Papers, *op. cit.*

[110] *Ibid.*

column report to his constituents published in the *Tribune* which opened:

Chosen by your favor to a seat in Congress through its brief Second Session, I have been an actor in or witness of some doings which may well seem to require farther explanation. It is not to be denied or disguised that the Session has been a failure, not only in view of the good it meditated, but judged solely with reference to what it might have done. . . . There was no good reason for failure of several important and beneficent measures which were not matured into laws at the late Session—no reason at all but the incompetency or unfaithfulness of a large portion of those clothed with the power and charged with the duty of enacting them. I do not choose to bear my equal portion of the blame, for I am confident I have not deserved it.[111]

In later years he recalled his association with Lincoln and said that there were men "on our side of the House" accounted abler than Lincoln but "that no other was more generally liked and esteemed than he." He doubted "whether five of us would have designated Abraham Lincoln [as] the man among us who would first attain the presidency."[112] He judged that A. H. Stephens of Georgia "was the most acute, and perhaps the ablest member of that House."[113] Lincoln also got a favorable impression of Stephens, writing to Herndon on February 2, 1848: "I just take my pen to say that Mr. Stephens, of Georgia, a little, slim, pale-faced, consumptive man, with a voice like Logan's, has just concluded the very best speech of an hour's length I ever heard. My old withered dry eyes are full of tears yet."[114]

In another statement Greeley left this impression of Congressman Lincoln:

Abraham Lincoln and Andrew Johnson (each of them about forty years old) were members of the House to which I was chosen, as Mr. Johnson had been of the two preceding and remained through the two following, when he was translated to the Senate. Mr. Johnson, being a Democrat, seldom visited our side of the hall, and I saw much less of him than of Mr. Lincoln, who was a Whig, and who, though a new member, was personally a favorite on our side. He seemed a quiet, good-natured man, did not aspire to leadership, and seldom claimed the floor. I think he made but one set speech during that session, and this speech was by no means a long one. Though a strong partisan, he voted against the bulk of his party once or twice, when

---

[111] *Tribune*, March 12, 1849.
[112] MS, Greeley's lecture on "Abraham Lincoln," *op. cit.*, pp. 14–15.
[113] Greeley, *op. cit.*, p. 227.
[114] Nicolay and Hay, *op. cit.*, I, 354.

that course was dictated by his convictions. He was one of the most mod-
erate, though firm, opponents of Slavery Extension, and notably of a buoy-
ant, cheerful spirit. It will surprise some to hear that, though I was often in
his company thenceforward till his death, and long on terms of friendly
intimacy with him, I never heard him tell an anecdote or story.[115]

Lincoln went home silent about the failures of the Thirtieth Congress
but disillusioned, disappointed, and keenly conscious of his own failure
to "distinguish" himself as his constituents had expected him to do.
He now dropped out of political prominence and went "to the practice
of law with greater earnestness than ever before."[116] Greeley went back
to his editorial chair confident that Congress had failed but that he had
not.

---

[115] Greeley, *op. cit.*, p. 226.
[116] Nicolay and Hay, *op. cit.*, VI, 37.

I am naturally antislavery. If slavery is not wrong, nothing is wrong. I cannot remember when I did not so think and feel.

Lincoln[1]

We have never been anything else than Anti-Slavery, either in word or deed.

Greeley[2]

4 The slavery issue

The slavery issue, characterized dramatically and prophetically by William H. Seward in 1858 as "an irrepressible conflict,"[3] engaged the minds of Lincoln and Greeley in one way or another throughout their lives. Lincoln died at the moment the "great and durable element of popular action"[4] was being determined, and Greeley lived to write its history and to see the worst days of reconstruction.[5] So far as the record goes, Greeley was inspired with a hatred of slavery at a very early age. It is difficult to determine just how far the intense feeling of his mature years influenced his memory of his boyhood attitude, but he recalled with his customary positiveness that before he was "yet half old enough to vote" he "heartily sympathized with the Northern uprising against the admission of Missouri as a Slave State."[6] During his apprenticeship days at East Poultney, he witnessed "a fugitive slave-chase" and shared the sense of "injustice and oppression" which it provoked in the community.[7]

Greeley was nine when the Missouri Compromise was enacted. He was already, in the light of his recollections, thinking in mature terms

---

[1] John G. Nicolay and John Hay, eds., *Complete Works of Abraham Lincoln*, X, 65.
[2] *Tribune*, February 1, 1844.
[3] Frederic Bancroft, *The Life of William H. Seward*, I, 459.
[4] Nicolay and Hay, *op. cit.*, II, 260.
[5] Horace Greeley, *The American Conflict*.
[6] Horace Greeley, *Recollections of a Busy Life*, p. 106.
[7] *Ibid.*, p. 65.

on the issues of slavery and reaching determinations which were to be reflected in his future conduct. Looking back on the formation of his views in those early days, he recalled that he had questioned the agitation of the abolitionists in the North because he could not see how the citizens of Vermont, however worthy their object, could bring about the overthrow of slavery in Georgia. "Hence," he said, "I for years regarded with complacency the Colonization movement."[8]

Lincoln left no first-hand record of his attitude on slavery as a boy and as a youth. He did declare that his father left Kentucky "partly on account of slavery, but chiefly on account of the difficulty in land titles."[9] On his two flatboat journeys to New Orleans, he had ample opportunity to see all the hateful aspects of slavery, but he left no record of his observations. Herndon's graphic account of Lincoln's reaction to witnessing a slave auction in New Orleans in 1831 is not convincing.[10] Lincoln may easily have seen such an auction with all its revolting details; but it is highly improbable that he then and there vowed that he would do something about it if he ever got the chance. According to Lincoln's own testimony, John Hanks, who started out with Lincoln and John Johnston on this trip, turned back at St. Louis.[11] Yet it was Hanks who told the tale to Herndon in 1865. Herndon also claimed that he had "heard Mr. Lincoln refer to it himself." This incident which has been accepted at full face value and repeated over and over by many writers is a good example of the wishful thinking frequently found in Lincolniana. In his prize-winning play, *Abe Lincoln in Illinois,* Robert E. Sherwood did not employ this incident. "I left that out," he explains in his supplementary notes, "because I don't believe any of it."[12]

Lincoln's first recorded views on slavery are to be found in the familiar resolutions of protest in which he joined with Dan Stone in the Illinois Legislature on March 3, 1837. In these resolutions he made it clear that he believed slavery to be "founded on both injustice and bad policy" but viewed "abolition doctrines" as calculated "rather to increase than abate its evils"; that the Congress of the United States had "no power under the Constitution to interfere with the institution of slavery in the different States"; and that while Congress had the power

---

[8] *Ibid.,* pp. 284–85.

[9] Nicolay and Hay, *op. cit.,* VI, 26.

[10] William H. Herndon and Jesse William Weik, *The Life of Lincoln,* I, 75–76.

[11] Nicolay and Hay, *op. cit.,* VI, 30.

[12] Robert E. Sherwood, *Abe Lincoln in Illinois,* p. 202. See also Roy P. Basler, *The Lincoln Legend,* pp. 134–38.

to abolish slavery in the District of Columbia, "the power ought not to be exercised, unless at the request of the people of the District." These views he did not thereafter alter except under the exigencies of war.[13]

Lincoln's first contact with slavery as a lawyer came before he retired from the legislature and culminated in an appeal before the Illinois Supreme Court, *Bailey* v. *Cromwell* et al. Cromwell had sold an alleged indentured Negro girl to Bailey and had taken Bailey's promissory note in payment. It was stipulated in the sale that Cromwell should produce proof that the girl was a slave. Cromwell did not produce proof, the girl left Bailey's service claiming that she was free, and Bailey refused to pay the note. The administrators of Cromwell's estate finally brought suit in Tazewell County and recovered judgment for the purchase price. Lincoln, as Bailey's counsel, took the case to the Illinois Supreme Court and was there met by his future law partner, Stephen T. Logan, as opposing counsel. The case had been heard in Circuit Court at the September term in 1839 and was determined by the Illinois Supreme Court in July, 1841.

Lincoln argued that the girl was free both under the Ordinance of 1787 and the Constitution of Illinois forbidding slavery, that no human being could be sold in a free state, and that there was, therefore, no consideration for the note and it should be held void. The Illinois Supreme Court sustained Lincoln's contention, reversed the Circuit Court, and held that "there was no consideration for the note and that it was void," and that "It is a presumption of law, in the State of Illinois, that every person is free without regard to color. The sale of a free person is illegal."[14]

Several years later Lincoln became involved as counsel on the opposite side of a similar case. On this occasion he was retained by a slave owner, Robert Matson, from Kentucky. Matson owned a farm in Coles County, Illinois, and was in the habit of bringing slaves from Kentucky to do the farm labor during the planting and harvesting season. He kept one slave, Anthony Bryant, on the Coles County farm continually. Under the law Bryant thus became a free man. In the spring of 1847 Matson brought Bryant's wife, a mulatto, the reputed daughter of Matson's brother, and four children from Kentucky with other slaves and sought to take them back in the fall. In the meantime, Mary

---

[13] Nicolay and Hay, *op. cit.*, I, 51–52.
[14] 3 Scammon, *Illinois Reports*, pp. 71–73; Rufus Rockwell Wilson, *Uncollected Works of Lincoln*, I, 457–58.

Corbin, Matson's housekeeper, quarreled with Jane Bryant and threatened to have her and her children sold by Matson for plantation labor in the far South. Anthony Bryant became alarmed and sought help from friends in the village of Oakland. A young doctor, Hiram Rutherford, and the proprietor of the village inn, Gideon M. Ashmore, gave Jane Bryant and her children refuge in the inn.

Unable to persuade the slaves to return to him, Matson made affidavit, and under a writ by William Gilman, justice of the peace, before whom the case was tried, the slaves were lodged in jail at Charleston as runaways. Excitement ran high. Application was made to the Circuit Court by the friends of the slaves for their release on a writ of habeas corpus. The situation was complicated by a suit for damages brought by Matson against Dr. Rutherford for having seized his slaves. Lincoln was in Charleston attending the sessions of the court, and his services were sought on both sides of the controversy. After some misunderstandings, he finally agreed to appear as the associate of Usher F. Linder for Matson. Opposing counsel held that the slaves were made free in Illinois through the Ordinance of 1787 and the Constitution of Illinois, the very argument Lincoln had made in *Bailey* v. *Cromwell,* but failed to cite the decision of the Illinois Supreme Court in this case. Lincoln held, in behalf of his client, that the sole question at issue was whether or not the slaves were *in transitu* or were meant to remain in Illinois. The slaves were released and declared free.[15]

Lincoln's first known account about slavery is in a "bread and butter" letter to Mary Speed, sister of his intimate friend Joshua Speed, on September 27, 1841. Lincoln had made a visit to the ancestral home of the Speeds in Kentucky and on his homeward journey traveled by steamboat from Louisville to St. Louis. Shortly after his return Lincoln wrote a long, chatty letter to Mary Speed in which he recounted his experience on the "Lebanon" on the way to St. Louis:

> *By the way, a fine example was presented on board the boat for contemplating the effect of condition upon human happiness. A gentleman had purchased twelve negroes in different parts of Kentucky, and was taking them to a farm in the South. They were chained six and six together. A small iron clevis was around the left wrist of each, and this was fastened to the main chain by a shorter one, at a convenient distance from the others, so that the negroes were strung together precisely like so many fish on a trotline. In this condition they were being separated forever from the scenes of*

---

[15] Albert J. Beveridge, *Abraham Lincoln,* I, 392–97. See also Duncan T. McIntyre, "Lincoln and the Matson Slave Case," *Illinois Law Review,* I, 386–91.

their childhood, their friends, their fathers and mothers, and brothers and sisters, and many of them from their wives and children, and going into perpetual slavery, where the lash of the master is proverbially more ruthless and unrelenting than any other where; and yet amid all these distressing circumstances, as we would think them, they were the most cheerful and apparently happy creatures on board. One whose offense for which he had been sold was an over-fondness for his wife, played the fiddle almost continually, and the others danced, sang, cracked jokes, and played various games with cards from day to day. How true it is that "God tempers the wind to the shorn lamb," or in other words, that he renders the worst of human conditions tolerable, while he permits the best to be nothing better than tolerable.[16]

There is no word in this letter about his own personal feelings. Fourteen years later, after he had recorded himself in unmistakable terms, he recalled this steamboat journey on the Ohio in a letter to Joshua Speed who had accompanied him:

You know I dislike slavery, and you fully admit the abstract wrong of it. So far there is no cause of difference. But you say that sooner than yield your legal right to the slave, especially at the bidding of those who are not themselves interested, you would see the Union dissolved. I am not aware that any one is bidding you yield that right; very certainly I am not. I leave that matter entirely to yourself. I also acknowledge your rights and my obligations under the Constitution in regard to your slaves. I confess I hate to see the poor creatures hunted down and caught and carried back to their stripes and unrequited toil; but I bite my lips and keep quiet. In 1841 you and I had together a tedious low-water trip on a steamboat from Louisville to St. Louis. You may remember, as I well do, that from Louisville to the mouth of the Ohio there were on board ten or a dozen slaves shackled together with irons. That sight was a continued torment to me, and I see something like it every time I touch the Ohio or any other slave border. It is not fair for you to assume that I have no interest in a thing which has, and continually exercises, the power of making me miserable.[17]

Herndon relates an incident which also shows how Lincoln's personal feelings were aroused by slavery. Sometime in 1855 an Illinois Negro working on a Mississippi steamboat found himself in New Orleans without "free papers" and in accordance with prevailing practice was clapped into jail. He was in grave danger of being sold as a slave to defray his prison expenses. His mother, Polly, who lived in Springfield,

---

[16] Nicolay and Hay, *op. cit.*, I, 178–79.
[17] *Ibid.*, II, 281–82.

went to Lincoln and Herndon for aid. They laid the case before Governor Matteson of Illinois who held that he was powerless to interfere. They then appealed to the governor of Louisiana and received the same answer. In a second interview with Governor Matteson, which resulted in nothing, Lincoln is said to have exclaimed: "By God, Governor, I'll make the ground in this country too hot for the foot of a slave, whether you have the legal power to secure the release of this boy or not." This alleged utterance suggests Herndon more than Lincoln. Dropping the case from a legal standpoint, they got up a subscription, paid the prison expenses in New Orleans, and "restored the prisoner to his overjoyed mother."[18]

Lincoln was no more of an abolitionist than Greeley, and like Greeley he long nourished the hope of the colonization of the Negroes. He reached his initial position on these issues through his discipleship of Henry Clay. In his eulogy on Clay he set forth Clay's views on slavery and on colonization and clearly indicated his agreement with these views. Although Clay owned slaves, he was opposed on principle and in feeling to slavery. On the question of human rights he perceived that the Negroes were not to be excepted from the human race, yet he could not perceive how slavery could be eradicated without producing an even greater evil to the cause of human liberty itself. Throughout his life Clay opposed both extremes of opinion on the subject. "Those who would shiver into fragments the Union of these States," said Lincoln, voicing his own views in eulogizing Clay, "tear to tatters its now venerated Constitution, and even burn the last copy of the Bible, rather than slavery should continue a single hour, together with all their more halting sympathizers, have received, and are receiving, their just execration; and the name and opinions and influence of Mr. Clay are fully and, as I trust, effectually and enduringly arrayed against them." Lincoln referred to Clay's continued support of the American Colonization Society and on his own account voiced the hope that its purposes might "indeed be realized." Continuing he said, "If, as the friends of colonization hope, the present and coming generations of our countrymen shall by any means succeed in freeing our land from the dangerous presence of slavery, and at the same time in restoring a captive people to their long-lost fatherland with bright prospects for the future, and this too so gradually that neither races nor individuals shall have suffered by the change, it will indeed be a glorious consummation."[19]

---

[18] Herndon and Weik, *op. cit.*, II, 378–79.
[19] Nicolay and Hay, *op. cit.*, II, 172–77.

An incident occurred at Alton, Illinois, on November 7, 1837, which stirred the nation and still further provoked the bitterness between pro-slavery and anti-slavery factions. Elijah P. Lovejoy, a young Presbyterian minister who had established a religious paper known as the *Observer* in St. Louis in 1833, had been obliged to move his paper from St. Louis to Alton because of the violent criticism his editorials against slavery had aroused. He insisted that he was not an Abolitionist but that he would continue to exercise his right as a free-born American citizen to express his views on slavery in his paper. He met with added criticism in Alton, and his press was twice thrown into the river. Declaring, "If I die, I have determined to make my grave in Alton," he persisted in his efforts. A new press was secured and stored in a warehouse, where Lovejoy and a group of his supporters fought off a mob which came to destroy it. During the night of November 7, the press was again destroyed; and in the encounter which ensued, Lovejoy was killed.[20]

The incident provoked the wrath of the Abolitionists throughout the country. In protest a great assembly was held at Faneuil Hall, Boston, on December 8, and at this meeting Wendell Phillips, then twenty-six, became famous as the "golden trumpet" of abolition. Lincoln at Springfield, only sixty miles from Alton, was silent. A few weeks later, on January 27, 1838, he delivered an address before a young men's lyceum in Springfield on the topic "The perpetuation of our political institutions." The discussion of the mob violence at Alton was still at high pitch, but Lincoln did not mention Lovejoy or Alton by name, although he did speak at length on the dangers of mob violence and referred cautiously to throwing printing presses into rivers and shooting editors.[21]

Greeley rarely hesitated to speak his mind. It took a little time for the circumstances of the Alton riot to reach the East, but on November 25 in an editorial headed "The Tragedy at Alton," he thundered:

We loathe and abhor the miserable cant of those that talk of Mr. Lovejoy as guilty of resisting public opinion. Public opinion forsooth! What right have five hundred or five thousand to interfere with the lawful expression of a freeman's sentiments because they happen to number more than those who think with him. We spurn the base tyranny—this utter denial of all rights, save as the tender mercies of a mob shall vouchsafe them. If Mr. L's views were erroneous, let them be refuted; if his motives were corrupt, (but this is not pretended,) let them be exposed and contemned; if his actions

---

[20] Joseph Cammet and Owen Lovejoy, *Memoir of Elijah Parish Lovejoy*, pp. 271–82.
[21] Nicolay and Hay, *op. cit.*, I, 41–42.

were unlawful, let them be lawfully punished. But, right or wrong, none of these were better or worse for the fact that they were unacceptable to a majority. He had as perfect and absolute a right to proclaim and defend his sentiments in Illinois, where nine-tenths may be opposed to them, as though they were all enthusiastic in their favor; and he who would deny or in the least degree abridge this right, is an enemy to freedom and a hypocrite if he dare pretend to republicanism.[22]

Lincoln and Greeley literally grew up with the issue of the long contemplated acquisition and annexation of Texas, which always provoked heated discussion of the slavery question. Lincoln was busy with his plans to go to Congress when annexation was finally accomplished, and at no time was he unduly alarmed at the inevitable extension of slavery which would come with annexation. Greeley, on the other hand, had always been vigorously opposed to territorial expansion, and he looked upon the annexation of Texas as a deliberate, if not malevolent, effort of the slave power to extend its domain.

Texas had become an undisputed Mexican possession in 1819 when Lincoln and Greeley were still small boys. In 1827 President John Quincy Adams, who later was bitterly opposed to annexation, proposed to offer Mexico one million dollars for Texas. The offer was never actually made. In 1829 President Andrew Jackson raised an actual offer to four or five million dollars but did not lure Mexico into selling. Texas proclaimed her independence on March 2, 1836, and then came the famous encounters of the Mexican General Santa Anna and General Sam Houston at the Alamo, Goliad, and San Jacinto. Santa Anna finally surrendered, and his so-called treaty with Houston recognized the independence of Texas. General Houston was inaugurated as President of the new republic on October 22, 1836. In March, 1837, the United States was first to acknowledge the independence of Texas, and was promptly followed by Great Britain, France, and Belgium.[23]

The question of annexation persisted.[24] Daniel Webster led the fight against it and frankly avowed his unwillingness to do anything that would extend slavery or add other slaveholding states to the Union. In August, 1837, an envoy from Texas went to Washington and proposed annexation. Martin Van Buren was then President, and the proposal was declined. Henry Clay was hardly less vehement against annexation than Webster but rather on grounds of expediency. He became in-

[22] The *New Yorker*, November 25, 1837.
[23] Greeley, *American Conflict*, I, 147–85.
[24] James Ford Rhodes, *History of the United States*, I, 75–86.

volved in the campaign of 1844 and, in an effort to please both the North and the South, was defeated for the presidency, largely on this issue, by James K. Polk. The election of Polk was the signal for annexation, and its proponents gained their objective even before he came into office. On February 27, 1845, with the adoption of a Joint Resolution by Congress, the annexation of Texas was decreed. The formal admission occurred in December, 1845. The third paragraph of section 2 of the congressional action, relating to slavery, read as follows:

Third. *New States of convenient size, not exceeding four in number, in addition to the said State of Texas, and having sufficient population, may hereafter, by the consent of said State, be formed out of the territory thereof, which shall be entitled to admission under the provisions of the Federal Constitution; and such States as may be formed out of that portion of said territory lying south of thirty-six degrees thirty minutes north latitude, commonly known as the Missouri Compromise line, shall be admitted into the Union with or without Slavery, as the people of each State asking admission may desire. And in such State or States as shall be formed out of said territory north of said Missouri Compromise line, Slavery or involuntary servitude (except for crime) shall be prohibited.*[25]

When the question of the annexation of Texas was determined in 1845, after years of agitation and bitter differences between Northern and Southern statesmen on the slavery issue involved, Lincoln seems at this time to have been singularly insensitive to the extension of slavery and to the significance of the issue which a few years later was to arouse him so deeply. In a letter to Williamson Durley, written on October 3, 1845, Lincoln stated his mild views: he had never been "much interested" in the Texas question; he could not see "much good" to come of annexation; he could not see how annexation would "augment the evil of slavery," believing that slaves would be taken there "in about equal numbers," with or without annexation.[26]

Lincoln was to express his convictions against the extension of slavery with more certainty when he came to blows with Douglas nine years later. But Greeley was uniformly and unqualifiedly against annexation from the beginning of the discussion of it. He was editing the *New Yorker* when Texas declared her independence. It taxes the imagination to conceive of the almost penniless printer, who had to hunt for work in New York in 1831, voicing positive and convincing views on national issues in a paper of his own five years later. Shortly before the

---

[25] *Cong. Globe*, 28th Cong., 2d sess., p. 363.
[26] Nicolay and Hay, *op. cit.*, I, 275–78.

inauguration of President Sam Houston, Greeley dealt at length with the Texas situation. He sympathized with the people of Texas in their gallant fight for independence and did not question the justice of their cause or the means they took to maintain it; but he urged that considerations of policy, safety, justice, and national honor should operate to forbid annexation. He also believed that the United States should not enlarge its boundaries and that there were many dangers in "extraordinary extension or aggregation of territory." Chief among the dangerous consequences attendant upon the annexation of Texas he held to be the revival of the slavery controversy which had nearly brought about the dissolution of the Union sixteen years earlier when the admission of Missouri was under consideration. "We wish them [Texans]," Greeley declared, "victory, glory, independence—anything but an amalgamation with the Federal Union. To this we stand inflexibly opposed."[27]

Greeley was ordinarily stubborn enough to stand by such a positive statement through thick and thin. He did so in this instance. He continued to fight annexation and paid his respects to it after its accomplishment. He steadily held that the annexation was conceived and inspired by a deliberate effort of the slave power to extend its domain and never yielded that view to other considerations. Transferring his ceaseless energy from the *New Yorker* to the *Tribune* he persisted in driving home his convictions. "Today, if the screws hold," he wrote in the *Tribune* on January 25, 1845, "the Annexation of Texas is to be driven through the House. . . . The mask is fairly off, and the strengthening of and securing of Slavery is boldly avowed to be the main object of Annexation, which, if this be not effected, is not desired at all. . . . The project was conceived in Slavery, and must be carried on as a Slavery-extending measure or it cannot be carried on at all."

On March 1 he declared that the "mischief" had been done and that the United States had thereby adopted a "ready made" war, that Mexico had been deliberately despoiled of her province by "our hypocrisy and our rapacity" and that she had no choice but to resist "the consummation of our flagitious designs." And finally on March 4 he said: "Texas is to be a great Slave country—a market for the Slave-breeders of our older Slave States, and a virgin soil for the Cotton and Sugar Planters of the newer States. That is the whole story."

Lincoln and Greeley were in complete agreement on the wisdom of the Wilmot Proviso. This proposal, which failed to become a law, was

---

[27] The *New Yorker*, October 8, 1836.

nevertheless an ominous sign of the growing tension between the North
and the South. It grew out of the effort to maintain the historic balance
between free soil and slave soil in the acquisition of new territory. A
plank in the platform of the Democratic party, adopted at its national
convention held at Baltimore in May, 1844, clearly illustrated this traditional principle. It read:

> Resolved, *That our title to the whole of the Territory of Oregon is clear
> and unquestionable; that no portion of the same ought to be ceded to Eng-
> land or any other power; and that the reoccupation of Oregon and the re-
> annexation of Texas at the earliest practicable period are great American
> measures, which this Convention recommends to the cordial support of the
> Democracy of the Union.*[28]

This "bargain of 1844" between northwestern Democrats and southern Democrats, which contemplated Texas as slave and Oregon as free
soil, was not kept.[29] Promptly after the Democratic victory in the campaign of 1844 Texas was annexed as a slave state, and Southern leaders
in Congress balked at keeping the Oregon end of the "bargain." Outraged at this "breach of faith" the northwestern Democrats seized the
first opportunity to retaliate. On August 8, 1846, President Polk asked
Congress to give him two million dollars as a basis for peace negotiations with Mexico. David Wilmot, a Democratic member of the House
from Pennsylvania, offered the following amendment to the appropria-
tion bill introduced in response to the President's message, which has
since been known as the Wilmot Proviso:

> Provided, *That, as express and fundamental condition to the acquisition
> of any territory from the Republic of Mexico by the United States, by virtue
> of any treaty which may be negotiated between them, and to the use by the
> Executive of the moneys herein appropriated, neither slavery nor involun-
> tary servitude shall ever exist in any part of said territory, except for crime,
> whereof the party shall first be duly convicted.*[30]

The bill as thus amended passed the House but was talked to death
in the Senate on the adjournment day of the first session of the Twenty-
ninth Congress.[31] It came up again in the following short session and
met a like fate.[32] The Proviso, or the principle involved in it, came to a

---

[28] Horace Greeley and John F. Cleveland, eds., *A Political Text-book*, p. 13.
[29] Clark E. Persinger, "The Bargain of 1844," *Annual Report of the American Historical
Association*, I, 189–95.
[30] *Cong. Globe*, 29th Cong., 1st sess., p. 1217.
[31] *Ibid.*, pp. 1220–21.
[32] *Ibid.*, 2d sess., pp. 425, 573.

vote five times in the Thirtieth Congress: three times in the first session and twice in the second session. Lincoln voted in favor of it on each occasion, and Greeley voted for it both times in the second session.[33] In the light of his *five* recorded votes on the issue Lincoln's recollection of his support of the Wilmot Proviso was peculiar. In his famous Peoria speech on October 16, 1854, he said: "In December, 1847, the new Congress assembled. I was in the lower House that term. The Wilmot Proviso, or the principle of it, was constantly coming up in some shape or other, and I think I may venture to say I voted for it at least forty times during the short time I was there. The Senate, however, held it in check, and it never became a law."[34] This recollection certainly ran in his mind, for he wrote his friend Speed on August 24, 1855: "When I was at Washington, I voted for the Wilmot Proviso as good as forty times."[35]

Beveridge insists that Lincoln was not guilty of inaccuracy or misstatement and explains that the expression "forty times" was merely a manner of speech, meaning "many" or "frequently."[36] This generous explanation would be the more convincing if Lincoln had not qualified the expression "forty times" with the phrases "at least" and "as good as." Lincoln may have been confusing actual votes with debates on the floor and discussions in the lobby of the House or with the table talk at Mrs. Spriggs's boarding house. There was ample opportunity during the Thirtieth Congress for Lincoln to voice his convictions on the exclusion of slavery from new territory more than "forty times."

Consistently opposed to the extension of slavery, Greeley fought hard for the establishment of the principle involved in the Wilmot Proviso. Although the Proviso failed, through the opposition of the Senate, in the closing hours of the first session of the Twenty-ninth Congress, Greeley regarded the favorable vote of the House "as a solemn declaration of the United North against the farther extension of Slavery under our Flag," and believed that no candidate for Congress from a free state would dare to avow himself in favor of receding from that position.[37] Discussing President Polk's message at the opening of the final session of the Twenty-ninth Congress in December, Greeley expressed the hope that Congress would grant the President's request

---

[33] *House Journal*, 30th Cong., 1st sess., pp. 454, 1154–55, 1243–46; 2d sess., pp. 99–100, 105.

[34] Nicolay and Hay, *op. cit.*, II, 200.

[35] *Ibid.*, p. 287.

[36] Beveridge, *op. cit.*, II, 246n.

[37] *Tribune*, August 12, 1846.

for "Two Millions" with which to make a satisfactory peace with Mexico, at the same time "carefully re-annexing to the grant the Wilmot Proviso against the farther extension of Slavery."[38]

Anxious to discover the attitude of Congress directly, Greeley went to Washington late in January "to glean information" on the progress of the Proviso and found the "indications less favorable" than he had hoped. His reports to the *Tribune* at this time dealt largely with this issue.[39] On his return home he declared: "Of course, we stand fast for the Wilmot Proviso, now and evermore."[40] The favorable vote of the House was announced "with surprise and gratification" in an editorial in the *Tribune* on February 16 under the heading "Freedom Triumphant." Greeley regarded this action as "among the most important and auspicious events of our time." Burning with his customary zeal he declared: "It is a victory to rank with Marathon and Marat, with Saratoga and Yorktown."[41] He was keenly disappointed at the later adverse vote of the Senate, but did not give up the fight. "The battle is not yet fought out," he said, "but the *end* is unmistakable."[42] After the adjournment of Congress the *Tribune* displayed at the head of its first editorial column in a box under the heading, "Betrayers of Freedom," a list of the five senators and twenty-six representatives from the free states who had voted against the Proviso and warned, "They shall have their reward."[43]

Greeley kept up a running fire against the extension of slavery in the fall of 1847 and through the first session of the Thirtieth Congress, of which Lincoln was a member, in 1848.[44] Greeley, also a member of the short session of the Thirtieth Congress, persisted in fighting extension and in urging the adoption of the Wilmot Proviso. He voted for it or the principle involved in it at every opportunity. After the adjournment of Congress, in reporting his action to his constituents under the heading "The Territories: Slavery," he told them that he had said openly to Southern members who railed against the Proviso: "I for one will meet you fully half way. Aid us to enact a law securing to New Mexico her ancient and rightful boundaries—aid us to protect and defend her

---

[38] *Ibid.*, December 10, 1846.

[39] *Ibid.*, February 1, 3, 4, 5, 1847.

[40] *Ibid.*, February 8, 1847.

[41] *Ibid.*, February 17, 1847.

[42] *Ibid.*, March 3, 1847.

[43] *Ibid.*, March 9, 1847.

[44] *Ibid.* See, particularly, editorials on August 17, 24; September 3, 10; October 12; November 3; December 4, 1847; also July 3, 19; August 4, 1848.

against the impudent claim of Texas to absorb and subjugate her—secure to the real People of New Mexico and California the right to decide conclusively whether they shall tolerate Slavery or not, and I will vote to organize these Territories without a Proviso against Slavery."[45]

Notwithstanding his declared disposition to go "half way" in settling the question of slavery in the territories, we find Greeley a year later still clinging to the basic principle of the Wilmot Proviso and saying, "But the Wilmot Proviso is the permanent medicine of the State—the grand heroic antidote for the evil passions that most excite the National rapacity and corrupt the National heart. Give us a proviso that there shall nevermore be Slavery in any territory of the Union, and the South would keep us carefully out of all wars of aggression and conquest thereafter."[46]

The Compromise of 1850, a distinct landmark in the history of the "irrepressible conflict," brought a temporary truce in the disputes between the pro-slavery and anti-slavery factions of the country. The compromise measures were advanced by Henry Clay who came back to the United States Senate in 1849, after an absence of seven years, expressly to employ his influence in preventing the secession which was threatened and to aid in the preservation of the Union. On January 29, 1850, Mr. Clay offered a series of eight resolutions in the Senate with the preliminary remark that, "Taken together, in combination, they propose an amicable arrangement of all questions in controversy between the free and slave states, growing out of the subject of slavery." These resolutions dealt with (1) the admission of California to the Union without any restriction "in respect to the exclusion or introduction of Slavery"; (2) the establishment of territorial governments by Congress in the territory acquired by the United States from the republic of Mexico outside the proposed boundaries of California, "without the adoption of any restriction or condition on the subject of Slavery"; (3) the establishment of the western boundary of the state of Texas, "excluding any portion of New Mexico, whether lying on the east or west of that [Rio del Norte] river"; (4) the payment by the United States of the legitimate and *bona fide* debt of Texas contracted before annexation, with the relinquishment by Texas of "any claim which she has to any part of New Mexico"; (5) the inexpediency of abolishing slavery in the District of Columbia without the consent of the state of Maryland and "without the consent of the people of the District, and with-

---

[45] *Ibid.*, March 9, 1849.
[46] *Ibid.*, January 29, 1850.

out just compensation to the owners of Slaves within the District"; (6) the expediency of the prohibition of the slave trade in the District; (7) the passage of a more effective Fugitive Slave Law; and (8) the inability of Congress "to prohibit or obstruct the trade in slaves between the Slaveholding States."[47]

The debates which ensued in Congress, especially in the Senate, were outstanding in the history of that body. Clay was supported by Webster, Cass, Douglas, and Foote; and opposed by Calhoun, who died shortly after the debates began, Seward, Chase, Hale, Benton, Jefferson Davis, and others. President Taylor threw the influence of the Administration against the measures. On April 18 a committee of thirteen, with Mr. Clay as chairman, was elected by the Senate to study and report upon various conflicting proposals which had been advanced.[48] This committee submitted its report on May 8 with a brief recapitulation of its views and recommendations.[49]

The so-called "Omnibus" bill springing out of the recommendations, after long debate, was dismembered and finally passed as "A bill to establish a Territorial Government for the Territory of Utah." Aided by the active support of Millard Fillmore, who succeeded to the presidency upon the death of General Taylor, Mr. Clay triumphed, however. During August and September, in addition to the Utah bill,[50] separate bills were passed admitting California to the Union as a free state, prohibiting the slave trade in the District of Columbia, revising and strengthening the Fugitive Slave Law, establishing the boundaries of Texas, and organizing territorial government in New Mexico. Utah and New Mexico were organized as territories without restriction as to slavery. It will thus be seen that the compromise at which Clay aimed gave concessions to the North in the admission of California and the prohibition of the slave trade in the District of Columbia; and concessions to the South in the organization of Utah and New Mexico and the passage of a new Fugitive Slave Law. The settlement of the Texas boundary question also silenced acrimonious debate. In the succeeding presidential campaign of 1852, the great political parties proceeded on the assumption that the differences between the North and the South on the slavery issue had been finally settled.

---

[47] *Cong. Globe*, 31st Cong., 1st sess., Pt. I, pp. 244–52. For full accounts of great debates, see also Beveridge, *op. cit.*, II, 70–141; and Rhodes, *op. cit.*, I, 99–196.
[48] *Ibid.*, p. 780.
[49] *Ibid.*, pp. 944–56.
[50] *Ibid.*, Pt. II, pp. 1504–2076.

The actions of the Congress which had enacted the compromise measures were widely heralded throughout the country. The speeches of Clay, Calhoun, and Webster were among the greatest in their long public careers. Indeed, Webster's effort stands in history as the "Seventh-of-March Speech."[51] In his maiden speech in the Senate, Seward coined the phrase, which was thereafter to be often repeated, "But there is a higher law than the Constitution."[52]

Lincoln and his partner, William Herndon, according to Herndon's testimony, "took such papers as the *Chicago Tribune, New York Tribune, Anti-Slavery Standard, Emancipator,* and *National Era.* On the other side of the question we took the *Charleston Mercury,* and the *Richmond Enquirer.*"[53] Lincoln undoubtedly also had the *Congressional Globe* at hand. He could not conceivably have missed the reports of the heated discussions in Congress that led to the Compromise of 1850. Neither could he have missed the voluminous newspaper accounts of the great debates. He was, beyond question, keenly interested in all the issues under discussion. The record of Lincoln's letters and papers is exceedingly scant for 1850. The dozen or more letters he wrote that year are mainly personal or related to business and give no sign of awareness of what was going on in Washington. Under date of July 1 the record contains notes for a lecture on Niagara Falls and for a law lecture.[54] The only recorded speech was the eulogy on Zachary Taylor delivered on July 25, and the only hint of knowledge of the problems which had confronted the President appears in the sentence, "I fear the one *great* question of the day, is not now so likely to be partially acquiesced in by the different sections of the Union, as it would have been, could General Taylor have been spared to us."[55] Two years later in his eulogy on Henry Clay, Lincoln dismissed the crowning undertaking of Clay's career with the words, "and more recently in the reappearance of the slavery question connected with our territory newly acquired of Mexico, the task of devising a mode of adjustment seems to have been cast upon Mr. Clay by common consent."[56] Herndon was right when he said that during this crisis in the country's history, "Lincoln lay down like the sleeping lion." In later years, as proof that he

---

[51] *Ibid.*, Pt. I, Appendix, pp. 269–76.
[52] *Ibid.*, p. 265.
[53] Herndon and Weik, *op. cit.*, II, 363.
[54] Nicolay and Hay, *op. cit.*, II, 134–43; Paul M. Angle, *New Letters and Papers,* pp. 61–77; Gilbert A. Tracy, *Uncollected Letters of Abraham Lincoln,* pp. 41–44.
[55] Angle, *op. cit.*, p. 75.
[56] Nicolay and Hay, *op. cit.*, II, 171.

knew well what was going on, he showed a ready familiarity with the terms of the compromise.[57] In his reply to Douglas at Jonesboro on September 15, 1858, he said: "I recollect that I, as a member of that [Whig] party, acquiesced in that compromise."[58]

Again Greeley was more demonstrative, more outspoken, than Lincoln, though the records show he blew hot and cold on the Compromise of 1850. Despite his discipleship of Clay and his belief that Clay's "heart" was "right" and his views "temperate and far-seeing,"[59] Greeley at first opposed any compromise and said "there remains one total, insuperable objection—it won't work. . . . Our tower of strength and of safety is the Wilmot Proviso."[60] Even at this relatively early date in the growing conflict, his words were an augury of the position he was to take in his criticism of President Lincoln a decade and more later: "Let the Union be a thousand times shivered rather than we should aid you to plant Slavery on Free Soil."[61] And again, in the same ominous vein, he said: "But of the two evils, Disunion or Slavery Extension, we prefer the former; of the two perils we consider the latter the more imminent."[62]

Through March, April, and May, 1850, Greeley continued to oppose compromise. He urged that the great men at Washington were deceiving themselves with respect to the strength of "the Anti-Slavery feeling among The People" and "that compromising and settling the main question around a table at Washington and settling it in the Country will turn out to be two very different things."[63] In the first part of June he spent several days in Washington and undertook "to keep cool and report from time to time."[64] Back home he strongly endorsed the speech of Seward in the Senate in which Seward held that "the Compromise is unnecessary, not fair and equal in its terms, humiliating to all the parties, and if adopted, will of necessity be utterly ineffectual."[65] In this connection, however, Greeley began to show a changed point of view holding that "The only thing that could ever make us assent to the [Omnibus] Bill was the danger that Texas might otherwise absorb New

---

[57] *Ibid.*, II, 202–03, Peoria speech, October 16, 1854.

[58] *Ibid.*, IV, 37.

[59] *Tribune*, January 31, 1850.

[60] *Ibid.*, February 1, 1850.

[61] *Ibid.*, February 20, 1850.

[62] *Ibid.*, February 23, 1850.

[63] *Ibid.*, April 22, 1850. See also, particularly, issues of March 9; April 15, 29; May 13, 20, 21, 25, 28, 1850.

[64] *Ibid.*, June 11, 1850.

[65] *Ibid.*, July 4, 1850.

Mexico and plant Slavery in free soil." By the last week in July he had come around to the view "that the passage of the bill would be more auspicious to the cause of Freedom than its defeat."[66]

He reversed himself so completely as to say that the Omnibus bill was "in truth a fair and equal compromise of the questions on which the North and the South are at issue."[67] At the end of July, Greeley went to Washington again and saw with his own eyes the Omnibus "smashed—wheels, axles and body." This new proponent of compromise taunted the opposition in these words: "Well, gentlemen hostile to the Compromise! the laboring oar is with you henceforth; We Compromisers have tried and failed, and it is your turn now, and we heartily wish you a pleasant job of it."[68] Under the caption "The Finale" Greeley announced the passage of the separate bills constituting the Compromise.[69]

Greeley, in 1864, recording the history of the great compromise, held that it was entirely proper for Congress to provide for the temporary government of all the territories acquired from Mexico and to settle boundary questions between Texas and New Mexico. He was not reconciled, however, to the payment of ten million dollars to Texas "for relinquishing her pretensions to territory never possessed by, nor belonging to her." And quite contrary to the views he had once voiced in the *Tribune* in 1850, he concluded his historical account with the declaration that "the net product was a corrupt monstrosity in legislation and morals which even the great name of Henry Clay should not shield from lasting opprobrium."[70] In 1868, fortified with further years of reflection and with the Civil War in the background, he contented himself with saying that the whole movement had been "fondly, but most mistakenly, calculated" to put "an end to Slavery agitation" and to usher in "a long era of fraternity and domestic peace."[71]

The year 1854 was momentous in the lives of Lincoln and Greeley and in the history of the nation. It was in that year that the Missouri Compromise, after having been the law of the land for thirty-four years, was set aside. It will be recalled that this Compromise, among the earlier efforts of Henry Clay to settle amicably the differences between the North and the South on the slavery question, provided that slavery

---

[66] *Ibid.*, July 23, 1850.
[67] *Ibid.*, July 27, 1850.
[68] *Ibid.*, August 2, 1850.
[69] *Ibid.*, September 9, 1850.
[70] Greeley, *American Conflict*, I, 210.
[71] Greeley, *Recollections*, p. 258.

should be prohibited in all the Louisiana Purchase lying north of 36° 30′ with the exception of Missouri which was admitted as a slave state. The year 1854 was also eventful in the life of Stephen A. Douglas, the "Little Giant" of Illinois. After a whirlwind career in public life, beginning in 1835, he had been in the United States Senate for seven years and was confidently, and with good reason, looking forward to the presidency. Always alert in building his political fences, Douglas thought he saw a way to assume Clay's mantle in 1854 by taking the leadership in promoting the organization of the territory of Nebraska which he had long sought. The course he now pursued, or was driven into, was attended with some embarrassment in the light of his past record.

Next to Clay and Webster, perhaps, Douglas had more to do with the promulgation of the Compromise of 1850 than any other member of Congress. He then held that the Missouri Compromise "had no practical bearing upon the question of slavery—it neither curtailed nor extended it one inch. Like the ordinance of 1787, it did the South no harm—the North no good—except that it had the effect to calm and allay an unfortunate excitement which was alienating the affections of different portions of the Union."[72]

Even before the Compromise of 1850, Douglas had unstintedly praised Clay as the possessor of "the proud sobriquet of the 'Great Pacificator'" and had said that the Missouri Compromise had "received the sanction and approbation of all parties in every section of the Union." He had also declared in 1849 that "All the evidence of public opinion at that day seemed to indicate that this Compromise had been canonized in the hearts of the American people, as a sacred thing which no ruthless hand would ever be reckless enough to disturb." In his Peoria speech on October 16, 1854, Lincoln quoted these utterances of Douglas.[73] Throughout the great debates on the Compromise of 1850 neither side contended that the Missouri Compromise was involved or impaired.

In the second session of the Thirty-second Congress a bill organizing the "Territory of Platte"[74] which finally emerged as the "Territory of Nebraska" was passed by the House[75] and defeated by the Senate,[76] where it was promoted by Douglas as Chairman of the Senate Commit-

---

[72] *Cong. Globe*, 31st Cong., 1st sess., Pt. I, Appendix, p. 570.
[73] Nicolay and Hay, *op. cit.*, II, 198.
[74] *Cong. Globe*, 32d Cong., 2d sess., pp. 7, 47.
[75] *Ibid.*, pp. 556–65.
[76] *Ibid.*, pp. 1020, 1113–17.

tee on Territories. This bill was opposed by the slavery interests because it was well recognized that it covered free-soil territory. The bill was, however, absolutely silent on slavery. On the opening day of the first session of the Thirty-third Congress, December 5, 1853, Senator Augustus C. Dodge of Iowa introduced a bill "to organize The Territory of Nebraska" which was referred to the Committee on Territories.[77] On January 4, 1854, Douglas reported the Nebraska bill with an accompanying committee report which contained the seeds of the forthcoming struggle.[78] On that day, if the fates could have spoken, they would have announced the march of Lincoln toward the presidency and the futility of the most cherished dreams of Douglas. While this report did not even hint that the restrictions imposed on the extension of slavery by the Missouri Compromise were removed by the Compromise of 1850, it did pointedly raise the question of the original validity of the Missouri restriction. This report also indicated that "in the opinion of those eminent statesmen who hold that Congress is invested with no rightful authority to legislate upon the subject of Slavery in the territories, the 8th section of the act preparatory to the admission of Missouri is null and void." The committee did "not feel themselves called upon to enter upon the discussion of these controversial questions." Still, the Nebraska bill did not meddle with the Missouri Compromise.

Douglas was soon in deeper water than he had anticipated. Senator Archibald Dixon of Kentucky gave notice of his purpose to move an amendment to the bill to provide "that the citizens of the several States or Territories shall be at liberty to take and hold their slaves within any of the Territories or States to be formed therefrom," as if the Missouri Compromise "had never been passed."[79] This proposed blunt abrogation or repeal of the Missouri restriction was more than Douglas had contemplated; but he was squarely caught, and his eagerness to win Southern favor led him, after the bill had been recommitted, on January 23 to report a totally new bill covering the area in question, designating the Southern portion as Kansas and the Northern as Nebraska, and opening the fight which ended at Appomattox.[80] Thus did the Kansas–Nebraska Act start on its stormy career: on March 3[81] the bill passed the Senate, on May 22[82] it passed the House, and on May

---

[77] *Cong. Globe*, 33d Cong., 1st sess., Pt. I, p. 1.
[78] *Ibid.*, p. 115. The report will be found in *Senate Reports*, Vol. I, No. 15.
[79] *Ibid.*, p. 175.
[80] *Ibid.*, pp. 221–22.
[81] *Ibid.*, pp. 531–32.
[82] *Ibid.*, Pt. II, pp. 1247–55.

30[83] it was approved by President Pierce. Douglas won a great parliamentary victory; but the Kansas–Nebraska Act settled nothing and merely fomented trouble. The "squatter sovereignty," which Douglas was to urge and which Lincoln and Greeley were to challenge for the next six years, died with slavery. The act led to the speedy disappearance of the Whig party, to the creation of the Republican party, and to the downfall of the Democratic party at the polls in 1860. Though he was still to fight valiantly and to pursue the presidency with added zeal, the act marked the turning point in the career of Douglas, and opened the way for Lincoln.

And it remained for Lincoln and Greeley, above all others on the platform and in the press, to point out the fallacies for which Douglas was responsible, and to mold public opinion on the cardinal and unavoidable issues which slavery brought before the American people for settlement. On their own testimony, they were stirred to action by the Kansas–Nebraska Act as they had never been before.

The "sleeping lion" at Springfield was thoroughly awakened. "From 1849 to 1854, both inclusive," Lincoln wrote in the sketch of his life which Jesse W. Fell had requested, "practiced law more assiduously than ever before. Always a Whig in politics; and generally on the Whig electoral tickets, making active canvasses. I was losing interest in politics when the repeal of the Missouri Compromise aroused me again."[84] In like vein he wrote in his brief autobiography, "In 1854 his profession had almost superseded the thought of politics in his mind, when the repeal of the Missouri Compromise aroused him as he had never been before."[85] "You know how anxious I am," he wrote J. M. Palmer on September 7, 1854, "that this Nebraska measure shall be rebuked and condemned everywhere."[86]

Herndon also left abundant record of Lincoln's renewed interest in politics. He wrote Weik,

At this time [after his return from Congress] he despaired of ever rising again in the political world; he was very sad and terribly gloomy, was unsocial and abstracted. The Kansas–Nebraska bill was introduced into Congress in 1854 by Senator Douglas. Lincoln saw his opportunity and Douglas' downfall; he instantly on the introduction of that bill entered into the political field, and by the force of his character, mind, eloquence, he became

[83] *House Journal*, 33d Cong., 1st sess., p. 957.
[84] Nicolay and Hay, *op. cit.*, V, 288.
[85] *Ibid.*, VI, 37.
[86] *Ibid.*, II, 187.

our abolition leader; he was too conservative for some of us, and I among them, and yet I stuck to Lincoln in the hopes of his sense of justice and the eternal right.[87] *[And again Herndon wrote Weik], he opposed slavery everywhere and at all times when to oppose it was political death. From 1820 to 1860 it was a time of "doughfaces" in the North. Lincoln turned his face to flint on this question and stood firm on his conscience. He opposed the repeal of The Missouri Compromise of 1819–20 with all his soul, first, on the grounds of policy and, secondly, on principle. The repeal was for a time Democratic, pro-slavery, and popular; but Lincoln and others made the repeal unpopular and justly odious. This repeal was his grand opportunity, and he seized it and rode to glory on the popular waves.*[88]

Soon after Congress adjourned in August, 1854, Douglas went home to Illinois to face the mounting criticism of the Kansas–Nebraska Act. He made an elaborate defense in the Hall of Representatives at Springfield on October 3, 1854,[89] and was answered at the same place by Lincoln the following day. Senator Beveridge devotes an entire chapter to this speech of Lincoln under the caption "First Great Speech."[90] "The anti-Nebraska speech of Mr. Lincoln," Herndon wrote in an editorial for the *Springfield Journal*, "was the profoundest in our opinion that he has made in his whole life."[91] The speech was reported at the time but was not released in full until its repetition in substance at Peoria on October 16, and is known as the Peoria speech.

This speech marked a turning point in Lincoln's career, and was perhaps the real beginning of his march toward the presidency. We need hardly look elsewhere for the summing up of his views on the slavery question up to this time; one can also find in it many, if not all, of the basic principles on which his arguments against the extension of slavery were to be made for the next six years. It is not possible to judge the full force of this epoch-making speech without reading it in its entirety. It is quotable throughout. Lincoln insisted that clear distinction should be kept between the existing institution of slavery and the extension of it. He acknowledged the constitutional rights of the South in slavery, "not grudgingly, but fully and fairly," and would sanction legislation "for the reclaiming" of fugitives. He had no prejudice against the Southern people and held that they were just what the North would be "in their situation." There was, however, no excuse for permitting slavery

---

[87] Emanuel Hertz, *The Hidden Lincoln*, p. 96.
[88] *Ibid.*, p. 173.
[89] *Illinois State Register*, October 4, 5, 1854.
[90] Beveridge, *op. cit.*, II, 218–90.
[91] Herndon and Weik, *op. cit.*, II, 368.

to go into free territory. He argued that slavery should be turned from its claims of "moral right" back upon its existing "legal rights" and that it should be returned to the "position our fathers gave it" and there be allowed to "rest in peace." He coined the famous phrase that "no man is good enough to govern another man without that other's consent." But, much as he hated slavery, he would consent to its extension rather than "see the Union dissolved." The question of whether a new country should be slave or free was a matter of "utter indifference" to Douglas. "Now, whether this view is right or wrong," Lincoln said, "it is very certain that the great mass of mankind take a totally different view. They consider slavery a great moral wrong, and their feeling against it is not evanescent, but eternal. It lies at the very foundation of their sense of justice and it cannot be trifled with. It is a great and durable element of popular action, and I think no statesman can safely disregard it."[92]

There was no side-stepping or change of front in Greeley's opposition to the Kansas–Nebraska Act. Indeed, in his whole career there were few situations which stirred his tempestuous soul more than what he called the "Iniquity."[93] Beginning early in January, 1854, he well-nigh exhausted his fertile dictionary of terms of opprobrium directed against Douglas and his cohorts. The following are random selections from the broadsides against the Kansas–Nebraska Act which appeared in the *Tribune* almost daily through January, February, March, April, and May, 1854:

January 10—*inebriated political morality*
    30—*measureless treachery and infamy*
February 2—*the most noxious things that ever vegetated on the dung-hill of political corruption*
    3—*the motive of it is as detestable as the act in contemplation is vile*
    13—*this piece of infernal rascality*
    17—*a gigantic act of political dishonesty*
March 14—*The fellows who propose to grab Nebraska are equal to any enormity.*
    15—*the conspirators at Washington*
    16—*miserable political funguses*
    28—*downright effrontery*
May 12—*Our dispatches from Washington last night show that the contest has begun on that infamous measure.*

---

[92] Nicolay and Hay, *op. cit.*, II, 190–262.
[93] *Tribune*, March 6, 1854.

Typical headings for vigorous editorials were "Slavery in the Field," January 6; "The Rascals at Washington," January 26; "Traitors and Doughfaces," February 6; "Is It a Fraud?" February 15; "Not One Reason," February 28; "The Shame and Disgrace of America," March 7; "Pulling the Wool," March 22; "An Ideal for the Conspirators," March 28; "Slavery and the Union," April 12.

There was cool, detached reasoning, as well as vituperation, in many of Greeley's attacks. He began by denouncing the proposal fostered by Douglas as a breach of solemn compact between the North and the South which would inevitably open the door to fresh and fierce agitation.[94] He uttered a warning that if slavery disowned its obligations and proved faithless to its own contracts, those who had hitherto admitted its rights under the Constitution would admit them no longer.[95] When the "Iniquity" passed the Senate he intimated that the time had come, since no compact was longer respected by the South, "to struggle earnestly, undauntedly, uncompromisingly for Universal Freedom."[96] The simple questions the North must ask herself with reference to the bill were: "Will the introduction of Slavery in the broad regions of Kansas and Nebraska tend to strengthen the Union, to make it more secure against explosion from within or assaults from without? Does justice require it? Will it promote the general welfare? Will it add new security to our liberties and to those of our descendants?"[97]

As the measure progressed in Congress, the *Tribune* carried "The Roll of Infamy" in a boxed heading on the first editorial column, from May 11 to May 22. The names in the roll were those representatives from free states who had voted on May 8 to take up the Kansas–Nebraska bill with a view to immediate passage. On May 13 the *Tribune* announced: "We yesterday hoisted the Stars and Stripes over the office of *The Tribune* in token of the extreme concern we feel in this important contest and shall keep it flying night and day while that contest continues. We hope never to strike it if that act shall herald the capitulation and dishonor of the Northern Representatives in this struggle."

Greeley rose to his most exalted mood when he saw that the immediate battle was lost. "The great struggle in Congress approaches its close. For good or evil, the verdict will be declared in the course of a few days. Whatever it may be, the gratitude of unborn millions will

---

94 *Ibid.*, January 6, 1854.
95 *Ibid.*, January 11, 1854.
96 *Ibid.*, March 6, 1854.
97 *Ibid.*, March 11, 1854.

be justly due and freely rendered to those who, against power, patronage, personal interest and party drill, have fought in either House the
battle of Freedom. Overborne they may be, beaten they cannot be, for
on their side are the instincts of Humanity, the spirit of our Age, the
hopes of Man and the justice of God."[98]

The day after he penned the above lines Greeley confessed that he
was "unable to find language of condemnation too strong to express the
depth of our indignation at the conduct of the men who are urging the
passage of the measure at this moment."[99] On May 23 the *Tribune* announced: "At 2 o'clock this morning we learn that the swindle was
passed by a majority of 13–113 voting for, and 100 against it";[100] and
on May 24 the *Tribune* blazed with the words: "THE REVOLUTION IS
ACCOMPLISHED and Slavery is King! How long shall this monarch
reign?" Greeley's final and prophetic words on the close of the battle
were: "And whatever may be the issue of the immediate struggle, we
will unswervingly trust that the forces are silently maturing which shall
rid our land ere many years of the scandal and crime of enslaving and
auctioneering the countrymen of Washington and Jefferson— Nay, we
will trust that even the outrage just consummated, which seems for
the moment so disheartening, shall in God's good providence be made
signally instrumental in hastening that glorious day when the sun shall
look down on no American slave."

Unwilling to let the guilty escape, the *Tribune* carried at the head
of its first editorial column from May 27 to June 1 this parting shot:

> *Be It Remembered*
> *Lists of Representatives*
> *and*
> *Senators of Free States*
> *who voted for the*
> *Kansas-Nebraska Bill*
>
> _____
> _____
> _____
>
> *Shall not Free People*
> *mark their betrayers?*

[98] *Ibid.*, May 18, 1854.
[99] *Ibid.*, May 19, 1854.
[100] *House Journal*, 33d Cong., 1st sess., p. 923.

The widespread agitation caused by the repeal of the Missouri Compromise was intensified by the Dred Scott decision of the United States
Supreme Court promulgated on March 6, 1857.[101] This case had for
eleven years been slowly finding its way to action by the Supreme Court.
In 1846 Dred Scott, a Negro, brought suit for his freedom against the
widow of his former master in the Missouri Circuit Court at St. Louis.
His plea was that his master had taken him into Illinois and later into
Minnesota (then a part of the Louisiana Territory), free territory under
the Ordinance of 1787 and the Missouri Compromise, and that the
freedom thus gained was not affected by his return to the slave state
of Missouri. He secured a verdict in January, 1850, which was set aside
on appeal by the Missouri Supreme Court in 1852, that tribunal holding that he had again become a slave upon his return to Missouri. In
November, 1853, a suit in Dred Scott's behalf was instituted in the
United States Circuit Court. Verdict was found against Scott on May
15, 1854, and on a writ of error the case was taken to the United States
Supreme Court. The case came up for argument on February 11, 1856,
and on May 12 a re-argument was ordered, which took place on December 15, 16, 17, and 18. Announcement of the decision of the court was
withheld until after the inauguration of President Buchanan on March
4, 1857.[102] The principal conclusions of the long opinion read by Chief
Justice Taney, and concurred in by a majority of the court, were thus
summarized by Nicolay and Hay:

> *That the Declaration of Independence and the Constitution of The
> United States do not include nor refer to negroes otherwise than as prop-
> erty; that they cannot become citizens of the United States nor sue in the
> Federal Courts.*
>
> *That Dred Scott's claim to freedom by reason of his residence in Illinois
> was a Missouri question, which Missouri law had decided against him.*
>
> *That the Constitution of The United States recognizes slaves as property,
> and pledges the Federal Government to protect it; and that the Missouri
> Compromise act and like prohibitory laws are unconstitutional.*
>
> *That the Circuit Court of The United States had no jurisdiction in the
> case, and must be directed to dismiss the suit.*[103]

---

[101] *Dred Scott v. Sandford* [sic], 19 How. 393. (Name is Sanford, but was recorded in
error.) For full accounts of all circumstances, see Beveridge, *op. cit.*, II, 443–520;
Rhodes, *op. cit.*, II, 207–27; Henry Wilson, *History of the Rise and Fall of the Slave
Power in America*, II, 523–33. See also Charles E. Snyder, "John Emerson, Owner of
Dred Scott," *Annals of Iowa*, XXI, No. 6, 441–61.

[102] Charles Warren, *The Supreme Court in United States History*, pp. 1–41.

[103] Nicolay and Hay, *Abraham Lincoln: A History*, II, 73. See also Allan Nevins, *The
Emergence of Lincoln*, I, 90–118.

The case had not attracted especial notice until it reached the United States Supreme Court. Greeley kept a wary eye on it. The correspondents of the *Tribune* in Washington watched the case closely and frequently reported on it.[104] Their predictions as to the outcome were remarkably close to the facts. The arguments of all the counsel in the final hearing were fully reported.[105]

It is not surprising, therefore, to find Greeley on March 7, 1857, announcing in his first editorial column that "The long trumpeted decision of the Supreme Court in the Dred Scott case was pronounced by Judge Taney yesterday, having been held over from last year in order not too flagrantly to alarm and exasperate the Free States on the eve of an important Presidential election." He then outlined the cardinal points as reported:

1. *A negro, because of his color, is denied the right of a citizen of the United States—even the right to sue in our Courts for the redress of the most flagrant wrongs.*

2. *A slave, being taken by his master into a Free State and thence returning under his master's sway, is not therefore entitled to his freedom.*

3. *Congress has no rightful power to prohibit Slavery in the Territories; hence the Missouri Restriction was unconstitutional.*[106]

He went on to say in this first announcement, also, that the decision was "an abominable judgment." This was mild language compared with what he had stored up. Soon "downright and bare-faced falsehood" became the "main staple" of the decision. "Any slave-driving editor or Virginia bar-room politician," he said, "could have taken the Chief Justice's place on the bench, and with the exception of a little bolder speaking-up, nobody would have perceived the difference." The decision he declared was "a mere collation of false statements and shallow sophistries got together to sustain a foregone conclusion."[107]

Provoked by the query put to him, "What do you propose to do about it?" Greeley set forth his views explicitly in a long editorial. He did not propose to resist the Federal authorities or to break up the Union, but he urged that when the doctrine came to be positively established it would be settled that "Slavery must pervade and control the whole Union or be expelled from every part of it." This in substance was what Lincoln said more effectively a year later in his famous Spring-

---

104 *Tribune*, February 18, 20, 26, 29; April 9, 10, 11, 12, 1856.
105 *Ibid.*, December 16, 17, 18, 19, 1856.
106 *Ibid.*, March 7, 1857.
107 *Ibid.*, March 10, 1857.

field speech. Greeley meant to make plain to his countrymen the iniquity and enormity of the Dred Scott decision "as a fatal blow to the rights and liberties of all." He proposed to show that a decision of the Supreme Court, though formidable, was not irreversible, and to "urge and effect" a readjustment of the basis on which the justices of the Supreme Court were apportioned. He meant to create and arouse an enlightened public sentiment which should ultimately place the Federal government, in all its departments, "in the hands of men who love the Constitution and the Union much, but Liberty, Eternal Justice and the inalienable Rights of Man, still more." And finally he said, "If there be treason in this, let the Federal District-Attorney hurry up his documents."[108]

True to this declaration, Greeley attacked the decision day after day, frequently in two- and three-column editorials denouncing the "decision of the five slaveholders" in blunt terms. Now and then the *Tribune* also published a blast from its Washington correspondent, J. S. Pike, who was as apt as his chief in the employment of adjectives.[109] Greeley's language was rarely as restrained as it appears in these excerpts. He charged the judges with "dense ignorance" or "willful misrepresentation" in dealing with the historical aspects of the case, and went so far as to say that the Chief Justice "seems to have totally forgotten the functions of a Judge, and to have relapsed into the character of an eager, artful, sophistical, jesuitical, lying advocate—for the suppression of the truth is lying to all intents and purposes."[110] Thereafter he entered into a complete analysis of the case,[111] and declared in a subsequent editorial that the dictum of the judges that Negroes were considered incapable of enjoying any social and political rights in Colonial times and at the period of the adoption of the Constitution was "absolutely and most glaringly and atrociously false."[112]

Greeley never modified his positive views on the Dred Scott decision. Seven years later he penned a soberer review of the decision but still insisted that the Chief Justice and his associates who concurred in the decision defied "history and common sense" and declared: "If twenty millions of freemen were unanimously and earnestly to insist that Freedom should be the law of their common territories, while but one

---

[108] *Ibid.*, March 16, 1857.
[109] *Ibid.*, March 17, 18, 19, 21, 27, 28; April 2, 9, 10, 11, 1857.
[110] *Ibid.*, May 20, 1857.
[111] *Ibid.*, May 28, 1857.
[112] *Ibid.*, June 5, 1857.

slaveholder should claim the privilege of taking his slaves to and holding them in said territories, the claim of this one slaveholder, according to the Court, would override and defeat, conclusively, the earnest demands of those twenty millions of freemen."[113]

Although Lincoln took strong ground against the Dred Scott decision, he bided his time and employed the careful language of the lawyer. His views on this disturbing question were expressed mainly in speeches in reply to Douglas before, during, and after their great debates.

In accordance with his custom Douglas came back to Illinois in the summer of 1857 to mend his political fences. On the night of June 12 Douglas spoke in the Hall of Representatives at Springfield on the issues of the day, devoting his address mainly to Kansas, Utah, and the Dred Scott decision. Lincoln heard Douglas,[114] and great preparations were made for a public meeting at which Lincoln was to answer Douglas. Herndon wrote his friend, Theodore Parker: "Douglas spoke here as represented. Lincoln will answer. *It will be an answer.* I know both men well, for long, long years. Lincoln is a gentleman; Douglas is—well, what shall I say?—an unscrupulous dog. He is a hybrid; Nature says to him Perish and Rot!"[115]

Greeley gave more than two columns to an analysis of Douglas' speech and quoted from it, employing italics of his own. With reference to some of Douglas' remarks on Kansas, Greeley wrote: "We have placed some of the more deliberate and atrocious falsehoods above in *italics*, so as to render them conspicuous; but in fact the insinuated calumnies are not less atrocious but only more cowardly."[116] This statement succinctly expressed Greeley's view of the entire speech, including the reference Douglas made to the Dred Scott decision.

Lincoln spoke in reply to Douglas in the Hall of Representatives on the night of June 26 and dealt at length with the Dred Scott decision. No doubt, without being aware of it, he took almost identically the position enunciated earlier by Greeley. He voiced his belief in obedience to and respect for the judicial department of government, but he frankly declared that the Dred Scott decision was erroneous. He would offer no resistance to it but he would do what he could to have it overruled. Previous decisions of the Supreme Court on vital issues had not

---

[113] Greeley, *American Conflict*, I, 251–64.
[114] *Illinois State Register*, June 15, 1857; Nicolay and Hay, *Complete Works*, II, 315.
[115] Joseph Fort Newton, *Lincoln and Herndon*, p. 119.
[116] *Tribune*, June 24, 1857.

necessarily controlled political action. The decision was based on assumed historical facts, especially in the expression of the opinion that "negroes were no part of the people who made, or for whom was made, the Declaration of Independence, or the Constitution of the United States." Lincoln finally put the issue, which was later to be determined on the battlefield, in these words:

> The Republicans inculcate, with whatever ability they can, that the negro is a man, that his bondage is cruelly wrong, and that the field of his oppression ought not to be enlarged. The Democrats deny his manhood; deny, or dwarf to insignificance, the wrong of his bondage; so far as possible crush all sympathy for him, and cultivate and excite hatred and disgust against him; compliment themselves as Union-savers for doing so; and call the indefinite outspreading of his bondage "a sacred right of self-government."[117]

Lincoln held tenaciously to these views in practically all of his important public addresses for the next three years. He repeated his arguments in the famous "house-divided" speech at Springfield on June 16, 1858, and adopted and pointedly emphasized the prevailing Republican view that the Dred Scott decision was the result of a conspiracy of the slavery advocates.[118] Disinterested students have since held that the charges of conspiracy were unfounded.[119] In this speech Lincoln also advanced the theory—the way now being open—that another "nice little niche" would soon be filled with a Supreme Court decision declaring that the Constitution of the United States does not permit a state to exclude slavery from its limits. He drove his views home time and again thereafter, without essential change in his basic argument.[120] Indeed, all that he had said on this momentous question must have come rushing back to his mind when he stepped out on the portico of the Capitol to deliver his First Inaugural, on March 4, 1861. True to his colors on constitutional questions, in the course of that address he said:

> I do not forget the position, assumed by some, that constitutional questions are to be decided by the Supreme Court; nor do I deny that such decisions must be binding, in any case, upon the parties to a suit, as to the object of that suit, while they are also entitled to very high respect and consideration in all parallel cases by all other departments of the government. And while it is obviously possible that such decision may be erro-

---

[117] Nicolay and Hay, *Complete Works*, II, 315–39.
[118] *Ibid.*, III, 1–15.
[119] Warren, *op. cit.*, III, 44–51.
[120] Nicolay and Hay, *Complete Works*, III, 38–41, 177–83, 252–55; IV, 56–63, 283–89, 320–22; V, 173–81.

neous in any given case, still the evil effect following it, being limited to that particular case, with the chance that it may be overruled and never become a precedent for other cases, can better be borne than could the evils of a different practice.

At the same time, the candid citizen must confess that if the policy of the government upon vital questions affecting the whole people, is to be irrevocably fixed by decisions of the Supreme Court, the instant they are made, in ordinary litigation between parties in personal actions, the people will have ceased to be their own rulers, having to that extent practically resigned their government into the hands of that eminent tribunal. Nor is there in this view any assault upon the court or the judges. It is a duty from which they may not shrink to decide cases properly brought before them, and it is no fault of theirs if others seek to turn their decisions to political purposes.[121]

From the passage of the Kansas–Nebraska Act in 1854 until the very beginning of the Civil War, Kansas was the preliminary battleground between the North and the South. The *Tribune* under Greeley's leadership gave an unconscionable amount of space, both in its editorial and news columns, to the border warfare which resulted from the clashes between pro-slavery and anti-slavery interests. Greeley was frequently asked impatiently, "When will you have done harping on frauds, wrongs and villainies in Kansas?" His answer was: "When those frauds and villainies cease to be perpetrated, and those wrongs are redressed."[122] He had earlier hit the nail a resounding whack on the head, as he had rare capacity for doing, when he said: "One thing only is needed to quiet Kansas—her Admission into the Union under a Constitution which is her free choice. Stop all quibbling and pettifogging as to the conclusions of an election from which the great body of her people—for reasons to them most satisfactory—stand aloof, and let the known will of the majority prevail."[123]

The majority of the settlers, of anti-slavery antecedents, had refused to recognize the territorial legislature chosen by what they called the "Missouri invaders," who sought desperately to fasten slavery permanently upon Kansas. Consequently, the two factions held their conventions and elections independent of each other. The territory became known as the "graveyard of Governors" who were sent from time to time by Federal authority to regulate its affairs. The pro-slavery legisla-

---

[121] *Ibid.*, VI, 179–80.
[122] *Tribune*, January 20, 1858.
[123] *Ibid.*, January 4, 1858.

ture, recognized at Washington as legal, called a Constitutional Convention, and the election for delegates was held on June 15, 1857. The free-state voters did not participate in this election, and the total vote polled was only about 2,200. The convention assembled at Lecompton on September 7, organized, and adjourned to await the result of a territorial election to choose a new legislature to be held on the first Monday of October. Upon the assurance of the territorial governor, Robert J. Walker, that a fair election would be held, the free-state interests nominated candidates and took part in the election. Over 11,000 votes were polled and after 2,800 had been rejected as fraudulent and irregular, it was found that the free-state party had carried the legislature and chosen the delegate to Congress.

The Constitutional Convention then reassembled at Lecompton and proceeded to formulate a pro-slavery constitution, which was allegedly submitted to the people at an election on December 21. Again the free-state men abstained from voting. The procedure was extraordinary, for the voters were not given opportunity to accept or reject the proposed constitution as a whole. The vote was taken merely "For the Constitution *with* Slavery" or "For the Constitution *without* Slavery." The result, of course, was the overwhelming adoption of the constitution with slavery, the vote being 6,266 to 567. In the meantime a special session of the new anti-slavery legislature had been held and had passed an act to submit the Lecompton Constitution fairly to the people on January 4, 1858. The Missouri invaders, not recognizing this action as valid, did not "come over to vote." The result was as follows: for the Lecompton Constitution *with* slavery, 138; for the Lecompton Constitution *without* slavery, 24; against the Lecompton Constitution, 10,266. It was clearly evident that a majority of the voters of Kansas were opposed to the adoption of this constitution in any form.[124]

In his annual message submitted to the first session of the Thirty-fifth Congress on December 8, 1857, President Buchanan discussed the Kansas situation at length and took the position that "it may well be questioned whether the peace and quiet of the whole country are not of greater importance than the mere temporary triumph of either of the political parties in Kansas."[125] The message was interpreted to indicate the President's willingness to accept the Lecompton Constitution, and immediate debate was provoked. In a special message submitted to Congress on February 2, 1858, the President again reviewed the Kansas

---

[124] Greeley, *American Conflict*, I, 249–50.
[125] *Cong. Globe*, 35th Cong., 1st sess., Appendix, pp. 1–7.

debacle and this time came out squarely for the admission of Kansas under the Lecompton Constitution.[126] The fight was on in dead earnest.

Senator Douglas broke with President Buchanan and led the fight against his own party. He took the ground that the constitution did not represent the will of the people of Kansas and that its acceptance and approval would be forcing something on them that they did not want. He was not concerned as to the wishes of the people regarding slavery. If they wanted it, they could authorize it in their constitution; if they did not want it, they could forbid it in their constitution. "It is none of my business which way the slavery cause is decided," he said. "I care not whether it is voted down or voted up."[127] A few months later Lincoln was to drive Douglas hard on his unconcern about slavery.

Despite the vigorous opposition of Douglas, Seward, and others, the Senate accepted the Lecompton Constitution—yeas 33, nays 25.[128] The House passed a substitute for the Senate bill, requiring a resubmission of the constitution to the people of Kansas under conditions that should insure a fair vote—yeas 120, nays 112.[129] The Senate rejected[130] the House bill, and a Conference Committee came forward with a measure known as the English bill, which passed both Houses.[131] This bill, an extraordinary document, provided for an election by the people of Kansas on August 3 when they should vote by ballot "Proposition accepted" or "Proposition rejected." A majority for acceptance would mean the immediate admission of Kansas to the Union under the Lecompton Constitution with certain grants of land and other perquisites—this the opponents of the measure regarded as a bribe. A majority for rejection would mean the formation and submission of a new constitution but not until the territory had a population equal to or exceeding the ratio of representation required for a member of the House of Representatives of the Congress of the United States—this the opponents of the measure regarded as a threat.

Greeley declared that the Lecompton Constitution subjected the majority of the people of Kansas to "the insolent, violent and fraudulent dictation of a petty minority" and insisted that this "new onslaught on the principles of democracy" was the work of pro-slavery disunion-

---

[126] *Senate Journal*, 35th Cong., 1st sess., pp. 153–62.
[127] *Cong. Globe*, 35th Cong., 1st sess., Pt. I, p. 18.
[128] *Senate Journal*, 35th Cong., 1st sess., pp. 275–80.
[129] *House Journal*, 35th Cong., 1st sess., pp. 572–80.
[130] *Senate Journal*, 35th Cong., 1st sess., p. 311.
[131] *Ibid.*, pp. 402–03; *House Journal*, pp. 709–10.

ists "bent on the establishment of a Southern Republic," who were using "the weak and pliant Mr. Buchanan as a tool for this end."[132] During the months of January, February, March, and April, while the Lecompton proposal was being thrashed out in Congress, the *Tribune* kept its readers fully informed day by day of what was going on in Washington. Greeley hardly let a day pass in the whole four months without some editorial reference to the "Lecompton Swindle,"[133] which from time to time he characterized as a "giant iniquity,"[134] "the will of the Slave Power,"[135] an "outrage,"[136] a "crime against Liberty,"[137] and an "abomination."[138] On February 25 the daily *Tribune* announced an extra, eight-page edition of the semi-weekly to be issued Saturday, February 28, dealing entirely with the Lecompton Constitution.

Greeley was outraged anew at the English bill and greeted it as a "modified Land-Grab thrown in by way of bait."[139] Then he called it "rascally ingenuity or ingenious rascality,"[140] and finally dubbed it Lecompton Junior—the English brat."[141] When the bill passed, he exclaimed: "Well; they have done it. Mr. English's Lecompton contrivance passed both Houses of Congress yesterday. . . . What then? Nothing but a very brief dismissal of the Kansas question from the floor of the two Houses. This bill settles nothing, establishes nothing, but leaves all at as loose ends as ever." He predicted at once that the people of Kansas would "spurn the bribe"[142] and on the day of the election confidently contemplated the defeat of the proposition.[143] He did not wait for the final returns from the polls to dismiss the affair from his mind with the crisp remark "That Lecompton, jr., has been unceremoniously strangled is hardly a piece of news."[144] The people of Kansas on August 3 refused the bribe, disregarded the threat, and voted by a majority of more than 10,000 to reject the proposition.

---

[132] *Tribune*, December 31, 1857.
[133] *Ibid.*, January 15, 1858.
[134] *Ibid.*, January 20, 1858.
[135] *Ibid.*, January 30, 1858.
[136] *Ibid.*, February 15, 1858.
[137] *Ibid.*, March 3, 1858.
[138] *Ibid.*, April 12, 1858.
[139] *Ibid.*, April 21, 1858.
[140] *Ibid.*, April 24, 1858.
[141] *Ibid.*, April 29, 1858.
[142] *Ibid.*, May 1, 1858.
[143] *Ibid.*, August 2, 1858.
[144] *Ibid.*, August 7, 1858.

Lincoln fully shared Greeley's views on the Lecompton Constitution but as usual was less vehement in expressing his own position. Since Lincoln and Douglas were in substantial agreement, which they did not conceal, in their determined opposition to the adoption of the Lecompton Constitution, their repeated thrusts at each other over this phase of the Kansas situation, in the light of history, seems to have been largely mere political jockeying. "Who killed Cock Robin?" seems to have concerned them both, in their race for the United States Senate, more than the vital issues of the case. Lincoln was at some pains to have it appear that he saw the enormity of the Lecompton maneuver before Douglas did and that Douglas could have made no headway against it without Republican aid.

In his Springfield speech on June 26, 1857, Lincoln defended the free-state men for not voting at the election of delegates to the Constitutional Convention and branded the procedure in the choice of delegates as "the most exquisite farce ever enacted."[145] In his Chicago speech on July 10, 1858, he took a fling at the claims of Douglas for "vast credit" for defeating the Lecompton Constitution and insisted that he and all Republicans were against it before Douglas was.[146] Again in his Springfield speech on July 17, in a defensive mood, he pointed out that nobody was opposing or had opposed the right of the people, when they formed a constitution, to form it for themselves. The dispute, he insisted, was on the question of fact, whether the Lecompton Constitution had been fairly formed by the people or not. "Lecompton in the raw," he said, "was defeated. It afterward took a sort of cooked-up shape, and was passed in the English bill."[147] Tucked away in "Notes for Speeches," under date of October 1, 1858, is Lincoln's most emphatic utterance on this question:

In the present aspect of affairs what ought the Republicans to do. I think they ought not to oppose any measure merely because Judge Douglas proposes it. Whether the Lecompton Constitution should be accepted or rejected is a question upon which, in the minds of men not committed to any of its antecedents, and controlled only by the Federal Constitution, by republican principles, and by a sound morality, it seems to me that there could not be two opinions. It should be throttled and killed as hastily and as heartily as a rabid dog.[148]

---

[145] Nicolay and Hay, *Complete Works*, II, 317–19.
[146] *Ibid.*, III, 27–29.
[147] *Ibid.*, III, 163–69.
[148] *Ibid.*, IV, 229.

Quite apart from the facts surrounding the Lecompton affair and Lincoln's attitude toward it, this debacle in history furnished him ammunition which he used with telling effect in his pursuit of Douglas. The remark of Douglas with reference to slavery in Kansas, "I care not whether it is voted down or voted up" became Lincoln's text henceforward. In the debates, in subsequent speeches, in the Cooper Institute address and in the First Inaugural, he drove home his contention that the issue turned upon whether slavery was right or wrong. If right, it could not be "voted down"; if wrong, it could not be "voted up." Douglas had trapped himself. He could not escape Lincoln's relentless insistence that slavery was wrong.

A new constitutional convention was assembled at Wyandot, Kansas, in March, 1859, and a free-state constitution was duly framed and ratified by the people in October. A bill providing for the admission of Kansas into the Union on the basis of this constitution passed the House on April 11, 1860: yeas 134, nays 73. The Senate, which was strongly Democratic, refused: yeas 32, nays 27.[149] It was not until January, 1861, that Kansas came into the Union as a free state. On the very day that Jefferson Davis and others abandoned their seats in Congress to take part in the Rebellion, the Senate voted to admit Kansas: yeas 36, nays 16. A week later the House voted: yeas 120, nays 42; and the long troubles of Kansas were soon forgotten in the pressure of the Civil War.[150]

The effect of the border warfare in Kansas reached all the way to Harper's Ferry, Virginia. John Brown's participation in the Kansas struggle had only served to strengthen his determination to undertake to free the slaves by force. On the night of October 16, 1859, with a little band of followers, and without an immediate, clear objective, John Brown seized the United States Arsenal at Harper's Ferry. "In the light of common sense," says Rhodes, "the plan was folly; from a military point of view it was absurd."[151] Even so, the hastily summoned local constabularies were not able to dislodge the raiders and their prisoners. Significantly enough it remained for a detachment of United States Marines, dispatched by President Buchanan, to bring the raid to a quick end on the morning of October 19. The first in command was Brevet Colonel Robert E. Lee, then the Lieutenant Colonel of the Second United States Cavalry; and his aide was First Lieutenant

---

[149] *Cong. Globe*, 36th Cong., 1st sess., Pt. II, p. 1672; Pt. III, p. 2625.
[150] *Ibid.*, 2d sess., Pt. I, pp. 489, 606.
[151] Rhodes, *op. cit.*, II, 355.

J. E. B. Stuart, of the First Cavalry. Lieutenant Israel Green led the Marines.

John Brown was Commander-in-Chief of the Provisional Army, as he called it, which numbered twenty-two: seventeen white men and five Negroes. Three of the band, including Brown's son Owen, were left in charge of arms and supplies at the Kennedy farm "headquarters" about five miles from Harper's Ferry. They escaped and were never apprehended. Of the little "army" of nineteen, ten were killed at Harper's Ferry (including Brown's sons, Oliver, aged 20, and Watson, aged 24); four escaped, two of whom were never apprehended; and five, including John Brown, were taken alive. These five and the two who were caught a few days later in Pennsylvania were tried, convicted of treason, and hanged at Charlestown. John Brown went first on December 2, 1859, four of his followers on December 16, and two on March 16, 1860. All but three of the twenty-two in the Provisional Army were under thirty years of age, and these three had not yet attained their majority.[152]

The reaction of Lincoln and Greeley to John Brown's raid at Harper's Ferry must be mentioned. Although the whole affair was only an incident, there is no measuring the depths to which both North and South were stirred by this mad scheme to free the slaves, or the degree to which their future conduct was determined by its repercussions.

Under the impression that Brown had been one of those killed at Harper's Ferry, Greeley wrote on October 19:

There will be enough to heap execration on the memory of these mistaken men. We leave this work to the fit hands and tongues of those who regard the fundamental axioms of the Declaration of Independence as "glittering generalities," believing that the way to universal emancipation lies not through insurrection, war, and bloodshed, but through peace, discussion, and the quiet diffusion of sentiments of humanity and justice. We deeply regret this outbreak; but remembering if their fault was grievous, grievously have they answered for it, we will not by one reproachful word disturb the bloody shrouds wherein John Brown and his compatriots are sleeping. They dared and died for what they felt to be right, though in a manner which seems to us fatally wrong. Let their epitaphs remain unwritten until the not distant day when no slave shall clank his chains in the shades of Monticello or by the groves of Mount Vernon.[153]

---

[152] Oswald Garrison Villard, *John Brown, A Biography Fifty Years After*, pp. 391–687.

[153] *Tribune*, October 19, 1859.

Possessed of all the facts later, Greeley expressed the view that the whole history of John Brown for two years previous leading up to Harper's Ferry was not "consistent with soundness of mind."[154] Greeley declared that slavery had killed Brown. He did not defend Brown's action in any way, and regarded his mode of combating evil as "unfit." Prophetically, however, he said: "Time will doubtless make plain the object and effect of this sacrifice, and show the errors of Man overruled and made beneficent by the wisdom and loving justice of God. So let us be reverently grateful for the privilege of living in a world rendered noble by the daring of heroes, the suffering of martyrs—among whom let none doubt that History will accord an honored niche to Old John Brown."[155]

Later in a long editorial under the heading, "Brown His Own Interpreter," Greeley held that even believers in the divine right of slaveholding would be obliged in their calm judgment to assign Brown a place among misguided enthusiasts. He predicted that the number who would revere his memory would increase as the years roll on, "until, in the good time coming, when American Slavery shall have passed away, mankind universally will hail him as a martyr."[156] Greeley was always impetuous and frequently wrong, but in his long career he never made a more prophetic statement. The well-beaten path to the grave of John Brown at North Elba, New York, worn anew each summer by thousands of reverent pilgrims, bears eloquent testimony to the discerning mind of the great editor.

Lincoln was silent on the John Brown raid until he made a series of political speeches in Kansas in the first week of December, 1859. On December 1, the day before Brown was hanged, he spoke at Elwood and according to the report briefly adverted to the Harper's Ferry affair. He expressed the view that Brown's undertaking was both illegal and futile. He held that the ballot was the medium through which the people, by the peaceful method provided in the Constitution, could voice their belief in regard to slavery. He believed with Governor Wise of Virginia that John Brown had shown great courage and rare unselfishness, but that no man North or South could approve of violence or crime.[157]

---

[154] *Ibid.*, November 25, 1859.
[155] *Ibid.*, December 3, 1859.
[156] *Ibid.*, December 10, 1859.
[157] Angle, *op. cit.*, p. 229.

The day after Brown's execution, December 3, Lincoln spoke at Leavenworth:

Old John Brown has just been executed for treason against a state. We cannot object, even though he agreed with us in thinking slavery wrong. That cannot excuse violence, bloodshed, and treason. It could avail him nothing that he might think himself right. So, if constitutionally we elect a president, and therefore you undertake to destroy the Union, it will be our duty to deal with you as old John Brown has been dealt with. We shall try to do our duty. We hope and believe that in no section will a majority so act as to render such extreme measures necessary.[158]

Deliberate effort was made by the Democrats in Congress to fasten responsibility for the Brown outrage on the Republican party. This view, largely held in the South, was strengthened by the zeal with which a small group of Brown's Northern supporters, including Theodore Parker, had on various occasions aided and abetted Brown. The fact that there was "an early exodus" of some of them to Canada was proof enough that they were at least privy to Brown's plans.[159] Jefferson Davis, in the Senate, branded the raid as "the invasion of a State by a murderous gang of abolitionists,"[160] and Senator Douglas, leaping to the attack, declared his "firm and deliberate conviction that the Harper's Ferry crime was the natural, logical, inevitable result of the doctrines and teachings of the Republican party." He held further that John Brown was inspired to his mad course by Lincoln's "house-divided-against-itself" doctrine and by Seward's picturing of the "irrepressible conflict."[161] Seward led the Republican forces in the Senate and was outspoken in the declaration that "while generous and charitable natures will probably concede that John Brown and his associates acted on earnest, though fatally erroneous, convictions, yet all good citizens will nevertheless agree that this attempt to execute an unlawful purpose in Virginia by invasion, involving servile war, was an act of sedition and treason, and criminal in just the extent that it effected the public peace and was destructive of human happiness and life."[162]

Lincoln's Cooper Institute speech on February 27, 1860, came while the congressional bickering was at fever heat. Addressing the South, in

---

[158] *Ibid.*, p. 235.
[159] Villard, *op. cit.*, p. 529.
[160] *Cong. Globe*, 36th Cong., 1st sess., Pt. I, p. 61.
[161] *Ibid.*, pp. 553–54.
[162] *Ibid.*, p. 913.

the carefully measured terms which characterize that notable summing up of the "durable question of the age," he said:

> You charge that we stir up insurrections among your slaves. We deny it; and what is your proof? Harper's Ferry! John Brown! John Brown was no Republican; and you have failed to implicate a single Republican in his Harper's Ferry enterprise. If any member of our party is guilty in that matter, you know it, or you do not know it. If you do know it, you are inexcusable for not designating the man and proving the fact. If you do not know it, you are inexcusable for asserting it, and especially for persisting in the assertion after you have tried and failed to make the proof. You need not be told that persisting in a charge which one does not know to be true, is simply malicious slander.
>
> Some of you admit that no Republican designedly aided or encouraged the Harper's Ferry affair, but still insist that our doctrines and declarations necessarily lead to such results. We do not believe it. . . . Republican doctrines and declarations are accompanied with a continual protest against any interference whatever with your slaves, or with you about your slaves. Surely, this does not encourage them to revolt. True, we do, in common with "our fathers who framed the government under which we live," declare our belief that slavery is wrong; but the slaves do not hear us declare even this. For anything we say or do, the slaves would scarcely know there is a Republican party. . . .
>
> John Brown's effort was peculiar. It was not a slave insurrection. It was an attempt by white men to get up a revolt among slaves, in which the slaves refused to participate. In fact, it was so absurd that the slaves, with all their ignorance, saw plainly enough it could not succeed. That affair, in its philosophy, corresponds with the many attempts, related in history, at the assassination of kings and emperors. An enthusiast broods over the oppression of a people till he fancies himself commissioned by Heaven to liberate them. He ventures the attempt which ends in little else than his own execution. Orsini's attempt on Louis Napoleon, and John Brown's attempt at Harper's Ferry, were, in their philosophy, precisely the same. The eagerness to cast blame on Old England in the one case, and on New England in the other, does not disprove the sameness of the two things.[163]

From the time of John Brown's raid until the first inauguration of Lincoln as President, the swiftly moving events leading to the Civil War were mainly political. From 1845 to 1861 both Lincoln and Greeley recorded themselves frequently on the developing slavery issue. Some of their statements during this period, largely confirming the de-

---

[163] Nicolay and Hay, *Complete Works*, V, 314–19.

tailed account here given of their views on slavery, appear in the following parallel columns:

Lincoln	Greeley
I hold it to be a paramount duty of us in the free States, due to the Union of the States, and perhaps to liberty itself (paradox though it may seem), to let the slavery of the other States alone; while, on the other hand, I hold it to be equally clear that we should never knowingly lend ourselves, directly or indirectly, to prevent that slavery from dying a natural death—to find new places for it to live in, when it can no longer exist in the old.[164]	*Until new light breaks upon us, however, we mean to be faithful to the American Union, alike in what it expressly requires of us, and what is fairly implied by its existence. Slavery having existed in the Southern States when that Union was formed and its continued existence being plainly anticipated and acquiesced in by the Federal Constitution, we cannot feel justified in warring,* as a citizen of the United States, *to overthrow that institution.*[165]
Little by little, but steadily as man's march to the grave, we have been giving up the old for the new faith. Near eighty years ago we began by declaring that all men are created equal; but now from that beginning we have run down to the other declaration, that for some men to enslave others is a "sacred right of self-government." These principles cannot stand together. They are as opposite as God and Mammon; and whoever holds to the one must despise the other.[166]	*Slavery is an evil which ought to be confined within its existing limits. Slavery is a blessing which ought to be extended as widely as possible. These are two antagonistic propositions which admit of no possible reconciliation nor compromise. From the moment of the passage of the Kansas-Nebraska bill, the North and the South will cease, so far as national political action is concerned, to have any ideas in common on the subject of Slavery.*[167]
We are now in the fifth year since a policy was initiated with the avowed object and confident promise of putting an end to slavery agita-	*Senator Douglas, in his Chicago speech, denounced as perilous the doctrine of Mr. Lincoln that Slavery or Freedom must ultimately prevail*

---

[164] *Ibid.*, I, 277, Lincoln to Williamson Durley, October 3, 1845.
[165] *Tribune*, April 3, 1845.
[166] Nicolay and Hay, *Complete Works*, II, 246–47, Peoria speech, October 16, 1854.
[167] *Tribune*, March 13, 1854.

Lincoln

tion. Under the operation of that policy, that agitation has not only not ceased but has constantly augmented. In my opinion, it will not cease until a crisis shall have been reached and passed. "A house divided against itself cannot stand." I believe this government cannot endure permanently half slave and half free. I do not expect the Union to be dissolved—I do not expect the house to fall—but I do expect it will cease to be divided. It will become all one thing, or all the other. Either the opponents of slavery will arrest the further spread of it, and place it where the public mind shall rest in the belief that it is in the course of ultimate extinction; or its advocates will push it forward till it shall become alike lawful in all the States, old as well as new, North as well as South.[168]

The real issue in this controversy —the one pressing upon every mind —is the sentiment on the part of one class that looks upon the institution of slavery as a wrong, and of another class that does not look upon it as a wrong. The sentiment that contemplates the institution of slavery in this country as a wrong is the sentiment of the Republican party. It is the sentiment around which all their actions, all their arguments, circle; from which all their proposi-

Greeley

in all our States, and in all sections of the Union. We do not concur in this denunciation. Most certainly Washington, Jefferson and a great majority of the eminent men of our Revolutionary age, held with Mr. Lincoln on this point, not with Mr. Douglas. They did not imagine that the Union should or would be dissolved because of the transformation of Slave into Free States. On the contrary, they looked hopefully for this transformation, as calculated to remove anomalies and incongruities, strengthen the bonds of affection between the several States and insure the perpetuity of the Union. We need hardly add that in this we entirely agree with them, and dissent from Mr. Douglas's dictum that "Our forefathers clearly perceived that the kind of domestic institutions which would suit New Hampshire would be totally unfit for the rice plantations of Carolina." [169]

The abolition of Slavery in the United States is often scouted at as a Utopian and chimerical idea, on the ground of the deep root which that institution has taken in our Southern States, the strength of the interests which it involves, and its thorough incorporation into the whole system of Southern society. . . . They no longer justify the continuance of Slavery on the ground of the magnitude of the interests involved in it and of the obstacles in

---

[168] Nicolay and Hay, *Complete Works*, III, 1–2, Springfield speech, June 16, 1858.
[169] *Tribune*, July 13, 1858.

Lincoln

tions radiate. They look upon it as being a moral, social, and political wrong; and while they contemplate it as such, they nevertheless have due regard for its actual existence among us, and the difficulties of getting rid of it in any satisfactory way, and to all the constitutional obligations thrown about it. . . . They insist that it, as far as may be, be treated as a wrong, and one of the methods of treating it as a wrong is to make provision that it shall grow no larger. They also desire a policy that looks to a peaceful end of slavery some time, as being a wrong.[170]

I think we want and must have a national policy in regard to the institution of slavery that acknowledges and deals with that institution as being wrong. Whoever desires the prevention of the spread of slavery and the nationalization of that institution, yields all when he yields to any policy that either recognizes slavery as being right, or as being an indifferent thing. Nothing will make you successful but setting up a policy which shall treat the thing as being wrong. When I say this, I do not mean to say that this General Government is charged with the duty of redressing or preventing all the wrongs in the world; but I do think that it is charged with preventing and redressing all wrongs which are wrongs to itself. This government is

Greeley

the way of getting rid of it. They have found it necessary to set up that Slavery is just and right in itself, a positive good to both masters and slaves, and the means best adapted for the material and moral development of the South. With a desperate hardihood they stake their whole case upon the maintenance of these points, and in bringing the public mind to contemplate the question from this point of view they are, perhaps, after all, under the guise of ultra advocates of Slavery, the real pioneers of emancipation.[171]

Of course, we resist the Extension of Slavery because we hate Slavery generally, and desire its extinction. We believe that, if Slavery had never gained a foot of new territory under our National flag, it would have died out of the Union ere this. We choose to seek laudable ends by lawful means. If we were to ask the People of our State to aid us in abolishing Slavery in Virginia, the obvious demurrer would be, "What right, what power have we to make or alter the laws of Virginia?" But when we ask them to aid in excluding Slavery from the Federal Territories—to prevent its extension—we ask them to do no more than was done by their fathers and ours—by Washington and Jefferson—by Slave States and Free States—what the Confedera-

---

[170] Nicolay and Hay, *Complete Works*, V, 59–60, reply to Douglas at Alton, October 15, 1858.
[171] *Tribune*, August 20, 1858.

<table>
<tr><td>

Lincoln

expressly charged with the duty of providing for the general welfare. We believe that the spreading out and perpetuity of the institution of slavery impairs the general welfare. We believe—nay, we know—that that is the only thing that has ever threatened the perpetuity of the Union itself.[172]

If slavery is right, all words, acts, laws, and constitutions against it are themselves wrong, and should be silenced and swept away. If it is right, we can not justly object to its nationality—its universality; if it is wrong, they can not justly insist upon its extension—its enlargement. All they ask we could readily grant, if we thought slavery right; all we ask they could as readily grant, if they thought it wrong. Their thinking it right and our thinking it wrong is the precise fact upon which depends the whole controversy. Thinking it right, as they do, they are not to blame for desiring its full recognition as being right; but thinking it wrong, as we do, can we yield to them? Can we cast our votes with their view, and against our own? In view of our moral, social, and political responsibilities, can we do this?

Wrong as we think slavery is, we can yet afford to let it alone where

</td><td>

Greeley

tion did, what the Union persisted in doing—what was never denied to be Constitutional until ten years back—what we and they have a clear right to do, and which their consciences must tell them that they ought to do. And we believe this is the true and most effective way to fight Slavery generally, and labor for its entire annihilation.[173]

But we are engaged in a great political controversy, whereof the relative justice, fitness and beneficence of the antagonistic systems of Free and Slave Labor are the real foundation. Messrs. Bell and Breckenridge believe Slavery essentially and eternally right—a proper and just relation through which service may be exacted and labor constrained. Mr. Douglas has—not once merely, but at least a hundred times—proclaimed his conviction that Slavery is, if not absolutely and universally right, at least right within certain latitudes and under certain conditions of soil, climate, and other industrial aptitudes. . . . Hence, he logically proclaims his perfect indifference as to Slavery's being "voted up or voted down" in any Territory or in any State.

The Republicans, on the contrary, hold Slavery to be essentially wrong, unjust, pernicious, and therefore resist its extension into, establishment

</td></tr>
</table>

---

[172] Nicolay and Hay, *Complete Works*, V, 230–31, Cincinnati speech, September 17, 1859.

[173] *Tribune*, April 8, 1859.

Lincoln

it is, because that much is due to the necessity arising from its actual presence in the nation; but can we, while our votes will prevent it, allow it to spread into the national Territories, and to overrun us here in these Free States?[174]

I hold that, in contemplation of universal law and of the Constitution, the Union of these States is perpetual. Perpetuity is implied, if not expressed, in the fundamental law of all national governments. It is safe to assert that no government proper ever had a provision in its organic law for its own termination. . . .

It follows from these views that no State upon its own mere motion can lawfully get out of the Union; that resolves and ordinances to that effect are legally void; and that acts of violence, within any State or States, against the authority of the United States, are insurrectionary or revolutionary, according to circumstances. . . .

In your hands, my dissatisfied fellow-country-men, and not in mine, is the momentous issue of civil war. The government will not assail you. You can have no conflict without being yourselves the aggressors. You have no oath registered in heaven to destroy the government, while I shall

Greeley

by, or recognition as already legally existing in, any of the Territories which are destined to become States of our Union. They seek to destroy it in the germ.[175]

The People of the Slave, and especially of the Cotton, States, have for thirty years been taught that the Union taxes and impoverishes them for the benefit of the North. Believing this, they are frequently impelled to menace us with Disunion, presuming that we will do or say nothing to avert that calamity to our section. It is high time that mischievous delusion were dispelled, since the North can have neither equality nor peace in the Union until it shall be. The issue having been fairly made up—Let the North recede from its principles or bid adieu to the Union—I do not see how we can make any concession of principle without dishonor.

Mr. Crittenden! The People of the Free States, with every respect for you, propose to stand by the Constitution as it is; to respect the rightful authorities, State and Federal; to let Congress enact such laws as to the majority shall seem good; and to back the Executive in enforcing these laws and maintaining the integrity

---

[174] Nicolay and Hay, *Complete Works*, V, 326–28, Cooper Institute address, February 27, 1860.
[175] *Tribune*, October 23, 1860.

Lincoln	*Greeley*
have the most solemn one to "pre-serve, protect, and defend it."[176]	*of the Union. For whatever troubles may impend or arise, those who conspire and rebel are justly responsible; if they would submit when beaten, as we do, there would be unbroken peace and prosperity.*[177]

It is thus apparent that Lincoln, the lawyer and politician, and Greeley, the editor and publicist, held very similar views on slavery for two decades before the Civil War. From their earliest recollections they believed slavery wrong, abhorred it, and hoped for its ultimate extinction. They were not abolitionists, however. They believed in the reign of law and the mandates of the Constitution. They long nourished the hope of compensated emancipation and, with Henry Clay, contemplated colonization. They were opposed to violence and ready to defend the rights of slavery where it existed under law. They found the Fugitive Slave Law distasteful but still believed it should be enforced with all other laws. They were stubbornly against the extension of slavery: Greeley always, and Lincoln gradually and finally with equal vigor. They were stirred as never before in their lives by the Kansas–Nebraska Act and labored valiantly against the principle involved in it. They regarded the Dred Scott decision as fundamentally unsound, were not held by it in political action, and argued with clear conscience for its reversal under law. They favored the Wilmot Proviso, sympathized with "bleeding" Kansas, and opposed and condemned the Lecompton Constitution. They believed John Brown a mad man and at no time sought the overthrow of slavery through violence. Broadly speaking, it may be said, as the crisis approached, that Lincoln and Greeley held substantially the same views on the slavery issue with one notable exception.

There was no place in Lincoln's mind for disunion. He believed the Union to be perpetual and conceived of no process by which it might be dissolved either by violence or by law. As early as 1856 he said to the South: "We do not want to dissolve the Union; you shall not."[178] He never departed from that view and solemnly repeated it in substance

---

[176] Nicolay and Hay, *Complete Works*, VI, 169–85, First Inaugural address, March 4, 1861.

[177] *Tribune*, January 7, 1861. Greeley to John J. Crittenden.

[178] Nicolay and Hay, *Complete Works*, II, 294, Galena speech, August (1?), 1856.

in the First Inaugural.[179] Greeley, on the other hand, regarded the extension of slavery as a greater evil than possible disunion and for a time nourished the delusion that the "Cotton States" might "be permitted to go in peace."[180] Lincoln consistently put the Union first. Greeley was often less concerned about the Union than about the restriction and ultimate extinction of slavery. In the midst of the great conflict the fundamental issue between them was joined.

[179] *Ibid.,* VI, 175.
[180] *Tribune,* November 16, 1860.

I have supposed myself, since the organization of the Republican party at Bloomington, in May, 1856, bound as a party man by the platform of the party then and since.

Lincoln[1]

I was a member of the first anti-Nebraska or Republican State Convention, which met at Saratoga Springs in September [1854].

Greeley[2]

5   Fellow Republicans

The Republican party was born of the slavery issue. The disastrous defeat of the Whigs in 1852 and the repeal of the Missouri Compromise in 1854 gradually fused the anti-slavery forces and led inevitably to a new political alignment. Definite movements across old party lines began before the passage of the Kansas–Nebraska Act. Although historians do not agree upon the genesis of the party and the choice of its name,[3] there are various claimants for first honors. Ripon, Wisconsin, emerges as perhaps the first place where a meeting of members of different political parties was held, looking to the formation of a new party on the slavery issue.[4] The meeting was held on February 28, 1854, presided over by its principal promoter, Alvan E. Bovay. Whigs, Free-Soilers, and Democrats joined in a resolution, if the Kansas–Nebraska bill, then pending, should pass, to "throw old party organizations to the winds, and organize a new party on the sole issue of the non-extension of slavery." A second meeting was held on March 20, after the Senate had passed the bill, and by a formal vote the town committees

---

[1] John G. Nicolay and John Hay, eds., *Complete Works of Abraham Lincoln*, III, 272.
[2] Horace Greeley, *Recollections of a Busy Life*, p. 314.
[3] Andrew Wallace Crandall, *The Early History of the Republican Party*, pp. 9–26.
[4] Francis Curtis, *The Republican Party*, I, 176–78. See also Henry Wilson, *History of the Rise and Fall of the Slave Power in America*, II, 409–10.

of the Whig and Free-Soil parties were dissolved and a new committee was chosen, consisting of three Whigs, one Free-Soiler, and one Democrat. Bovay suggested at this meeting that an appropriate name for the new party would be "Republicans," and he later wrote: "We went into the little meeting Whigs, Free-Soilers, and Democrats. We came out of it Republicans, and we were the first Republicans in the Union."[5]

The Kansas–Nebraska Act, having passed the House on May 22, was signed by President Pierce on May 30. The first state-wide convention in protest against the act and in support of a united anti-slavery party was held at Jackson, Michigan, on July 6, 1854, in response to a call for a mass meeting signed by more than ten thousand persons from all parts of the state. This day and place may fairly be said "to be the birthday and birthplace of the Republican party."[6] This assemblage nominated a complete ticket for state offices pledging the candidates to a platform in a notable series of resolutions which branded slavery as "a great moral, social and political evil," declared it to be "a violation of the rights of man as man," condemned the repeal of the Missouri Compromise as "an act unprecedented in the history of the country," demanded "the repeal of the fugitive slave law, and an act to abolish slavery in the District of Columbia," and recommended the calling of a general convention of the free states and such of the slaveholding states, or portions thereof, as might desire to be represented, "with a view to the adoption of other more extended and effectual measures in resistance to the encroachments of slavery." The convention also fixed unmistakably the label of the new party it was creating when it

Resolved, *That in view of the necessity of battling for the first principles of republican government, and against the schemes of an aristocracy, the most revolting and oppressive with which the earth was ever cursed, or man debased, we will co-operate and be known as* Republicans *until the contest be terminated.*[7]

The movement thus definitely inaugurated in Michigan spread rapidly to other states. Republican tickets were run in state elections in 1854 in Illinois, Indiana, Iowa, Maine, Michigan, Ohio, and Wisconsin; and in 1855 in Massachusetts, New York, and Vermont.[8] On June 19, 1855, "The Republican Association of Washington, D.C." was organized and committed to the propositions, "*First*, That Con-

---

[5] Curtis, *op. cit.*, I, 178.
[6] *Ibid.*, p. 2. See also Wilson, *op. cit.*, II, 412.
[7] Wilmer C. Harris, *Public Life of Zachariah Chandler*, pp. 20–29, 89–118.
[8] Curtis, *op. cit.*, I, 206.

gress possesses no power over the institution of slavery in the several States; but that, outside of State jurisdiction, the constitutional power of the Federal Government should be extended to secure *life, liberty,* and *happiness* to all men, and therefore, *Second,* There should be neither slavery nor involuntary servitude, except for the punishment of crime, in any of the Territories of the United States."[9]

This organization issued a circular "to the friends of the Republican movement throughout the United States," on January 17, 1856. On the same date the chairmen of the state Republican committees of Indiana, Maine, Massachusetts, Michigan, New York, Ohio, Pennsylvania, Vermont, and Wisconsin issued an invitation "To the Republicans of the United States" to attend an informal convention at Pittsburgh to be held on February 22 "for the purpose of perfecting the National Organization, and providing for a National Delegate Convention of the Republican Party, at some subsequent day, to nominate candidates for the Presidency and Vice-Presidency, to be supported at the election in November, 1856."[10]

At this convention there were delegates present from all the free states and from Kentucky, Maryland, Missouri, South Carolina, and Virginia. The resolutions adopted demanded the "repeal of all laws allowing the introduction of Slavery into Territories once consecrated to Freedom, and the resistance by constitutional means of the existence of Slavery in any Territory," and urged the "Republican Organization to resist and overthrow the present National Administration, as it is identified with the progress of the Slave power to national supremacy."[11]

A National Executive Committee was constituted, and this committee on March 27 issued an invitation—to "The People of the United States, without regard to past political differences or divisions, who are opposed to the repeal of the Missouri Compromise, to the policy of the present administration, to the extension of slavery into the territories, in favor of the admission of Kansas as a free state, and of restoring the action of the Federal Government to the principles of Washington and Jefferson"—to send three delegates from each congressional district and six at large from each state to a convention to be held in Philadelphia on June 17, 1856, "for the purpose of recommending candidates to be supported for the offices of President and Vice-

---

[9] *Ibid.*, p. 249.
[10] *Ibid.*, pp. 250–51.
[11] Charles W. Johnson, comp., *First Three Republican National Conventions*, p. 11.

President of the United States."[12] On the date indicated the first Republican National Convention was held at Philadelphia, attended by 565 delegates representing all the free states and Delaware, Kentucky, and Maryland.

As usual Greeley was prompter to get into action, more voluble and aggressive, but less astute than Lincoln, in the political game. Greeley was off at the crack of the starting pistol in the history of the new party; and the perennial itch for office, from which neither Lincoln nor Greeley was ever quite free, broke out into a visible rash while the Republican party was forming. The decisive defeat of General Scott for the presidency in 1852 prompted Greeley to look about for a new means of recording his determined opposition to the extension of slavery, and shortly after the election he let go:

> *We have said that we considered the Whig party crushed by the defeat of General Scott—not simply by the fact of such defeat, nor yet by its overwhelming extent—but mainly by reason of the treachery and destitution of principle which that defeat revealed. . . . This then is the alternative now practically presented to us—"Cease to expose the iniquities of Slavery or cease to be regarded as Whigs."—"Very well," we reply; "we cannot stifle our convictions respecting Slavery; we choose to go out of the Whig party, if we must, rather than to remain in it subjects, servants, or prisoners."*[13]

Greeley had an amazing number of far-flung private contacts. His personal correspondence, of which he left abundant evidence, must have taken as much of his time as his arduous editorial duties. In a letter to a friend written on June 19, 1854, he said: "I presume I write 2000 letters each year, which I think is my share, considering what I have to do besides."[14] It is not surprising, therefore, to find that Alvan E. Bovay of Ripon, Wisconsin, was one of his private correspondents. While the Kansas–Nebraska bill was pending, Bovay wrote to Greeley on February 26, 1854, expressing his belief that the bill would become a law and urging Greeley to advocate in his paper—"now a power in the land"—the calling of the opponents of the bill "in every church and schoolhouse in the free states." He went further and asked the editor to "Urge them to forget previous political names and organizations, and to band together under the name I suggested to you at Lovejoy's Hotel in 1852. I mean the name 'Republican.' It is the only one that will serve

---

[12] *Ibid.*, p. 14.

[13] *Tribune*, November 30, 1852.

[14] Greeley Papers, Library of Congress, Washington, D.C., Greeley to Mrs. M. B. O. Thomas, June 19, 1854.

all purposes, present and future—the only one that will live and last."[15]

Greeley was reluctant to believe that the glorious days of the Whig party, such as they had been, were gone with Clay and Webster. Impetuous as he was, he was not quite ready to embrace a new party label, and so he wrote Bovay on March 7:

> *I faintly hope the time has come which Daniel Webster predicted when he said, "I think there will be a North." But I am a beaten, broken-down, used-up politician, and have the soreness of many defeats in my bones. However, I am ready to follow any lead that promises to hasten the day of northern emancipation. Your plan is all right if the people are right. . . . However, we will try and do what we can. But remember that editors can only follow where the people's heart is already prepared to go with them. They can direct and animate a healthy public indignation, but not "create a soul beneath the ribs of death."*[16]

A few weeks later another correspondent of Greeley's bobbed up, A. N. Cole of Allegany County, New York, editor of the *Genesee Valley Free Press.* Mr. Cole, who later claimed to be the "Father of the Republican Party," also early felt the need of a new party to express the growing common views of the North on the slavery question. He wrote his friend Greeley of his plans to call a meeting for the purpose of promoting a new party in Allegany County to be held at Friendship, New York, on May 16, 1854, and asked him what name to give the new party. Greeley wrote Cole, no doubt recalling Bovay's suggestion, "Call it Republican, no prefix, no suffix, but plain Republican." Cole's meeting was not well attended, but the few who were present perfected an organization, adopted the name Republican, and authorized a committee to call a county-wide nominating convention. Such a convention was held at Angelica, New York, on October 15 and a county ticket put in the field and subsequently elected.[17]

In the meantime Bovay kept after Greeley and wrote in retrospect, "I was an intimate friend of Horace Greeley's, and he would always listen to me on political matters. . . . He did not always assent to my propositions, but in the end he did to most of them, and he did to this one after a good deal of nagging. It was not one letter that I wrote him, but many, before he displayed the Republican flag in the *Tribune's* columns. I was more solicitous about the name than about the organiza-

---

[15] Curtis, *op. cit.,* I, 177.

[16] *Ibid.*

[17] *Ibid.,* pp. 202–05.

tion. . . . My friend Greeley valued names too lightly. . . . I wanted the name to appear early in the *Tribune,* and it did."[18]

Bovay was quite right in his judgment of Greeley's attitude. On June 16, 1854, in an editorial in the *Tribune* headed "Party Names and Public Duty," Greeley set forth his view that the country greatly needed emancipation from "party names and party shackles." He regretted to see good men who held the same fundamental views against the extension of slavery divided and defeated because of adherence to mere party labels. He wished strongly to see a union of all those members of the two parties "who believe resistance to the extension of Slave Territory and Slave Power the most urgent public duty of our day." He was not much concerned about the name for such a union. It might be called "Whig," "Free Democratic," or something else; but he thought "some simple name like 'Republican' would more fitly designate those who had united to restore our Union to its true mission of champion and promulgator of Liberty rather than propagandist of Slavery."

Greeley, in quietly contemplating the emergence of a new party, was quite willing that it should carry him into high office in his own state. Smarting with bitterness at the passage of the Kansas–Nebraska Act and its approval by President Pierce, he took a fling at the Administration early in August and declared that its chief characteristic was "imbecility." "Others," he said, "may incline to the opinion that it is a morally bad administration rather than a mentally weak one; but we think that its lack of principle is far excelled by its lack of sense. Certainly the most depraved politicians, if gifted with ordinary discretion, would never commit the acts of wickedness and folly which have not merely broken up and destroyed the great party that bore Mr. Pierce into office, but have rendered his Executive career a record of shame and ridicule, to such a degree that the Presidency of John Tyler shines with glory in comparison."[19]

The Republican movement in the New York State election in 1854 took shape in the principles advanced and supported at the polls rather than in the immediate adoption of the name "Republican." Thurlow Weed, editor of the *Albany Evening Journal,* political boss and power behind the throne in the Whig party, and Senator William H. Seward, the party's chief officeholding representative, were reluctant to give up the Whig name. They were both strongly anti-slavery, however, and were instrumental in the fusing of all the anti-slavery factions in the

---

[18] *Ibid.,* p. 178.
[19] *Tribune,* August 5, 1854.

fall election in support of Myron H. Clark for governor. Clark had two clear-cut planks in his political platform—"opposition to negro Slavery in the Nation; and anti-Rum in the State,"[20]—and was nominated by the Whigs, the Prohibitionists, the Free-Soil Democrats, and the newly organized Anti-Nebraskans. His running mate as lieutenant-governor was Henry J. Raymond, editor of the *New York Times,* who had served his apprenticeship under Greeley, first on the *New Yorker* and later on the *Tribune.* Clark and Raymond were elected, and a legislature favorable to the re-election of Senator Seward was chosen. Greeley and Raymond participated in an Anti-Nebraska Convention composed of Whigs, Free-Soilers, and independent Democrats held at Saratoga in August. This convention did not nominate candidates but passed resolutions supporting "the sacred cause of freedom, free labor and free soil."[21] At an adjourned meeting in September the Anti-Nebraska forces got behind the Clark and Raymond ticket.[22]

In the meantime Greeley's desire for office took a strange turn. He had long been identified with the political firm of "Seward, Weed, and Greeley," and now thought it was time for the reward of office. He called on Weed at the Astor House in New York City and asked if Weed "did not think that the time and circumstances were favorable to his nomination for Governor." Weed replied that the time and circumstances were favorable to Greeley's election, if nominated, but he pointed out that Clark, the anti-slavery and prohibitionist candidate, had "stolen his thunder." Greeley accepted Weed's verdict cheerfully, but turned up a few days later in Weed's office at Albany with the question: "Is there any objection to my running for Lieutenant-Governor?" The astute Weed had no objection whatever, but he quietly pointed out the undesirability of having a strong temperance advocate at both ends of the ticket. Again Greeley accepted the situation; but when the Whig State Convention, meeting at Syracuse on September 20, 1854, nominated Henry J. Raymond, his former apprentice and present newspaper rival, to run as lieutenant-governor with Clark, he was deeply outraged. He held Weed responsible for Raymond's nomination and believed that Weed had concealed his intention during their discussion of his own candidacy.[23]

---

[20] Curtis, *op. cit.,* I, 205.
[21] *Ibid.*
[22] Frederic Bancroft, *The Life of William H. Seward,* I, 365–74.
[23] Harriet A. Weed and Thurlow Weed Barnes, eds., *The Life of Thurlow Weed,* II, Memoir, 225–27. See also Francis Brown, *Raymond of the Times,* pp. 137–40.

Toward the end of the campaign, Greeley wrote Seward on October 25:

Just as soon as this election is over, I want to have an earnest talk with you. I have held in as long as I can, or shall have by that time. I don't think we can absolutely be beaten, but relatively we must be—simply for want of courage and common-sense. And if we are beaten, anyhow I shall endeavor to show why. I have tried to talk to Weed, but only with partial success. Weed likes me, and always did—I don't think he ever had a dog about his house he liked better—but he thinks I know nothing about politics. . . . If there are any plans for the future, I want to know what they are, and if there are none, I want to know that fact, and I will try to form a plan of some sort for myself.[24]

Greeley was too impatient to wait for an opportunity for an "earnest talk" with Seward. On November 11, in a letter to Seward, he let out his apparently long accumulated wrath and gave notice of the dissolution of the "political firm of Seward, Weed and Greeley." This letter, unconsciously on Greeley's part, was a self-portrait of the man with whom Lincoln was to deal throughout the trying days of the Civil War, and it figured largely in the acrimonious discussions that took place after Seward's defeat by Lincoln in the Wigwam Convention in Chicago in May, 1860. Greeley gave the letter to the public in the *Tribune* on June 14, 1860; he also published it in his *Recollections of a Busy Life,* and then said he saw nothing in it "that requires explanation."[25] The letter contained more than two thousand words and was petulant, almost childish, in tone. Greeley complained bitterly that Weed and Seward had sought his aid in advancing their own political interests but had ignored him completely as eligible for office and had overlooked him when pecuniary emoluments were available. This letter stands perhaps as the most discreditable note in the whole career of the famous editor.

Seward did not allow Greeley's letter to upset him. On the day he received it he wrote Weed that he had received a letter from Greeley "full of sharp, pricking thorns" but absolving him because of his "at the bottom, nobleness of disposition" from "saying or doing anything wrong or unkind." Seward also said that it was sad to see Greeley so unhappy and asked whether there might not be opportunity during the winter to secure his appointment to the Board of Regents.[26] He also

---

[24] Bancroft, *op. cit.,* I, 371–72.
[25] Greeley, *op. cit.,* pp. 311–22.
[26] Bancroft, *op. cit.,* I, 373.

wrote a careful, if not even soothing, letter to Greeley, which unfortunately was not preserved. It brought a response from Greeley almost as strange as the original explosion but much less vehement. He wrote as an old man in a half-apologetic tone, saying that his "political life" was ended, and that "it would have been precious" to him "to have had some public and palpable recognition" that he was "accorded worthy among others." He implied that there was nothing left for him to do but to sell his interest in the *Tribune* and retire to his little farm.[27] Greeley was then forty-three, and eighteen years later he *did* leave his editorial desk along enough to run for the presidency, but the day after his defeat he was back at his desk.

During the summer and fall of 1854, while Greeley was nursing his hopes and his hurts in New York, the Republican party was germinating in Illinois. Lincoln, according to Herndon, "was always calculating and always planning ahead. His ambition was a little engine that knew no rest."[28] This active little engine had prompted Lincoln to get into line to succeed General James Shields, whose term in the United States Senate was to expire in 1855. An Anti-Nebraska group with abolition leanings was scheduled to hold a state convention with plans for a Republican party in Springfield on October 5.[29] Herndon, in the thick of this movement, was wise enough to know that Lincoln's hopes for the senatorship made it unwise for him to be identified with that group. When an effort was made to have Lincoln speak at a hastily planned meeting the night of October 4, Herndon persuaded Lincoln to get out of town, in order that he might not be dragged into it and might escape the necessity of declining to attend. Thus, less than six years before he was to be nominated for the presidency by the Republican party, Lincoln ran away from the prospect of being called a Republican. In his absence he was named a member of the embryonic State Committee set up by the convention; but, cleverly shy of affiliating himself with any new party movement which savored of abolition, he declined to serve. There is no doubt that Lincoln and Herndon were both long-headed politicians. In the debates with Douglas in 1858, Douglas tried, and failed dismally, to brand Lincoln as responsible for certain resolutions alleged to have been adopted by the "Black Republicans" at the Springfield Convention in question.[30] Lincoln did admit that he had left

---

[27] Greeley Papers, *op. cit.*, Greeley to William H. Seward, November 24, 1854.

[28] William H. Herndon and Jesse William Weik, *The Life of Lincoln*, II, 375.

[29] *Transactions of McLean County Historical Society*, III, 43–47.

[30] Herndon and Weik, *op. cit.*, II, 371–72. See also Nicolay and Hay, *op. cit.*, III,

Springfield at the time, but he did not state his reasons for leaving then.

Like Greeley, Lincoln did not conceal his wish for office, but there was no "political firm" in Illinois quite comparable to that of "Seward, Weed, and Greeley" in New York to which he could go to voice his wish to become a United States senator. His "restless ambition" which "found its gratification only in the field of politics" was now employed, as it was when he had sought election to Congress in 1846, by sounding out his friends and district leaders.[31] He no doubt wrote many letters which have never come to light. Among the known letters, the two which follow are typical:

Clinton, DeWitt Co., November 10, 1854

[To Charles Hoyt]
Dear Sir: You used to express a good deal of partiality for me, and if you are still so, now is the time. Some friends here are really for me, for the U. S. Senate, and I should be very grateful if you could make a mark for me among your members. Please write me at all events giving me the names, post-offices, and "political position" of members round about you. Direct to Springfield.

Let this be confidential.

Yours truly
A. Lincoln[32]

Springfield, November 27, 1854

[To T. J. Henderson]
My Dear Sir: It has come around that a Whig may, by possibility, be elected to the United States Senate; and I want the chance of being the man. You are a member of the legislature and have a vote to give. Think it over, and see whether you can do better than go for me. Write me at all events, and let this be confidential.

Yours truly,
A. Lincoln[33]

Quite contrary to his wishes, Lincoln had been elected to the lower House of the legislature on November 7. When it became apparent that he had a chance of being chosen for the United States Senate, he re-

---

205–12, 223–30; Horace White, "Abraham Lincoln in 1854," *Illinois State Historical Society*, January, 1908.

[31] Herndon and Weik, *op. cit.*, II, 335.

[32] Nicolay and Hay, *op. cit.*, II, 262–63, Lincoln to Charles Hoyt, November 10, 1854.

[33] *Ibid.*, p. 263, Lincoln to T. J. Henderson, November 27, 1854. For similar letters, see *ibid.*, pp. 265–73; Gilbert A. Tracy, *Uncollected Letters of Abraham Lincoln*, pp. 52–53.

signed from the legislature. In the special election to fill the vacancy, much to his discomfiture, a Democrat was chosen. The Anti-Nebraska forces had a majority in the legislature made up of Whigs and Anti-Nebraska Democrats. The two Houses met by agreement in joint convention to choose a senator on February 8, 1855. The Whigs were mainly for Lincoln, and the Douglas Democrats were for Shields. The Anti-Nebraska Democrats divided their vote, and a few of them at the outset supported Lyman D. Trumbull. Lincoln led when the balloting began but was checkmated when Governor Joel A. Matteson appeared as a dark horse candidate. Shields was eliminated, Lincoln began to lose, and the contest settled down between Matteson and Trumbull. On the tenth and final roll call, Lincoln turned his fifteen remaining votes to Trumbull, who was elected by a majority of one.[34] Lincoln felt bad at his defeat, but it did not prevent him from congratulating Trumbull at a reception at the home of Ninian W. Edwards in Springfield that evening.[35] The next day, February 9, 1855, he was in a wholesome philosophical mood, which permitted him to write a letter to Elihu B. Washburne explaining his defeat, and closing with the words:

> *I regret my defeat moderately, but I am not nervous about it. I could have headed off every combination and been elected, had it not been for Matteson's double game—and his defeat now gives me more pleasure than my own gives me pain. On the whole, it is perhaps as well for our general cause that Trumbull is elected. The Nebraska men confess that they hate it worse than anything that could have happened. It is a great consolation to see them worse whipped than I am. I tell them it is their own fault—that they had abundant opportunity to choose between him and me, which they declined, and instead forced it on me to decide between him and Matteson.*
>
> *With my grateful acknowledgments for the kind, active and continued interest you have taken for me in this matter, allow me to subscribe myself*
> Yours forever,
> A. Lincoln[36]

In his autobiography, written five years later, Lincoln did not mention his defeat for the Senate and recalled only that he took the stump in the autumn of 1854 "with no broader political aim or object than

---

[34] For dependable accounts of this election, see Horace White, *op. cit.*, pp. 15–19; and Albert J. Beveridge, *Abraham Lincoln*, II, 275–90.

[35] Horace White, *The Life of Lyman Trumbull*, p. 45.

[36] Nicolay and Hay, *op. cit.*, II, 274–77, Lincoln to E. H. Washburne, February 9, 1855. See also Emanuel Hertz, *Abraham Lincoln—A New Portrait*, II, 65, Lincoln to W. H. Henderson, February 21, 1855.

to secure, if possible, the reelection of Hon. Richard Yates to Congress. His speeches at once attracted a more marked attention than they had ever done before."[37]

The tense excitement of this senatorial election in Illinois did not reach the East. In due time the *Tribune* reported on its editorial page that the Hon. Lyman Trumbull, a Free-Soil Democrat, had been chosen by the Illinois Legislature to succeed General Shields in the United States Senate and did not mention the defeated Lincoln. "This glorious result," the announcement read, "is a fitting finale to the Repeal of the Missouri Compromise by Douglas and Co., who have made their boasts that the result of the recent Illinois election was a Nebraska triumph, and that there would be no election for Senator this winter."[38] A letter to the *Tribune* signed "Chicago" headed "The Triumph of Freedom in Illinois," published three days later, dealt with the election of Trumbull but did not refer to Lincoln's participation in the contest.

In a business letter written on March 10, 1855, Lincoln said: "When I received the bond I was dabbling in politics, and of course neglecting business. Having since been beaten out I have gone to work again."[39] He was as good as his word. From this time until May 29, 1856, when he joined the Republican party, he kept discreetly in the political background. Holding his unalterable opposition to the extension of slavery, he carefully avoided participation in controversial issues which divided the anti-slavery forces. Thus he kept out of the bitter prohibition fight waged in Illinois at this time, and he also kept out of the discussion of the violence taking place in Kansas and the furor aroused over the assault on Charles Sumner in the United States Senate on May 22, 1856. Greeley was living night and day with the Kansas question, and he coined the term "Border Ruffians" during this period.[40] He was also leading the fight for temperance in the East,[41] and was outraged at the attack on Sumner.[42]

Lincoln said nothing publicly, and very little privately, on the vital issues in these twenty months which were stirring men to assert themselves in vigorous terms. He did, however, write three significant letters in August, 1855, which showed how closely he was watching the

---

[37] Nicolay and Hay, *op. cit.*, VI, 37.

[38] *Tribune*, February 9, 1855.

[39] Nicolay and Hay, *op. cit.*, II, 278, Lincoln to Sanford, Porter, and Striker.

[40] *Tribune*, April 10, 12, 1855.

[41] *Ibid.*, November 7, 1854.

[42] *Ibid.*, May 23, 1856.

troubled scene and how religiously he was sticking to the fundamental issues on the slavery question. In the first, on August 11, he wrote Owen Lovejoy,

I am quite busy trying to pick up my lost crumbs of last year. . . . Not even you are more anxious to prevent the extension of slavery than I. And yet the political atmosphere is such, just now, that I fear to do anything, lest I do wrong. Know Nothingism has not yet entirely tumbled to pieces. Nay, it is even a little encouraged by the late elections in Tennessee, Kentucky and Alabama. Until we can get the elements of this organization there is not sufficient material to successfully combat the Nebraska democracy with. We cannot get them so long as they cling to a hope of success under their own organization; and I fear an open push by us now may offend them and tend to prevent our ever getting them. About us here, they are mostly my old political and personal friends, and I have hoped this organization would die out without the painful necessity of my taking an open stand against them. Of their principles I think little better than I do of those of the slavery extensionists.[43]

In the letter to George Robertson, written on August 15, he struck the note which he was to emphasize later, concerning the permanence of the nation—"forever—half slave and half free."[44] In the letter to Joshua F. Speed on August 24, he discussed the Kansas problem with entire familiarity and declared that "I shall advocate the restoration of the Missouri Compromise so long as Kansas remains a Territory, and when, by all these foul means, it seeks to come into the Union as a slave state, I shall oppose it."[45]

On February 22, 1856, a group of Illinois Anti-Nebraska editors under the leadership of Paul Selby, editor of the *Morgan Journal* of Jacksonville, held a meeting at Decatur, which marked the real beginning of the Republican party in the state. Lincoln was present and seems to have been the only outsider admitted to the deliberations. The record does not indicate how he became identified with the meeting. The resolutions adopted bore "the stamp of his peculiar intellect" and pledged the editors to disavow any intention of interfering with slavery in the states; to protest against the introduction of slavery into territory already free; to demand the restoration of the Missouri Compromise; to insist upon the maintenance of the doctrine of the Declaration of Independence as essential to freedom of speech and the press; to op-

---

[43] Tracy, *op. cit.*, pp. 59–60, Lincoln to Owen Lovejoy, August 11, 1855.
[44] Nicolay and Hay, *op. cit.*, II, 278–81, Lincoln to George Robertson, August 15, 1855.
[45] *Ibid.*, pp. 281–87, Lincoln to Joshua F. Speed, August 24, 1855.

pose "Know Nothingism"; and to seek reform in the state government. Lincoln spoke at the post-prandial affair in the evening and waived aside the suggestion of one of the editors that he be made the candidate for governor. He urged that an Anti-Nebraska Democrat, such as Colonel William H. Bissell, would be more available than an old-line Whig like himself. The conference adopted an independent resolution which recommended that a state convention be held at Bloomington on May 29.[46]

Meanwhile, the lively and astute Herndon knew well enough that an "old-line Whig" had no political future. "Mere hatred of slavery and opposition to the injustice of the Kansas-Nebraska legislation were not all that were required" of Lincoln. "He must be a Democrat, Know-Nothing, Abolitionist, or Republican, or forever float about in the great political sea without compass, rudder, or sail."[47] Herndon decided to take matters into his own hands. In Lincoln's absence on the circuit, he "drew up a paper for the friends of freedom to sign," calling a county convention in Springfield to select delegates for the forthcoming Republican State Convention in Bloomington, and signed Lincoln's name at the head of the call.[48] After the call came out, fearing that he had gone too far, Herndon wrote Lincoln, who was attending court in Tazewell County, what he had done and asked him to send his approval or disapproval at once. The answer came promptly: "All right; go ahead. Will meet you—radicals and all."[49]

On May 24, Lincoln and Herndon were among the delegates from Sangamon County, chosen to attend the Bloomington Convention. This celebrated meeting, while the name Republican did not appear in the call or in the report of the proceedings, stands in history as the first Illinois State Republican Convention, and it marks Abraham Lincoln's unequivocal affiliation with the Republican party. A state ticket, headed by the Anti-Nebraska Democrat, William H. Bissell, for governor, the man who was suggested by Lincoln at Decatur, was chosen and subsequently elected. Lincoln was named as an elector for the state at large and as a delegate to the forthcoming National Convention at Philadelphia. The resolutions adopted were closely in line with the views already expressed by Lincoln. He was not a member of the committee but his intimate friend, Orville H. Browning, was chairman of it

---

[46] *Transactions of McLean County Historical Society*, III, 30–43.
[47] Herndon and Weik, *op. cit.*, II, 382.
[48] *Ibid.*, p. 382. See also *Illinois State Journal*, May 14, 1856.
[49] Herndon and Weik, *op. cit.*, p. 383.

and Lincoln was close at hand throughout its deliberations. The new Republican doctrine, which Lincoln was now to espouse, was based on the frank determination "to wrest the government from the unworthy hands" controlling it, to "prevent the extension of slavery into territories heretofore free," to brand the repeal of the Missouri Compromise as "unwise, unjust and injurious," to favor the immediate admission of Kansas "under the constitution adopted by the people of said territory," and to defend the Union "to the last extremity."[50]

And as if to set the gauge of future battle for Lincoln, the convention paid its compliments to Douglas in a separate, heated resolution as follows:

Resolved, *That* STEPHEN A. DOUGLAS, *having laid his "ruthless hand" upon a sacred compact, which had "an origin akin to that of the constitution," and which had "become canonized in the hearts of the American people," has given the lie to his past history, proved himself recreant to the free principles of this government, violated the confidence of the people of Illinois, and now holds his seat in the senate while he misrepresents them.*[51]

Lincoln no doubt had a hand in the resolution counseling the "foregoing" of "all former differences of opinion upon other questions." There was need of such counsel. There were both radicals and conservatives in the meeting, old-line Whigs, Anti-Nebraska Democrats, Know-Nothings, Free-Soilers, and Abolitionists. Feeling ran high. The assault of Preston S. Brooks on Charles Sumner had occurred only the week before, and on the morning the convention opened, the Chicago papers were full of the sacking of Lawrence, Kansas, by the "Border Ruffians." It remained for Lincoln to harmonize the differences and to crystallize the common view. He accomplished this difficult task in what is known as his "Lost Speech." Herndon's glowing account of this speech, first publicly made in 1866 and confirmed later, is not without foundation.[52] At the meeting of the McLean County Historical Society commemorative of the Bloomington Convention of May 29, 1856, held on May 29, 1900, forty-four years later, several of the prominent men who participated in the convention, including the venerable John M. Palmer, who had presided at the original meeting, were present and still recalled Lincoln's "Lost Speech" as one of the most impressive they had ever

---

[50] *Transactions of McLean County Historical Society*, III, 160–61, copied from the *Illinois State Journal*, May 30, 1856.

[51] *Ibid.*, p. 163.

[52] Herndon and Weik, *op. cit.*, II, 384–85.

heard.[53] They preferred to hold the speech in memory rather than to accept the version of it written in 1896 by Henry C. Whitney from notes he had taken at the time.[54]

Impressive as Lincoln's speech seems to have been, two reports of the Bloomington Convention, published in the *Tribune* on June 3, went into considerable detail but did not even notice the presence of Lincoln. A third report signed "Spirit of '76," published on June 9, furnished the information that "Speeches were made by the ablest men in the State," mentioned one or two others but said nothing of Lincoln's speech.

Illinois Republicanism was keeping pace with the nation in 1856. On Washington's birthday when the little group of Anti-Nebraska editors were exchanging views, listening to Lincoln, and planning for the state convention to be held at Bloomington on May 29, the national meeting was organizing the Republican party at Pittsburgh, with Horace Greeley in the thick of it, and making plans for the first National Republican Nominating Convention to be held at Philadelphia on June 17. The Bloomington Convention was held just in time to give delegates their credentials for Philadelphia. Although Lincoln had been chosen as a delegate, he was busy on the circuit and did not go to Philadelphia.

Greeley attended both the Pittsburgh and the Philadelphia conventions. In publishing the call for the informal Pittsburgh meeting he said: "What is contemplated is the beginning of a National movement designed to unite all the opponents of Slavery Extension in the Presidential contest before us."[55] On February 24, he reported from Pittsburgh, "I have no guess, no choice, as to who shall be its candidates for President and Vice-President; but the intelligence, the earnestness, the moral weight of this Convention assure me that they will be capable and worthy."[56] Later in the spring he declared his purpose to hold himself free to support Seward, McLean, Chase, Frémont, "or whoever

---

[53] *Transactions of McLean County Historical Society*, III, 81–82, 91, 93–94, 124. See also Sherman Day Wakefield, *How Lincoln Became President*, pp. 57–69; and Reinhard H. Luthin, *The First Lincoln Campaign*, pp. 69–91.

[54] Whitney's version of Lincoln's "Lost Speech" may be found in *McClure's Magazine*, VII (1896), 315–31; in Ida M. Tarbell, *The Life of Abraham Lincoln*, II, 306–21; and in a "Souvenir of the 11th Annual Dinner of the Republican Club of the City of New York," February 12, 1897.

[55] *Tribune*, January 17, 1856.

[56] *Ibid.*, February 25, 1856.

else, being heartily in favor of and openly committed to the cause of Free Kansas, may be nominated by the Philadelphia Convention."[57] Ten days before the convention he discussed the availability of Seward, Chase, Sumner, McLean, and Frémont and expressed willingness to take any one of them, but preferred Seward.[58] During these pre-convention months Greeley did not let up on his characterization of Douglas as the chief proponent of the "infamous Nebraska bill."[59] He found it difficult to follow the "pettifogging lawyer around the barren stump of discussion where he seeks to dodge the blows struck at him."[60] He pictured Douglas as "the arch-traitor from Illinois" vomiting "his rage upon the Senate,"[61] as adding to his profession "that of a bully,"[62] as "Benedict Arnold Douglas,"[63] and as guilty of "impudent sophistry and unblushing misrepresentation."[64]

Taken to task by some of his fellow editors for his rough treatment of Douglas, Greeley almost outdid himself:

Our portrayal of the essential characteristics of Senator Douglas appears to have shocked the sensibilities of some of our contemporaries. In our estimation, the annals of public affairs can show no greater criminal than the man who, at this age, in a Republican Government, sells out free territory to be coerced and blackened with the hideous crime and curse of African Slavery; aims to cover the transaction by pretending its harmony with the beneficent designs of the great National Charter of our liberties; defends, by glaring falsehoods, the outrages and tyranny engendered by the incipient processes of this traitorous surrender; and then dares insolently to threaten to "subdue" by powder and ball and the hangman's cord, the opponents and the victims of the stupendous crime and swindle. What sort of language is applicable to such a man, but that which describes the morals of the slaver, the pirate, and the traitor? If human doom is to be commensurate with human offense, what, short of moral crucifixion, should be the penalty of such gigantic wickedness?[65]

Two years later we shall find Greeley urging the Republicans of Illinois to support Douglas for re-election to the United States Senate, and finally, because his advice was not heeded, giving half-hearted support

---

[57] Ibid., April 29, 1856.
[58] Ibid., June 16, 1856.
[59] Ibid., July 4, 1855.
[60] Ibid., March 14, 1856.
[61] Ibid., March 24, 1856.
[62] Ibid., April 11, 1856.
[63] Ibid., June 4, 1856.
[64] Ibid., June 20, 1856.
[65] Ibid., April 18, 1856.

to Lincoln against Douglas in their epoch-making campaign of 1858.

The lines formed slowly for the political battle of 1856. The Whigs had disappeared in the West, and the new Republican party faced the Democrats squarely. In the East there was more diversity, where four principal parties were active: Whigs, Democrats, Know-Nothings, and Republicans. In the South the Democrats stood firm, and the old-line Whigs had largely gone over to the American party. A national council of the American party met at Philadelphia on February 19 and on February 22 organized as a nominating convention and named ex-President Millard Fillmore of New York for President and Andrew Donelson of Tennessee for Vice-President. The anti-slavery delegates from the East and the North withdrew before action was taken and, calling themselves North Americans, nominated John C. Frémont of California for President and William F. Johnston of Pennsylvania for Vice-President. Johnston subsequently withdrew in favor of William L. Dayton of New Jersey. The Democrats met at Cincinnati on June 2, with a three-cornered fight on their hands, President Pierce, James Buchanan of Pennsylvania, and Douglas seeking the nomination. Pierce was eliminated on the sixteenth ballot, and on the seventeenth Buchanan was nominated. John C. Breckenridge was named for Vice-President.[66] The sadly decimated Whig party met on September 17 at Baltimore and accepted Fillmore and Donelson as candidates by resolution.

On hearing the news of Buchanan's nomination, Lincoln wrote Lyman Trumbull that a good many Whigs "of conservative feelings, and slight pro-slavery proclivities" were likely to go for him unless "the Anti-Nebraska nomination" should divert them. He thought that the man to hold these Whigs was Judge John McLean. He questioned whether they would "go for Buchanan," as against Chase, Banks, Seward, Blair, or Frémont. He thought they would stand for Blair or Frémont for Vice-President—"but not more." He felt that something should be done to pacify the Whigs since nine-tenths of the Anti-Nebraska votes had to come from them. For himself he was "*in*" and ready to go "for any one nominated" unless he should be " 'platformed' expressly, or impliedly" on some ground which he thought wrong.[67]

Greeley spent several months in Washington in the winter and spring of 1856, sending "Editorial Correspondence" to the *Tribune*. The nomination of Fillmore and Donelson at Philadelphia prompted him

---

[66] Curtis, *op. cit.*, I, 262–63.
[67] Tracy, *op. cit.*, pp. 66–68, Lincoln to Lyman Trumbull, June 7, 1856.

to say: "The nomination of Fillmore falls like a wet blanket on the Americans here. I cannot find one who ever believed in or wished to see a North who sustains it. It seems to be generally felt, even by Know-Nothings—in earnest, that it is a grave mistake for a new party to select as its standard bearer a hackneyed and discarded politician."[68] Later he felt that the nomination ought to unite the North on the Republican platform while dividing the South between the two pro-slavery parties.[69] As the time approached for the Republican Convention, the *Tribune* was determined to hold a position from which "we can enter upon the support of Gov. Seward, Judge McLean, Gov. Chase, Col. Frémont, or whoever else, being heartily in favor of and openly committed to the cause of Free Kansas, may be nominated by the Philadelphia Convention."[70] Ten days before the convention met, the *Tribune* believed that Seward, Chase, or Sumner should be the Republican nominee if the "opponents of Slavery Extension" could "elect whomsoever they may choose to nominate." In the event that the "Anti-Nebraska" sentiment should be deemed strong enough to elect a President only, in concurrence with other influences working against the Cincinnati nominees, then the man for the crisis might be Banks, Bissell, Frémont, or McLean. Greeley was already really picking Frémont.[71] He had received Buchanan's nomination mildly, compared to the language he was to use later in the campaign. He recognized Buchanan as "a man respectable in every personal relation—a good citizen and neighbor—a man of fair talents and unsullied private character"; but he held that Buchanan's election "would be in the highest degree disastrous to our country and prejudicial to the advance of Freedom and Justice throughout the world."[72]

It was pretty clearly anticipated, when the first National Republican Convention assembled at Philadelphia on June 17, that John C. Frémont would be the standard bearer.[73] The first day was given over to the appointment and organization of committees and to warming-up speeches. To employ Lincoln's phrase, the convention solemnly "platformed" its candidates on the second day before proceeding to choose them. David Wilmot of Pennsylvania, of Proviso fame, presented the

---

[68] *Tribune*, February 27, 1856.

[69] *Ibid.*, February 28, 1856.

[70] *Ibid.*, April 29, 1856.

[71] *Ibid.*, June 6, 1856. See also Jeter A. Isely, *Horace Greeley and the Republican Party*, pp. 151–95.

[72] *Tribune*, June 7, 1856.

[73] William Starr Myers, *The Republican Party—A History*, p. 64.

platform as chairman of the committee appointed for that purpose. It might have been written by either Lincoln or Greeley so closely did it follow the common views they had held up to this time. The Kansas plank could not have been too strong to suit Greeley; and Lincoln might have preferred it more pacific in tone. The platform as a whole was a faithful elaboration of the position of the new party as expressed in the preamble:

This convention of delegates, assembled in pursuance of a call addressed to the people of the United States, without regard to past political differences or divisions, who are opposed to the repeal of the Missouri Compromise; to the policy of the present Administration; to the extension of Slavery into Free Territory; in favor of the admission of Kansas as a Free State; of restoring the action of the Federal Government to the principles of Washington and Jefferson; and who purpose to unite in presenting candidates for the offices of President and Vice-President, do resolve as follows. . . .[74]

Before the convention proceeded to an informal ballot on the choice for President, the names of Seward, McLean, and Chase were withdrawn from consideration; but the withdrawal of McLean's name was subsequently rescinded. The informal ballot resulted as follows: Frémont, 359; McLean, 190; Banks, 1; Sumner, 2; Seward, 1. A formal ballot was then taken, after lengthy discussion, which was announced as follows: Frémont, 520; McLean, 37; Seward, 1. The convention then, on motion of General J. W. Webb of New York, adopted the following resolution:

Resolved, That this Convention do unanimously nominate John C. Fremont of California, to be the Republican candidate for President of the United States, at the ensuing election.

On the third and last day the choice of a running mate for Frémont was taken up. The names of William L. Dayton of New Jersey, Abraham Lincoln of Illinois, David Wilmot of Pennsylvania, and John A. King of New York were proposed from the floor. John Allison of Pennsylvania proposed Lincoln's name and Colonel William B. Archer and "Hon. Judge Palmer" of Illinois seconded the proposal. An informal vote resulted as follows: Dayton, 253; Lincoln, 110; Banks, 46; Wilmot, 43; Sumner, 35; King, 9; and scattering votes for nine other candidates. There were several withdrawals before the formal balloting began. In the midst of the balloting Judge Palmer arose and said:

---

[74] Johnson, *op. cit.*, pp. 43–45.

In behalf of the delegation of the State of Illinois, I return thanks to such members of this Convention as have honored the favorite of our State with their vote. Illinois asks nothing for herself in this contest. She is devoted— and I trust that the result of the next election will prove that she is devoted —to the great cause that has brought us together. [Cheers.] She knew that in Abraham Lincoln we had a soldier tried and true. We offered him to the Republican party of the United States for the position that we have indicated, but we are content to prefer harmony and union to the success even of our cherished favorite. Therefore, we say to those of our friends who have honored us, we commend them to withdraw the votes thus cast for Mr. Lincoln and give them that direction that will make the vote unanimous and harmonious for Wm. L. Dayton.

The withdrawal of Lincoln's name was the signal for the ensuing switch to Dayton, and the final tabulation of the formal ballot showed him unanimously chosen. With a final round of speech-making and the speedy transaction of routine business "and nine tremendous cheers for the candidates, in the best of feeling, the convention adjourned."[75]

Lincoln was in court at Urbana on Friday, June 20, when the Chicago papers brought the report of the vote for Vice-President. Expressing surprise, he said the vote must have been for a great man by the name of Lincoln in Massachusetts.[76] John Van Dyke, a delegate to the convention, who had been in Congress with Lincoln, made a rousing speech after Dayton was nominated in the course of which he mentioned Lincoln in most kindly terms.[77] Lincoln promptly wrote to thank him for his "kind notice." He asked Van Dyke to present his respects to Judge Dayton and to tell him, "I think him a far better man than I for the position he is in, and that I shall support both him and Colonel Frémont most cordially."[78]

Greeley and his reporters sent full accounts of the proceedings to the *Tribune* day by day. When Frémont was nominated by acclamation, Greeley wired his paper, "The enthusiasm is tremendous."[79] The *Tribune* published in its news columns all the references to Lincoln during the choice of the candidate for Vice-President.[80] Greeley promptly gave

---

[75] *Ibid.*, pp. 15–82.
[76] Henry C. Whitney, *Life on the Circuit with Lincoln*, p. 80.
[77] Johnson, *op. cit.*, p. 71.
[78] Nicolay and Hay, *op. cit.*, II, 289–90.
[79] *Tribune*, June 19, 1856.
[80] *Ibid.*, June 20, 1856.

editorial approval to the ticket but said: "We do not enter upon the contest before us in any spirit of overweening confidence. We admit that the apparent odds are greatly in favor of our adversaries."[81] In discussing the choice for Vice-President, Greeley had this to say: "New Jersey in good faith presented the name of Mr. Dayton—Illinois that of Mr. Lincoln. They are both true and able men—they were severally urged as certain to conciliate support in their respective localities. We do not know that Mr. Dayton is an older or better soldier than Mr. Lincoln; but his proximity to Pennsylvania and his relations with her citizens decided the question in his favor. And, while we know Mr. Lincoln well and esteem him highly, we believe this choice was judicious."[82]

The campaign which followed was long to be remembered. "Never in our history, and probably never in the history of the world," says Rhodes, "had a more pure, more disinterested, and more intelligent body of men banded together for a noble political object than those who now enrolled themselves under the Republican banner."[83] Rhodes also says that the "cause" was "much stronger than the candidate."[84] Lincoln had preferred McLean, and Greeley had preferred Seward; but they gave themselves to the support of the ticket unreservedly. Lincoln recalled that he made over fifty speeches, no one of which so far as he remembered was printed;[85] however, fragments of his speeches at this time have been preserved.[86] Herndon says Lincoln was in constant demand throughout the campaign and that almost every county seat in the state wanted him. Iowa, Indiana, and Wisconsin sought his help.[87] Busy at home, he made only one speech outside of the state, at a Republican demonstration at Kalamazoo, Michigan, on August 27.[88] Throughout the campaign he held to his fundamental thesis that slavery should not be extended and that the Union should be preserved. He took it upon himself to counteract Fillmorism. He wrote letters widely to "wean away Fillmore's adherents." Herndon quoted this one as characteristic:

---

[81] *Ibid.*

[82] *Ibid.*, June 21, 1856.

[83] James Ford Rhodes, *History of the United States*, II, 166.

[84] *Ibid.*, p. 192.

[85] Nicolay and Hay, *op. cit.*, VI, 38.

[86] *Ibid.*, II, 292–95, 299–307.

[87] Herndon and Weik, *op. cit.*, II, 386–87.

[88] Paul M. Angle, *Lincoln Day by Day, 1854–1861*, p. 139; and Thomas I. Starr, *Lincoln's Kalamazoo Address*.

Springfield, September 8, 1856

Harrison Maltby, Esq.
Dear Sir:

I understand you are a Fillmore man. Let me prove to you that every vote withheld from Fremont and given to Fillmore in this State actually lessens Fillmore's chance of being President.

Suppose Buchanan gets all the slave States and Pennsylvania and any other one State besides; then he is elected, no matter who gets all the rest. But suppose Fillmore gets the two slave States of Maryland and Kentucky, then Buchanan is not elected; Fillmore goes into the House of Representatives and may be made President by a compromise. But suppose again Fillmore's friends throw away a few thousand votes on him in Indiana and Illinois; it will inevitably give these States to Buchanan, which will more than compensate him for the loss of Maryland and Kentucky; it will elect him, and leave Fillmore no chance in the House of Representatives or out of it.

This is as plain as adding up the weight of three small hogs. As Mr. Fillmore has no possible chance to carry Illinois for himself it is plainly to his interest to let Fremont take it and thus keep it out of the hands of Buchanan. Be not deceived. Buchanan is the hard horse to beat in this race. Let him have Illinois, and nothing can beat him; and he will get Illinois if men persist in throwing away votes upon Mr. Fillmore. Does some one persuade you that Mr. Fillmore can carry Illinois? Nonsense! There are over seventy newspapers in Illinois opposing Buchanan, only three or four of which support Mr. Fillmore, all the rest going for Fremont. Are not these newspapers a fair index of the proportion of the votes? If not, tell me why.

Again, of these three or four Fillmore newspapers, two at least are supported in part by the Buchanan men, as I understand. Do not they know where the shoe pinches? They know the Fillmore movement helps them, and therefore they help it.

Do think these things over and then act according to your judgment.

Yours very truly,
A. Lincoln[89]

Confidential

Greeley also believed that Buchanan was a "hard horse to beat" and bent every effort throughout the campaign to beat him. The *Tribune* issued a campaign life of Frémont which had a wide distribution and which was translated into German and Welsh.[90] Greeley, of course, kept the Kansas situation constantly before his readers and desired to

---

[89] Herndon and Weik, *op. cit.*, II, 388n.
[90] *Tribune*, August 2, 1856.

see both Buchanan and Fillmore beaten in order that Kansas should "be unequivocally and speedily admitted as a Free State."[91] He was especially severe with Buchanan. Digging up praise of Frémont by Buchanan uttered four years earlier, he employed his bent for vivid imagery:

> We have caught the old rat at last! We have him secured in the square jaws of a steel trap, with a firm, safe, stiff spring, so that he cannot get away. He would gladly pull off his tail, or gnaw off a paw even, as many of his race have done, to escape, if that was all that held him. But, unfortunately, the jaws are closed fixedly around his neck, and the old rat cannot get away.
>
> In THE TRIBUNE of to-day our readers will find JAMES BUCHANAN squarely out in favor of JOHN C. FREMONT! They will read with deep interest what the hoary-headed libeler of to-day said about the gallant and dashing young hero who is now his antagonist, four years ago, when he had no motive to speak anything but the bare, simple, naked truth.[92]

The day before election Greeley summed up the issue as he saw it. He declared that no question had ever been submitted to the judgment of the American people of "more awful magnitude" than that which they would have to decide at the ballot box. The big question was whether Kansas and the territory west of it to the Pacific should be "blessed with Freedom or cursed with Slavery." James Buchanan was the candidate of the "slave driving Democracy." John C. Frémont was the candidate of the "liberty loving Republican party."[93]

The "cause" won a victory, but the "candidate" lost. The insistent threat of disunion by the South if Frémont should be elected, the apprehension of many voters, who favored the cause, that he would not bring a steady hand to the helm, and the votes of the "seedy Fillmoreites," brought about the realization of Lincoln's worst fears and Greeley's apprehensions. Buchanan had a popular vote of 1,838,169, and carried nineteen states, including Illinois and Indiana, which gave him an electoral vote of 174. Frémont had a popular vote of 1,341,264, and carried eleven states, including Massachusetts and New York, which gave him an electoral vote of 114. Fillmore had a popular vote of 874,534, and carried Maryland with eight electoral votes.[94]

Lincoln and Greeley were disappointed but not discouraged. "We

---

[91] *Ibid.*, August 6, 1856.
[92] *Ibid.*, September 20, 1856. For other typical pungent comments during the campaign, see issues of September 17, 22; October 8, 10, 18, 22, 24, 1856.
[93] *Ibid.*, November 3, 1856.
[94] Curtis, *op. cit.*, I, 267.

have lost a battle," said Greeley tne day after the election. "The Bunker Hill of the new struggle for Freedom is past; the Saratoga and York-town are yet to be achieved."[95] In December in a speech at a Republican banquet in Chicago, celebrating the complete victory of the state ticket, Lincoln launched into the recent message of President Pierce to Congress in which the President said that the people were responsible for Buchanan's victory.[96] Lincoln pointed out that the "people" who voted for Buchanan were in a minority of the whole people, as shown by the election, by about four hundred thousand votes. "We were divided between Fremont and Fillmore," he said. "Can we not come together for the future? . . . Thus let bygones be bygones; let past differences as nothing be; and with steady eye on the real issue, let us reinaugurate the good old 'central ideas' of the republic. We can do it. The human heart is with us; God is with us."[97]

The next major battle was four years away, but Lincoln and Greeley kept up their fire at the advance guard of the enemy, Stephen A. Douglas. The continued turbulence in Kansas and the announcement of the Dred Scott decision, withheld until after Buchanan's inauguration, gave them constant occasion for keeping on the trail of Douglas. Greeley had reason enough to pursue Douglas from a wholly impersonal standpoint, for Douglas was the incarnation of the Kansas–Nebraska Act which Greeley had fought day in and day out. Lincoln shared Greeley's view on the "Iniquity," but he also had a personal reason for keeping a wary eye on Douglas: he hoped to succeed him in the United States Senate in 1859. Douglas spoke in Springfield on June 12, 1857, on "Kansas, Utah, and the Dred Scott decision,"[98] and Lincoln replied on June 26.[99] Two days before Lincoln's reply, Greeley had devoted two and a half columns to an analysis of Douglas' speech. Greeley was true to his editorial form in referring to what Douglas had said about the Kansas situation.[100] He repeated his appraisal of Douglas a few days later in commenting on the support of Douglas by Charles H. Lanphier, editor of the *Illinois State Register* at Springfield: "Mr. Stephen A. Douglas, after several ineffectual trials, has provided himself with a home organ after his own heart—one whose capacities for

---

[95] *Tribune*, November 5, 1856.
[96] *Cong. Globe*, 34th Cong., 3d sess., Appendix, pp. 1–6.
[97] Nicolay and Hay, *op. cit.*, II, 308–12.
[98] *Illinois State Register*, June 13, 1857.
[99] Nicolay and Hay, *op. cit.*, II, 315–39.
[100] *Tribune*, June 24, 1857.

ribaldry, misrepresentation and falsehood are exceeded only by his own!"[101]

On July 6 the *Tribune* published in its news columns correspondence from Springfield, under date of June 30, headed "Lincoln's Reply to Douglas," which contained a review of the recent speeches of Lincoln and Douglas and included a personal reference to Lincoln: "Mr. Lincoln is too well known in Illinois to need a word of commendation; but it may be interesting to Republicans at a distance to be informed that there is not a man in this State whose opinions on political subjects command more universal respect by all classes of men than his. The party may well be proud of such an advocate." This issue also contained a reprint of correspondence from Springfield to the *Chicago Tribune* about Lincoln's speech under date of June 27, and also a report of Senator Trumbull's speech in reply to Douglas made at Springfield, June 29. Commenting editorially in this same issue, Greeley said:

The Hon. Stephen A. Douglas having seen fit to open a fresh discussion of the political topics on which the American people are called to act, his example has been followed by his Republican colleague, the Hon. Lyman Trumbull, and by the late leading candidate on the Fremont Electoral Ticket, the Hon. Abraham Lincoln of Springfield who formerly represented that district in Congress. We print herewith a synopsis of Mr. Lincoln's speech from the pen of a Springfield correspondent, with half of the full report of the speech of Mr. Trumbull. We need not commend these able efforts to the careful attention of political readers.

In the summer and fall of 1857 Lincoln was keeping a sharp eye out for the election of a legislature which would favor his choice for the United States Senate in 1859.[102] Before Congress assembled in December, 1857, rumors were afloat that trouble was brewing in the Democratic camp at Washington over the Lecompton Constitution. Lincoln sounded out Senator Trumbull on what he thought of the probable " 'rumpus' among the Democracy." He felt that the Republicans should stand clear of any squabble because in their view both the President and Douglas were wrong.[103] Arriving in Washington a few days in advance of the opening of Congress, Douglas promptly let it be known that he

---

[101] *Ibid.*, July 4, 1857.

[102] Tracy, *op. cit.*, p. 78, Lincoln to Dr. B. Clarke Lundy, August 5, 1857. See also Paul M. Angle, *New Letters and Papers of Lincoln*, pp. 168–69, Lincoln to R. Yates, September 30, 1857.

[103] Tracy, *op. cit.*, p. 82, Lincoln to Lyman Trumbull, November 30, 1857.

was opposed to the Lecompton Constitution, and immediately pounced on Buchanan's message, in which the President displayed a willingness to accept it.[104] Lincoln wrote to Trumbull again telling him that the Democrats in Illinois were sticking to Douglas but "hobbling along with the idea" that there was "no split between him and Buchanan." The Democrats, he told Trumbull, were indulging in "the most extravagant eulogies on B., & his message" and insisting that he had not endorsed the Lecompton Constitution.[105]

Greeley put his stock of choice adjectives, reserved for the vilification of Douglas, into cold storage about the time the rumors began to spread of the break between Douglas and Buchanan. Before Congress assembled he questioned whether the anti-Lecomptonites were *"really"* to have the help of Douglas and others. "Having seen Stephen A. Douglas," he said, "stand up day after day in the Senate and pettifog the case of the enslavers and ravagers of Kansas against the clearest demonstration of their infamy, it will be hard for us to believe that he will now take the side of justice and true democracy. We are ready to yield to the force of evidence, but it must be evidence about which there can be no mistake." He even ventured the suggestion that "Herod and Pilate" might "become once more such friends as they formerly were."[106]

On the day Buchanan's message was submitted to Congress, the correspondence from Washington in the *Tribune* made very clear that a breach had come between the President and Douglas. Editorially, Greeley said: "The career of Senator Douglas has not been such as to inspire in us an exalted confidence in either his philanthropy or his political conscientiousness. We never saw reason for either liking or trusting him. His shrewdness, however, is indisputed."[107] Recalling the epithets Greeley had applied to Douglas repeatedly during the last three years to express his utter lack of confidence in him and his downright contempt for him, Lincoln, in his personal concern and anxiety, may have looked upon this mild statement as praise. Then he no doubt magnified his imagined hurts when Greeley presently said that he was more and more assured that Douglas would triumph in his present policy "and bring 'Old Buch' to his marrow-bones";[108] and that he had no

---

[104] *Tribune*, December 4, 1857.
[105] Tracy, *op. cit.*, p. 83, Lincoln to Lyman Trumbull, December 18, 1857.
[106] *Tribune*, December 2, 1857.
[107] *Ibid.*, December 8, 1857.
[108] *Ibid.*, December 12, 1857.

part in the controversy into which so many Republican journals had plunged concerning the motives and the sincerity of Douglas.[109]

Later editorials in December apparently disturbed Lincoln greatly. One denied any wish to embark on the "sea of speculation" concerning the effects of the struggle on Mr. Douglas' "presumed aspirations or prospects," but intimated that he would probably save his party in Illinois from defeat the next year and thus insure his re-election.[110] In another, Greeley declared it no part of his business to defend the consistency of Senator Douglas on the Kansas question; but did not see the justice of some of the assaults made on him "in certain Administration prints. . . . Because Senator Douglas may have been willing," he said, "to allow Kansas to become a Slave State, because for the sake of helping on that object he was willing for a time to shut his eyes to the reign of violence and usurpation of which Kansas has been the scene, it by no means follows that he is therefore bound to support the Lecompton schedule, or that the ground which he has taken as to that document fairly exposes him to any charge of treachery to his party associates, or abandonment of any position which he has ever assumed."[111]

This was, to be sure, strange language to Lincoln, coming from the distinguished critic of the "arch-conspirator" of the Kansas–Nebraska legislation. Lincoln's concern over any possible advantage Douglas might get over him was revealed in a complaining letter to Trumbull, which also shows the thoroughness with which he was now following Greeley in the *Tribune*:

Bloomington, Dec. 28, 1857

Hon. Lyman Trumbull.

Dear Sir: What does the "New York Tribune" mean by its constant eulogizing, and admiring, and magnifying Douglas? Does it, in this, speak the sentiments of the Republicans at Washington? Have they concluded that the Republican cause, generally, can be best prompted by sacrificing us here in Illinois? If so we would like to know it soon; it will save us a great deal of labor to surrender at once.

As yet I have heard of no Republican here going over to Douglas; but if the "Tribune" continues to din his praises into the ears of its five or ten thousand Republican readers in Illinois, it is more than can be hoped that all will stand firm.

---

[109] *Ibid.*, December 16, 1857.
[110] *Ibid.*, December 21, 1857.
[111] *Ibid.*, December 23, 1857.

I am not complaining—I only wish a fair understanding. Please write me at Springfield.

> Your Obt. Servt.
> A. Lincoln[112]

This letter reveals Lincoln in one of his rare exhibitions of frightened petulance as an office seeker. He was a little later to have substantial ground for his apprehension that Greeley was disposed to undermine him in his enthusiastic commendation of Douglas for his stand against Buchanan on the Lecompton issue. Up to this time, in the *Tribune* at least, Greeley had not eulogized or admired or magnified Douglas, nor dinned his praises into anybody's ears, but Lincoln had a sixth sense in politics. He was moved not so much by what Greeley had said as by what his words implied for the future. Lincoln knew better than the famous editor did himself where he was headed.

The very day after Lincoln wrote to Trumbull, Greeley committed himself in such a way as to indicate that he had not yet contemplated the position he was soon to take in urging the Republicans of Illinois to support Douglas for re-election to the United States Senate. He held that the Republicans were under no sort of obligation to Douglas for his current attitude on the Kansas question, and that it would have been better for the Republicans if Douglas had gone with Buchanan and tried to force the Lecompton Constitution through Congress. He would thus have seriously damaged his own party and at the same time have failed in his object. Douglas was no Republican, and if this casual cooperation with the Republicans in resistance to an outrageous wrong should result in a schism among the Democrats so much the better for the Republicans. "We apprehend, however," Greeley said, "nothing of the sort. The Lecompton fraud once beaten, as beaten it must be, its advocates will be glad enough to sink all remembrance of it, and act with their former brethren, as if nothing had ever separated them."[113] In January, advices from Washington led Greeley to believe that "Buchanan and the fire-eaters" were "broken down." "Walker, Douglas and Wise," he said, "carry the day, and remain the leaders of the National Democratic party. Thanks to them, the people of Kansas are saved from the continuance of a usurpation under whose bloody and outrageous sway they have suffered from the beginning. We say thanks to them, but in reality the thanks are due to the great and formidable Republican party, and not to any number of frightened Democrats,

---

[112] Tracy, *op. cit.*, pp. 83–84, Lincoln to Lyman Trumbull, December 28, 1857.
[113] *Tribune*, December 24, 1857.

fearful not only of the annihilation of their party, but of their own personal annihilation as well."[114]

Lincoln communicated his apprehensions about Greeley's attitude to Herndon,

I think Greeley is not doing me, an old Republican and a tried anti-slavery man, right; he is talking up Douglas, an untrue and an untried man, a dodger, a wriggler, a tool of the South once and now a snapper at it—hope he will bite 'em good; but I don't feel that it is exactly right to pull me down in order to elevate Douglas. I like Greeley, think he intends right, but I think he errs in this hoisting up of Douglas, while he gives me a downward shove. I wish that someone would put a flea in Greeley's ear, see Trumbull, Sumner, Wilson, Seward, Parker, Garrison, Phillips and others, and try and turn the currents in the right direction. These men ought to trust the tried and true men.[115]

This report "in substance" of what Lincoln had said to Herndon was made by Herndon in a letter to Jesse W. Weik, written on December 23, 1885, four years before *The Life of Lincoln* by Herndon and Weik was published. The account in the published work is similar but not identical.[116] The report of the conversation in the letter is couched in the characteristic style of Herndon rather than that of Lincoln, but there is no doubt that Lincoln did say something of the sort to Herndon.

In any event, early in March, on the assumption that Lincoln wished him to do so, Herndon set out for Washington, New York, and Boston.[117] In Washington, he recorded in a letter to Weik that he had seen Trumbull, Seward, Sumner, and Wilson, and had found, "They were all right and doing all they could to stem the rising tide of Douglasism." In *The Life of Lincoln*, Herndon also gave account of a call on Douglas whom he found ill in bed. Douglas said he was not standing in Lincoln's way and sent his regards to him.

Herndon wrote Weik from New York, saying that he had seen Greeley. "We had a long conversation, but this is the shell and substance of it. Greeley said to me, as I *inferred*, as I understood it, that he would most assuredly assist Douglas in all honorable ways; that he liked Lincoln, had confidence in him, and would not injure him; that he would somewhat change tactics, and be careful in the future." Greeley introduced Herndon to many of the leading Republicans in

---

[114] *Ibid.*, January 12, 1858.
[115] Emanuel Hertz, *The Hidden Lincoln*, pp. 113–15.
[116] Herndon and Weik, *op. cit.*, II, 391–93.
[117] Joseph Fort Newton, *Lincoln and Herndon*, p. 150, Herndon to Theodore Parker.

New York City and to Henry Ward Beecher who sent greetings to Lincoln. Herndon also wrote Weik from Boston, saying that he had seen Governor Banks, Theodore Parker, William Garrison, and Wendell Phillips, and that he had "put them all right, if they were not before."

From Boston, Herndon wrote to Lincoln:

> *Revere House,*
> *Boston, Mass., March 24, 1858*
>
> *Friend Lincoln.*
>
> *I am in this city of notions, and am well—very well indeed. I wrote you a hasty letter from Washington some days ago, since which time I have been in Philadelphia, Baltimore, New York, and now here. I saw Greeley, and so far as any of our conversation is interesting to you I will relate. And we talked, say twenty minutes. He evidently wants Douglas sustained and sent back to the Senate. He did not say so in so many words, yet his feelings are with Douglas. I know it from the spirit and drift of his conversation. He talked bitterly—somewhat so—against the papers in Illinois, and said they were fools. I asked him this question, "Greeley, do you want to see a third party organized, or do you want Douglas to ride to power through the North which he has so much abused and betrayed?" and to which he replied, "Let the future alone; it will come out all right. Douglas is a brave man. Forget the past and sustain the righteous." Good God, righteous, eh!*
>
> *Since I have landed in Boston I have seen much that was entertaining and interesting. This morning I was introduced to Governor Banks. He and I had a conversation about Republicanism and especially about Douglas. He asked me this question, "You will sustain Douglas in Illinois, wont you?" and to which I said "No, never!" He affected to be much surprised, and so the matter dropped and turned on Republicanism, or in general— Lincoln. Greeley's and other sheets that laud Douglas, Harris, et al., want them sustained, and will try to do it. Several persons have asked me the same questions which Banks asked, and evidently they get their cue, ideas, or what not from Greeley, Seward, et al. By-the-bye, Greeley remarked to me this, "The Republican standard is too high; we want something practical."*
>
> *This may not be interesting to you, but however it may be, it is my duty to state what is going on, so that you may head if off—counteract it in some way. I hope it can be done. The Northern men are cold to me—somewhat repellent.*
>
> *Your friend,*
> *W. H. Herndon.*[118]

---

[118] Herndon and Weik, *op. cit.*, II, 394–95. See also David Donald, *Lincoln's Herndon*, pp. 112–25.

This letter shows that Greeley was not alone among the Republicans of the East in the disposition to be charitable to Douglas at this juncture. Herndon apparently was confused in his letter to Weik when he included Wilson among those he found "all right" at Washington. He referred to Henry Wilson, senator from Massachusetts. Senator Wilson had already written Theodore Parker: "I say to you in confidence that you are mistaken in regard to Douglas. He is as sure to be with us in the future as Chase, Seward or Sumner. I leave motives to God; but he is to be with us; and he is today of more weight to our cause than any ten men in the country. I know men and I know their power, and I know that Douglas will go for crushing the Slave Power to atoms."[119]

Herndon's journey confirmed Lincoln's apprehensions. He was disturbed at the attitude of other Eastern Republicans but chiefly concerned at the effect of Greeley's views upon the voters in Illinois, where the *Tribune* was widely read and accepted as a political bible. There was less shock and surprise that others should come to the support of Douglas so quickly; Greeley was about the last man anyone would expect ever to tolerate Douglas. It must be remembered how religiously and consistently Greeley had opposed the extension of slavery and how vigorously he had condemned slavery as a great moral wrong. The Kansas–Nebraska Act had been conceived and furthered by Douglas for whom Greeley had not been able to find enough satisfactory terms of opprobrium. Douglas had declared in January that he did not care whether slavery was "voted up or voted down"; and now in March, Greeley, of all men, found Douglas "righteous." It was enough to make Lincoln suspicious of the renowned editor.

Greeley's course for the next six months does not enhance his reputation for candor and good sportsmanship. Although "Lecompton Junior —the English brat" had passed both Houses of Congress on April 30 and the Kansas issue had temporarily been put aside, Greeley continued to give the Republicans of Illinois anxiety. The Illinois Democratic State Convention had been held at Springfield on April 21. The Douglas Democrats were in control, and a small group of Buchananites bolted the convention. Douglas and the Democratic delegation in the House were roundly endorsed, and—without mention of Buchanan directly—the Administration was approved so far as it had or would carry out "the principles of the Democratic party as expressed in the

---

[119] Newton, *op. cit.*, p. 148, Henry Wilson to Theodore Parker, February 28, 1858. See also Wilson, *op. cit.*, II, 567.

Cincinnati platform."[120] The Republicans were jubilant at the split among the Democrats and immediately made plans for a Republican State Convention to be held on June 16.[121] They were outraged, however, at the pressure from the East to support Douglas for re-election to the Senate. On May 4 the *Chicago Daily Journal*, voicing the common Republican view in Illinois, paid its respects to the (Massachusetts) *Springfield Republican*. Unable to keep out of a newspaper fight and correctly suspecting that the *Chicago Daily Journal* had the *New York Tribune* in mind also, Greeley kicked up the dust and still further disturbed Lincoln and the Republican managers in Illinois by a long editorial. He straddled the issue more than was his custom, recognized Lincoln as the possible candidate of the Republican party for the Senate, said that he was "widely known as one of the truest and most effective advocates of Republican principles," and admitted that the Republicans of Illinois had the "undoubted right to name their own candidate." Then he got down off the fence and praised Douglas for being "faithful" in the Lecompton struggle. There was only one interpretation to be put upon this disingenuous harangue—Greeley believed strongly that the Republicans of Illinois should not hesitate to support Douglas.[122]

Lincoln wrote no more complaining letters, but began soberly to prepare for battle. He was now at some pains to point out to his correspondents, before he began speechmaking, that there still remained all the difference there ever was between Douglas and the Republicans. This was the very point which Greeley and other Eastern Republicans seemed wholly to overlook. He understood the Republicans to insist that Congress should, and Douglas to insist that Congress should not, keep slavery out of the territories before and up to the time they formed state constitutions. No Republican had ever contended, when a constitution was to be formed, that any but the people of the territory should form it. No Republican had ever contended that Congress should dictate a constitution to any state or territory. On the other hand, the Republicans had contended that the people should be perfectly free to form their constitution in their own way—"as *perfectly free from the presence* of Slavery amongst them, as from every other improper influence." Lincoln concluded therefore that in voting together in opposition to the Lecompton Constitution "neither Judge Douglas

---

[120] James W. Sheahan, *The Life of Stephen A. Douglas*, p. 394.
[121] Beveridge, *op. cit.*, II, 554.
[122] *Tribune*, May 11, 1858.

nor the Republicans" had "conceded anything which was ever in dispute between them."[123]

In the middle of May, the *Chicago Tribune* drew Greeley's fire, and he naively convicted himself while stoutly proclaiming his innocence. He was so deeply enamored of his own views that he almost came to believe that he was always right. The record has to be searched minutely to find him acknowledging himself in the wrong. Tenacious and constant along some lines, he was wholly inconsistent along others. In his reply to his Chicago cotemporary he bade the Illinois Republicans to "choose for their second Senator precisely as they see fit," reiterated his view that Douglas' course on the Lecompton question had not been "merely right—it had been conspicuously, courageously, eminently so." Protesting that he had no counsel to give any party in Illinois, he climbed on the fence again and said: "We *know* that Mr. Lincoln will prove an excellent Senator if elected; we *believe* Mr. Douglas cannot henceforth be otherwise."[124] In his reply to the *Chicago Daily Journal* on May 11, Greeley had alluded to a "secret coalition" between the Republicans and Buchananites in Illinois. Now the *Chicago Democrat* turned the tables on Greeley and intimated that he was a party to a deal with Douglas. Greeley indignantly denied the charges.[125]

It remained for "A Republican," writing to the *New York Tribune* from Chicago on May 13, to bring Greeley to earth and to put an end to his direct editorial support of Douglas. He apparently pondered over this communication, for he did not publish it until May 27. "A Republican" was polite but pointed and employed Lincoln's line of reasoning as well as his direct style of expression. It is not beyond the realm of possibility that Lincoln was the author. He could easily have sent it to Chicago for mailing; indeed, he could even have gone to Chicago for that purpose. The record for that week, beyond the dates of letters written on May 10 and 15 from Springfield, does not give definite evidence of his whereabouts.[126] In any event the communication was such as few persons except Lincoln could have written at that time, and it stumped Greeley. "It astonishes us," the letter ran, "that the Re-

---

[123] Angle, *New Letters and Papers*, p. 176, Lincoln to J. F. Alexander, May 15, 1858. See also *ibid.*, p. 178, Lincoln to Samuel Wilkinson, June 10, 1858; Tracy, *op. cit.*, pp. 87–88, Lincoln to Lyman Trumbull, June 23, 1858; Nicolay and Hay, *op. cit.*, II, 356–58, 361–64, Lincoln to E. B. Washburne, April 26, May 27, 1858; and *ibid.*, p. 358, Lincoln to J. M. Lucas.
[124] *Tribune*, May 17, 1858.
[125] *Ibid.*, May 22, 1858.
[126] Angle, *Lincoln Day by Day*, p. 228.

publicans of the Eastern States can desire the defeat of Lincoln to make place for Douglas, who is no Republican, and who desires to be elected only as a Democrat." Then "A Republican" asked the editor some embarrassing and pointed questions, such as were later to be put to Douglas by Lincoln:

The Republicans of Illinois believe that Congress has the legal power to interdict Slavery from the Territories. Does Douglas?

They believe that the Constitution regards slaves as persons and not as chattels, wherever it refers to them. Does Douglas?

They believe that it carries Slavery nowhere, and that Slavery can have no legal existence outside of State limits. Does Douglas?

They believe that colored men have rights that whites are bound to respect. Does Douglas?

They indignantly repudiate the doctrine laid down in the Dred Scott decision and its obiter dicta. Does Douglas?

Greeley contented himself with repeating the charge of a coalition between the Republicans and the Lecomptonites as "a veritable thing" and dismissed the pertinent questions by saying, "Having already given full expression to our views on the subject generally, we cheerfully give place to our Illinois correspondent and allow him the last word."[127]

Herndon had no use for Douglas, and after his return from his trip East he was very suspicious of Greeley.[128] He apparently scolded Greeley for his attitude, as he was quite capable of doing, in a letter written on May 7. Greeley kept it three weeks and replied to it two days after his brief dismissal of "A Republican."

New York, May 29, 1858

Friend Herndon:

I have yours of the 7th. I have not proposed to instruct the Republicans of Illinois in their political duties, and I doubt very much that even so much as is implied in your letter can be fairly deduced from anything I have written.

Let me make one prediction. If you run a candidate against Harris and he is able to canvass, he will beat you badly. He is more of a man, at heart and morally, than Douglas, and has gone into the fight with more earnestness and less calculation. Of the whole Douglas party, he is the truest and best. I never have spoken a dozen words with him in my life, having met him but once; but if I lived in his district, I should vote for him. As I have never

---

[127] *Tribune*, May 27, 1858.
[128] Donald, *op. cit.*, p. 117.

spoken of him in my paper, and suppose I never shall, I take the liberty to say this much to you. Now paddle your own dugout.

Yours,
Horace Greeley[129]

Greeley shortly changed his figure of speech from "paddling a dugout" to "shouldering an elephant." In a letter to Joseph Medill, editor of the *Chicago Tribune,* on July 24, 1858, he said: "You have got your Elephant— You would have him—now shoulder him! He is not very heavy after all." Mr. Medill sent the letter to Lincoln who carefully copied it in his own hand omitting the names of Medill and Greeley and put it away among his papers.[130]

After he got over his initial nervousness, Lincoln's capacity for calmness in time of stress was well illustrated in these days. He scanned the enemy's breastworks with poise and discrimination; and no sector of the battlefield escaped his notice. He watched Greeley from a distance and kept in close touch with friendly Chicago editors. On June 1 he wrote to the editor of the *Chicago Daily Journal* summing up the situation:

My Dear Sir: *Yours of yesterday, with the enclosed newspaper slip, is received. I have never said or thought more, as to the inclination of some of our Eastern Republican friends to favor Douglas, than I expressed in your hearing on the evening of the 21st of April, at the State library in this place. I have believed—I do believe now—that Greeley, for instance, would be rather pleased to see Douglas reëlected over me or any other Republican; and yet I do not believe it is so because of any secret arrangement with Douglas. It is because he thinks Douglas's superior position, reputation, experience, ability, if you please, would more than compensate for his lack of a pure Republican position, and therefore his reëlection do the general cause of Republicanism more good than would the election of any one of our better undistinguished pure Republicans. I do not know how you estimate Greeley, but I consider him incapable of corruption or falsehood. He denies that he directly is taking part in favor of Douglas, and I believe him. Still his feeling constantly manifests itself in his paper, which, being so extensively read in Illinois, is, and will continue to be a drag upon us. I have also thought that Governor Seward, too, feels about as Greeley does, but not being a newspaper editor, his feeling in this respect is not much manifested. I have no idea that he is, by conversation or by letter, urging Illinois Republicans to vote for Douglas.*

---

[129] Newton, *op. cit.,* p. 164, Greeley to Herndon, May 29, 1858.
[130] David C. Mearns, *The Abraham Lincoln Papers,* I, 214–15.

As to myself, let me pledge you my word that neither I, nor any friend so far as I know, has been setting stake against Governor Seward. No combination has been made with me, or proposed to me, in relation to the next presidential candidate. The same thing is true in regard to the next governor of our State. I am not directly or indirectly committed to any one, nor has any one made any advance to me upon the subject. I have had many free conversations with John Wentworth; but he never dropped a remark that led me to suspect that he wishes to be governor. Indeed, it is due to truth to say that while he has uniformly expressed himself for me, he has never hinted at any condition.

The signs are that we shall have a good convention on the 16th and I think our prospects generally are improving some every day. I believe we need nothing so much as to get rid of unjust suspicion of one another.

Yours very truly,
A. Lincoln[131]

It *was* a *good* convention which the Republicans of Illinois held at Springfield on June 16, despite the ugly rumors afloat in advance of it that Long John Wentworth, editor of the *Chicago Democrat*, was out to displace Lincoln for the nomination for the United States Senate to succeed Douglas.[132] Lincoln's interests were safe, however, in the hands of his friend, Norman B. Judd, of Chicago, chairman of the Republican State Committee. Well-laid plans were carried out without a hitch. The candidates for office were "platformed" in "pure" Republican fashion in a document drawn by Orville H. Browning which "was adopted without dissent."[133] The convention answered Greeley and other Republicans of the East, who had been hinting, suggesting, and openly recommending support of Douglas, by the enthusiastic and unanimous adoption of a resolution proposed by Charles L. Wilson, editor of the *Chicago Daily Journal*:

Resolved, *That Abraham Lincoln is the first and only choice of the Republicans of Illinois for the United States Senate, as the successor of Stephen A. Douglas.*[134]

At the evening session of the convention, Lincoln delivered his famous "house-divided" speech, and launched his campaign for the

---

[131] Nicolay and Hay, *op. cit.*, II, 362–63, Lincoln to Charles L. Wilson, June 1, 1858.
[132] Beveridge, *op. cit.*, II, 565–68.
[133] Theodore Calvin Pease and James G. Randall, eds., *The Diary of Orville Hickman Browning*, I, 327.
[134] *Illinois Daily State Journal*, June 17, 1858.

Senate. "I believe this government cannot endure permanently half slave and half free" was an old text which Lincoln now adopted for himself and elaborated in his own simple, direct fashion. Greeley had said as much two years before when he declared, "It is the nature of Freedom, as of Slavery, to advance or die. Slavery feels that its time is short, and it will rage within the next four years as it has never yet done."[135] The task before the Republicans, Lincoln said, was to meet and overpower "the present political dynasty," and he departed from the lofty tone of his speech long enough to give Greeley and the other Eastern Republicans something to think about:

There are those who denounce us openly to their own friends, and yet whisper us softly that Senator Douglas is the aptest instrument there is with which to effect that object. They wish us to infer all from the fact that he now has a little quarrel with the present head of the dynasty; and that he has regularly voted with us on a single point upon which he and we have never differed. They remind us that he is a great man, and that the largest of us are very small ones. Let this be granted. But "a living dog is better than a dead lion." Judge Douglas, if not a dead lion for this work, is at least a caged and toothless one. How can he oppose the advances of slavery? He don't care anything about it. His avowed mission is impressing the "public heart" to care nothing about it.[136]

The *Tribune* gave brief notices of the convention on June 17 and 18, and on June 21 Greeley said on the editorial page that "Abraham Lincoln was also among the speakers, and was received with overwhelming enthusiasm, he being the unanimous choice for U. S. Senator" and printed the resolution of the convention. He took his time to deliberate upon what he should say about the rejection of his advice, but on June 24 he printed Lincoln's speech in full in the news columns of the *Tribune* and rather grudgingly commended Lincoln editorially, while sticking to his strange notion that Douglas had somehow become the chief opponent of the "Cotton Oligarchy":

We print elsewhere the compact and forcible speech of the Hon. ABRAHAM LINCOLN before the late Republican State Convention at Springfield, Ill., setting forth the distinctive position and views of the Republicans of Illinois, as distinguished from those of Senator Douglas and his supporters. We need not ask attention to this concise and admirable statement. Mr.

[135] *Tribune*, November 25, 1856.
[136] Nicolay and Hay, *op. cit.*, III, 13.

Lincoln never fails to make a good speech, when he makes any, and this is one of his best efforts. And its leading positions will be heartily indorsed by the great body of the Republicans of other States, as they already have been by those of Illinois.

In the actual state of things, a determined contest between the Republicans of Illinois and the great mass of the Democrats of that State who sympathize with Mr. Douglas, is inevitable. We have earnestly hoped that this contest might be avoided. So long as the Slave Power remains in possession of the Federal Government, and dispenses for its own aggrandizement the Sixty or Eighty Millions which annually flow from the Treasury, it has seemed to us desirable, in the light of principle no less than in that of policy, to soften and efface whatever differences may at any time exist between those who, from whatever cause, are arrayed in practical opposition to the aspirations and the rule of the Cotton Oligarchy. We have looked to and labored for a union in 1860 of all who were found arrayed in opposition to the late flagitious attempt to impose a Slave Constitution on Kansas by the power of the Federal Government and in notorious opposition to the clearly-expressed will of the People thus sought to be subjugated. As a step toward this consummation, we have desired and labored for a substantial accord in their approaching Elections between the Republicans of Illinois and that immense majority of the Democrats who stand with Douglas on the platform of Popular Sovereignty.

Our expectations have been disappointed. Our efforts are, for the present, baffled. Illinois is to be the arena this year of a desperate contest which we would have gladly aided to avert. We lay no blame on this side nor on that. We do not say that this contest was not inevitable. We only fear that its effect will be, as its tendency certainly is, to drive back One Hundred Thousand Illinois Democrats into a position of open alliance with and virtual subserviency to the Slave Power. Should such be the result, it will be our unfailing consolation that we have done what we could to prevent it.

With this melancholy pronouncement in mind, let us now follow Greeley step by step through the famous campaign which resulted in the re-election of Douglas to the United States Senate. On June 26 the *Tribune* printed a half-column communication from Collinsville, Illinois, under date of June 15, the day before the State Convention, signed "W," which was headed, "Sketch of the Hon. Abraham Lincoln," and which commended him highly as a match for Douglas. On the evening of June 9, fresh from his victorious fight in Congress against the Lecompton Constitution, Douglas spoke to a vast multitude from the balcony of the Tremont House in Chicago.[137] Lincoln, who was present

---

[137] *Chicago Times*, July 10, 1858.

to hear Douglas, replied to him from the same rostrum on the following night.[138] On June 12 Greeley devoted a column and a half to a discussion of Douglas' Chicago speech; he declared that if the Democratic party was to be saved from "utter wreck and dissolution in the Free States," it would be through the "sagacity and courage of Judge Douglas"; and he again voiced the view that Douglas' course in the recent session of Congress had "achieved for him a high place among our statesmen" and earned for him the "grateful affection" of the people. Greeley mildly regretted that Douglas had seen fit to plant himself on the quicksands of "Squatter Sovereignty," and predicted that he could not fail to be beaten on that ground unless his opponents should "be so unwise as to degrade the contest from the high ground of principle into the mire of personality."

On July 12, in a long editorial referring to Douglas' Chicago speech, commending Douglas personally without sustaining his argument, Greeley forecast the great debates when he said: "We trust Messrs. Lincoln and Douglas will speak together at some fifteen or twenty of the most important and widely accessible points throughout the State, and that the controversy will be prosecuted, through the rival candidates of the Lower House, at every county seat and considerable town." On July 13, the *Tribune* printed Douglas' speech in full, and Greeley made this comment: "Senator Douglas in his Chicago speech denounces as perilous the doctrine of Mr. Lincoln that Slavery or Freedom must ultimately prevail in all our states, and in all sections of the Union. We do not concur in this denunciation. Most certainly Washington, Jefferson, and a great majority of the eminent men of our Revolutionary age, held with Mr. Lincoln on this point, not with Mr. Douglas."

On July 14 Greeley discussed the doctrine of "Popular Sovereignty" as advanced by Douglas and wanted it "distinctly understood" that he did not accept it. He repeated and extended this view in another editorial on July 15.

On July 15 the *Tribune* printed Lincoln's Chicago speech, as clipped from the *Chicago Press and Tribune* of July 12, and on the following day Greeley thawed out slightly:

The admirable and thoroughly Republican speech of Mr. Lincoln in reply to Judge Douglas, published in our last, seemed to require no comment; yet a single remark with reference to the origin and attitude of the rival can-

---

[138] Nicolay and Hay, *op. cit.*, III, 19–52.

vassers may not be out of place. Judge Douglas, who regards Slavery as an affair of climate and latitude, is a native of Free Vermont; Mr. Lincoln, who esteems Slavery a National evil, and hopes that our Union may one day be all Free, was born and reared in slaveholding Kentucky. These gentlemen would seem respectively to have "conquered their prejudices" founded in early impressions. We shall watch with interest the progress of their canvass.

The Republicans of Illinois, reading the great editor eagerly and ordinarily with hearty approval, felt that they had a right to expect Greeley to do more than "watch with interest." It must be remembered, however, that he had told Herndon to "paddle his own dugout," and his subsequent conduct furnishes additional proof that he meant what he said.

Douglas spoke in the Courthouse Square at Bloomington on July 16, and then proceeded to Springfield where he spoke the following day.[139] Lincoln heard the Bloomington speech and was called upon to reply but declined on the ground that the meeting had been arranged for Douglas and it would not be fair for him to take advantage of the audience.[140] He did not hear Douglas at Springfield on July 17 but busied himself in the preparation of the address he was to deliver that evening in the Hall of Representatives.[141] The *Tribune* did not notice these important addresses either in its news columns or on the editorial page.

On July 22 the *Tribune* printed an article, clipped from the *Chicago Press and Tribune* entitled "The Passage-at-arms Between Lincoln and Douglas in 1854," which reviewed their appearances at the State Fair at Springfield and at Peoria in that year. On this date also the *Tribune* quoted from a letter from a Chicago correspondent comparing Lincoln and Douglas:

A correspondent at Chicago sends us a letter on the opening of the contest between Messrs. Douglas and Lincoln from which we take the following brief description of the powerful antagonist of the "Little Giant":

As well informed as Douglas in political and constitutional history, he is his superior in legal lore and acumen. His equal in logic, he is his master in ready, keen, yet quiet wit. If he cannot match him in invective, he is an over-match in powers of genuine sarcasm.

Inferior to the Senator in the variety, brilliancy and rounded fullness of his rhetoric, he is vastly his superior in the faculty of impressing a popular

---

[139] *Illinois State Register*, July 19, 1858; and Nicolay and Hay, *op. cit.*, III, 54–154.
[140] *Bloomington Pantagraph*, July 17, 1858.
[141] Nicolay and Hay, *op. cit.*, III, 155–58.

audience with the idea of his perfect sincerity, and of winning and carrying their attention by his familiar colloquial, yet pointed style of speaking. He will prove himself to be equal to his antagonist, fertile, powerful, unscrupulous, as he is!

In like vein, a correspondent from St. Louis, who signed himself "Philo," wrote an article under date of July 20, which the *Tribune* published July 26. This article read in part: "Douglas has been heard at Chicago and Springfield, and I think he has disappointed your expectations. You have been too charitable to him, and given him credit for qualities he does not possess. The people of Illinois know him better than you, and facts are now verifying their estimation. He opposed Lecompton because his State was otherwise lost to him; and that lost, his Presidential aspirations were nowhere."[142]

The seven formal debates in which Lincoln and Douglas participated in August, September, and October, 1858, constitute one of the great events of American history. The contest was not merely for the prize of the United States senatorship. It was the preliminary academic battlefield of the Civil War, and was widely so recognized throughout the country. No debate in Congress was ever more fully reported to the people. The *Chicago Press and Tribune* and the *Chicago Times* employed skilled correspondents who traveled with the debaters and reported the speeches verbatim. The *St. Louis Republican,* Forney's *Philadelphia Press,* and the *New York Evening Post* were among the leading papers which sent special writers to the scene and kept their readers fully informed of the progress of the debates.[143] Rhodes was quite right when he said that "Even among the Republicans of the East the contest seemed noteworthy only because Douglas was engaged in it. Before making the Springfield speech that opened the campaign, Lincoln was generally regarded as a backwoods lawyer who had more temerity than discretion in offering to contest the senatorship with Douglas, against the advice of the wisest Republicans of the East."[144] There is less ground, however, for Rhodes's declaration that "The *Tribune,* in spite of Greeley's deprecating the contest . . . gave Lincoln a loyal support."[145]

There was ample reason why Greeley and his paper should have

---

[142] See also *Tribune* editorial on Douglas, July 28, 1858.
[143] Edwin Erle Sparks, eds., *Semi-centennial of the Lincoln-Douglas Debates,* pp. 75–84. See also Allan Nevins, *The Emergence of Lincoln,* I, 374–99.
[144] James Ford Rhodes, *History of the United States,* II, 297.
[145] *Ibid.*

taken an interest in the debates and should have reported and analyzed them for their readers. The *Tribune* was the leading official organ of the Republican party. Greeley not only attended the main political conventions and carried a staff of reporters with him, but he also frequently went to Washington when great issues were at stake; and the regular daily reports of the doings of Congress were fully and intelligently reported by his paper. Greeley was a tireless news gatherer, had a discriminating sense of what constituted news, and was well aware of the popularity of his paper in Illinois. But quite beyond the news value presented by the debates, the issue which was being fought out by these two forensic gladiators had absorbed Greeley's thought for years. Little that concerned the slavery issue escaped his notice and analysis. He knew well enough before the debates began what turn the discussion would take. He knew Douglas, fore and aft, and he was one editor of an Eastern newspaper who knew where Lincoln stood. His whole career dictated that he should now espouse the cause Lincoln represented.

Lincoln was to declare that slavery was inherently wrong and that the country could not permanently endure half slave and half free; Douglas was to deny the existence of a moral issue and discuss slavery from the standpoint of climate and latitude. Lincoln was to stand squarely upon the Declaration of Independence and hold that the Negro had *human* rights; Douglas was to put the Negro outside the pale of the Declaration and deal with him as a *chattel*. Lincoln was to brand the Kansas–Nebraska Act as a disgraceful breach of national faith; Douglas, as chief instigator, was to defend and glorify the act. Lincoln was to show that the Dred Scott decision was based on historical error and that it opened the way for nationalizing slavery; Douglas was to defend the decision and to brand as disloyal and unpatriotic anyone who sought its repeal. There was no difference, as Lincoln had clearly pointed out, between Douglas and the Republicans on the Lecompton issue; moreover, it was already dead and buried.

On all the live issues of the debates, Greeley had eloquently voiced in the *Tribune* the arguments now to be advanced by Lincoln. His sole ground, along with other Eastern Republicans, for urging that the Republicans of Illinois support Douglas for re-election was the stand Douglas had taken in the last session of Congress against the Buchanan Administration on the adoption of the Lecompton Constitution. Douglas was bold enough to insist that he remained a Democrat and did not want "Black Republican" support.

What did the *Tribune* and Greeley do during the seven encounters

between Lincoln and Douglas? The answer is simple. The *Tribune* lost
one of the greatest opportunities in its long and honorable career to
report a great event adequately to its readers; and its justly celebrated
and distinguished editor sulked in his tent.

Lincoln challenged Douglas on July 24. Correspondence ensued between them and they had one chance conference. Douglas accepted by
letter on July 30 and named the dates and places as follows:

Ottawa, La Salle County	*August 21, 1858*
Freeport, Stephenson County	" 27 "
Jonesboro, Union County	*September* 15 "
Charleston, Coles County	" 18 "
Galesburg, Knox County	*October* 7 "
Quincy, Adams County	" 13 "
Alton, Madison County	" 15 "

Lincoln acceded by letter on July 31 and the public was at once informed.[146] Throughout the debates there was no indication in the *Tribune* that anything unusual was going on in Illinois. A three-line announcement without comment read: "Messrs. Douglas and Lincoln
have agreed to a joint discussion at one prominent point in each Congressional district of Illinois, alternately to open and close."[147] The
Tribune apparently had no representative on the ground. No two of
the news items published during the period in any way referring to the
debates were signed by the same correspondent. There was no mention
of any of the news items on the editorial page.

The first debate at Ottawa on August 21 was reported in full in the
semi-weekly *Tribune* on August 27, as clipped from the *Chicago Press
and Tribune* of August 23. None of the later debates was reported in
detail. During the period, Greeley published articles on horse taming,
addresses on farming by Ralph Waldo Emerson and Edward Everett
at county fairs in Massachusetts, detailed accounts of the laying of the
Atlantic cable, and Bayard Taylor's correspondence relating his travels
in Europe. The semi-weekly *Tribune* of September 10 devoted an entire
page to Greeley's address on "The Needs of American Agriculture" at
a fair in Indiana. The semi-weekly also gave a full page on October 22
to a prize fight between Heenan and Morrissey, and on October 26 deplored the fight editorially but justified the space given to it on the
ground of "Catering to the Public."

---

[146] Nicolay and Hay, III, 189–97; Sparks, *op. cit.*, pp. 55–74.
[147] *Tribune*, August 4, 1858.

There were, however, during the debates four leading editorials in the *Tribune* dealing with Douglas, one of which mentioned "the electioneering speeches" he was then making in Illinois. These editorials were directed at the criticism of Douglas by the *Washington Union* which had supported Buchanan, and their import was that Buchanan sought the overthrow of Douglas in order to have him out of the way in 1860. They came dangerously near to being an invitation to the opponents of Buchanan to support Douglas.[148] Lincoln was not mentioned.

Several speeches made by Republican leaders on national issues during the time of the debates were published in the *Tribune* in full. Three of these speeches took Douglas to task and presented the very arguments Lincoln was making almost every day in Illinois. One speech made by Senator Trumbull in Chicago was too long for publication but Greeley praised it highly:[149] "For years we have day by day set forth the vital truths so lucidly and forcibly presented by Mr. Trumbull, and we rejoice that they seem to be taking firm root in the magnificent West which bears in its bosom the destinies of our country." And then he went on to say: "Mr. Trumbull is an admirable debater—always knowing what he wants to say, and therefore saying it. He crowds his colleague very hard—harder we think than Mr. Lincoln has done in any of his published speeches—with regard to his support of the 'Toombs bill' for pacifying Kansas, passed by the Senate, but defeated in the House, in the Summer of 1856." Senator Trumbull spoke again at Alton, Illinois, on August 25. Greeley again referred to Trumbull's Chicago speech and printed the Alton speech in full.[150]

Carl Schurz delivered a notable address at Chicago on September 28. The *Tribune* printed it in full, and Greeley called it "one of the ablest and cleanest expositions yet made of the chief political question to be settled in the pending elections."[151] Seward delivered his famous "irrepressible conflict" speech at Rochester on October 26, and the *Tribune* printed it in full, with Greeley finding it "clear, calm, sagacious, profound and impregnable."[152]

Early in September, while "the magnificent West," on the prairies of Illinois, was bearing "in its bosom the destinies of our country,"

---

[148] *Ibid.*, August 3, September 6, 7, 14, 23, 1858.
[149] *Ibid.*, August 18, 1858.
[150] *Ibid.*, September 7, 1858.
[151] *Ibid.*, October 18, 1858.
[152] *Ibid.*, October 28, 1858.

Greeley, according to his associate editor, Charles A. Dana, went out "to Indiana to deliver his agricultural address, and also to be absent when he is nominated for Governor, or isn't." No wonder the letters between "Friend Herndon" of Springfield and "Friend Parker" of Boston blistered with indignation. "Greeley is not fit for a leader," wrote the Boston Abolitionist, Theodore Parker, to Herndon. "He is capricious, crochety, full of whims, and as wrong headed as a pig."[153] And Herndon replied: "I wholly agree with you about Greeley, but dared not say so before you. . . . By the bye, Greeley has done us infinite harm here in Illinois, and is still doing so; he 'sorter, sorter'—is this way and that—is no way, and this course injures us here very much."[154] Now that Parker had opened the way, Herndon let out all his wrath against Greeley: "Greeley is acting a great dog, is he not? Just look at the power of his great paper, with its world-wide circulation, and does he state who he is for, what he wants, what Illinois is doing, what freedom is struggling for, and how, with intensity, etc.? Nothing of the kind. He does not seem to know there is such a man as Lincoln, such a struggle as 1858–9, and such a State as Illinois. Does he keep his own people 'posted'? Who would know by Greeley's paper that a great race for weal or woe was being fought all over the wide prairies of Illinois? Who would? It is strange indeed!"[155]

Herndon must have given Greeley a piece of his mind again; Greeley's response was neither reassuring nor convincing:

New York, N.Y., October 6, 1858

W. H. Herndon, Esq.

My Dear Sir:—It seems to me that my name ought not to be used to distract and disorganize the Republicans of your State. My personal conviction is that Col. Harris and Mr. Morris are two as clear-seeing, reliable, conscientious men on the slavery question as need be sent to Congress, and that it is a public misfortune that they are not recognized and supported as such. I do not wish to deny you to qualify this belief. The case is different with regard to Senator Douglas, who, in his present position I could not, of course, support, but he need not have been in this position had the Republicans of Illinois been as wise and farseeing as they are earnest and true. I shall not disguise my regret that the Republicans of your and the Quincy district did not see fit to support Messrs. Morris and Harris. I think they might have done so without a sacrifice either of principle or policy; but,

153 Newton, *op. cit.*, p. 202, Theodore Parker to Herndon, August 28, 1858.
154 *Ibid.*, p. 209, Herndon to Theodore Parker, September 11, 1858.
155 *Ibid.*, pp. 222–23, Herndon to Theodore Parker, October 4, 1858.

seeing that things are as they are, I would not wish to be quoted as authority
for making trouble and division among our friends.

Yours,
Horace Greeley[156]

After the formal debates were concluded at Alton on October 15,
Lincoln and Douglas carried on their campaigns separately, speaking
almost every day until the election on November 2. The Republican
state ticket was elected and the popular vote was for Lincoln by a plurality of about 4,000. The apportionment then in force, coupled with
the number of hold-over members of the legislature, left a majority in
favor of Douglas. The election of a United States senator by the legislature was a mere formality on January 6, 1859, when Douglas received
fifty-four votes and Lincoln forty-six.

The result was of course known as soon as the returns were in from
the November election. On November 4 the *Tribune* reported that
"Senator Douglas telegraphed last evening to his Eastern friends that
he has positively triumphed in Illinois by the election of a Legislature
which will return him to the U. S. Senate," and that "Mr. Douglas has
achieved a great personal triumph." The next day Greeley devoted a
column editorial to Douglas, speaking of his "hard-won, brilliant, conclusive triumph" and speculating upon the effect his present success
would have upon his future political fortunes. He now began to hedge
a bit as he contemplated the possibility of Douglas reaching the White
House, and came to the conclusion that he had failed in the campaign
"to elicit any evidence of his possessing those lofty and admirable qualities without which the Presidency can afford no heartfelt satisfaction
and confer no enduring fame."[157] There was as yet no mention of the
man who had carried the Republican banner in Illinois and who,
though he had failed to win a seat in the Senate, had been chiefly responsible for the election of the Republican state ticket.

Greeley knew well enough that the Republicans of Illinois strongly
resented the suggestion he had made in the spring that they support
Douglas for re-election and that they regarded his silence throughout
the campaign as distinctly hostile to Lincoln's interests. Always trucu-
lently sure of his own ground, Greeley now felt obliged to explain his
position.[158] He made lame excuses and stubbornly stuck to his view

[156] *Ibid.*, pp. 223–24, Greeley to Herndon, October 6, 1858.
[157] *Tribune*, November 5, 1858.
[158] *Ibid.*, November 12, 1858.

that the true policy of the Republican party would have been to rally around Douglas and "uphold him on his new platform of practical resistance to the behests of the Slave Power." He could not refrain from telling the Illinois Republicans to do their worst.

The Republicans of Illinois have been aware throughout their late canvass that, though we did what we could to aid them after the battle was set,[159] *we regretted that they deemed it necessary to join issue with Mr. Douglas rather than with the common adversary. We have been repeatedly given to understand that we were booked to suffer, after the Election, for our demur to their course, through a large withdrawal of Illinois subscriptions. We have made this exposition as full and frank as possible, in order that those who have threatened us with the resentment of Illinois may have tangible grounds on which to proceed in their work of vengeance. And we will give them an additional advantage by adding that we decidedly regret that such faithful and worthy representatives as Messrs. Thomas L. Harris and Isaac N. Morris proved themselves last Winter are returned with the Republican votes against them rather than for them.*[160]

This bold unconcern of the editor about Illinois subscriptions must have attracted the attention of his more canny business manager. A few days later the editor thought it well to take some notice of the man who had opposed Douglas and now found that "Mr. Lincoln's campaign speeches were of a very high order. They were pungent without bitterness and powerful without harshness. The brief address at Springfield in which he opened the canvass was a model of compactness, lucidity, and logic. As a condensed statement of the issues which divide the Republicans from the Democrats of our day, it has rarely or never been exceeded." Never quite able to bestow praise unreservedly, Greeley thought Lincoln might have pressed Douglas harder, especially on the issue of "Squatter Sovereignty." "While we think no man could have upborne the Republican standard more gallantly than Mr. Lincoln has done, it seems to us possible to have done so more skillfully—therefore more effectively. If this criticism seems unkind, we shall regret the misapprehension, not the frankness which impelled it."[161]

It must have amused Lincoln and his friends in Illinois to be blithely told by Greeley, after the battle was set, that he had done what he could

---

[159] Emphasis on the matter in roman type is by the present author.

[160] Harris and Morris, Democratic congressmen from Illinois, opposed the Lecompton Constitution, and were re-elected to the 36th Congress. Harris died before his new term began. See *Biographical Directory of the American Congress*, pp. 1066, 1536.

[161] *Tribune*, November 17, 1858.

to aid them. Douglas must have lifted his bushy eyebrows and shaken his mane when he discovered from this editorial that Greeley's chief concern in urging the Republicans to support him was to separate him from all Southern support and thus to render him helpless in the future. Douglas did not have long to wait to discover that the whimsical editor was not his friend for life. Douglas visited New York City toward the end of the year and was greeted editorially in this wise by the man who had urged the Republicans of Illinois to support him: "It is true that his mental constitution, as exhibited in his political career, is not of the sort to command the admiration of severe critics or to assure him a place among the great statesmen and orators of the country. It lacks at once the charm of the imagination and the fascinations of both wit and sentiment; while it seems equally destitute of the guiding influence of a sacred love of truth; and a careful observance of the lines which sunder her domains from those of falsehood."[162]

In plain English, which Greeley could but did not always use, Douglas was now characterized as a hard-boiled, second-rate, humorless politician, in addition to being a rogue and a liar.

Herndon wrote Parker that one of the causes of Lincoln's defeat was that "Greeley never gave us one single, solitary, manly lift. On the contrary, his silence was his opposition. This our people felt. We never got a smile or a word of encouragement outside of Illinois from any quarter during all this great canvass. . . . Greeley is a natural fool, I think, in this matter—his hearty Douglas position."[163] He grew a bit more charitable in a letter to Parker (it proved to be a last letter, for Parker was soon to pass away), but not less keenly analytical: "Greeley is getting quite conservative: he is a timid man; he is willing to agitate for an idea during its abstract state, but he shudders when it is about to concrete itself amidst living events, human conditions, social, religious, or political. He *will not do* for a great leader of America's present events: he will do to lead in small and unimportant events, political or social; but not where absolute principles will squeeze out blood, if necessary, to get themselves applied; he is fine for theoretic principles—not for heaven-high ones applied. Greeley is, however, an honest man and I still like him somewhat."[164]

Herndon must have paid his respects to Greeley shortly after the November election, for he received this letter from him:

---

[162] *Ibid.*, December 31, 1858.
[163] Newton, *op. cit.*, pp. 234–35, Herndon to Theodore Parker, November 8, 1858. See also pp. 241–43, November 23, 1858; and pp. 245–47, November 27, 1858.
[164] *Ibid.*, p. 265, Herndon to Theodore Parker, December 15, 1858.

New York, N.Y. Nov. 14, 1858

Friend Herndon:—*I do not think I could write editorials that would seem to you lucid or satisfactory. Perhaps you will not be able to understand me when I advise you privately that:* (1) *Mr. Douglas would be the strongest candidate that the Democratic party could present for President; but* (2) *they will* not *present him. The old leaders won't endure it.* (3) *As he is doomed to be slaughtered at Charleston it is good policy to fatten him meantime. He will cut the better at killing time.*

The Republicans of Illinois might have had Douglas with them in their late struggles, as those of Pennsylvania had Hickman, Indiana had Davis, New Jersey had Adrian, and New York had H. F. Clark and Haskins. Some of these may treat us badly; but a majority of them will prove sound coin. But the Republicans of Illinois chose to have the anti-Lecompton Democrats against rather than with them. In consequence, the State will cast a majority of its votes next December ('59) for a Democrat Speaker, while Pennsylvania will throw 21 to 4; New Jersey 5 to 0; and New York 28 to 4 on the right side. Your course may prove wiser in the long run; but ours vindicates itself at the outset. A gain of 25 members of Congress in three contiguous States is our answer to all gainsayers.

Yours,

HORACE GREELEY[165]

There were, as might have been expected, repercussions from the senatorial campaign which obliged Greeley to enter into many explanations. The *Chicago Press and Tribune* kept on Greeley's trail and severely arraigned him in an article published on February 2, 1859, with a challenge to Greeley to reproduce it in his paper. Greeley was rarely frightened by his adversaries; he promptly published the article in the *New York Tribune* and called special attention to it on his editorial page. His comment on the Chicago article led him to refer to his correspondence with Herndon and to declare that Herndon fully agreed with him on the occasion of his visit to New York in March, 1858, that the Republicans of Illinois should support Douglas for re-election.[166] Herndon's letter to Lincoln from Boston and his several letters to Parker, clearly indicate that he took or thought he took exactly the opposite position. The purpose of Herndon's visit to the East was to win Greeley and other Eastern Republicans to the support of Lincoln. It is possible that the New York editor talked the Illinois lawyer into circles, and it is also possible that Herndon may have been fortified with liquor before he called on Greeley and remembered later what he had meant

---

[165] *Ibid.*, p. 240, Greeley to Herndon, November 14, 1858.
[166] *Tribune*, February 12, 1859.

to say as what he actually said. It is hardly necessary to draw the conclusion that either Greeley or Herndon deliberately lied about the conversation between them.

The whole subject of Greeley's interference in Illinois politics was thoroughly aired in the early days of the Thirty-sixth Congress. The Congress assembled on December 5, 1859, and the long contest over the choice of a Speaker in the House was at once precipitated. Greeley went to Washington at the opening of Congress, and a dispatch he sent to the *Tribune* dated December 5 and printed the next day incensed William Kellogg, a Republican congressman from Illinois and a close friend of Lincoln. On December 7 Kellogg on the floor of the House said: "I charge that Mr. Greeley was again and again, with others, in consultation in the parlor of Judge Douglas, planning and scheming the election of Judge Douglas to the Senate of the United States from the State of Illinois."[167] The same day Douglas wrote Congressman J. A. McClernand of Illinois, in response to an inquiry, that many politicians of all shades of opinion were callers at his house, that Greeley may have called upon him, but he declared as wholly untrue the charge that there had ever been any deal between him and Greeley concerning his re-election.[168] Greeley wrote at once to Kellogg and published his letter, admitting that he had called at Douglas' house in Washington during the fight over the Lecompton Constitution, but flatly denying that he had ever on any occasion discussed with Douglas his candidacy for any office.[169]

How closely Lincoln was following the deliberations of Congress and the columns of the *Tribune* at this time may be understood from a letter he now dispatched to Congressman Kellogg. Incidentally, it also illustrates his ability to submerge his personal feelings in the exercise of political caution:

> Springfield, Ills. Dec. 11, 1859
>
> Hon. William Kellogg.
> My Dear Sir:
>
> *I have been a good deal relieved this morning by a sight of Greeley's letter to you, published in the Tribune. Before seeing it, I much feared you had, in charging interviews between Douglas & Greeley, stated what you believed, but did not certainly know to be true; and that it might be untrue,*

---

[167] *Cong. Globe*, 36th Cong., 1st sess., Pt. I, pp. 40–43.
[168] *Ibid.*, p. 84.
[169] *Tribune*, December 8, 1859. See also *Cong. Globe*, 36th Cong., 1st sess., Pt. IV, Appendix, pp. 157–65.

and our enemies would get an advantage of you. However, as G. admits the interviews, I think it will not hurt you that he denies conversing with D. about his re-election to the Senate. G. I think, will not tell a falsehood; and I think he will scarcely deny that he had the interview with D. in order to assure himself from D.'s own lips, better than he could from his public acts and declarations, whether to try to bring the Republican party to his support generally, including his re-election to the Senate. What else could the interview be for? Why immediately followed in the Tribune the advice that all Anti-Lecompton democrats should be re-elected? The world will not consider it anything that D.'s re-election to the Senate was not specifically talked of by him and G. Now, Wash, I do not charge that G. was corrupt in this. I do not think he was, or is. It was his judgment that the course he took was the best way of serving the Republican cause. For this reason, and for the further reason that he is now pulling straight with us, I think, if I were you, I would not pursue him further than necessary to my own justification. If I were you I would however be greatly tempted to ask him if he really thinks D.'s advice to his friends to vote for a Lecompton and slave Com. man is "plucky."

Please excuse what I have said in the way of unsolicited advice. I believe you will not doubt the sincerity of my friendship for you.

Yours very truly,
A. Lincoln[170]

Early in 1860 the man whom Greeley had wanted returned to the Senate was branded in the homely and quite unmistakable language of which Greeley was capable when he chose to employ it:

He has done more than any other man to produce the present political state of the country, through hateful scheming, and reckless legislation. But for Douglas and Pierce, there would have been no repeal of the Missouri Compromise, no outrages in Kansas, no John Brown, and no inroad upon Virginia. Yet the man who is at the bottom of these things is the busiest man in the country today, with fresh contrivances to still further disturb the public peace and perplex our national affairs. If there was any power which could take Mr. Douglas affectionately by the arm and walk him into retirement, and mention to him in a confiding but decisive manner, "Friend Douglas, thee has done mischief enough in thy day and generation for a whole regiment of politicians, and henceforth thee must betake thyself in private to contrition and repenting of thy sins," it would be a happy thing for the country, and a useful lesson to political charlatans in the future. Nothing is clearer than that justice and tranquillity demand such a disposition of this great political sinner. He has been a walking magazine of mis-

---

[170] Angle, *New Letters and Papers*, pp. 237–38, Lincoln to William Kellogg, December 11, 1859.

*chief to his own political friends from the time he reported his Kansas–
Nebraska bill. . . . Certainly such a man ought to be turned out to grass
like another Nebuchadnezzar.*[171]

And yet Greeley clung as long as he lived to the idea that the Republicans of Illinois should have supported Douglas in 1858. It was
almost impossible for him to find himself inconsistent or in the wrong.
Reviewing these days, ten years later, he repeated in substance the lame
excuses which he had first voiced in the *Tribune* in November, 1858,
and said that the friends of Lincoln "did not, for a while, incline to forgive me for the suggestion that it would have been wiser and better not
to have opposed Mr. Douglas' return; *but I still abide in that conviction.*"[172] There was prophetic insight in the comment which Joseph
Medill or one of his associates made in the *Chicago Press and Tribune*
in 1859 in seeking an explanation for Greeley's attitude on the re-
election of Douglas: "It is only to be accounted for on the belief entertained by hundreds of the friends of the N. Y. Tribune and its chief
editor, that having fixed upon a policy, however visionary, he will follow
it into the jaws of Tophet, rather than to admit that he was mistaken."[173]

Lincoln felt his defeat keenly but took it in good part and did not
blame anyone directly. He absolved Senator Crittenden, who had vigorously supported Douglas, from "anything dishonorable"[174] and wrote
the chairman of the Republican State Committee, N. B. Judd, that he
was "convalescent" but determined that "the fight must go on."[175] He
also wrote Judd that he had been on expenses so long without earning
anything that he was "absolutely without money now for even household purposes."[176] In February, 1859, he dusted off a so-called popular
lecture on "Discoveries, Inventions and Improvements" and sought
opportunities to deliver it to add to his depleted treasury,[177] although
early in March he declined an invitation to deliver this lecture at Rock
Island because he was "unable, from press of business to comply therewith."[178]

There is nothing in the record to show that Lincoln remonstrated

---

[171] *Tribune*, January 25, 1860.
[172] Greeley, *op. cit.*, p. 358. The italics are the author's.
[173] *Chicago Press and Tribune*, February 2, 1859.
[174] Nicolay and Hay, *op. cit.*, V, 90–91, Lincoln to J. J. Crittenden, November 4, 1858.
[175] *Ibid.*, pp. 91–92, Lincoln to N. B. Judd, November 15, 1858.
[176] *Ibid.*, p. 93, Lincoln to N. B. Judd, November 16, 1858.
[177] Angle, *Lincoln Day by Day*, pp. 267, 269.
[178] Tracy, *op. cit.*, p. 104, Lincoln to T. J. Pickett, March 5, 1859.

with Greeley directly concerning his attitude during the senatorial campaign of 1858, or that he ever scolded Greeley afterward. We get good illustration of Lincoln's consummate political skill in his approach to Greeley and the Eastern Republicans generally after Douglas' victory. He cleverly and prophetically pointed out that there would be another "blow up" among the Democrats, in that Douglas had managed to gain support as the best instrument to *"break down"* and at the same time to *"up-hold"* the slave power.[179] Lincoln held that no ingenuity could long keep up this double position. He therefore cautioned the Republicans against being broken up "to form the tail of Douglas' new kite."[180] He kept a close eye on Douglas, and we may be quite sure he continued to read the *Tribune*. He bided his time to get in a polite—but straight from the shoulder—blow at the Republicans who had been disposed to support Douglas. It is also quite apparent that he was thoroughly familiar with Herndon's correspondence with Greeley and had pondered over Greeley's letter of November 14 in which he bragged to Herndon about the wisdom displayed by the Republicans in New Jersey, New York, and Pennsylvania in supporting anti-Lecompton Democrats for re-election to Congress.

On March 1, 1859, Lincoln spoke in Chicago at a celebration of a municipal victory by the Republicans. This brief address has largely escaped notice in the biographies and various Lincoln studies, perhaps because of the utter simplicity and matter-of-fact common sense with which Lincoln turned the tables on Greeley and the other Eastern Republicans. He took this opportunity to demonstrate so that a child could understand—even if the stubborn Greeley refused to do so—the fallacy of Republican support of Douglas on any grounds. Lincoln declared that he had not said "an unkind word of any one" who had entertained the opinion that the Republicans of Illinois should have supported Douglas for the Senate. He held, however, that such support would have resulted in the destruction of the Republican party throughout the Union. The Republicans would not have absorbed Douglas, he would have absorbed them; he would in time have been claiming their support for all his doctrines and dogmas; and "the harmony and strength around the Republican banner" would have been dissolved. Lincoln went on to add a word "bearing on the future," which was strongly in his mind. "The Republican principle, the profound central truth that slavery is wrong and ought to be dealt with as a wrong," he said, ". . . cannot

---

[179] *Ibid.*, p. 96, Lincoln to Dr. B. Clarke Lundy, November 26, 1858.
[180] *Ibid.*, pp. 96–98, Lincoln to Lyman Trumbull, December 11, 1858.

advance at all upon Judge Douglas's ground; that there is a part of the country in which slavery must always exist; that he does not care whether it is voted up or down." If the Republicans should be led upon that ground "the great living principle" upon which the party was organized would be surrendered.[181]

---

[181] Nicolay and Hay, *op. cit.*, V, 114–24.

The taste is in my mouth a little.

Lincoln[1]

My choice was Edward Bates of St. Louis.

Greeley[2]

6   Bigger game

Whitney believed that Lincoln first thought of himself as a candidate for President either at the time of his highly successful "Lost Speech" at the Republican State Convention at Bloomington, Illinois, on May 29, 1856, or on June 19 of that year when he was surprised by the vote he received for Vice-President at the first Republican National Convention at Philadelphia.[3] Certainly the notice he received in Illinois and in the Middle West generally during the encounter with Douglas in 1858, despite the coolness and indifference of the East, put the presidential bee permanently in his bonnet. His intimate friends on the circuit and the Republican newspapers of Illinois were quick to recognize his availability, and with all his quiet modesty Lincoln never really shrank from letting his political ambitions be known in strategic quarters. He now took definite steps on his own account. He purchased outright a moribund German newspaper in Springfield, the *Illinois Staats-Anzeiger*, and put an editor, a former owner, in charge, who was to bear all expense and take all profits.[4] The contract, however, obliged the editor not to depart in political sentiment "from the Philadelphia and Illinois Republican platforms," and Lincoln admonished him in a letter "against letting down the Republican standard a hair's-breadth."[5] He

---

[1] Gilbert A. Tracy, *Uncollected Letters of Abraham Lincoln*, Lincoln to Lyman Trumbull, April 29, 1860.

[2] Horace Greeley, *Recollections of a Busy Life*, p. 389.

[3] Henry C. Whitney, *Life on the Circuit with Lincoln*, p. 82.

[4] Paul M. Angle, *New Letters and Papers of Lincoln*, pp. 204–05, contract with Theodore Canisius.

[5] John G. Nicolay and John Hay, eds., *Complete Works of Abraham Lincoln*, V, 129–30, Lincoln to Theodore Canisius, May 17, 1859.

wrote Schuyler Colfax of his desire to see him to discuss political matters which he could not put into a letter and especially "to hedge against division in the Republican ranks generally, and particularly for the contest of 1860."[6]

The evolution of his acknowledgment of his candidacy to his friends and political correspondents was consciously and cautiously unfolded. In April, 1859, he did not in candor think himself "fit for the presidency."[7] In July, he was still of the same opinion but looking "anxiously" for further letters from a correspondent who had made the suggestion.[8] In November, he was willing to "labor faithfully in the ranks" of the Republican party unless the "judgment of the party" should assign him to a different position.[9] In December, pledged not to enter a struggle with Trumbull for a seat in the Senate, he "would rather have a full term in the Senate than in the presidency."[10] In December, also, at the suggestion of Jesse W. Fell, he prepared a "sketch" of his life and career. "There is not much of it," he said, "for the reason I suppose, that there is not much of me." He wished it not to appear as having been written by himself, but had no objection to the incorporation of extracts from his speeches.[11] In February, 1860, Lincoln was out in the open. He then felt he was not in a position where it would hurt much if he were not nominated on the national ticket, but as he wrote Judd, "where it would hurt some for me to not get the Illinois delegates. . . . Can you not help me a little in this matter in your end of the vineyard?"[12]

Despite the fact that Lincoln was in danger of going "to the wall for bread and meat" if he neglected his business, he busied himself daily in writing letters, saw to it that the debates with Douglas were printed for distribution, and was almost constantly burdened with the preparation of a speech.[13] He delivered long, carefully prepared addresses at Columbus and Cincinnati in September,[14] and spoke en route at Dayton and Indianapolis.[15] He spoke at the Wisconsin State Fair at Mil-

---

[6] *Ibid.*, pp. 131–33, Lincoln to Schuyler Colfax, July 6, 1859.
[7] *Ibid.*, pp. 127–28, Lincoln to T. J. Pickett, April 16, 1859.
[8] *Ibid.*, pp. 136–38, Lincoln to Samuel Galloway, July 28, 1859.
[9] *Ibid.*, pp. 257–58, Lincoln to W. E. Frazier, November 1, 1859.
[10] *Ibid.*, pp. 281–82, Lincoln to N. B. Judd, December 9, 1859.
[11] *Ibid.*, pp. 286–89, Lincoln to J. W. Fell, December 20, 1859.
[12] *Ibid.*, pp. 290–91, Lincoln to N. B. Judd, February 5, 1860.
[13] *Ibid.*, pp. 138–39, Lincoln to Hawkins Taylor, September 6, 1859.
[14] *Ibid.*, pp. 140–89, 190–235. See also Angle, *op. cit.*, pp. 208–19.
[15] Paul M. Angle, *Lincoln Day by Day, 1854–1861*, pp. 300, 309–10.

waukee and also in Beloit and Janesville, and in early December he made a series of speeches in Kansas.

The culmination of his public utterances on the slavery issue came in his Cooper Institute address in New York City on February 27, 1860.[16] Indeed, the Cooper Institute address may be regarded as the valedictory of his long experience in the discussion of public issues as a private citizen. The measure of the man he had become is to be found in this address. Its language indicates the skill he had acquired in clarity of statement, in simplicity of style, and in effective straightforward thinking. The orderly, coherent, and unassailable logic of this speech gives evidence of the lawyer and politician at his best. The careful research on which it was based, the knowledge of the Constitution and the history of his country, of which it revealed him possessed, gave him the unmistakable rank of a statesman; and the courage and unabashed naturalness with which he addressed this distinguished audience in the East singled him out as presidential timber.[17]

The editor of the *Tribune* behaved handsomely. The Saturday preceding Lincoln's speech, the *Tribune* published a sketch of his career:

ABRAHAM LINCOLN *of Illinois will, for the first time, speak in this Emporium, at Cooper Institute, on Monday evening. He will speak in exposition and defense of the Republican faith; and we urge earnest Republicans to induce their friends and neighbors of adverse views to accompany them to this lecture. The Association which has taken the responsibility of drawing Mr. Lincoln from his Western home and business, to give our citizens this gratification and the Republican cause this aid, have deserved well of their compatriots, and we shall wisely encourage them to similar efforts in the future. . . .*

In 1858, he was unanimously designated by the Republican State Convention to succeed Mr. Douglas in the Senate, and thereupon canvassed the State against Mr. D. with remarkable ability. Mr. Douglas secured a majority of the Legislature and was elected, but Mr. Lincoln had the larger popular vote. . . .

—Such is ABRAHAM LINCOLN *of Illinois—emphatically a man of the People, a champion of Free Labor, of diversified and prosperous Industry, and of that policy which leads through peaceful progress to universal intelligence, virtue and freedom. The distinguishing characteristics of his political addresses are clearness and candor of statement, a chivalrous courtesy to op-*

---

[16] Harlan Hoyt Horner, *The Growth of Lincoln's Faith*, pp. 109–10
[17] Nicolay and Hay, *op. cit.*, V, 293–328.

ponents, and a broad genial humor. Let us crowd the Cooper Institute to hear him on Monday night.[18]

On Monday morning, February 27, the *Tribune* admonished its readers: "Remember Abraham Lincoln's Address at the Cooper Institute tonight and ask your friends who are not Republicans to accompany you to hear it. It is not probable that Mr. Lincoln will be heard again in our City this year, if ever. Let us improve the present opportunity."

And then as if recalling his experience with the Illinois Republicans in 1858, Greeley penned a characteristic editorial—and he must have envisioned the Cooper Institute speaker of that evening as one of his readers—which he headed with the one word, "Douglas."

We are quite obliged to our numerous friends who write remonstrating with us for stating that Mr. Douglas is the strongest candidate for next President that can be run by the Democratic party, whence we infer that he will be nominated at Charleston. Our displeased correspondents in no case object that our estimate of Mr. Douglas's strength is mistaken—on the contrary, they all either expressly or tacitly admit that it is quite true, but that we ought to have suppressed it on that account. We differ with these friends on every point. We hold it our duty to apprise our readers of all interesting and important truth that comes to our knowledge, and that it can never be impolitic to do so. We hold, moreover, that if Mr. Douglas be indeed the strongest candidate that our adversaries can select, their National Convention will be quite likely to know the fact, even though we did not apprise them of it. We hold, too, that the leading Lecompton conspirators will do their utmost to defeat Douglas's nomination,—wherein they may possibly succeed; and in that case, we shall have some remarks to offer which would be divested of all their force if it were supposed that we made them simply because Douglas was ruled off the course. And still further: we trust both friends and adversaries believe that we say what is true because it is true, without always waiting to decide that it is also politic; and we mean to deserve that reputation.

—Just a word more; We hold that the Democratic Party ought to nominate Douglas; we hold also that the People ought to defeat him. Not merely because his doctrines and inculcations respecting Slavery are unsound, but because he is the responsible author of a perilous and damaging agitation, do we wish to see him a candidate, and well beaten.[19]

David Dudley Field called the Cooper Institute meeting to order, and William Cullen Bryant presided and presented the speaker. Horace

---

[18] *Tribune,* February 25, 1860.
[19] *Ibid.,* February 27, 1860.

Greeley sat on the platform and spoke briefly, as did two or three others, at the conclusion of Lincoln's address. Lincoln went to the *Tribune* office at midnight to read the proofs of his address for publication the next day, and the night editor that Greeley had assigned to the task dropped the original manuscript into the wastebasket when the work was finished.[20]

The next day the speech appeared in full in the *Tribune* with this glowing comment by Greeley on the editorial page:

The Speech of ABRAHAM LINCOLN *at the Cooper Institute last evening was one of the happiest and most convincing political arguments ever made in this City, and was addressed to a crowded and most appreciating audience. Since the days of Clay and Webster, no man has spoken to a larger assemblage of the intellect and mental culture of our City. Mr. Lincoln is one of Nature's orators, using his rare powers solely and effectively to elucidate and to convince, though their inevitable effect is to delight and electrify as well. We present herewith a very full and accurate report of his Speech; yet the tones, the gestures, the kindling eye and the mirth-provoking look, defy the reporter's skill. The vast assemblage frequently rang with cheers and shouts of applause, which were prolonged and intensified at the close. No man ever before made such an impression on his first appeal to a New York audience.*

Mr. Lincoln speaks for the Republican cause tonight at Providence, R. I., and it is hoped that he will find time to speak once or more in Connecticut before he sets his face homeward.

We shall soon issue his Speech of last night in pamphlet form for cheap circulation.

In the same issue in an editorial headed "Presidential" the *Tribune* pledged itself to support with all its power the candidate of the forthcoming Republican National Convention. "Whether it be Mr. Seward, Mr. Chase, Mr. Bates, Mr. Fremont, Mr. Fessenden, Mr. Lincoln or any other man, we shall do our best to secure his election, not from any personal love for the man, but because the triumph of the Cause is identified with his success."

Lincoln now did "find time," on a visit to his son Robert at Phillips Exeter Academy, to speak at Providence, Concord, Manchester, Dover, Exeter, Hartford, New Haven, Meriden, Woonsocket, Norwich, and Bridgeport. Small wonder he wrote to Mrs. Lincoln from Exeter on March 4: "I have been unable to escape this toil. If I had foreseen it, I think I would not have come East at all. The speech at New York, being

---

[20] George Haven Putnam, *Abraham Lincoln*, pp. 205–66.

within my calculation before I started, went off passably well and gave me no trouble whatever. The difficulty was to make nine others, before reading audiences who had already seen all my ideas in print."[21]

While Lincoln was visiting Robert between speeches in New England, the *Tribune* brought out the Cooper Institute speech in one of its "Campaign Tracts" and offered it for sale by the thousand and over at *one cent* per copy.[22] Greeley now called the speech "the most systematic and complete defense yet made of the Republican position with regard to Slavery. We believe no speech has yet been made better calculated to win intelligent minds to our standard. Will the friends of the Cause everywhere aid us to circulate it?"

It was indeed a busy two weeks for Lincoln. On March 12 the *Tribune*, having done its full duty, speeded the departing guest: "Abraham Lincoln spoke on Friday at Norwich, Conn., and on Saturday evening at Bridgeport, whence he came on by the Night Express to this City, attending the churches of Drs. Beecher and Chapin yesterday. He leaves this morning for home, by way of the Erie Railroad, having spoken once in New England for each secular day since his address in our City, two weeks ago. Mr. Lincoln has done a good work and made many warm friends during this visit."

The Cooper Institute speech went more than "passably well." Its author returned to Springfield a national figure. Answering a letter shortly thereafter from R. M. Corwine, who was to be a delegate to the Chicago Convention from Ohio, concerning prospects in Illinois, Lincoln told Corwine that he might not be the "fittest person" to answer his questions for the reason that "when not a very great man begins to be mentioned for a very great position, his head is very likely to be a little turned." Allowances would therefore have to be made for his views. "I think Mr. Seward," he wrote, "is the very best candidate we could have for the North of Illinois, and the very *worst* for the South of it. The estimate of Gov. Chase here is neither better nor worse than that of Seward, except that he is a newer man. They are regarded as being almost the same, seniority giving Seward the inside track. Mr. Bates, I think, would be the best man for the South of our State, and the worst for the North of it. If Judge McLean was fifteen, or even ten years younger, I think he would be stronger than either, in our state, taken as

---

[21] *Ibid.*, p. 49.
[22] *Tribune*, March 6, 1860.

a whole. . . . I feel myself disqualified to speak of myself in this matter."[23]

On April 29, Lincoln confessed in a letter to Senator Trumbull, who was watching the approaching convention battle from the vantage point of Washington: "The taste *is* in my mouth a little." That fact, he apprehended, as in his letter to Corwine, disqualified him from forming correct opinions. He nevertheless wanted it understood that his own "pretensions" would not "be pressed to the point of endangering our common cause." Then he proceeded to analyze the Illinois situation again:

> *Now, as to my opinions about the chances of others in Illinois. I think neither Seward nor Bates can carry Illinois if Douglas shall be on the track; and that either of them can, if he shall not be. I rather think that McLean would carry it with D. on or off; in other words, I think McLean is stronger in Illinois, taking all sections of it, than either S. or B.; and I think S. the weakest of the three. I hear no objection to Mr. McLean except his age; but that objection seems to occur to everyone; and it is possible it might leave him no stronger than the others. By the way, if we should nominate him, how would we save to ourselves the chance of filling his vacancy in the Court? Have him hold on up to the moment of his inauguration? Would that course be no draw-back upon us in the canvass?*
>
> *Recurring to Illinois, we want something here quite as much as, and which is harder to get than, the electoral vote—the Legislature. And it is exactly in this point that Seward's nomination would be hard upon us. Suppose he should gain us a thousand votes in Winnebago, it would not compensate for the loss of fifty in Edgar.*[24]

Leaving out of consideration his honesty of purpose and his high patriotic motives—which a world now canonizing him universally acknowledges—we have here a clear self-portrait of Lincoln the politician. He was an eager aspirant for office who shrewdly watched for opportunity to advance his own interests. He looms the larger in history if we will remember that he was no superman. Seward couldn't win in the south of Illinois, Bates couldn't win in the north; neither could win with Douglas on the track, and everybody knew Douglas would be on the track. Moreover, Seward couldn't win the legislature, and Chase was merely neck and neck with Seward. McLean was too old, and besides there was the chance of losing his place on the United States Su-

---

[23] Tracy, *op. cit.*, pp. 138–39, Lincoln to R. M. Corwine, April 6, 1860.
[24] *Ibid.*, pp. 142–44, Lincoln to Lyman Trumbull, April 29, 1860.

preme Court. Who could win Illinois, north and south? Who could secure a Republican legislature along with the electoral ticket? Who could win with Douglas on the track? It wasn't necessary to tell Corwine and Trumbull who the man was, they could read between the lines as we now can. Let this "be strictly confidential," Lincoln had said to Corwine. "Let no eye but your own see this," he had said to Trumbull. And now, there being no reason for obeying these injunctions, these two letters help us to sane appraisal of the lawyer from Springfield who wanted to be President. They paved the way, too, for the action Lincoln profoundly hoped the Illinois Republicans would take at their state convention scheduled to be held in Decatur on May 9. The story of that convention is now quite as legendary as it is historical. John Hanks and the rails from the Sangamon bottom carried the day, and Lincoln's hopes were realized in this resolution:

> Resolved, *That Abraham Lincoln is the choice of the Republican party of Illinois for the Presidency, and the delegates from this State are instructed to use all honorable means to secure his nomination by the Chicago Convention, and to vote as a unit for him.*[25]

Buried in a short paragraph in the *Tribune* on May 11, listing the nominations for state offices at the Decatur Convention, this sentence alone appeared: "*Abram* Lincoln was declared the choice of the Republicans of Illinois for the Chicago Presidential Nomination."

Now let us see what Greeley was doing to influence the deliberations of the forthcoming Republican National Convention. Here again we may leave out of our consideration his honesty of purpose and his high patriotic motives—they too are not questioned by posterity—and let Greeley give us another portrait of himself. He had begun as early as June, 1858, to give signs that he was already thinking seriously of the presidential election of 1860. He assured his readers, however, that the *Tribune* would have no candidate until November or December, 1859.[26]

In a long editorial on April 26, 1859, entitled "The Presidency in 1860," Greeley remarked that a *new* President was to be chosen in the next year, and he explained his use of the word "new" by saying that not more than a half dozen persons, including "the Hon. James Buchanan" himself, had "any idea of reelecting that eminent functionary." Buchanan out of the way, he insisted, contrary to rumors then afloat,

[25] Osborn H. Oldroyd, *Lincoln's Campaign*, p. 9.
[26] *Tribune*, June 10, 1858.

the *Tribune* was not laboring to nominate and elect *A*, *B*, or *C*; the end the *Tribune* had in view was a union of the "opposition" to assure Republican success. A union of the electors who supported Frémont and Fillmore in 1856, he pointed out, would bring success in 1860. The elevation of this or that man to the presidency, he admitted, might seem desirable, "but the triumph of our cause," he said, "is of infinitely greater importance." The *Tribune* would prefer an "original Republican—Gov. Seward or Gov. Chase, for instance"—but would "heartily and zealously support" a candidate "like John Bell, Edward Bates, or John M. Botts" with the assurance that "his patronage, his power, if chosen President" would "be used not to extend Slavery, but to confine it to the States that see fit to uphold it."[27] This was hardly "laboring to nominate" any one person, although it is perfectly clear from his subsequent procedure that Greeley slipped in the name of Bates as a trial balloon. He was quite capable of reasoning himself into the belief that the "cause" was his sole concern so long as he had not come out openly for any particular candidate. The record is clear that he was adroitly "building-up" Bates for nearly a year ahead of convention time.[28]

Perhaps the fullest presentation of Greeley's views—which also shows the working of his mind in the pursuit of his own ends—is demonstrated in a long editorial appearing in the *Tribune* on February 20, 1860.

THE PRESIDENCY

We judge that there is no longer a shadow of hope that the National Committee will change the time originally designated for the meeting of the Chicago Convention. We have not within the last six weeks met a Republican outside of that Committee who did not consider the postponement of that Convention to the middle of June a deplorable mistake—as in effect giving away the two best months of the campaign. Until the nominations shall have been made, very little will or can be done to secure success in the ensuing election. We shall be wrangling with each other about our prospective candidates, rather than rallying and organizing our forces for effective service against the common adversary. Delegations will be packed to secure the nomination of this or that aspirant, and many will go to Chicago not to hear, to consider and decide by what instrumentalities the Good Cause

---

[27] *Ibid.*, July 25, 1859; January 19, 1860.

[28] See, especially, *Tribune*, May 16, August 25, November 14, 1859; February 10, March 26, April 2, 1860. See also Jeter A. Isely, *Horace Greeley and the Republican Party*, pp. 255–86.

can best be subserved, but to carry out a prearranged programme, no matter at what risk or cost. Thus the bright idea of waiting to let the Slave Democracy quarrel and fall to pieces at Charleston is quite likely to result in serious and damaging dissensions if not positive disruption in our own ranks. But weak men will do anything sooner than admit that they have made a blunder; so we must consider the time of holding the Convention settled beyond further controversy. . . .

We hold, then, that if the Republican party is strong enough to elect as next President whomsoever it will, there are two men who, above all others, are entitled to consideration at Chicago. Those men are WILLIAM H. SEWARD *of New-York and* SALMON P. CHASE *of Ohio. Being members of the Federal Senate when Mr. Douglas introduced, remodeled and pressed through his Nebraska bill, they opposed and exposed it with a promptness, energy, address and resolution which have rarely been equaled. Others did nobly; but it is preeminently due to these two that the country was early and generally apprised of the real character and purpose of that iniquitous measure and that the hollow hypocrisy of its claims to justification on the basis of "Popular Sovereignty" were held up to the indignant gaze of all who were not willfully blind. As Mr. Douglas is very likely to be the candidate of the Sham Democracy, there would be eminent fitness in pitting against him one of his two chief antagonists in the memorable struggle which dissolved old organizations and called the Republican party into being. Each of them is, by original character, by training, by experience, emphatically a statesman of unquestioned ability, unsullied integrity, broad National views and feelings, and thoroughly Republican principles and aspirations. No sane American, no matter of what section, would have any fear that the National interests or honor would suffer under the sway of Seward or Chase, while the noisy swash of disunion would be rebuked and exploded by the election and administration of either of them, and stand exposed to all the world as the hollow mask it really is. No earnest Republican, surely, could refuse to work as well as vote for either Chase or Seward, or to do every honorable thing within his power to secure the election of whichever should be nominated. . . .*

And it does seem to us—though we hold this view subject to the representations of the delegates to Chicago from the doubtful States—that, if we cannot probably elect Seward or Chase, it will be vain to nominate instead either Banks, or Fessenden, or Dayton, or Cameron, or Lincoln. Good men and true are they all; but wherein or on what ground can we rationally hope to obtain for either of them any considerable support which will not be accorded to Chase or Seward? All of these are simply and thoroughly Republicans, who fought with us the good fight of 1856, and bear the scars of that well fought and glorious, though unsuccessful, struggle. No one will seriously contend that either of them is abler, more eminent, more deserving, than they who led the forlorn hope against Douglas and his Iniquity in

1854. On what plausible ground could we hope to secure for them the votes denied us in 1856? . . .

If, then, our Convention shall decide that it cannot safely nominate Seward or Chase, we hold, with due submission, that the man for the hour is EDWARD BATES *of Missouri. Mr. Bates is commended to our judgment, because, while essentially a Republican, he has not hitherto been identified with our party, and is not exposed to the unjust prejudices which incessant misrepresentation has excited against our veteran leaders. Born, reared, and always residing in a Slave State, it will be morally impossible to make anybody believe that he meditates disunion as a means of getting rid of Slavery, or that his election would result in disunion. A practical Emancipationist, it would be hard work to make him odious to sane Abolitionists, while we might safely count, in his behalf, on the noisy, malignant, untiring denunciations of the little handful of Disunion Abolitionists who refuse to vote even for Seward or Chase, yet insist on damaging these statesmen by speaking well of them. . . .*

But enough for the day. If the Chicago Convention shall see fit to nominate one of our most pronounced Republicans, we shall receive this as authentic evidence that the Republican party is stronger than we had supposed it, and shall go to work with a will to justify that confidence in its strength. If, on the other hand, it shall present the name of Edward Bates, we shall feel a double assurance that the domination of the Slave Power in our National Councils will finally cease and determine on the 4th of March, 1861.[29]

Greeley's method of eliminating candidates he did not want in favor of the man he did want was not unlike the method Lincoln followed in his letters to Corwine and Trumbull. Two men stood out above all others as eminently qualified for the high office—Seward and Chase; but they could not carry Pennsylvania, New Jersey, and Illinois. "Good men and true" were Banks, Fessenden, Dayton, Cameron, and Lincoln; but they were "simply and thoroughly Republicans" who could not command as much support as Seward and Chase; if neither Seward nor Chase could be elected, it would therefore "be vain" to nominate any of these lesser lights. What in this extremity was to be done? Greeley had the answer. Unlike Lincoln he did not leave it to be read between the lines. "With due submission"—and it may be said with months of planning—"the man for the hour" was Edward Bates. Greeley let his armor down for a moment only in this whole pronouncement. When he raised questions about the choice of Seward or Chase, he said: "We have our opinions with respect to them; but we do not desire that the Convention shall be governed or influenced by them." His desires were

---

[29] The convention was finally held May 16–18, 1860.

greatly modified by the time the convention opened, for no man worked harder to have the convention governed *and* influenced by his own ideas than Greeley.

As the day for the memorable Wigwam Convention approached, Lincoln and Greeley believed that above all else they were first and foremost for the "Cause"; and so far, perhaps, as it is possible for ordinary mortals to submerge personal aims and selfish purposes this was true. The "Cause" for which they had battled since early manhood—each in his own way—was common to them. Lincoln had expressed that common cause in his Cooper Institute address, and Greeley had said that this was the best defense of it that had yet been made. Although the human equation was apparently subordinate, it was nevertheless urgent: Lincoln was for Lincoln, and Greeley was for Bates.

Murat Halstead's account of the proceedings of the Wigwam Convention held in Chicago, May 16–18, 1860, still makes refreshing reading to this day.[30] Lincoln discreetly stayed at home.[31] Greeley, not being in the good graces of the Weed-Seward organization, had no official standing in his own state; but he managed, not feeling "at liberty" to refuse the invitation, to be a delegate from Oregon with instructions that Judge Bates was "the decided choice of Oregon for President."[32] He arrived early, and Halstead reported that "the principal lions" at the Tremont House were Greeley and Senator Frank P. Blair. "The way Greeley is stared at as he shuffles about, looking as innocent as ever, is itself a sight. Wherever he appears there is a crowd gaping at him, and if he stops to talk a minute with someone who wishes to consult him as the oracle, the crowd becomes dense as possible, and there is the most eager desire to hear the words of wisdom that are supposed to fall on such occasions."[33] The Seward men arrived in large numbers wearing badges of silk with Seward's likeness and name. The day before the convention opened, some wag pinned one of the Seward badges to Greeley's back, and he created a sensation as he "hitched about."[34]

Halstead was not impressed about the talk of harmony. One could not "stay long among the Seward men at the Richmond House," he said, "without hearing unkind and profane expressions used respecting

---

[30] Murat Halstead, *Caucuses of 1860*, pp. 120–54. See also, especially, William E. Baringer, *Lincoln's Rise to Power*, pp. 188–245.

[31] Angle, *Lincoln Day by Day*, p. 333.

[32] *Tribune*, May 22, 1860.

[33] Halstead, *op. cit.*, p. 121.

[34] *Ibid.*, p. 123.

brother delegates of conservative notions. He would very frequently hear brother Greeley, for example, who is hated intensely by them, called a 'd———d old ass!' "

The Hon. George Ashmun of Massachusetts, who had been in Congress with Lincoln and Greeley, was made permanent chairman. Greeley received an ovation when the roll was called and his credentials from Oregon were presented. He was named a member of the Committee on Resolutions which was assigned the task of drafting the platform. He no doubt had a leading hand in it, for on his own testimony he was kept out of the active canvass by the deliberations of the committee Wednesday night and most of Thursday.[35] Conclusive proof that he helped materially is to be found in his statement: "I think no former Platform ever reflected more fairly or fully the average conviction of a great National party." All accounts indicate that Greeley was one of the busiest men at the convention, going about constantly, when he was free from committee work, urging that Seward could not be elected and that Bates should be chosen. He put it very mildly eight years later: "I did not hesitate to avow my preference though I may have withheld some of my reasons for it."[36] "It was a fearful week," he wrote Pike immediately after the convention, "such as I hope and trust I shall never see repeated."[37]

Lincoln was "nervous, restless, and laboring under more or less suppressed excitement," according to Herndon. The day before the nomination he hustled the editor of the *Illinois State Journal*, E. L. Baker, off to Chicago with a copy of the *Missouri Democrat* in which he had marked references to Seward's position on the slavery question. On the margin of the paper he wrote in pencil: "I agree with Seward in his 'Irrepressible Conflict,' but I do not endorse his 'Higher Law' doctrine." And then he added an injunction intended for Judge David Davis, his manager, which he carefully underscored: "*Make no contracts that will bind me.*"[38] Judge Davis was not greatly moved by the instructions and went right on promising portfolios in the Cabinet and diplomatic posts to Pennsylvania, Indiana, New Jersey, and other hesitating states he was ardently wooing. It was wise to have such an injunction in the record; but the long intimacy and close understanding between the

---

[35] *Tribune*, May 22, 1860.
[36] Greeley, *op. cit.*, p. 389.
[37] James S. Pike, *First Blows of the Civil War*, pp. 519–20, Greeley to Pike, May 21, 1860.
[38] William H. Herndon and Jesse William Weik, *The Life of Lincoln*, III, 462.

circuit rider and the judge made it quite possible that Lincoln apprehended that Davis would be no less a skillful politician than he was himself.

The platform, which Greeley had helped to draft and which he thoroughly approved, was unanimously adopted, after some changes and debate, on the second day of the convention. It could have been written in its entirety by either Lincoln or Greeley. There were seventeen planks, covering the usual criticism of the opposition and the promises of the party seeking power. The substance of the platform touching the vital issues of the day appeared in sections 4, 5, 7, and 8 as follows:

4. That the maintenance inviolate of the rights of the States, and especially the right of each state to order and control its own domestic institutions according to its own judgment exclusively, is essential to that balance of powers on which the perfection and endurance of our political fabric depends; and we denounce the lawless invasion by armed force of the soil of any state or territory, no matter under what pretext, as among the gravest of crimes.

5. That the present Democratic Administration has far exceeded our worst apprehensions, in its measureless subserviency to the exactions of a sectional interest, as especially evinced in its desperate exertions to force the infamous Lecompton Constitution upon the protesting people of Kansas; in construing the personal relation between master and servant to involve an unqualified property in persons; in its attempted enforcement, everywhere, on land and sea, through the intervention of Congress and of the Federal Courts of the extreme pretensions of a purely local interest; and in its general and unvarying abuse of the power entrusted to it by a confiding people.

7. That the new dogma that the Constitution, of its own force, carries slavery into any or all of the territories of the United States, is a dangerous political heresy, at variance with the explicit provisions of that instrument itself, with contemporaneous exposition, and with legislative and judicial precedent; is revolutionary in its tendency, and subversive of the peace and harmony of the country.

8. That the normal condition of all the territory of the United States is that of freedom: That as our Republican fathers, when they had abolished slavery in all our national territory, ordained that "no person should be deprived of life, liberty or property, without due process of law," it becomes our duty, by legislation, whenever such legislation is necessary, to maintain this provision of the Constitution against all attempts to violate it; and we deny the authority of Congress, of a territorial legislature, or of any indi-

viduals, to give legal existence to slavery in any territory of the United States.[39]

The balloting took place on Friday, May 18. Greeley almost gave up the fight and wired the *Tribune* at midnight on Thursday that the opposition would not be able to concentrate on any other candidate and that Seward would probably be nominated.[40] Three votes were taken as follows:[41]

	Votes		
	1st	2d	3d
Whole number of votes	465	465	465
Necessary for a choice	233	233	233
William H. Seward of New York	173½	184½	180
Abraham Lincoln of Illinois	102	181	231½
Simon Cameron of Pennsylvania	50½	2	0
Salmon P. Chase of Ohio	49	42½	24½
Edward Bates of Missouri	48	35	22
William L. Dayton of New Jersey	14	10	1
John McLean of Ohio	12	8	5
Jacob Collamer of Vermont	10	0	0
Scattering number of votes	6	2	1

Before the third ballot could be announced, Ohio had switched four votes to Lincoln, and other delegations promptly followed bringing his total to 354. On motion of William M. Evarts of New York, seconded by John A. Andrew of Massachusetts, the nomination of Abraham Lincoln as the Republican candidate for President was made unanimous. After two ballots Hannibal Hamlin of Maine was chosen for Vice-President, and his nomination was also made unanimous.

The modest and yet truthful Lincoln told the Notification Committee in his parlor at Springfield on May 21 that he could "almost" wish that the great responsibility "had fallen upon some one of the far more eminent and experienced statesmen whose distinguished names were before the convention." And then the cautious and practical politician told the committee that by its leave he would "consider more fully the resolutions of the convention, denominated the platform," and respond

---

[39] Charles W. Johnson, comp., *First Three Republican National Conventions*, pp. 131–33; and Francis Curtis, *The Republican Party*, I, 355–58.

[40] *Tribune*, May 18, 1860.

[41] Edward Stanwood, *A History of the Presidency*, I, 294–95. See also Reinhard H. Luthin, *The First Lincoln Campaign*, pp. 136–67.

in writing, "not doubting that the platform will be found satisfactory, and the nomination gratefully accepted."[42]

Two days later in a formal letter he accepted the nomination and gave his approval to the platform in these words: "The declaration of principles and sentiments which accompanies your letter meets my approval; and it shall be my care not to violate or disregard it in any part."[43]

Before Greeley got home from the convention, the *Tribune* printed a long editorial on Saturday, May 19, entitled "Honest Old Abe." It could hardly have been written by Greeley, but it fairly expressed the views he now held when he was able to detach himself from his zeal to defeat Seward. It contained a brief sketch of Lincoln's career which for the time was remarkably free from errors. The title "Honest Old Abe" was a mark of affection of the masses for Lincoln. He was made of "sterling stuff" and could be relied upon "for perfect integrity and constant fidelity to duty." His nomination would be satisfactory to all Republicans and the "moderation of his character, and the conservative tendencies of his mind" would commend him to all sections of the opposition. His election was *a thing that can be done.* The *Tribune* urged organization, discussion, and the arousing of patriotic citizens to this end.

On the following Tuesday a two-column article on the editorial page of the *Tribune* signed "H. G." dealt with "Last Week at Chicago." As an illustration of the "self-made man who worships his Creator" it is a classic. Greeley was still mentally fuming about the lobbies of the Tremont House with the Seward badge pinned on his coattail. His mind, he confessed, had been "long before deliberately made up that the nomination of Gov. Seward for President was unadvised and unsafe." He had resolved to avoid this convention and went to Chicago finally at the insistence of friends in Oregon to do his "best to nominate Judge Bates." He acknowledged that there was "no truer, more faithful, more deserving Republican than Abraham Lincoln" and that "probably no nomination could have been more conducive to a certain triumph." He even admitted that the nomination of Judge Bates "would have fallen like a wet blanket on nearly the whole party, that thousands would have sworn never to support it, and that counter nominations would have been got up or seriously threatened."

With "nearly the whole party" disaffected, Greeley still expected

---

[42] Nicolay and Hay, *op. cit.*, VI, 12–13.
[43] *Ibid.*, pp. 14–15.

"the great body of conservative and quiet voters" who had "hitherto stood aloof from the Republican organization" to elect Bates. "And now," he said, "when all the world is raining bouquets on the successful nominee, so that, if he were not a very tall man, he might stand a chance to be smothered under them, when thousands are rushing to bore him out of house and home, and snowing him white with letters, and trying to plaster him all over with their advertising placards, I, who knew and esteemed him ten years ago, reiterate that I think Judge Bates, to whom I never spoke nor wrote, would have been the wiser choice." Employing the mystical logic Lincoln was soon to encounter on more vital issues, Greeley further held that "the selection of Edward Bates would have been more far-sighted, more courageous, more magnanimous," and he put the final seal of his approval on this portrait he was drawing of himself in these words: "My first attendance on a National Convention was at Harrisburg, in December, 1839, when the nominations were made which swept the country in 1840. I then acted with some of those whom I this time acted against: *I am sure we were right then; I feel confident that I was not wrong this time.*"[44]

Seward had confidently expected the nomination, and with abundant justification. He left Washington shortly before the Chicago Convention announcing to his friends that his senatorial duties were ended and retired to his home at Auburn, New York, to await the expected news from Chicago.[45] He was deeply disappointed, but no defeated aspirant for the presidency ever conducted himself with better grace.[46] His friends were less discreet, particularly Weed, his manager, the owner of the *Albany Evening Journal*, and Henry J. Raymond, one of Weed's principal lieutenants, editor of the *New York Times*, which had powerfully supported Seward.[47] The fat was soon in the fire. Raymond stopped at Auburn to see Seward on his way back from Chicago, and sent off a letter dated Auburn, May 22, to his own paper in which he castigated Greeley scathingly and with the fine sarcasm of which he was capable.[48] Raymond awarded Greeley full credit, which, in his modesty he would not claim for himself, for the success of the main business which had taken him to Chicago—"the defeat of Gov. Seward." He also said that Greeley was indebted to those upon whom

[44] The italics are the author's.
[45] Pike, *op. cit.*, p. 516.
[46] Frederic Bancroft, *The Life of William H. Seward*, I, 541–53.
[47] Harriet A. Weed and Thurlow Weed Barnes, eds., *The Life of Thurlow Weed*, II, Memoir, 268–90. See also Francis Brown, *Raymond of the Times*, pp. 188–91.
[48] *New York Times*, May 24, 1860.

he waged warfare for refraining from making public the fact that, nearly six years earlier, he "had privately, but distinctly repudiated all further political friendship for, and alliance with Gov. Seward, and menaced him with his hostility wherever it could be made most effective, for the avowed reason that Gov. S. had never aided or advised his elevation to office."

Greeley was easily beguiled into labored efforts to justify himself, and loving nothing more than wordy combat, he leaped to the attack. In a series of broadsides, which, contrary to his usual custom, he signed with his name or initials, he took on the *New York Times*, the *New York Courier and Inquirer*, the *Albany Evening Journal*, and any other assailant who showed his head.[49] He unmasked all his guns in his first attack on Raymond on May 25, and thereafter largely employed the same type of shells. After quoting a considerable part of Raymond's letter, Greeley analyzed the "artful mixture of truth and misrepresentation" it contained. He admitted that he had done what he could to prevent the nomination of Seward, not on personal grounds, but because he firmly believed Seward could not be elected. He called on Raymond to produce the letter he had written Seward in 1854, saying that he had no copy of it, and promising to publish it in full if the original should be put into his hands. "To my mind," he said, "it was the imperative duty of the Convention to regard the triumph of the cause first, and the gratification of personal feelings or aspirations a long way afterward."

Greeley's letter of November 11, 1854, to Seward, dissolving the "political firm of Seward, Weed, and Greeley," was finally sent to Greeley through Weed. Greeley boldly published the letter in full, admitting that he had had "no idol" since 1854 but insisting that he had "uttered more praise with less blame" of Seward "than of any other living statesman."[50] Characteristically, he found himself right all along the line. "And if ever in my life I discharged a public duty in utter disregard of personal considerations, I did so at Chicago last month. . . . Need I add that each subsequent day's developments have tended to strengthen my confidence that what I did was not only well meant but well done." Greeley disposed finally of his controversy with Raymond

---

[49] *Tribune*, May 25, 28; June 2, 14, 1860. The *Albany Evening Journal*, the *New York Times*, the *New York Courier and Inquirer*, and other New York papers reveal the full details of this unbecoming squabble. See also Robert S. Harper, *Lincoln and the Press*, pp. 49–61.

[50] *Tribune*, June 14, 1860.

and Weed by saying: "I want to improve all the space in these columns that can be spared from other uses in aid of the election of Lincoln and Hamlin, and I do not think it will be possible to tempt me into further allusion to the warfare waged upon me."[51]

The lines of the campaign of 1860 were being drawn. The long-heralded Democratic National Convention had been held at Charleston, South Carolina, from April 23 to May 3 and resulted in a split with most of the Southern delegates withdrawing and organizing a separate convention. After fifty-seven ballots, in all of which Douglas led, the regular convention adjourned to meet at Baltimore on June 18. The seceders adjourned to meet at Richmond on June 11 and again adjourned to await action at Baltimore.

The Baltimore Convention resulted in an additional split between the Northern and Southern delegates. Another secession took place, and the regular convention, or what called itself regular, proceeded with the nomination of Stephen A. Douglas for President and Benjamin Fitzpatrick of Alabama for Vice-President. Fitzpatrick declined the nomination, and the National Committee named Herschel V. Johnson of Georgia as the candidate. The seceders at Baltimore set up a separate organization and nominated John C. Breckenridge of Kentucky for President and Joseph Lane of Oregon for Vice-President. The Charleston seceders now promptly endorsed the nominations of Breckenridge and Lane. In the meantime the Constitutional Union party had met at Baltimore on May 9 and nominated John Bell of Tennessee for President and Edward Everett of Massachusetts for Vice-President, and the Republicans had named Lincoln and Hamlin at Chicago on May 18. Thus there were four tickets in the field, and the Democratic party was hopelessly divided.

The slavery issue was paramount. The Republicans held that slavery existed only by state law, that Congress could not establish it anywhere and was bound to prohibit and exclude it from all Federal territory. The Southern Democrats held that Congress should protect slavery in Federal territory and that the citizen of any slave state had a right to migrate to any territory taking his slaves with him as property to be protected with or without support of the territorial legislature. The Northern Democrats held to the doctrine of popular sovereignty, that the people of a territory were free to permit or prohibit slavery as they chose without interference by Congress. The Constitutional party, avoiding spe-

---

[51] *Ibid.*, June 18, 1860.

cific issues, ambiguously declared itself for "the Constitution, the
Union, and the enforcement of the laws."[52]

When the *Tribune* printed the letters of acceptance of Lincoln and
Hamlin, Greeley said, "Our candidates are now fairly in the field, and
we have nothing to do but to go forward and elect them";[53] and the
Tribune labored earnestly and consistently to that end throughout the
campaign. Announcement was made on June 30 of a "Campaign Edition" of the semi-weekly *Tribune* to be continued until after the election. Dozens of campaign tracts were issued, with especial emphasis on
Lincoln's Cooper Institute address and the Lincoln-Douglas debates,
and a "Life of Abraham Lincoln" by an "Illinois Republican" was
brought out. Greeley and Cleveland issued their *Political Text-book*
which was in some ways an effective Republican campaign document.
The news columns of the *Tribune* printed many clippings from other
papers complimentary to Lincoln and strongly advocated the support
of the Republican ticket. Notable speeches during the campaign by Republican leaders were published in full and commented upon editorially. Especial notice was taken of the speeches of Seward and Carl
Schurz. The platforms of the four tickets in the field were analyzed, and
no opportunity was lost to get in a blow at the enemies. On September
19, after Republican electors were designated in New York and candidates named for state offices, the state ticket led by Lincoln and Hamlin appeared at the masthead of the *Tribune*.

Douglas was the only one of the candidates who took the field and
carried on an aggressive campaign on the stump. He spoke almost daily,
and often two or three times a day, and traveled to nearly every state in
the Union. The *Tribune* had something to say in its news columns or
on the editorial page about Douglas almost daily. Greeley devoted
many editorials to pursuit of him and entitled one of them, "Douglas
the Wanderer."[54] He did not employ the vicious adjectives to which
he had resorted during the debates on the Kansas–Nebraska bill but
mainly contented himself with pointing out the fallacies of Douglas'
position. Typical editorials were headed as follows:

> *July 17—Popular Sovereignty—Douglasism*
> " 20—*The Doom of Douglas*

---

[52] Halstead, *op. cit.*, pp. 104–20; James Ford Rhodes, *History of the United States*, II,
396–421; James Albert Woodburn, *American Politics. Political Parties and Party
Problems in the United States*, pp. 106–07; and Horace Greeley, *The American Conflict*, I, 309–26.

[53] *Tribune*, June 9, 1860.

[54] *Ibid.*, October 24, 1860.

> *August* 2—*Mr. Douglas on the Stump*
> " 21—*Douglas Dumb*
> " 31—*The Degradation of Douglas*
> *September* 3—*Douglas at the South*
> " 18—*Mr. Douglas Smoked Out*

He grew a little more severe as the campaign progressed and moved from the "eminent Squatter-Sovereign"[55] and the candidate "reckless of truth and probability"[56] to the declaration: "It is a shame to our politics that any public man should in his public capacity so equivocate and deceive, so abandon the truth and so stick to falsehood, that, were it done in private life and done openly, he would be left without name and credit enough to buy a pint of rum on trust in a corner grocery."[57]

After the initial announcements and editorials concerning Lincoln which had appeared in the *Tribune* following the Wigwam Convention, the editorial page gave singularly little notice to him until after the election. Indeed, Lincoln was scarcely mentioned editorially in July, August, September, and October, except incidentally in discussion of campaign issues. Greeley showed none of the warmth of support which he had given Clay in 1844. While his paper loyally supported the Republican ticket and steadily fired at the three opposing tickets, the great editor did not seize the opportunity which stared him in the face. Lincoln, the opponent of Douglas, and Lincoln, the debater and stump speaker, through the copies of speeches printed and sold in quantity by the business office of the *Tribune*, was becoming widely known; but there was a real need, an opportune occasion, for an introduction of Lincoln the man to an Eastern audience. No editor in America was better equipped than Greeley to couple with the logic of Lincoln's reasoning the personality and character of the man. None of the campaign lives or campaign tracts did this service as well as Greeley might have done it in the *Tribune*. He missed one of the greatest editorial opportunities of his life. He was ordinarily quick to portray human qualities, and he put much emphasis on the man behind a doctrine. An explanation of his almost studied indifference to Lincoln the man may be that Greeley with all his perspicacity had not yet discovered Lincoln. Toward the end of the campaign in a long editorial entitled "Rail-Splitting," the *Tribune* did get around to thinking of the Rail-

---

[55] *Ibid.*, August 21, 1860.
[56] *Ibid.*, August 28, 1860.
[57] *Ibid.*, October 6, 1860.

Splitter as well, but even then he fell into the error of having Lincoln obliged as a youth "to support his widowed mother and her younger children." In part the editorial read:

ABRAHAM LINCOLN *illustrates our position and enforces our argument. His career proves our doctrine sound. He is Republicanism embodied and exemplified. Born in the very humblest White stratum of society, reared in poverty, earning his own livelihood from a tender age by the rudest and least recompensed labor, soon aiding to support his widowed mother and her younger children, picking up his education as he might by the evening firelight of rude log cabins, clearing off primeval forests, splitting rails at so much per thousand, running a flat-boat, and so working his way gradually upward to knowledge, capacity, esteem, influence, competence, until he stands to-day the all but elected President of this great, free People—his life is an invincible attestation of the superiority of Free Society, as his election will be its crowning triumph. . . .*[58]

On election day, Greeley predicted: "To-day ABRAHAM LINCOLN will be chosen President and Hannibal Hamlin Vice-President unless Fraud shall prevent it for Apathy will not."

In accordance with his own judgment and on the advice of his friends, Lincoln adopted the policy immediately after his nomination at Chicago of saying nothing and of writing nothing for public consumption on the issues of the campaign. It was a difficult task to maintain silence. Visitors and correspondents, friends and strangers, who were sometimes watching for opportunity to take advantage of him, besought him almost daily to give his views on this or that question. Thus he was asked to state his views on the Fugitive Slave Law, on the tariff and the protection of American industry; to write a disclaimer of his intention to interfere with the slaves or slavery in the states; and to set forth his conservative as well as his radical views. To all such requests and suggestions he steadfastly turned a deaf ear and politely referred his questioners and advisers to the printed record of his speeches.

It would be both imprudent and contrary to the reasonable expectation of my friends for me to write or speak anything on doctrinal points now.[59]

. . . The convention which nominated me, by the twelfth plank of their platform, selected their position on this question [the tariff]; and I have declared my approval of the platform, and accepted the nomination.[60]

---

[58] *Ibid.*, October 23, 1860.
[59] Nicolay and Hay, *op. cit.*, VI, 48–49, Lincoln to T. A. Cheney, August 14, 1860.
[60] *Ibid.*, p. 58, Lincoln to G. Yoke Tams, September 22, 1860.

. . . I certainly am in no temper, and have no purpose to embitter the feelings of the south; but whether I am inclined to such a course as would in fact embitter their feelings, you can better judge by my published speeches than anything I would say in a short letter, if I were inclined now, as I am not, to define my position anew.[61]

. . . Those who will not read or heed what I have already publicly said would not read or heed a repetition of it. "If they hear not Moses and the prophets, neither will they be persuaded though one rose from the dead."[62]

. . . If I were to labor a month I could not express my conservative views and intentions more clearly and strongly than they are expressed in our platform and in my speeches already in print and before the public.[63]

Lincoln even declined to speak on August 9 when the Illinois Republicans held an immense rally in Springfield to celebrate his nomination.[64]

Lincoln was given a room in the Statehouse during the campaign where he received a long line of visitors daily, sat for portrait painters and photographers, and endeavored to read his endless mail. While he said and wrote nothing for the public on "doctrinal" issues, he did not hesitate to confer with political leaders and to write letters of advice and caution to those in whom he had confidence. He came up to election day, however, keeping religiously to the promise to himself and to the public to stand on the platform adopted at Chicago and by his well-known views already widely circulated in his published addresses. On Tuesday, November 6, 1860, he voted a straight Republican ticket, after having carefully cut the name of Abraham Lincoln from the top of the ballot.[65]

Lincoln carried all of the free states except New Jersey, where a fusion ticket resulted in the choice of four electors for Lincoln and three for Douglas. There was no Lincoln ticket in Alabama, Arkansas, Florida, Georgia, Louisiana, Mississippi, North Carolina, Tennessee, and Texas. In South Carolina the electors were chosen by the legislature and were for Breckenridge and Lane. There was a relatively small number of votes cast for Lincoln in Delaware, Kentucky, Maryland, Missouri, and Virginia. While Lincoln had 180 electoral votes to 123 for the three other candidates, his popular vote was nearly a million

---

[61] Tracy, *op. cit.*, pp. 165–66, Lincoln to L. Montgomery Bond, October 15, 1860.
[62] Nicolay and Hay, *op. cit.*, VI, 63–64, Lincoln to W. S. Speer, October 23, 1860.
[63] *Ibid.*, pp. 66–67, Lincoln to George D. Prentice, October 29, 1860.
[64] Angle, *Lincoln Day by Day*, p. 345.
[65] *Ibid.*, p. 358; and *Tribune*, November 7, 8, 1860.

less than the combined vote of the three others. The popular vote and the electoral vote stood as follows:[66]

	Popular Vote	Electoral Vote
Lincoln and Hamlin	1,857,610	180
Douglas and Johnson	1,291,574	12
Breckenridge and Lane	850,082	72
Bell and Everett	646,124	39

In the first national election in which the Republican party had participated in 1856, a united South triumphed over a divided North; now the tables were turned, and a united North triumphed over a divided South. The triumph was confined to the presidency, however, for the anti-Republicans still held the Supreme Court and Congress.

The meaning of the election [says Rhodes] was that the great and powerful North declared slavery an evil, and insisted that it should not be extended; that while the institution would be sacredly respected where it existed, the conduct of the national government must revert to the policy of the fathers and confine slavery within bounds; that they hoped, if it were restricted, the time might come when the Southern people would themselves acknowledge that they were out of tune with the enlightened world and take steps gradually to abolish the system. The persistent and emphatic statement that the Republicans were the radical party had fixed that idea in the public mind; but in truth they represented the noblest conservatism. They simply advocated a return to the policy of Washington, Jefferson, and Madison. The North had spoken. In every man's mind rose unbidden the question, What would be the answer of the South?[67]

Southern threats of secession in the event of Lincoln's election had been made throughout the campaign. Events now moved rapidly and the threats were promptly realized. On the very day before the national election, the Legislature of South Carolina met at Columbia and listened to the message of the governor in which he said: "I would earnestly recommend that, in the event of Abraham Lincoln's election to the Presidency, a Convention of the people of this State be immediately called, to consider and determine for themselves the mode and measure of redress."[68] Within a week such a convention was called, and on December 20 the presiding officer of the convention announced: "The ordinance of secession has been signed and ratified, and I pro-

---

[66] Greeley, *American Conflict*, I, 328–29; and Greeley, *Recollections*, pp. 392–93.
[67] Rhodes, *op. cit.*, II, 458.
[68] Greeley, *American Conflict*, I, 331.

claim the State of South Carolina an independent commonwealth."[69] Mississippi followed on January 9, 1861; Florida on January 10; Alabama on January 11; Georgia on January 19; Louisiana on January 26; and Texas on February 1. Delegates from South Carolina, Mississippi, Florida, Alabama, Georgia, and Louisiana met on February 4 at Montgomery, Alabama; and on February 9, after having adopted a constitution, took oath of allegiance to the "Confederate States of America" and elected Jefferson Davis as President and Alexander H. Stephens as Vice-President. Inauguration ceremonies were held on February 18.

In the meantime the second session of the Thirty-sixth Congress assembled on December 3 and listened to the annual message of President Buchanan in which he made the ominous statement, "The long-continued and intemperate interference of the northern people with the question of slavery in the Southern States has at length produced its natural effects."[70] The message did not promote harmony. On the contrary, it provoked debate which lasted until the expiration of the Congress a few hours before Lincoln's inauguration. The President argued himself into a circle and confessed his helplessness.

In the course of the debate in the Senate, John P. Hale of New Hampshire characterized the President's position accurately according to the judgment of both sides of the controversy: "South Carolina has just cause for seceding from the Union; that is the first proposition. The second is, that she has no right to secede. The third is, that we have no right to prevent her from seceding."[71] Reviewing these stirring days later, Greeley said of the President's message: "To expose its inconsistency with notorious facts were a waste of time and effort; to lose temper over it were even a graver mistake: the proper, fittest frame of mind wherein to contemplate it is one of silent wonder."[72]

Special committees were appointed in the House and in the Senate.[73] The committee in the House, consisting of one member from each state, was to consider "so much of the President's message as relates to the present perilous condition of the country." The committee in the Senate, consisting of thirteen members, was to consider "so much of the President's message as relates to the present agitated and distracted condition of the country and the grievances between the slaveholding

---

[69] Henry Wilson, *History of the Rise and Fall of the Slave Power in America*, III, 110.

[70] *Cong. Globe*, 36th Cong., 2d sess., Pt. II, Appendix, pp. 1–7.

[71] *Cong. Globe*, 36th Cong., 2d sess., Pt. I, p. 9.

[72] Greeley, *American Conflict*, I, 368.

[73] *House Journal*, 36th Cong., 2d sess., p. 36, December 4, 1860; and *Senate Journal*, p. 49, December 18, 1860.

and non-slaveholding States." Various proposals for conciliation and compromise were advanced, which came to nought, notably the famous Crittenden Compromise[74] proposed as a Joint Resolution in the Senate by the venerable John J. Crittenden of Kentucky, and a radical amendment of the Constitution advanced in the House by C. L. Vallandigham of Ohio.[75] The sum total of three months of bitter debate was the adoption by the House of a report of its Special Committee, presented by Thomas Corwin of Ohio, calculated to placate the South and to prevent disunion,[76] although the Crittenden Compromise was debated hotly and rejected on the last day of the session.[77] A separate Joint Resolution proposed by Mr. Corwin, providing for an amendment to the Constitution and denying to Congress any power to interfere with slavery "until every State in the Union by its individual State action shall consent to its exercise," was passed by both Houses and approved by the President.[78]

A "Peace Congress" assembled in Washington February 4 on invitation of the Legislature of Virginia. It was attended by delegates from twenty-two states and was presided over by former President John Tyler.[79] Its recommendations were submitted to Congress, but all efforts at compromise were fruitless. Civil war was the answer.

Greeley looked on the election of Lincoln as a "conspicuous and glorious triumph." He did not expect immediate "political harmony and quiet," but did feel that the agitation raised in the South would "gradually and surely subside into peace" without damage to "the integrity of the Union."[80] "We are not a bit sorry for Lincoln's success," he said, "on the contrary, we like it hugely; and the antics of the Chivalry only make us gladder and gladder that they have ceased to be our rulers. And let them nullify, secede, form a new Southern Republic, or do what they will, we shall still be glad that Lincoln is elected."[81]

He now set his face against war and against compromise, and the second day after the election, as yet undisturbed by the threats of secession, he counseled that if the "Cotton States" should decide that they could do better out of the Union than in it, they should be allowed

---

[74] *Cong. Globe*, 36th Cong., 2d sess., Pt. I, p. 114.
[75] *Ibid.*, pp. 794–95, February 7, 1861.
[76] *House Journal*, 36th Cong., 2d sess., pp. 407–21, February 27, 1861.
[77] *Cong. Globe*, 36th Cong., 2d sess., Pt. II, pp. 1336–1413, March 2, 1861.
[78] *House Journal*, 36th Cong., 2d sess., p. 574.
[79] Wilson, *op. cit.*, III, 83–95; and Greeley, *American Conflict*, I, 396–403.
[80] *Tribune*, November 9, 1860.
[81] *Ibid.*, November 17, 1860.

to "go in peace." "We must ever resist the asserted right of any State to remain in the Union, and nullify or defy the laws thereof: to withdraw from the Union is quite another matter. And, whenever a considerable section of our Union shall deliberately resolve to go out, we shall resist all coercive measures designed to keep it in. We hope never to live in a republic, whereof one section is pinned to the residue by bayonets."[82]

This view Greeley voiced frequently and emphatically throughout November.[83] A typical utterance at this time ran in this wise:

But if the Cotton States generally unite with her [South Carolina] in seceding, we insist that they cannot be prevented, and that the attempt must not be made. Five Millions of People, more than half of them of the dominant race, of whom at least a Half a Million are able and willing to shoulder muskets, can never be subdued while fighting around and over their own hearthstones. If they could be, they would no longer be equal members of the Union, but conquered dependencies. Suppose they could be overcome and their military forces destroyed: what then? Can you compel them to send members to Congress? Can you make them accept Federal offices? Can you prevent their tarring and feathering those who do? If not, how idle to talk of subduing them.[84]

The editor again thought he wanted office. Shortly after the election, Greeley wrote his friend Beman Brockway, editor of the (New York) *Watertown Times*, "As to myself, I *would* like to go to the Senate, and would not like to go into the Cabinet."[85] It was even then anticipated that Seward would be called to the service of the new Administration and would retire from the Senate at the end of his term on March 4, 1861. The Republicans were clearly in control of the New York Legislature in the winter of 1860–61 but were sharply divided into two "wings." The wing in power had long been dominated by Seward and Weed. Weed was the "boss," and the opposition wing was out to rid the state of "one-man" rule. This wing, however, while agreeing in principle and purpose, was divided into two factions when it came time to nominate a candidate to succeed Seward. Weed put forward William M. Evarts. The larger anti-Weed group favored Greeley, and the smaller group favored Judge Ira Harris of Albany. There was much

---

[82] *Ibid.*, November 9, 1860.
[83] *Ibid.*, see, especially, issues of November 13, 16, 19, 26, 1860.
[84] *Ibid.*, November 30, 1860.
[85] Greeley Papers, Library of Congress, Washington, D.C., Greeley to Beman Brockway, November 4, 1860.

log-rolling for several weeks before the contest. It was clear that the Republican nominee would be elected. The Democrats nominated Horatio Seymour. The caucus of the Republican members took place Saturday night, February 2. The whole number of votes was 115. For seven ballots Evarts and Greeley polled about 40 votes each, Harris about 20, and the balance was scattered among other candidates. Discovering that he could not name Evarts, Weed chose the lesser of the two evils: he abandoned Evarts and threw his support to Harris on the eighth ballot, and on the ninth ballot Harris was chosen.[86] On February 5 the two Houses of the legislature balloted separately and then met in joint session to consummate the election of Judge Harris. The vote in the House[87] was Harris 88, Seymour 31; in the Senate,[88] Harris 22, Seymour 9.

Greeley talked less about peaceable secession as the days wore on; but he clung to the possibility of such an outcome of the struggle until after Lincoln's inauguration. He put himself squarely on record again in January in a signed, open letter to J. L. O'Sullivan who had urged that the choice of alternatives was "reconciliation by acceptable compromise" or "peaceable separation."

> As to Secession, I have said repeatedly, and here repeat, that, if the People of the Slave States, or of the Cotton States alone, really wish to get out of the Union, I am in favor of letting them out as soon as that result can be peacefully and constitutionally attained. . . . I want no States kept in the Union by coercion. . . . Let there be an open and full canvass—let the champions of the Union have a fair opportunity to present and argue the matter to the People, secure against violence and outrage—let the vote be so taken that quiet, peaceful, Union-loving men may vote as they think, without apprehension or insult—and if the South declares for Disunion, I will join you in urging the requisite change in the Constitution to let them out.[89]

In a second letter to O'Sullivan he declared that he wanted proof that the Southern people really desired separation from the "Free States" and again said he would "joyfully" cooperate with them to secure the end they sought when assured of their settled wish.[90]

Willing that the slave states should "go in peace," Greeley was heat-

---

[86] *Tribune*, February 4, 1861.
[87] *New York Assembly Journal*, 84th sess., pp. 247–48, February 5, 1861.
[88] *New York Senate Journal*, 84th sess., p. 137, February 5, 1861.
[89] *Tribune*, January 14, 1861.
[90] *Ibid.*, January 21, 1861.

edly opposed to compromise or conciliation on any ground, and fought all of the measures advanced to that end. He insisted that there should be no bribing, no coaxing, no wheedling those to stay in the Union who wanted to get out.[91] And so he continued to hammer home the futility of compromise. "But to make concessions involving vital principles because some State or section threatens to secede, is to incite constant bullying and menace by proffering rewards for turbulence and giving bounties for treason."[92] He would "hold no parley with conspirators and traitors."[93] For a month before the inauguration the *Tribune* carried in italics at the head of its editorial column under the title "Mottoes for the Day" this quotation from a statement made by Lincoln to Dr. C. H. Ray of the *Chicago Tribune*:

I will suffer death before I will consent or advise my friends to consent to any concession or compromise which looks like buying the privilege of taking possession of the Government to which we have a Constitutional right; because, whatever I might think of the merit of the various propositions before Congress, I should regard any concession in the face of menace as the destruction of the Government itself, and a consent on all hands that our system shall be brought down to a level with the existing disorganized state of affairs in Mexico. But this thing will hereafter be, as it is now, in the hands of the people; and if they desire to call a Convention to remove any grievances complained of or to give new guarantees for the permanence of vested rights it is not mine to oppose.[94]

Preceding "Mottoes for the Day" for the last ten weeks before the adjournment of Congress, this heading blazed forth in the *Tribune*:

NO COMPROMISE

NO CONCESSIONS TO TRAITORS!

The Constitution as it is

Coupled with all his repeated assurances of his willingness to let the Southern states "go in peace" and his bristling hostility to compromise, there was an undercurrent, which sometimes made it exceedingly difficult for his readers to know just where he stood, in Greeley's utterances which indicated both his hope and his belief that the difficulties would be adjusted and that the Union would be preserved once the new Ad-

[91] *Ibid.*, November 19, 1860.
[92] *Ibid.*, December 12, 1860.
[93] *Ibid.*, January 21, 1861.
[94] *Ibid.*, February 8, 1861.

ministration was in power. "Do not meddle," he counseled. "Do not compromise. Be patient. Be forbearing. The Secession movement under a firm administration will settle itself."[95] He hinted to the South that the seceding states would put themselves into a worse position, so far as slavery was concerned, than that in which they already stood.[96] He talked about what the seceding states owed to the Union,[97] and entreated all "who meditate Treason to pause ere it is too late, and avoid at once the traitor's crime and his doom."[98] He published and answered in the *Tribune* on December 28 a letter of December 23 from Gen. Leslie Combs. In his reply he proposed that the territorial question be settled by the adoption of Thomas Jefferson's proposition as reported to Congress in April, 1784, and he would apply this proposition to all territories present and prospective. With characteristic innocence, having a hundred times opposed compromise, Greeley blithely offered his own solution to all other slavery questions:

I. *Let each State cherish or prohibit Slavery as it shall see fit.*

II. *Let each citizen like or dislike Slavery as to him shall seem good, and be at perfect liberty to give his reasons for the faith that is in him.*

III. *Let every Slave owner manage his own negroes, so long as he shall retain them in some Slave State; if any runs out of such State, let the owner be at perfect liberty to persuade or entice him back into servitude, free from any impertinent intermeddling. Should any third party poke his nose into what is none of his business, let the master be at liberty to cowhide him for the intrusion. But let the laws of every Free State hold every man free who does not choose to be a slave.*

IV. *If any person goes from a Free into a Slave State and there attempts to stir up rebellion, or interfere in any way between masters and slaves, let him be dealt with as the law of that Slave State shall direct.*

If this ready-made solution of the troubles that beset him met the eye of the President-elect as he snatched a glance at the *Tribune* on Thursday, February 28, in the midst of his stream of callers at Willard's in Washington, he must have recalled a letter he had received from the editor back in December as well as his visit with Greeley at a Springfield hotel on February 5. According to Nicolay and Hay, disturbed by Greeley's "damaging vagaries about peaceable secession," Lincoln had

---

[95] *Ibid.*, January 22, 1861.
[96] *Ibid.*, December 3, 1860.
[97] *Ibid.*, December 8, 1860.
[98] *Ibid.*, December 28, 1860.

written Greeley a word of caution, apparently on December 19, for
Lincoln had received a reply dated December 22. In his letter Greeley
said that a state could no more secede at pleasure from the Union than
a stave could secede from a cask; that if eight or ten contiguous states
sought to leave, then he should say,

*There's the door—go! But, if the seceding State or States go to fighting and
defying the laws, the Union being yet undissolved save by their own say-so,
I guess they will have to be made to behave themselves. . . . I fear nothing,
care for nothing, but another disgraceful back-down of the Free States.
That is the only real danger. Let the Union slide—it may be reconstructed;
let Presidents be assassinated, we can elect more; let the Republicans be
defeated and crushed, we shall rise again. But another nasty compromise,
whereby everything is conceded and nothing secured, will so thoroughly
disgrace and humiliate us that we can never raise our heads, and this country
becomes a second edition of the Barbary States, as they were sixty years ago.
"Take any form but that."*[99]

On a lecture tour in the Middle West, Greeley landed in Springfield
on the morning of February 5, where he was to lecture that evening. In
the afternoon the President-elect called on the editor at his hotel. The
dispatch from Springfield to the *Tribune* said the interview "lasted several hours."[100] Greeley urged an anti-compromise policy on Lincoln and
is said to have received "gratifying assurances." Cabinet appointments
were discussed. Greeley was opposed to Cameron and favored Chase
and Colfax. The dispatch volunteered the information that, despite
the fact that he had just been defeated at Albany in his race to succeed
Seward in the United States Senate, Greeley did not ask anything either
for himself or his friends.

Somewhere along the line in this Western journey, Greeley penned
a unique letter to Lincoln under date of February 6, 1861. After repeating what he had undoubtedly said to Lincoln in their interview, that he
did not want anything for himself, Greeley intimated that it would be
difficult for the President, in view of Seward's presence in the Cabinet,
to do justice to the anti-Weed Republicans in the distribution of
patronage in New York. He naively suggested that the President recognize the two "wings" or factions and alternately recognize them in ap-

---

[99] John G. Nicolay and John Hay, *Abraham Lincoln—A History*, III, 258. See also
David C. Mearns, ed., *The Abraham Lincoln Papers*, II, 349–50, Greeley's letter to
Lincoln, December 22, 1860.
[100] *Tribune*, February 6, 1861.

pointing New Yorkers to office. Lincoln might in this way settle all New York appointments "in a single sitting" and thus promote sadly needed party unity.

Then in a postscript, Greeley proceeded to recommend candidates for district attorney, surveyor of the port, and government printer. He also urged the President to name John C. Frémont as Minister to France, saying, "It is due to the Fremonters of '56 that he be offered a position of dignity and honor. . . . Nobody who is fit for an office really needs one or will rebell because some other good man is preferred, provided we are not sacrificed because we took the course which led to your nomination." This letter was a forerunner of the frequent unsolicited advice Greeley was to offer Lincoln in the days to come.[101]

Anxious that the anti-Weeds should not be overlooked, on April 8, 1861, George Opdyke, David Dudley Field, and James S. Wadsworth joined Greeley in urging the appointment of a surveyor of the port "in full accord and sympathy" with the collector already appointed. The collector, it was pointed out, is the head of the revenue service and the surveyor, his right hand. Disagreements would weaken the Administration. Moreover, most of the appointments thus far had been made from the other side of the party.

On the envelope in which this recommendation was made, this notation, which seems to be in Lincoln's handwriting, appears: "Greely [sic], Opdycke [sic], Field & Wadsworth, in favor of having two big puddings on the same side of the board."[102]

A dispatch from Springfield on the following day indicated that Greeley had lectured the night before to a "very large audience" but did not indicate the presence of Lincoln at the lecture. "The radical Republicans," the dispatch said, "derive a good deal of comfort from the invigorating influence his emphatic anti-compromise declarations are presumed to have upon the wavering members of the party. They are in high glee over the gratifying assurance he is claimed to have received of the intention of the President-elect to adhere firmly to the doctrines embodied in the Chicago platform. He [Greeley] expressed a fear during his stay that a sufficient number of weak-backed Congressmen could be mustered to secure the passage of a compromise measure before the 4th of March." Greeley had intended to go from Springfield to lecture

---

[101] Robert Todd Lincoln Collection, Library of Congress, Washington, D.C. (7198), Greeley to Lincoln, February 6, 1861.

[102] *Ibid.* (8881), Greeley, George Opdyke, David D. Field, and James S. Wadsworth to Lincoln, February 8, 1861.

at St. Louis but changed his plans because "leading Republicans had advised him that he would probably be mobbed should he attempt to lecture."

Three days after Greeley's visit with Lincoln at Springfield, the *Tribune* said: "The vital question for the Republican party is, Will ABRAHAM LINCOLN stand firm in this trying hour? We answer, He will! Other men whom the people have trusted may falter and flee from danger, equally to be pitied whether cowards or traitors, but we are sure that Lincoln will STAND FIRM."[103]

The next day the *Tribune* hopefully predicted that a firm hand was all that was needed:

We beg the Republican compromisers to stay their hand. We beg them not to consummate the suicide of their principles and their party. The Republicans are masters of the situation. Nothing is wanting but a firm hand and a steady rein, and a most glorious and overwhelming triumph awaits us. Secession will cure itself, and without war or ruin to anybody but those who pertinaciously drag those evils down upon their own heads. It is true the Government is enveloped in a storm. But its foundations are strong and immovable, for they repose in the hearts of the people. It can stand the strain put upon it. Let it not abate a hair of its just authority. Let it not concede an inch, but let it bide its time in confidence and patience, exercising forbearance, but demanding obedience, and rejecting all propositions of surrender, whatever form or guise they may assume. So it will save itself from demoralization and come forth with a new prestige and accumulated vitality.[104]

It would be interesting to know the exact genesis of this editorial. It appeared four days after Greeley had left Springfield, but before he had returned home from his lecture trip.[105] And yet this declaration was in the tone of the inaugural address on which Lincoln was at work and indeed could have formed its text. Greeley may have dispatched it to Dana, his associate, in its actual form, or he may have written Dana about his talk with Lincoln so as to enable Dana to formulate it. Whatever its source, it served for the moment, at least, to put the President-elect and the *Tribune* on substantially the same ground.

˙Overtures were apparently made to Lincoln to interfere in the New York senatorial election. The day before Greeley's conference with Lincoln at Springfield, Lincoln wrote Thurlow Weed:

---

[103] *Tribune*, February 8, 1861.
[104] *Ibid.*, February 9, 1861.
[105] *Ibid.*, February 20, 1861.

Springfield, Illinois,
February 4, 1861

Dear Sir: *I have both your letter to myself and that to Judge Davis, in relation to a certain gentleman in your State claiming to dispense patronage in my name, and also to be authorized to use my name to advance the chances of Mr. Greeley for an election to the United States Senate.*

It is very strange that such things should be said by any one. The gentleman you mention did speak to me of Mr. Greeley in connection with the senatorial election, and I replied in terms of kindness toward Mr. Greeley, which I really feel, but always with an expressed protest that my name must not be used in the senatorial election in favor of, or against, any one. Any other representation of me is a misrepresentation.

As to the matter of dispensing patronage, it perhaps will surprise you to learn that I have information that you claim to have my authority to arrange that matter in New York. I do not believe that you have so claimed; but still so some men say. On that subject you know all I have said to you is "Justice to all," and I have said nothing more particular to any one. I say this to reassure you that I have not changed my position.

In the hope, however, that you will not use my name in the matter, I am,

Yours truly,
A. Lincoln[106]

It is clear that Greeley did not go to Springfield, as has frequently been alleged, to seek Lincoln's support of his candidacy. The formal election of Judge Harris was taking place at about the same hour that Lincoln called on Greeley on February 5; and while he was traveling about on a lecture tour, Greeley could not have failed to know the result of the Republican caucus three days before. Weed may have discussed the coming senatorial election in New York with Lincoln on the occasion of his visit to Springfield on December 20, but he was too skilled in political management not to know that the President-elect could not safely dabble in state politics. There is no intimation in Weed's full account of his visit with Lincoln that this question was mentioned, though he does say that Lincoln commented on the fact, when he was about to go, that he had "made no application, suggestion or allusion to appointments."[107]

After the election Lincoln adhered to the policy he had set for himself during the campaign, and made no public declarations on the issues

---

[106] Nicolay and Hay, *Complete Works*, VI, 104–05, Lincoln to Thurlow Weed, February 4, 1861.
[107] Weed and Barnes, *op. cit.*, I, 602–14.

before the American people until he started on his journey to Washington. His time was consumed in meeting the hordes of office seekers who constantly besieged him, in watching as closely as possible the secession movement in the South and the abortive efforts at compromise at Washington, in receiving national political leaders at Springfield and in corresponding with others, and in thinking about an inaugural address and the make-up of his Cabinet. He continued to resist efforts to draw him into public discussion. "I feel constrained, for the present at least," he wrote Truman Smith on November 10, "to make no declaration for the public. . . . I could say nothing which I have not already said, and which is in print, and open for the inspection of all."[108] Writing to the editor of the *New York Times* about the disposition of "political fiends" to misuse any declaration he might make, Lincoln employed a free quotation from the Scriptures, "They seek a sign, and no sign shall be given them."[109]

There was no occasion for Greeley to journey to Springfield to discover whether Lincoln would stand firm. He stuck literally to the views he had already expressed and to the Chicago platform to which he subscribed. He did not hesitate to urge responsible leaders in whose good sense he had confidence to stand squarely against the extension of slavery and the various compromises that were now being widely proposed. "Entertain no proposition for a compromise in regard to the extension of slavery," he counseled Congressman William Kellogg. "The instant you do they have us under again; all our labor is lost, and sooner or later must be done over."[110] The same advice was given Congressman E. B. Washburne: "Prevent, as far as possible, any of our friends from demoralizing themselves and our cause by entertaining propositions of compromise of any sort on 'slavery extension.' "[111] He wrote Senator Trumbull, with whom he kept in close touch, "The tug has to come & better now than any time hereafter. . . .[112] If any of our friends do prove false, and fix up a compromise on the territorial question, I am for fighting again—that is all."[113]

Perhaps the most positive statement of his opposition to compromise that Lincoln made in this period is to be found in a "Private and confi-

---

[108] Nicolay and Hay, *Complete Works*, VI, 68–69, Lincoln to Truman Smith, November 10, 1860. See also *ibid.*, pp. 70–71, Lincoln to N. P. Pascall, November 16, 1860.

[109] *Ibid.*, pp. 74–75, Lincoln to Henry J. Raymond, November 28, 1860.

[110] *Ibid.*, pp. 77–78, Lincoln to William Kellogg, December 11, 1860.

[111] *Ibid.*, pp. 78–79, Lincoln to E. B. Washburne, December 13, 1860.

[112] Tracy, *op. cit.*, p. 171, Lincoln to Lyman Trumbull, December 10, 1860.

[113] *Ibid.*, pp. 171–72, Lincoln to Lyman Trumbull, December 17, 1860.

dential" letter to Seward, written after Seward had signified his willingness to become Secretary of State:

I say now, however, as I have all the while said, that on the territorial question—that is, the question of extending slavery under the national auspices—I am inflexible. I am for no compromise which assists or permits the extension of the institution on soil owned by the nation. And any trick by which the nation is to acquire territory, and then allow some local authority to spread slavery over it, is as obnoxious as any other. I take it that to effect some such result as this, and to put us again on the high road to a slave empire, is the object of all these proposed compromises. I am against it. As to fugitive slaves, District of Columbia, slave-trade among the slave States, and whatever springs of necessity from the fact that the institution is amongst us, I care but little, so that what is done be comely and not altogether outrageous. Nor do I care much about New Mexico, if further extension were hedged against.[114]

The temptation to take the platform in these days must have been great, but Lincoln adhered to his policy to make no speeches. A "ratification" meeting was held by the Republicans at Springfield on November 20. Lincoln merely greeted the assemblage in a few words and asked to be excused from making a speech. In those few words, however, he managed to suggest that those who were rejoicing over the victory should not "cherish any hard feelings" against the opposition.[115] Senator Trumbull made the principal address and copied literally into his remarks a memorandum furnished him by Lincoln. In this way the President-elect kept off the platform and yet could not resist this opportunity to have the Republican principles for which he stood enunciated.

I have labored in, and for, the Republican organization with entire confidence that whenever it shall be in power, each and all of the States will be left in as complete control of their own affairs respectively, and at as perfect liberty to choose, and employ, their own means of protecting property, and preserving peace and order within their respective limits, as they have ever been under any administration. Those who have voted for Mr. Lincoln, have expected, and still expect this; and they would not have voted for him had they expected otherwise. I regard it as extremely fortunate for the peace of the whole country, that this point, upon which the Republicans have been so long, and so persistently misrepresented, is now to be brought to a practical test, and placed beyond the possibility of doubt. Disunionists per se are now in hot haste to get out of the Union, precisely

---

[114] Nicolay and Hay, *Complete Works*, VI, 102–04, Lincoln to Seward, February 1, 1861.
[115] *Ibid.*, p. 72.

because they perceive they can not, much longer, maintain apprehension among the Southern people that their homes, and firesides, and lives are to be endangered by the action of the Federal Government. With such "Now, or never" is the maxim. I am rather glad of this military preparation in the South. It will enable the people the more easily to suppress any uprisings there, which their misrepresentation of purpose may have encouraged.[116]

The day after the Springfield celebration Lincoln went to Chicago to keep an appointment with the Vice-President-elect, Hannibal Hamlin. En route he greeted briefly the crowds that assembled at the stations at Lincoln and at Bloomington and managed not to enter "upon any discussion of the political topics of the day."

On December 20, the day South Carolina led the procession of the seceding states, Lincoln was in a conference with Thurlow Weed whom he had invited to come to see him. To his surprise Weed found the President-elect "at ease and undisturbed."[117] They found much in common. Before leaving Albany, Weed had written editorials for his paper, the *Albany Evening Journal*,[118] in which he had foreshadowed secession and rebellion and urged that the North should stand together, if war came, for the preservation of the Union. In his interesting account of this day with Lincoln, Weed revealed the fact that he took back East with him direct to Washington a letter from Lincoln to John A. Gilmer, a member of the House from North Carolina, tendering him a place in the Cabinet. This action Weed had urged on Lincoln. Weed does not record the fact that he was also the bearer of a message to Trumbull in which Lincoln seems to have been moved to propose conciliatory measures himself. His conference with Weed may have prompted him to this course. The next day he wrote Trumbull:

Springfield, Ill., Dec. 21st, 1860

Hon. Lyman Trumbull.

My Dear Sir: Thurlow Weed was with me nearly all day yesterday, and left last night with three short resolutions which I drew up, and which, or the substance of which, I think, would do much good if introduced and unanimously supported by our friends. They do not touch the territorial question. Mr. Weed goes to Washington with them; and says that he will first of all confer with you and Mr. Hamlin. I think it would be best for Mr. Seward to introduce them and Mr. Weed will let him know that I think

---

[116] Tracy, *op. cit.*, p. 186.
[117] Weed and Barnes, *op. cit.*, I, 602–14.
[118] *Albany Evening Journal*, December 5, 6, 8, 17, 1860.

so. Show this to Mr. Hamlin, but beyond him do not let my name be known in the matter.

> *Yours as ever,*
> A. Lincoln[119]

The "three short resolutions" to which Lincoln referred were lost until Frederic Bancroft found them in Seward's papers in Lincoln's handwriting:

Resolved:

That the fugitive slave clause of the Constitution ought to be enforced by a law of Congress, with efficient provisions for that object, not obliging private persons to assist in its execution, but punishing all who resist it, and with the usual safeguards to liberty, securing free men against being surrendered as slaves—

That all state laws, if there be such, really, or apparently, in conflict with such law of Congress, ought to be repealed; and no opposition to the execution of such law of Congress ought to be made—

That the Federal Union must be preserved.[120]

There was not much room in Lincoln's thinking for secession. He did not tolerate the idea of it. "I believe you can pretend to find but little, if anything, in my speeches about secession," he wrote Weed. "But my opinion is, that no State can in any way lawfully get out of the Union without the consent of the others; and that it is the duty of the President and other governmental functionaries to run the machine as it is."[121] This view was confirmed in Lincoln's response a week later to the request of Governor Curtin of Pennsylvania for his guidance in the preparation of his inaugural address as governor.

Confidential

Springfield, Ills. Dec. 21, 1860

Hon. A. G. Curtin
My Dear Sir

Yours of the 14th was only received last night. I am much obliged by your kindness in asking my views in advance of preparing your inaugeral [sic]. I think of nothing proper for me to suggest except a word about this secession and disunion movement. On that subject, I think you would do well to express, without passion, threat, or appearance of boasting, but nevertheless, with firmness, the purpose of yourself, and your state to maintain the Union at all hazzards [sic]. Also, if you can, procure the Legislature

---

[119] Tracy, *op. cit.*, p. 172, Lincoln to Lyman Trumbull, December 21, 1860.

[120] Frederic Bancroft, *The Life of William H. Seward*, II, 10n.

[121] Nicolay and Hay, *Complete Works*, VI, 82, Lincoln to Thurlow Weed, December 17, 1860.

to pass resolutions to that effect. I shall be very glad to see your friend, the Attorney General, that is to be; but I think he need scarcely make a trip merely to confer with me on the subject you mention.

Yours very truly
A. Lincoln[122]

Lincoln's purpose "to maintain the Union at all hazards" was fixed and unalterable. Apprehensive that the wavering Buchanan would surrender the Charleston forts, he early indicated in confidential letters his judgment that if the forts fell or were surrendered they should be retaken. Thus he wrote in response to a letter from an old friend:

Confidential

Springfield, Ill. Dec. 22, 1860

Hon. P. H. Silvester
My Dear Sir:

Your kind letter of Nov. 16th, was duly received. Want of time has delayed me so long before acknowledging the receipt of it. This, even now, is the most I can do.

The political horizon looks dark and lowering; but the people, under Providence, will set all right.

If Mr. B. surrenders the forts, I think they must be re-taken.

Yours truly,
A. Lincoln[123]

One searches in vain in Lincoln's published letters from election day to Inauguration Day for any evidence of nervousness or lack of his ordinary poise. Accustomed all his life to deep fits of melancholy and despondency, so far as the public was concerned, at least, he seems to have escaped from them at this time. The patience and the nerves of those who were informed of what was going on, North and South, were tried almost to the point of despair. Thomas Corwin, chairman of the Committee of Thirty-three in the House, vainly seeking a basis of compromise, wrote Lincoln in January:

---

[122] Angle, *New Letters and Papers*, p. 260, Lincoln to Governor A. G. Curtin, December 21, 1860.

[123] Lincoln to P. H. Silvester, December 22, 1860. Silvester, a member of Congress from New York, was in the House with Lincoln in 1847–49. The original letter was presented by Silvester's son to Mr. Martin T. Nachtmann of Albany, N. Y. It is now printed for the first time through the courtesy of Mr. Nachtmann's daughter, Mrs. Townsend R. Morey. See also Nicolay and Hay, *Complete Works*, VI, 84–85, Lincoln to E. B. Washburne, December 21, 1860; p. 86, Lincoln to Major David Hunter, December 22, 1860; pp. 93–94, Lincoln to J. T. Hale, January 11, 1861; Tracy, *op. cit.*, p. 173, Lincoln to Lyman Trumbull, December 24, 1860.

I have been for thirty days in a Committee of Thirty-Three. If the States are no more harmonious in their feelings and opinions than these thirty-three representative men, then, appalling as the idea is, we must dissolve, and a long and bloody civil war must follow. I cannot comprehend the madness of the times. Southern men are theoretically crazy. Extreme Northern men are practical fools. The latter are really quite as mad as the former. Treason is in the air around us everywhere. It goes by the name of patriotism. Men in Congress boldly avow it, and the public offices are full of acknowledged secessionists. God alone, I fear, can help us. Four or five States are gone, others are driving before the gale. I have looked on this horrid picture till I have been able to gaze on it with perfect calmness. I think, if you live, you may take the oath.[124]

Whatever Lincoln's emotions may have been, to the outside world he seemed to be gazing on the troubled scene "with perfect calmness." To all appearances he was the steadiest man in America.[125] It would almost seem that he yet failed to comprehend the full force of his own utterance, "I believe this government cannot endure permanently half slave and half free,"[126] or the equally prophetic utterance of Seward, "It is an irrepressible conflict between opposing and enduring forces, and it means that the United States must and will, sooner or later, become either entirely a slave-holding nation or entirely a free-labor nation."[127] He yet nourished the hope that the sense of justice and considerate dealing he carried in his own heart, which he subconsciously expected to put into practical operation at Washington, would win the South back and save the Union.

There is a distinctly new note in Lincoln's public utterances from the day he left Springfield for Washington. With all his good comradeship on the circuit and his reputed capacity for story telling, he was a self-sustained and self-reliant figure. Up to this time he had given little evidence of reliance in any way upon other men or upon a higher power.

---

[124] Nicolay and Hay, *Abraham Lincoln*, III, 218, Thomas Corwin to Lincoln, January 16, 1861.

[125] One finds widely divergent views on this question in the Lincoln literature. Nathaniel W. Stephenson, *Lincoln*, pp. 120–21, holds that Lincoln was "terribly unhappy" and that his last days at Springfield "were days of mingled gloom, desperation, and the attempt to recover hope." William E. Barton, on the other hand (*The Life of Abraham Lincoln*, I, 462), finds no evidence in support of Stephenson's view and holds that Lincoln's "prevailing mood was happy at this time." See also Kenneth M. Stampp, *And the War Came*, pp. 178–203; and William E. Baringer, *A House Dividing*.

[126] Nicolay and Hay, *Complete Works*, III, 2.

[127] Bancroft, *op. cit.*, I, 459.

His letter to his old associate in Congress, now published for the first time, is the only one in the record of this period of waiting in which he mentions "Providence." In the pathetic little address of farewell to the people of Springfield on the morning of February 11, now engraven upon the hearts of the American people, he reached out beyond himself in a way he had hardly ever done before for the "assistance of that Divine Being" without whose help he could not "succeed," with whose help he could not "fail."[128] From this day forth, the record is unmistakable, this hitherto self-reliant man put his chief trust in the Providence of God.[129]

Despite this new note in his public utterances, which was voiced again and again on the way to Washington, his brief addresses en route represent the low-water mark in his whole career on the platform. All along the way, aroused by the secession that was then in progress, the people watched and waited for a challenge in behalf of the Union from the President-elect; and he mainly spoke awkward platitudes. The legislatures of Indiana, Ohio, New York, New Jersey, and Pennsylvania were in session, and he appeared before them confessing that he was unprepared and insisting that he should remain silent on public policies until he was in office. He was called upon to speak to vast audiences in Cincinnati, Pittsburgh, Cleveland, Buffalo, Rochester, Syracuse, New York City, and Philadelphia, and gave little sign of the man he had been or was to be.

With six states out of the Union, with forts and arsenals seized by the secessionists, with panic among the people North and South, with Fort Sumter besieged and with the inauguration of Jefferson Davis as President of the Confederate States of America taking place while he was journeying to Washington, Lincoln declared at Pittsburgh on February 15, "there is no crisis excepting such a one as may be gotten up at any time by turbulent men aided by designing politicians,"[130] and again at Cleveland on the same day, "I think there is no occasion for any excitement. I think the crisis, as it is called, is altogether an artificial one. . . . Why all this excitement? Why all these complaints? As I said before, this crisis is altogether artificial. It has no foundation in fact. It can't be argued up, and it can't be argued down. Let it alone, and it will go down of itself."[131] At Philadelphia he drove home this

---

[128] Nicolay and Hay, *Complete Works*, VI, 110–11.
[129] Horner, *op. cit.*, pp. 127–71.
[130] Nicolay and Hay, *Complete Works*, VI, 125.
[131] *Ibid.*, pp. 130–31.

strange idea with which he seemed possessed in an almost Pollyanna statement:

I have felt all the while justified in concluding that the crisis, the panic, the anxiety of the country at this time, is artificial. If there be those who differ with me upon this subject, they have not pointed out the substantial difficulty that exists. I do not mean to say that an artificial panic may not do considerable harm; that it has done such I do not deny. The hope that has been expressed by your mayor, that I may be able to restore peace, harmony, and prosperity to the country, is most worthy of him; and most happy, indeed, will I be if I shall be able to verify and fulfill that hope. I promise you that I bring to the work a sincere heart. Whether I will bring a head equal to that heart will be for future times to determine. It were useless for me to speak of details of plans now; I shall speak officially next Monday week, if ever. If I should not speak then, it were useless for me to do so now. If I do speak then, it is useless for me to do so now. When I do speak, I shall take such ground as I deem best calculated to restore peace, harmony, and prosperity to the country, and tend to the perpetuity of the nation and the liberty of these States and these people.[132]

The stage had been set splendidly throughout the journey for a declaration of purpose from the one man in the nation clothed with the authority to make it. Lincoln's performance was disappointing; he missed one of the greatest opportunities ever given to any man to rally his fellows to the support of a cause by the employment on the public platform of the eloquence and will and mind and heart he possessed. Samuel Bowles made a severe indictment of the man who was neither the Lincoln of his yesterday nor of his tomorrow, when he said: "Lincoln is a simple Susan."[133]

Save for the hurried secret flight from Harrisburg to Washington at the end, it was a triumphal journey even if the central figure did not rise to his own proportions, and the *Tribune* chronicled it faithfully day by day in its news columns. At Pittsburgh Lincoln's remark that "We should do neither more nor less than we gave the people reason to believe we would do when the people gave us their votes,"[134] prompted the *Tribune* editorially to say, "There spoke Old Abe! Honest Old Abe of the West, who means to make good in March what he promised in November."[135] On February 16 at Girard, Ohio, Greeley

---

[132] *Ibid.*, pp. 155–56.

[133] George S. Merriam, *The Life and Times of Samuel Bowles*, I, 318, Samuel Bowles to H. L. Dawes, February 26, 1861.

[134] Nicolay and Hay, *Complete Works*, VI, 126–27.

[135] *Tribune*, February 16, 1861.

unexpectedly boarded the presidential train, "equipped with a valise and his well-known red and blue blankets." He was at once conducted into the car of the President, who came forward to greet him. He got off at Erie after traveling about twenty miles with the company.[136] The interview unfortunately has been lost to history. Two days later as the train bearing Lincoln and his party left Buffalo for Albany, it was reported that "Among the distinguished gentlemen on the train besides those previously reported as accompanying Mr. Lincoln was Horace Greeley of New York."[137] Greeley apparently joined the party again and went as far as Albany.[138]

A committee of the Common Council of New York City journeyed to Albany to present an engrossed invitation to the President-elect and his suite to be the guests of the city during their stay in the metropolis.[139] The whimsical editor of the *Tribune* greeted the city's distinguished guest on the morning of February 20 with a "Card" at the head of the first editorial column, signed "Horace Greeley," in which he took a whack at his own opponents. In the course of this untimely diatribe he harked back, as he had promised not to do, to his support of Bates at Chicago.

It is alleged that I wanted a conservative for President in 1860. What I wanted was that candidate who being inflexibly opposed to Slavery Extension, could poll the largest vote, and whose nomination would most effectually repel the calumny that the Republican is a sectional party. I still believe that Mr. Bates was that man[140]—that he would have secured thousands of votes which were actually cast against us, and that disunion could have made no headway against a President who has always resided below the slave line, and is very widely esteemed and confided in at the South as well as in the North. I sought that man by whom the Republican principle could most surely and with least convulsion be established; there are some who seem to regard the principle only as a means of advancing the fortunes of their man. When assured that Mr. Lincoln was as available as I knew him to be worthy, I went heartily for him.

In a parallel column, as if to atone for this exhibition of bad manners, he called the city's guest the "Champion, Defender and Friend" of the people.

Greeley must have followed the presidential suite to Washington, for

---

[136] *Ibid.*, February 18, 1861.
[137] *Ibid.*, February 19, 1861.
[138] *Ibid.*, February 20, 1861.
[139] *Ibid.*, February 18, 1861.
[140] Emphasis on the matter in roman type is by the present author.

on February 28, we find him writing his friend Brockway from the capital city: "My friend, let us be patient. Old Abe is honest as the sun and means to be true and faithful; but he is in the web of very cunning spiders and cannot break out if he would. Mrs. Abe is a Kentuckyian and enjoys flattery."[141]

One of the "cunning spiders" Greeley had in mind was Seward, the prospective Secretary of State. On the very morning of Inauguration Day, Lincoln was engaged in preventing Seward from taking the "first trick."[142] Just before the inauguration, Lincoln dispatched a note to Seward politely but firmly requesting him to countermand the withdrawal he had sent the President-elect only two days before.[143] With this new development and his inaugural address on his mind, not to mention the inaugural ball and the agony of his new white kid gloves, it is doubtful whether Lincoln found time that day to scan the editorial page of the *Tribune*.

We do not expect to approve every act, much less every appointment of the new Administration. We expect to have every reason to dissent from some of its views and demur to certain of its acts; and we shall, if we see cause, express that dissent with entire frankness. But the men whom we did our best to elect can never forfeit our confidence nor incur our hostility so long as they shall remain faithful to the noble Platform on which they were nominated and elected. Let us all at this auspicious moment give it fresh and careful reading. [Here followed in full the Republican Platform adopted at the Wigwam Convention.]

That the new President will steer his course by this chart, we cannot doubt; and though storm and darkness envelop the outset of the voyage we joyfully predict that its progress will be successful and its close glorious. And so with a hearty good will, we bid him God-Speed.

The inaugural address prepared in "a dingy, dusty, and neglected back room"[144] over a store across the street from the Statehouse at Springfield had been printed before the journey to Washington began, and Lincoln's careful guarding of it accounts in no little part for his failure to rise to his own level in his other speeches on the way. Certain minor changes were made in it at the suggestion of Orville H. Browning and Seward, and one or two fundamental points of view were modified

---

[141] Greeley Papers, Library of Congress, *op. cit.*, Greeley to Beman Brockway, February 28, 1861.

[142] Clarence Edward Macartney, *Lincoln and His Cabinet*, pp. 126–27.

[143] Nicolay and Hay, *Complete Works*, VI, 185.

[144] Herndon and Weik, *op. cit.*, III, 478.

on Seward's advice; but it was delivered substantially as its author intended it should be.[145]

It was indeed a dramatic scene on the east portico of the Capitol at noon on March 4, 1861. Buchanan was there to release his feeble hold on a government he had well-nigh turned over to the secessionists. Chief Justice Taney was there to administer the oath of office to Lincoln. Douglas was there to hold the President's hat. And Greeley was there, sitting just behind the President as the inaugural was delivered, as he said afterward, "on a bright, warm, still March day, expecting to hear its delivery arrested by the crack of rifle aimed at his heart; but it pleased God to postpone the deed, though there was forty times the reason for shooting him in 1860 that there was in '65, and at least forty times as many intent on killing or having him killed. No shot was then fired, however; for his hour had not yet come."[146]

The next day the North breathed easier, and Greeley passed a fair judgment on the inaugural.

It is marked by no useless words and no feeble expression: "he who runs may read it," and to twenty millions of people it will carry the tidings, glad or not, as the case may be, that the Federal Government of the United States is still in existence with a Man at the head of it. . . .

The address cannot fail to exercise a happy influence upon the country. The tone of almost tenderness with which the South is called upon to return to her allegiance, cannot fail to convince even those who differ from Mr. Lincoln that he earnestly and seriously desires to avoid all difficulty and disturbance, while the firmness with which he avows his determination to obey the simple letter of his duty, must command the respect of the whole country, while it carried conviction of his earnestness of purpose, and of his courage to enforce it.

A fuller analysis of "Mr. Lincoln's Address," in a later issue of the *Tribune*, left nothing to be desired.[147] The high character of the document met with universal satisfaction; its sagacity was as striking as its courage. It acknowledged and proclaimed the "dry legal obligation" of fulfilling all that the Constitution required as regarded slavery. The declaration that the policy of the government was not to be fixed irrevocably by the Supreme Court, to which the Constitution gave no political power, was as sound common sense as it was good law.

---

[145] Nicolay and Hay, *Abraham Lincoln*, III, 317–44.

[146] Greeley, *Recollections*, p. 404. See also Mearns, *op. cit.*, Greeley to Herndon, December 26, 1860.

[147] *Tribune*, March 6, 1861.

The editorial in the *Tribune* continued, highly laudatory in tone,

But it is in the admirable treatment of the Secession question that Mr. Lincoln is most entitled to the gratitude of the country, and must certainly, it seems to us, command the support of all good citizens. The duty of the head of the Government to assert the rights of the Government itself is so self-evident a truth that the truth of the corollary is no less so—that those will be guilty of commencing civil war, if any shall arise, who shall attempt to hinder the Federal Government from occupying its own property. The avowal of his purpose, in this regard, is unequivocal, unhesitating, firm, and earnest. One thing only can be understood from it—he means to execute the laws. But as there is no hesitation, so there is no haste; and the firmness of his purpose is tempered by mercy. He means evidently to provoke no unnecessary hostilities, and only where his duty is perfectly clear to protect the rights of the whole will he assert the authority of the Federal Government. If in the interior of the Southern States foolish people will not permit the presence of Federal officers, they will be permitted to do without them, as they only are the losers; but where revenue is to be collected which belongs to the whole people, or where forts are to be reoccupied which no more belong to the section where they happen to be than they do to the people of the most distant corner of the Union, then the laws must be executed, and the power of the Federal Government asserted. But time, no doubt, will be given to the unhappy people, betrayed by an imbecile Government into excesses which four months ago they never contemplated, to return to their allegiance, and restore the property of which they have possessed themselves under a lamentable delusion.

The clearness with which the President states his position on this point is as remarkable as its firmness, and so persuaded will the country be that it is a wise plan, and that it is a plan which must confine all further disturbances to a few localities in settling the differences with the South, and that no disastrous consequences will follow it to any of the interests of the country, that we predict that the people will now turn to their several affairs, the mechanic to his craft, the farmer to his plow, the merchant to his merchandise, all men to their usual callings, satisfied that they may safely leave the question in the hands of one perfectly able to manage it, who will bring order out of seeming chaos, reason out of folly, safety out of danger, and that in so doing he will not sacrifice the national honor or jeopard any of the national interests.

As the "voyage" began, enveloped in "storm and darkness," to all appearances, at least, Lincoln and Greeley were disposed to chart almost identical courses. They subscribed unreservedly to the "noble Platform." They were uncompromisingly against the extension of slavery. They had no purpose to interfere with it in the states where it existed. They recognized the "dry legal obligation" of according it the protection the Constitution gave it. They favored the enforcement of the Fugitive Slave Law—at least Greeley thought at times he did, though he was beginning to talk about "letting every man catch his own slaves."[148] They refused to recognize the Dred Scott decision as determining or fixing a rule of political action. They believed that no state could lawfully leave the Union without the consent of the others. They believed that the President should live up to his oath of office and firmly enforce the laws; they were ready and willing, however, to practice patience and forbearance and to take every possible step to avoid hostilities. If they now differed at all basically, it was in their conception of the significance of the Union and the importance of its maintenance. Lincoln held the Union to be perpetual and put its preservation above all else. Greeley in his love of peace, his fear of war, his hatred of slavery, was not so sure of the beneficence of the Union. The burdens of the nation were now on the shoulders of the President. It remains to be seen how far the editor aided and supported him.

They were grievously wrong—these two eager, honest, patriotic, liberty-loving, peace-loving men—in their common assumption that the new Administration with its firm procedures, its honest purposes, its considerate dealing, could and would bring "order out of chaos, reason out of folly, safety out of danger" without war and without sacrifice of national honor. With all their interest in the "durable question of the age," their close contact with their fellows and their capacity to judge men and events, they did not yet sense the force and passion and determination of the Rebellion. Six weeks from the day when Greeley had "joyfully" predicted a "successful" and "glorious voyage"[149] and Lincoln had held out the olive branch to the South with the words, "We are not enemies, but friends,"[150] the President called on "the Militia of the several States of the Union to the aggregate number of 75,000" to control "combinations too powerful to be suppressed by the ordinary course of judicial proceedings, or by the powers vested in the marshals by law" and "to cause the laws to be duly executed."[151]

Looking back upon these historic days seven years later, Greeley was able to see that Lincoln's "faith in reason" had been misplaced, but, living always in the convictions and judgments of the day of his pro-

---

[148] *Ibid.*, February 22, 1861.
[149] *Ibid.*, March 4, 1861.
[150] Nicolay and Hay, *Complete Works*, VI, 185.
[151] *Ibid.*, pp. 246–47.

nouncements, he was wholly unable to recall that he had adopted and applauded Lincoln's views as the "voyage" began. He truthfully and guilelessly penned these words in 1868: "Mr. Lincoln entered Washington the victim of a grave delusion. A genial, quiet, essentially peaceful man, trained in the ways of the bar and the stump, he fully believed that there would be no civil war,—no serious effort to consummate Disunion. His faith in Reason as a moral force was so implicit that he did not cherish a doubt that his Inaugural Address, whereon he had bestowed much thought and labor, would, when read throughout the South, dissolve the Confederacy as frost is dissipated by a vernal sun."[152]

---

[152] Greeley, *Recollections*, p. 404.

It is now recommended that you give the legal means for making this contest a short and decisive one: that you place at the control of the government for the work at least four hundred thousand men and $400,000,000.

Lincoln[1]

Instead of energy, vigor, promptness, daring, decision, we had in our councils weakness, irresolution, hesitation, delay.

Greeley[2]

7 Forward to Richmond

"Lincoln is slow as molasses in making up his mind," said Miss Tarbell, in an interview in 1937 two days before her eightieth birthday, to a reporter of the *New York Herald Tribune,* "but when he has thought things out, his ideas are always sound. He knows things have to be worked out gradually and that you cannot bring about reform by ukase."[3]

"He thought the world might be reformed in a day—in his day," wrote Beman Brockway in 1891 of his old friend, Greeley. "When a thing was to be done, his idea was that it was to be done now—this very day and hour."[4]

This temperamental difference between Lincoln and Greeley, basic in their personal contacts and in their approach to public issues, accounts perhaps for the lack of any warmth or cordiality of feeling between them and for their inability to see certain things alike. The "irrepressible conflict," come to a head, was bound to find them taking radically different points of view.

The President found on his desk at nine o'clock on the morning of

---

[1] John G. Nicolay and John Hay, eds., *Complete Works of Abraham Lincoln,* VI, 311.
[2] Horace Greeley, *Recollections of a Busy Life,* p. 403.
[3] *New York Herald Tribune,* November 3, 1937.
[4] Beman Brockway, *Fifty Years in Journalism,* pp. 152–53.

his first working day in office the countermanding of the withdrawal he had asked his prospective Secretary of State to send him!

March 5, 1861

My Dear Sir: Deferring to your opinions and wishes as expressed in your letter of yesterday, and in our conversation of last evening, I withdraw my letter to you of the 2d instant, and remain, with great respect and esteem,

Your most obedient servant,
WILLIAM H. SEWARD[5]

The President of the United States.

At twelve noon on that day John G. Nicolay, one of Lincoln's secretaries, carried the President's nominations for his Cabinet to the Senate, then convened in extra session.[6] Lincoln was, it is true, ordinarily "slow as molasses." Yet on Wednesday, November 7, 1860, the day after his election, he had "made up" his Cabinet, and it was substantially the same as the one he submitted to the Senate on March 5, 1861.[7] Although during the intervening four months he had deliberately sought the advice and suggestion of various political leaders on the composition of the Cabinet and was besieged by the friends of aspirants, he remained unmoved by the public clamor which took place. Seward, Chase, Bates, Welles, and Blair, it may fairly be said, were his own choice. Cameron and Smith were to some extent forced on him by the commitments made by his friends at the Wigwam Convention; and, strangely enough, they were the first to go.

The battle for a place in the Cabinet centered around Seward and Chase. Weed was for Seward; Greeley greatly favored Chase[8] and was assumed to be violently opposed to Seward.[9] Greeley stoutly denied, however, that he had at any time opposed the choice of Seward; and his own record, at least, sustains his contention. Early in January, when it was known that Lincoln had proffered the portfolio of Secretary of State to Seward and when there were rumors afloat that he would decline, Greeley said: "We sincerely trust that he will not decline. There are few men in the country who could conduct its foreign relations with the ability, dignity and tact which Mr. Seward would bring to the duty."

---

[5] John G. Nicolay and John Hay, *Abraham Lincoln—A History*, III, 372.
[6] *Ibid.*
[7] Edgar T. Welles, ed., *The Diary of Gideon Welles*, with an introduction by John T. Morse, Jr., I, 82.
[8] *Tribune*, January 5, 1861.
[9] Ralph Ray Fahrney, *Horace Greeley and the Tribune*, pp. 68–70. See also Henry B. Stanton, *Random Recollections*, pp. 220–22.

There was talk of Greeley as Postmaster General. The wife of a newly elected judge of the Superior Court in New York City on the Republican ticket wrote Lincoln saying that she and her husband were warm personal friends of Mr. Greeley, calling attention to his "unwearied and faithful labors during this last campaigne," and indicating that his friends were looking for a place for him in the Cabinet. "It will cause *great disappointment*," she said, "should he not receive a favor worthy of his acceptance. He is a man who will never approach or present the slightest claim himself, his sensitive, high-minded pride will prevent him from doing so, but I do not know a man who better understands what should be recognized by the Higher powers as due to him."[10]

After the nominations had been confirmed, Greeley was still being taken to task by his contemporaries for his opposition to Seward and declared: "The *Tribune* promptly and heartily approved the selection of Gov. Seward for the State Department. It early and sincerely offered to support his reelection to the Senate, while it was understood that Mr. S. would take no appointment. It never in any manner opposed his selection for the Cabinet or for whatever post under President Lincoln he might choose to accept. . . ." Greeley was openly and frankly at war with Weed, and, in this connection, expressed the hope that "our good friends who protest our warring upon the [*Albany Evening*] *Journal* will allow us this liberty."[11]

That the editor was not craftily distinguishing between the declarations of his paper and his own personal conduct and attitude is shown by a subsequent statement, over his own name, in the *Tribune*, in which he said: "I am charged with having opposed the selection of Governor Seward for a place in President Lincoln's Cabinet. That is utterly, absolutely false, the President himself being my witness. I might call many others, but one such is sufficient."[12]

Color was given to the widespread belief that Greeley was maneuvering to keep Seward out of the Cabinet by his unhesitating opposition to Seward's efforts at conciliation and compromise with the South.[13] Greeley was disposed to rush to the defense of his own ideas and to grow feverish in abstract argument, but his shafts were rarely aimed at or intended for the individual who questioned his views. He was quite capable, therefore, of deeming Seward fitted to be Secretary of State

---

[10] David C. Mearns, ed., *The Abraham Lincoln Papers*, II, 341–42, Mrs. Rhoda E. White to Lincoln, December 15, 1860.

[11] *Tribune*, March 13, 1861.

[12] *Ibid.*, July 25, 1861.

[13] *Ibid.*, February 9, 1861.

while he was severely criticizing his conduct in the Senate. His criticism of Seward shortly before and promptly after the inauguration made it doubly difficult at the time for anyone to believe that he was willing to see Seward in the Cabinet. Thus the week before the inauguration, with uncanny accuracy, in the light of Seward's subsequent conduct during the month of March, Greeley had pointed out that Seward regarded himself "as the center and soul of the incoming Administration, and Mr. Lincoln as but an ornamental appendage thereto."[14] In this statement there is abundant evidence to show he was voicing the literal truth. Seward was promptly to discover that the President—not the self-styled Premier—was to rule. Greeley thought, contrary to the view held in many high circles that Lincoln would be only a figurehead and would be dominated by his ministers, that it would be more consistent with the genius of the government to consider Lincoln as the head of the incoming Administration and to await the official exposition of his views before other hands should assume to shape his policy.

A few days after the inauguration Greeley took Seward to task again. He insisted that he did not question Seward's motives and purposes; but he was fearful that his policy was fatally mistaken and perilous.[15] Seward's tone demanded explanation. His former square stand on fundamental Republican principles seemed to be forgotten. He was now ignoring the question of extending slavery and addressing himself solely to saving the Union, or so it seemed to Greeley. "It is a good thing to save the Union," said Greeley, "but something more than sentiment is needful to effect that object. If the only policy of Mr. Seward is to save the Union, and if all other questions are as nothing compared with that, why should he not avow that he is willing to yield up all those principles in which he has helped to educate the public mind, and which he has helped to plant in hearts which cannot discard them, for the sake of a Union which will enforce degradation on the North and restore the insolent domination of the South?"[16]

But vastly more important than the nomination and confirmation of a Cabinet, and the question of whether it was or was not satisfactory to the editor of the *Tribune*, was the task to be undertaken by the President and his Cabinet. The day before the inauguration the *Tribune's* celebrated Washington correspondent had penned a letter to his paper in which he graphically and truthfully, and in language quite worthy of

---

[14] *Ibid.*, February 27, 1861.
[15] *Ibid.*, March 8, 1861.
[16] *Ibid.*, March 11, 1861.

his chief, described the situation confronting the new Administration. "Brushing away," he said, "all the treasonable complicities, all the hesitant and trembling imbecilities, all the pernicious and demoralizing dogmas of constitutional interpretation, all the delinquencies of official corruption, and all the purulent influences generated by a noxious social condition, which have so signally and fatally imbued and ruined Mr. Buchanan's administration, the new Government must march boldly to its work."[17]

On the morning of March 5 Lincoln found the first piece of work toward which the government was expected boldly to march. A communication from the War Department brought the disquieting information from Major Robert Anderson that Fort Sumter must be reinforced or abandoned. Recalling the words he had in all honesty and sincerity uttered the day before, "The power confided to me will be used to hold, occupy and possess the property and places belonging to the government, and to collect the duties and imposts," the idea of abandoning Fort Sumter was repugnant to the President.[18] But he had also said, "beyond what may be necessary for these objects, there will be no invasion, no using of force against or among the people anywhere." The conflict between the discharge of his constitutional duty and his disposition to exercise forbearance contributed to the delay which led finally to the surrender of the fort on April 13. The cautious steps the President took to make sure the South should fire the first shot prompted Nicolay and Hay to say that "No act of his will gain him greater credit than his kindly forbearance and patient wisdom in allowing full time and reflection for the ultimate decision at this supreme juncture."[19]

One decision, wholly behind the scenes, came out of these early troubled days, namely, that the President was to control the Administration. Seward had entered upon his duties fully convinced that the guiding hand was to be his. He was vigorously opposed to relieving Fort Sumter and urged its evacuation. Going ahead on his own initiative, as he anticipated doing regularly, he became involved in private conversations with the "Commissioners" from the provisional government at Montgomery, greatly to his own embarrassment and to the dangerous confusion of the President's plans to send provisions to Fort Sumter and reinforcements to Fort Pickens. After he knew definitely that Lin-

---

[17] *Ibid.*, March 6, 1861.
[18] Nicolay and Hay, *Complete Works*, VI, 175–76.
[19] Nicolay and Hay, *Abraham Lincoln*, IV, 63.

coln was determined to send "bread" to Major Anderson, Seward submitted a memorandum to the President on April 1, entitled "Some
Thoughts for the President's Consideration." In this strange document
he insisted that the Administration was yet without a policy, foreign
or domestic; he proposed to change the question before the public from
slavery to union or disunion; he repeated his opposition to relieving
Fort Sumter; and then he made the preposterous declaration that explanations should be sought at once from Great Britain, Russia, Spain,
and France, and that if the two latter governments did not give satisfactory explanations, Congress should be convened and war declared
upon them. He ended this deliberate proposal to take control of the
government with these words: "It is not in my especial province; but I
neither seek to evade nor assume responsibility."[20]

The President's brief answer, made on the same day, determined the
issue between him and his Secretary of State.

*. . . Upon your closing propositions—that "whatever policy we adopt, there
must be an energetic prosecution of it.*

*"For this purpose it must be somebody's business to pursue and direct
it incessantly*

*"Either the President must do it himself, and be all the while active
in it, or*

*"Devolve it on some member of his cabinet. Once adopted debates on
it must end, and all agree and abide"—I remark that if this must be done,
I must do it.[21]*

When Lincoln penned that remark he became President in fact as
well as in title, and Seward's subsequent conduct atoned for his temporary aberration. There is no record that Lincoln ever referred to the
matter again with Seward or that he ever mentioned it to other members of the Cabinet. Seward's memorandum and the President's reply
were tucked away in the files and not brought to light until after the
death of both President and Secretary.

Aside from the sharp eye Greeley kept on Seward—and he was wiser
than he knew in that—Greeley started out with the best of intentions
toward the new Administration. It was very evident, however, that he
was having as much trouble as the President and his Cabinet in getting
bearings for an assured position. He talked almost in the same breath

---

[20] Nicolay and Hay, *Complete Works*, VI, 234–36. See also Kenneth M. Stampp, *And
the War Came*, pp. 170–76, 272–80.
[21] Nicolay and Hay, *Complete Works*, VI, 236–37.

about permitting as many Southern states as wished to withdraw from the Union to do so through a national convention,[22] and about the urgent necessity of the Administration's being prepared "to meet force with force, and maintain the honor and independence of the United States at all hazards."[23] If the means of the government were insufficient to meet the demands put upon it, it was the duty of the President to call an extra session of Congress and ask for the means required.

Two weeks after the inauguration he came to the defense of the Administration when the *Boston Courier* complained of the delay at Washington in establishing order in the country. He humbly submitted to the "superior judgment" of the *Boston Courier* that two weeks or two months, or two years, or even two presidential terms, might not be too long a time in which to restore the Union to a perfectly sound condition. He counseled his Boston contemporary that "the Union to be worth anything must be preserved in its original constitutional vigor," that no "political bolus" could now effect a cure, and that the restoration of the Union was a work requiring "time, labor and thoughtful consideration."

Never able to be "humble" very long in any wrangle with a fellow editor, Greeley dropped the Boston critic to the mat with this blow:

Is it reasonable to expect that President Lincoln and the Republicans should, in two weeks, have made any perceptible progress in restoring what for twenty years the architects of ruin have been employed in undermining? Let us remember that the crash which has come in the last four months was no sudden failure of a single pillar or arch of the Union, due to some inherent weakness or original baseness of material and which, from its limited nature, might be capable, with skill and energy, of a speedy remedy. It is more than twenty years that Southern disorganists, first under the name of Nullifiers, then of Secessionists, then of Cooperationists, next of Democrats, and finally of Unionists, have been diligently and enthusiastically at work sapping the very foundation of the Union.[24]

This attitude was, to be sure, a quick change from the contemplation of a national convention to permit the disaffected states to withdraw from the Union; but this promising evidence of editorial forbearance and patience must have been comforting to the President who on the very day of its utterance was finding his army and navy advisers at loggerheads and his Cabinet against him as to action on Fort Sumter.

[22] *Tribune,* March 12, 1861.
[23] *Ibid.,* March 16, 1861.
[24] *Ibid.,* March 20, 1861.

If Lincoln got any satisfaction from the intimation that the leading Republican journal of the country was resolved to hold up his hands, it was short-lived. Hardly had another two weeks elapsed when out from the *Tribune* editorial sanctum came a thundering demand, "Come to the Point!"

If there be any point on which the opinions of the American People may be said to be substantially unanimous, it is that of impatience with the present state of uncertainty and anarchy, and desire that it should be brought to an end at the earliest moment. Hence the obvious dissatisfaction with the present attitude of the Federal Administration—a discontent which does not imply a belief that the President and his Cabinet are taking, doing or meditating a wrong step, but only that they still consider when they should already have decided, and pause when they ought to act. We do not say that this is right or wise—we simply chronicle an obvious fact. The country, with scarcely a show of dissent, cries out— If we are to fight, so be it; if we are to have peace, so much the better; if the Union can be preserved or restored, good; but, if it cannot be, let us understand the fact and acquiesce in it. At all events, let this intolerable suspense and uncertainty cease! . . .

If the disaffected States—even the so-called Border States, will clearly indicate their willingness to be satisfied with the Constitutional Amendment recently initiated by Congress—that which guards the Slave States, whether they be many or few, against any interference with their domestic institutions by Congress—we will zealously and faithfully commend that proposition to the acceptance of Republicans. If they prefer the calling of a National Convention, with powers limited only by the right of revision by the People, we will go in as heartily for that. . . .

Again we say, Let the Administration, as soon as may be, proclaim its policy, so plainly that it cannot be mistaken. If the Union is to be maintained at all hazards, let the word be passed along the line that the laws are to be enforced, and the People stand ready with heart and hand. If the Secession of the Gulf States—and any more of them that choose to follow— is to be regarded as a fixed fact, let that be proclaimed, and let the line of Revenue collection be established and maintained this side of them. At all events, let us have a clearly defined programme, and let it when once proclaimed, be lived up to. We only ask that it embody no waiting on contingencies, no prolongation of the present suspense, but that it shall be such as will bring matters to a focus at the earliest moment possible.[25]

In between warning the *Boston Courier* to be "Not Quite So Fast" and exercising his own demand upon the Administration to "Come to

---

[25] *Ibid.*, April 3, 1861.

the Point!" Greeley was also dealing in a detailed academic fashion with the vital issue of what should be done about Fort Sumter and Fort Pickens. He held that evacuation of Fort Sumter, as a military necessity, humiliating as it might be, would not be due "to any negligence or feebleness of the present Administration" but would be regarded as "one of the last bitter drops in the cup left in our hands by the Government which has so long weighed us down and which has now hardly passed out of our sight."[26] Without knowing it, Greeley took almost the identical position Lincoln held when he said that the abandonment of Fort Sumter must be justified, if at all, "upon the square, plump, and only tenable ground of want of power to preserve the fort from being captured."[27] Greeley urged that abandonment of Fort Pickens be avoided if possible and that relief be sent to the fort at the time Lincoln already was taking steps to that end.

The very day after Greeley's exhibition of impatience and his insistence that matters be brought to a focus, when it was evident that relief was to be sent to Major Anderson, the *Tribune*—could Greeley have written it?—expressed the belief that the new Administration had done right in hesitating, pausing, considering, taking account of stock before rushing upon the formidable batteries that surrounded Fort Sumter.[28] There seems no doubt, however, that the hand that penned the stirring "Come to the Point" editorial on April 3 also wrote the article on "Military and Naval Movements," published April 6; the same kind of double somersault of which Greeley was so capable is clearly exhibited in both:

Some English traveler in this country once said that the Americans expect everything to be done in twenty minutes. The force of the remark has been strongly illustrated by the recent popular clamor about the inactivity of the present Administration. In their feverish impatience for news the people have forgotten that it is but a single month since Mr. Lincoln and his Cabinet entered upon office, at a period when the whole machinery of Government had become rotten and disorganized, partly through treason, and partly through imbecility. . . .

In four weeks Mr. Lincoln's Administration silently, quietly, without unnecessary alarm has raised the Government from its disorganized, bankrupt state, and put it in condition to face with some degree of efficiency a very formidable rebellion.[29]

[26] *Ibid.*, March 11, 1861.
[27] *Ibid.*, March 16, 1861.
[28] *Ibid.*, April 4, 1861.
[29] *Ibid.*, April 6, 1861.

Following this new editorial viewpoint, the Washington correspondent of the *Tribune* made the discovery that while the Administration had been charged with inertness and the absence of a vigorous policy, it had been prudently preparing measures to meet the exigency and to fortify itself with the necessary resources. When Mr. Lincoln came into office he had found an empty treasury, a demoralized army, and treasonable defection throughout the civil service. And he had had to feel his way into public confidence against a factious opposition and to ascertain the extent of resources at his command before proceeding to carry out the principles announced in his inaugural, which had never been abandoned for an instant.[30] Confirming this view, two days later the Washington correspondent wrote: "It is the opinion of the best and most experienced officers of the Government, that no former Administration, in 30 years, had so quietly and efficiently matured and directed its policy as that now in power."[31]

When word came of the bombardment of Fort Sumter, Greeley repeated the view he had now definitely adopted that the Administration had exhausted concessions while quietly preparing for action; and that no honorable course was left open to the government but to attempt to relieve its heroic garrison at all hazards.[32] On Monday, April 15, the *Tribune* published at the head of its first editorial column the President's proclamation calling for 75,000 militia and convening Congress in extra session; and the editor declared: "Fort Sumter is lost, but Freedom is saved. . . . Live the Republic!"

Catching the prevailing war fever at once, Greeley took the view that the chief business of the American people for the year must be to prove "that they have a Government and that Freedom is not another name for Anarchy."[33] Always serene in his confidence in his own position, he did not hesitate to offer immediate advice to the Administration: he would raise the President's call from 75,000 to a "Half Million" at once; he would make a "patriotic loan" of $100,000,000 and send to Europe, for delivery within thirty days, for 100,000 firearms and for 1,000 "choice" field guns.[34] Blithely he declared, "We will not undertake to

---

[30] *Ibid.*, April 8, 1861.

[31] *Ibid.*, April 10, 1861.

[32] *Ibid.*, April 13, 1861. For detailed discussion of Sumter, see Avery O. Craven, *The Coming of the Civil War*; David M. Potter, *Lincoln and His Party in the Secession Crisis*; and Stampp, *op. cit.*

[33] *Tribune*, April 17, 1861.

[34] *Ibid.*, April 22, 1861.

say what the Government should do at this juncture," and then proceeded in the same breath to lay down a six-point policy.

> *First, Military occupancy of Maryland.*
>
> *Second, Advance upon Richmond and the armed holding of that city.*
>
> *Third, Military occupancy of Norfolk, Charleston, Savannah, Mobile and New Orleans.*
>
> *Fourth, the proclamation of martial law in all the rebellious States.*
>
> *Fifth, the offering of large rewards for the arrest of Jefferson Davis and his conspirators.*
>
> *Sixth, their trial and execution under martial law.*[35]

The President had only to ask for "men and money" to carry out this "bold policy" and was warned: "The man who knows wisely how to take at the flood this tide in our affairs, now sweeping on toward its hight [*sic*], will identify his name forever with the glory of the country he will help to achieve; while, if he miss it and suffer the safety and character of the country to be stranded by its ebb, he will be swept away in the depths of oblivion, if not of infamy. But the country will survive."

The busy editor also took time to offer "practical suggestions" for the benefit of the Quartermaster General. Everything should contribute to the efficiency, comfort, and ability of the individual soldier; bright-colored scarfs, belts, sashes, etc. should be avoided; flannel underwear should be provided for the soldiers but not red; target practice should be frequent; soldiers should be lightly loaded on march; Minié rifles with sword bayonets were preferable; the cavalry and the artillery should be greatly increased; women should provide flannels and socks, lint and bandages.[36]

By the middle of June, Greeley was talking about "A Short War" but had reached the conclusion that the contest could not be finished "during the summer solstice." During the hot weather he would be content with the blockading of the rebel ports and the dispersing of the "armed traitors" in the states lying along the Potomac, the Ohio, and the upper Mississippi. The hot months over, the government should be ready to move "heavy columns" along the Atlantic Coast, through the central regions, and down the Mississippi valley; and "the war should be closed in triumph within one year from the time it was commenced."[37]

---

[35] *Ibid.*, May 2, 1861.
[36] *Ibid.*, May 12, 1861.
[37] *Ibid.*, June 19, 1861.

For two months after the fall of Sumter, Greeley was alternately sympathetic with the Administration and appreciative of its tremendous problems, severely critical of it, patient and forbearing, restive and insistent upon action. The President's call for 75,000 militia had hardly reached the governors of the states before Greeley was insisting that "long-abused credulity" should give way to "awakened energy," and ironically warning "good Uncle Abe" about the danger of reading "another essay" to the secessionists proving that he never meant them any harm. He was also warning Secretary Seward about delivering "another oration" to them on the glories and blessings of the Union. Essays and orations would have to be promptly promulgated, for Jefferson Davis and Henry A. Wise would soon be capturing Washington and would not delay hanging the President and his Secretary of State "ten minutes for any manner of nonsense." The country should be advised forthwith if the Administration had not yet packed its trunk.[38]

Old-time adjectives, employed upon other occasions, came into play again. The President and Mr. Seward endeavored to deal discreetly with Governor Hicks's request that Northern troops be excluded from Maryland and his suggestion that Lord Lyons, British Minister at Washington, should be asked to act as mediator between the Washington and the Montgomery governments. Greeley railed at the audacity, the "sublimity of impudence" of "this sniveling, whiffling traitor" in daring to address the President at all. The answer to Governor Hicks should have been "through the guns of Fort McHenry." And to the "Men in Power in Washington!" he thundered, "the loyal States look to you for words of cheer—words replete with the dignity of conscious justice and strength—in this our Country's hour of deadly peril. Better that you had never been born than that they should thus look in vain."[39]

New York merchants deemed talk about using troops for the protection of the capital as "pedantic twaddle."[40] The pugnacious editor was ready to obliterate Baltimore. "If the passage of our armies be disputed over our own highways," he said, "and if Senators of the United States have to steal away privily to escape being torn in pieces by the inhabitants of Baltimore, the sooner that city be burned with fire and leveled to the earth, and made an abode for owls and satyrs, and a place for fishermen to dry their nets, the better."[41]

---

[38] *Ibid.*, April 22, 1861.
[39] *Ibid.*, April 25, 1861.
[40] *Ibid.*, April 26, 1861.
[41] *Ibid.*, May 2, 1861.

The evolution of the shift from a kindly, judicial attitude to a carping, fault-finding view in the editorial office of the *Tribune*, in these early days of the Administration, may perhaps best be demonstrated by presenting in parallel columns extracts from two editorials appearing in May:

May 2, 1861	May 16, 1861
Defensive Warfare	*Sham Unionism*

Who of us expected that sublime unanimity of the Northern People in rallying around their insulted flag? Why should we require of Mr. Lincoln a more prophetic spirit than we possessed ourselves? That the imminence and the magnitude of the Crisis at hand was not generally apprehended, we think is very clear from the neglect of the late Congress to invest the President with the power and means necessary to meet it. At the time of the Inauguration, the public opinion of the country, always sluggish to change its direction or to increase its force, was not in advance of the doctrines of the Inaugural. A defensive policy, the protection of the places and property of the Government, and the recovery of such as had been wrested from it, and the collection of the revenue, was all the issue the North was then ready to make up with the South.

History will blame the new Administration that it seemed to yield a passive, negative assent to this state of things even for an hour. It had no business, no right to do so. The Proclamation which it postponed for six weeks should have been prepared beforehand, and issued the very day of its accession to power. To relieve the beleaguered forts and vindicate the authority of the Union in the rebellious states was a work of time, the Government having been treacherously disarmed and disabled by the late Cabinet, but the Proclamation of April 15th ought to have appeared on the morning of March 5th, and been promptly followed by the most decisive action. The Government hesitated, temporized, waited, forbearing for a month even to attempt the relief of sorely-pressed Sumter.

While Greeley was alternately counseling patience and urging decisive action, the President was tremendously occupied with minor issues, the petty concerns of office absorbing his time and energy even more than the high affairs of state. Nicolay and Hay graphically described the conditions under which Lincoln worked in these trying days:

The city was full of strangers; the White House full of applicants from the North. At any hour of the day one might see at the outer door and on

*the staircase, one line going, one coming. In the anteroom and in the broad
corridor adjoining the President's office there was a restless and persistent
crowd,—ten, twenty, sometimes fifty, varying with the day and hour,—each
one in pursuit of one of the many crumbs of official patronage. They walked
the floor; they talked in groups; they scowled at every arrival and blessed
every departure; they wrangled with the door-keepers for the right of en-
trance; they intrigued with them for surreptitious chances; they crowded
forward to get even as much as an instant's glance through the half-opened
door into the Executive chamber. They besieged the Representatives and
Senators who had privilege of precedence; they glared with envy at the
Cabinet Ministers who, by right and usage, pushed through the throng and
walked unquestioned through the doors. At that day the arrangement of
the rooms compelled the President to pass through this corridor and the
midst of the throng when he went to his meals at the other end of the
Executive Mansion; and thus, once or twice a day, the waiting expectants
would be rewarded by the chance of speaking a word, or handing a paper
direct to the President himself—a chance which the more bold and persistent were not slow to improve.*[42]

If it was not the postmastership of Cleveland or Providence which
harassed the President, it was the embarrassing application from
"Cousin Lizzie" for that office in Springfield. If it was not the Pawnee
Indian Agency which took a forenoon, it was the vacancy in the super-
vising inspectorship of steamboats in the district of Baltimore. If it
was not an appraisership in New York City which kept him awake at
night, it was a land office job in the far West. The high office of the
"Superintending Architect of the Treasury Department connected with
the Bureau of Construction" also took the President's time. It was held
"by a man by the name of Young, and wanted by a gentleman by the
name of Christopher Adams." In a letter to Secretary Chase, Lincoln
inquired, "Ought Mr. Young to be removed, and if yea, ought Mr.
Adams to be appointed? Mr. Adams is magnificently recommended;
but the great point in his favor is that Thurlow Weed and Horace Greeley join in recommending him. I suppose the like never happened before, and never will again; so that it is now or never. What say you?"[43]

Larger issues pressed in upon the President constantly. The appointment of George P. Marsh as minister to Sardinia and of Anson Burlingame to Austria gave him as much concern as the appointment of
Minister Charles F. Adams to England and Minister William L. Dayton to France. To Secretary Seward, Lincoln wrote:

---

[42] Nicolay and Hay, *Abraham Lincoln*, IV, 68–69.
[43] Nicolay and Hay, *Complete Works*, VI, 268–69, Lincoln to Chase, May 8, 1861.

*These gentlemen all have my highest esteem but no one of them is orig-
inally suggested by me except Mr. Dayton. Mr. Adams I take because you
suggested him, coupled with his eminent fitness for the place. Mr. Marsh
and Mr. Burlingame because of the intense pressure of their respective
States, and their fitness also. The objection to this card is that locally they
are so huddled up—three being in New England and two from a single
State. I have considered this and will not shrink from the responsibility.
This, being done, leaves but five full missions undisposed of—Rome, China,
Brazil, Peru, and Chili. And then what about Carl Schurz; or, in other
words, what about our German friends? Shall we put this card through, and
arrange the rest afterward? What say you?*[44]

Not so important but equally disturbing were the conflicting desires
of "Mr. Senator King" and "Mr. Speaker Grow" for patronage. Lincoln
was put to it to "find a place for each a man."[45]

But finding places to satisfy congressmen, governors, and other political leaders was not as trying as the shaping of national policies and of
relations with foreign nations. Even before Lincoln's ministers reached
England and France, it became evident that these powers were disposed
to favor the South. Before Minister Adams reached London, the British
Minister of Foreign Affairs, Lord John Russell, had received representatives of the Southern Confederacy unofficially, and upon Adams' arrival
he found that Queen Victoria's proclamation of neutrality had been
published, raising the Confederacy to the position of a belligerent
power.

Secretary Seward framed the first draft of the response of the United
States government to this action. Seward had apparently not yet learned
fully that "the President is the best of us," for the language he used was
ill-advised and calculated to make a wider breach between the Federal
government and England and France, if not indeed to lead to war. Lincoln's alterations in the dispatch show the wisdom and timeliness of
his intervention and the basic quality of his statesmanship.[46] In spite of
all these vital problems, Lincoln found time to write a letter of condo-
lence to the parents of Colonel Ellsworth, closing with the words: "May
God give you that consolation which is beyond all earthly power. Sincerely your friend in a common affliction, A. Lincoln."[47]

In his proclamation on April 15, 1861, calling 75,000 militia, the
President also called an extra session of Congress to meet on July 4

[44] *Ibid.*, p. 223, Lincoln to Seward, March 18, 1861.
[45] *Ibid.*, pp. 329–30.
[46] *Ibid.*, pp. 277–86.
[47] *Ibid.*, pp. 287–88.

"then and there to consider and determine such measures as, in their wisdom, the public interest and safety may demand."[48] As the time approached for the extra session, urgent demand for decisive action against the Rebels had developed throughout the North. Lincoln was importuned by Northern governors to move against the enemy, and the Northern press clamored for action. As late as June 23, however, the *Tribune* had counseled that the campaign should be prosecuted with energy but that no forward step should be taken that would have to be retracted. Following upon the heels of this wise caution, the *Tribune* came out on June 26 with this startling announcement at the top of the second column of the editorial page:

THE NATION'S WAR-CRY

Forward to Richmond.   *Forward to Richmond!*
The Rebel Congress must not be allowed to meet there on the 20th of July. BY THAT DATE THE PLACE MUST BE HELD BY THE NATIONAL ARMY.

This war cry was carried in each issue of the *Tribune* up to the day that Congress met. While it undoubtedly voiced the prevailing and overwhelming view of the North, there is no direct evidence that its publication changed or especially influenced the action of the government. "The President and his advisers," recorded Nicolay and Hay, "comprehended the necessity of meeting the just expectations of the free States, of sustaining the popular enthusiasm which had filled the three months' quota of volunteers, and to which they looked for a like completion of the projected three years' army."[49]

On June 29, less than a week before Congress was to assemble, Lincoln called his Cabinet and the principal military officers into conference upon what immediate steps should be taken.[50] It was decided to undertake a campaign against the Rebels at Manassas. Scott, the infirm but doughty old General-in-Chief, was opposed to the movement. He was against war by "piecemeal." He had previously urged a carefully planned campaign down the Mississippi River in the autumn and winter, coupled with the blockade of the Eastern seaports in an over-all enveloping of the South. This plan had been widely condemned by the press and came to be known as "Scott's Anaconda."[51] The old Gen-

---

[48] *Ibid.*, pp. 247–48.
[49] Nicolay and Hay, *Abraham Lincoln*, IV, 321. See also William B. Hesseltine, *Lincoln and the War Governors*, pp. 115–35.
[50] Nicolay and Hay, *Abraham Lincoln*, IV, 322–23.
[51] *Ibid.*, pp. 298–307.

eral was overruled by the President and his Cabinet, but he loyally gave his approval and support to the plan for immediate action advanced by General McDowell.

In the last few days of June, with his mind filled with plans for an immediate mass movement of troops against the enemy, one wonders how Lincoln found time to prepare his message to Congress. No ghost writer touched it. In every line it is Lincolnesque in simplicity, in directness, and in the calm, judicial approach which mainly characterized his public utterances throughout his presidency.

In a matter-of-fact way he first discussed the existing situation, the suspension of the functions of the Federal government by the Southern states, the seizure by them of government property, the Fort Sumter incident which left the government no choice but to call out the war power. He explained the call for militia and for volunteers, and declared that these measures, whether strictly legal or not, were ventured upon under what appeared to be a popular demand and a public necessity, with the expectation that Congress would readily ratify them. He also explained at length the necessity for the suspension of the writ of habeas corpus and justified such action under the express terms of the Constitution.

Lincoln then frankly pointed out that the South had invented the sophism that any state of the Union may consistently with the national Constitution, and therefore lawfully and peacefully, withdraw from the Union without the consent of the Union or of any other state. Sovereignty he defined as a political community without a political superior and repeated the view he had often expressed before that the states have their status in the Union and that they have no other status.

Looking forward confidently to the suppression of the Rebellion, Lincoln deemed it proper to say that it "would be his purpose then, as ever, to be guided by the Constitution and the laws." Thus he refused to recognize secession and held out the olive branch to the Southern states as he had in the inaugural address. A paragraph in this great document has not had the attention it deserves from the historians and biographers. It reads:

Our popular government has often been called an experiment. Two points in it our people have already settled—the successful establishing and the successful administering of it. One still remains—its successful maintenance against a formidable internal attempt to overthrow it. It is now for them to demonstrate to the world that those who can fairly carry an election can also suppress a rebellion; that ballots are the rightful and peaceful successors of bullets; and that when ballots have fairly and con-stitutionally decided there can be no successful appeal back to bullets; that there can be no successful appeal, except to ballots themselves, at succeed-ing elections. Such will be a great lesson of peace: teaching men that what they cannot take by an election, neither can they take it by a war; teaching all the folly of being the beginners of a war.[52]

The *Tribune* printed the message in full on July 6 and editorially said:

This Message eschews episodes and circumlocution, and goes straight to the work. Not a sentence in it bespeaks the phrase-monger. It gushes out from the earnest heart of the author, and goes straight to the hearts of the patriotic millions. Utterly devoid of rhetorical embellishment and official reserve, its positions will be comprehended and its arguments appreciated by every rational mind. . . .

We have on hand the simple business of crushing out the great rebellion, and we trust every care will be taken that it be not complicated with any other. No compromise with Treason; but the most energetic efforts for its suppression! such is the National duty and the National will. We rejoice to find the President so emphatically faithful to the one and so responsive to the other.

Perhaps no condensed statement has since better epitomized the life and service of Lincoln. Greeley was right. Lincoln was faithful to na-tional duty and responsive to the national will. Greeley spoke better than he knew. His subsequent treatment of Lincoln on many occasions might have been more considerate and just if he had kept constantly in mind his own splendid characterization of the troubled President.

The advance of the Federal forces planned by Lincoln and his ad-visers before Congress assembled culminated in the disaster of Bull Run on July 21. Twenty-five years after this memorable event, Nicolay and Hay were able to fix the responsibilities of government and com-manders with "easy precision."

When Lincoln, on June 29, assembled his council of war, the com-manders, as military experts, correctly decided that the existing armies— properly handled—could win a victory at Manassas and a victory at Win-chester, at or near the same time. General Scott correctly objected that these victories, if won, would not be decisive; and that in a military point of view it would be wiser to defer any offensive campaign until the following

---

[52] Nicolay and Hay, *Complete Works*, VI, 297–325. See also J. G. Randall, *Constitu-tional Problems Under Lincoln*, pp. 51–59.

autumn. Here the President and the Cabinet, as political experts, inter-
vened, and on their part decided, correctly, that the public temper would
not admit of such delay. Thus the Administration was responsible for the
forward movement, Scott for the combined strategy of the two armies,
McDowell for the conduct of the Bull Run battle, Patterson for the escape
of Johnston, and Fate for the panic; for the opposing forces were equally
raw, equally undisciplined, and as a whole fought the battle with equal
courage and gallantry.[53]

Confusion, dismay, and alarm at the time prompted efforts to find a
scapegoat. The second day after the battle the *Tribune* charged the
"shipwreck of our grand and heroic army" squarely to the Administration, confessed its inability to conjecture what apology the government
could offer "to the humiliated and astounded country," declared that
whatever apology might be offered would "be found altogether insufficient and unsatisfactory," and demanded "the immediate retirement
of the present Cabinet from the high places of power, which, for one
reason or another, they have shown themselves incompetent to fill."[54]

Greeley's contemporaries in New York City, especially Henry J. Raymond of the *Times*[55] and James Gordon Bennett of the *Herald*, turned
the tables on him and insisted that he was himself responsible for the
debacle by goading the Administration to premature action through
the "Forward to Richmond" war cry in the *Tribune*. Both Raymond
and Bennett branded the "Forward to Richmond" slogan as "insane"
clamor; Raymond announced the "retirement of General Greeley"
and Bennett wrote of "Massa Greeley in a flood of tears."[56] The press
widely adopted this monstrous charge, and soon poor Greeley was put
on the rack. It did not suffice that it was promptly shown that the celebrated war cry had been written by Fitz-Henry Warren, then Washington correspondent of the *Tribune*, and placed on the editorial page,
in Greeley's absence, by Charles A. Dana, the managing editor.[57] Nor
did Greeley's immediate protestation that he was not responsible for
the war cry and did not approve of it and that he did not write the editorial criticizing the Administration and calling for the retirement of
the Cabinet quiet the clamor.

Greeley was deeply distressed and departed from his usual practice

---

[53] Nicolay and Hay, *Abraham Lincoln*, IV, 360.
[54] *Tribune*, July 23, 1861.
[55] *New York Times*, July 23, 25, 26, 30; August 2, 1861.
[56] *New York Herald*, July 23, 24, 25, 26, 1861. See also Robert S. Harper, *Lincoln and the Press*, pp. 100–06.
[57] Henry Luther Stoddard, *Horace Greeley, Printer, Editor, Crusader*, pp. 213–15.

by answering his critics in the *Tribune* over his own signature on July 25. In the course of a long article entitled "Just Once" he said:

> It is true—I have no desire to conceal or belittle it—that my ideas as to the general conduct of the War for the Union are those repeatedly expressed by myself and others through THE TRIBUNE, and of course are not those on which the conduct of that war has been based. It is true that I hold and have urged that this war cannot, must not, be a long one—that it must be prosecuted with the utmost energy, promptness and vigor, or it will prove a failure—that every week's flying of the Secession flag defiantly within a day's walk of Washington renders the suppression of the revolt more difficult if not doubtful. It is true that I think a Government that begins the work of putting down a rebellion by forming "camps of instruction," or anything of that sort, is likely to make a very long job of it. It is true that I think our obvious policy, under the circumstances, would have been to be courteous and long-suffering toward foreign powers but resolute and ready in our dealings with armed rebels; and it seems to me the opposite course has been taken. But the watchword "Forward to Richmond!" is not mine, nor anything of like import. I wish to evade no responsibility, but to repel a personal aspersion. . . .
>
> I wish to be distinctly understood as not seeking to be relieved from any responsibility for urging the advance of the Union Grand Army into Virginia though the precise phrase "Forward to Richmond!" is not mine, and I would have preferred not to iterate it. I thought that that Army, One Hundred Thousand strong, might have been in the Rebel capital on or before the 20th inst., while I felt that there were urgent reasons why it should be there if possible. And now, if anyone imagines that I, or anyone connected with THE TRIBUNE, ever commended or imagined any such strategy as the launching of barely Thirty Thousand of the One Hundred Thousand Union Volunteers within fifty miles of Washington against Ninety Thousand Rebels enveloped in a labyrinth of strong intrenchments and unreconnoitered masked batteries, then demonstration would be lost on his closed ear. But I will not dwell on this. If I am needed as a scapegoat for all the military blunders of the last month, so be it! Individuals must die that the Nation may live. If I can serve her best in that capacity, I do not shrink from the ordeal.
>
> Henceforth, I bar all criticism in these columns on Army movements past or future, unless somebody should undertake to prove that Gen. Patterson is a wise and brave commander. He seems to have none to speak his praises, so if there is anything to be said in his behalf, I will make an exception in his favor. Other than this the subject is closed and sealed. Correspondents and reporters may state facts, but must forbear comments. I know that there is truth that yet needs to be uttered on this subject, but

this paper has done its full share—and all that it ought, and perhaps more than it could afford to do—and henceforth stands back for others. Only I beg to be understood—once for all—that if less than half the Union Armies directly at hand are hurled against all the rebel forces that could be concentrated—more than double their number—on ground specially chosen and strongly fortified by the traitors, THE TRIBUNE *does not approve and should not be held responsible for such madness. Say what you, will of the past, but remember this for the future, though we keep silence.*

Henceforth, it shall be THE TRIBUNE'*s sole vocation to rouse and animate the American People for the terrible ordeal which has befallen them. The Great Republic imminently needs the utmost exertions of every loyal heart and hand. We have tried to serve her by exposing breakers ahead and around her; henceforth, be it ours to strengthen, in all possible ways, the hands of those whose unenviable duty is to pilot her through them. If more good is thus to be done, let us not repine that some truth must be withheld for a calmer moment, and for less-troubled ears.*

The journal which is made the conduit of these personal assaults on me attributes the course of THE TRIBUNE *to resentment "against those who have ever committed the inexpiable offense of thwarting Mr. Greeley's raging and unsatisfied thirst for office."*

I think this justifies me in saying that there is no office in the gift of the Government or of the People which I either hope, wish, or expect, ever to hold. I certainly shall not parade myself as declining places that are not offered for my acceptance; but I am sure the President has always known that I desired no office at his hands; and this not through any violation of my rule above stated, but through the report of mutual and influential friends, who at various times volunteered to ask me if I would take any place whatever under the Government, and were uniformly and conclusively assured that I would not.

Now let the wolves howl on! I do not believe they can goad me into another personal notice of their ravings.

HORACE GREELEY

July 24, 1861

The public justifiably conceived of the *Tribune* as Greeley, for in literal fact it was. "Just Once" was therefore not accepted at its face value, and Raymond and Bennett both gave it wide publicity. It is difficult even after the passing of the years not to read Greeley's characteristic *thinking*, if not his deliberate *acting*, into the war cry and into the editorial after Bull Run. Greeley was honest. His words must be accepted; but his very explanation is naive and clearly shows that he was anxious to see the Federal forces move "Forward to Richmond!" More than that, he had already upon many occasions severely castigated the

Administration. His excuse seems lame even today, but he had been stampeded by the disaster and no doubt with good reason felt that his professional career and the stability of his paper were endangered. A few weeks after he penned "Just Once," Greeley wrote his friend Moncure Daniel Conway that he had been very ill and was yet too weak to work and declared: "The Tribune *did* suffer considerably by the truth told by Warren, etc., about the want of purpose and management at Washington, and I think would have been ruined had I not resolved to bend to the storm. I did it very badly, for I was all but insane, yet I hope all will yet be well with us."[58]

In the light of Greeley's collapse and of his realization that he was obliged "to bend to the storm," his assurances concerning the future policy of the *Tribune* may be better understood. They deceived no one save perhaps himself. The public at least had no notion that the trenchant editor would be able to halter himself and had no wish to see him do so. Nobody in or out of the *Tribune* office believed that the editor would henceforth "bar all criticism" of Army movements, past and future; that he would live up to his assurance that, in the future, correspondents and reporters "may state facts but must forbear comments"; and that the "sole vocation" of the *Tribune* would thereafter be "to arouse and animate the American people." Nor did anyone but Greeley believe that he was correctly interpreting his own inner yearnings and impulses when he said, as he was in the habit of doing, from time to time, that he did not "hope, wish, or expect, ever to hold" public office.

In these anxious days following the humiliating defeat at Bull Run, the first violent setback of the war, we find perhaps the best measure we shall discover of the stamina, poise, and resoluteness of character of Greeley and Lincoln. Greeley broke under extraordinary stress. Lincoln did not. On the night following the battle of Bull Run, Lincoln lay awake on a sofa in the Executive Office formulating plans for the future.[59] From time to time he received excited officers and civilians who were arriving in Washington after their inglorious flight from the battlefield. In the midst of these interruptions he sketched the policy and military procedure he deemed expedient to meet the new situation. The memoranda he began on that fateful night stand in the record under the dates of July 23 and 27. Greeley's "Just Once" was written on July

---

[58] Moncure Daniel Conway, *Memories and Experiences*, p. 336.
[59] Nicolay and Hay, *Abraham Lincoln*, IV, 368.

24. His brain fever had reached its height when he addressed a letter to the President on July 29. Lincoln's memoranda and Greeley's letter are presented in parallel columns.

Lincoln's Memoranda	*Greeley's Letter*
(July 23, 1861.)	*(New York, Monday, July 29, 1861 Midnight.)*

1. *Let the plan for making the blockade effective be pushed forward with all possible despatch.*

Dear Sir: This is my seventh sleepless night—yours too, doubtless—yet I think I shall not die, because I have no right to die. I must struggle to live, however bitterly. But to

2. *Let the volunteer forces at Fort Monroe and vicinity under General Butler be constantly drilled, disciplined, and instructed without more for the present.*

business. You are not considered a great man, and I am a hopelessly broken one. You are now undergoing a terrible ordeal, and God has thrown the gravest responsibilities upon you. Do not fear to meet them. Can the rebels be beaten after all that has occurred, and in view of the actual state of feeling caused by our late, awful disaster? If they can,

3. *Let Baltimore be held as now, with a gentle but firm and certain hand.*

—and it is your business to ascertain and decide,—write me that such is your judgment, so that I may know and do my duty. And if they cannot be beaten,—if our recent disaster is fatal,—do not fear to sacrifice yourself to your country. If

4. *Let the force now under Patterson or Banks be strengthened and made secure in its position.*

the rebels are not to be beaten,—if that is your judgment in view of all the light you can get,—then every drop of blood henceforth shed in this quarrel will be wantonly, wickedly shed, and the guilt will rest heavily on the soul of every promoter of the crime. I pray you to decide quickly and let me know my

5. *Let the forces in Western Virginia act till further orders according to instructions or orders from General McClellan.*

duty.

If the Union is irrevocably gone, an armistice for thirty, sixty, ninety, one hundred and twenty days—

6. [Let] General Fremont push forward his organization and operations in the West as rapidly as possible, giving rather special attention to Missouri.

7. Let the forces late before Manassas, except the three-months men, be reorganized as rapidly as possible in their camps here and about Arlington.

8. Let the three-months forces who decline to enter the longer service be discharged as rapidly as circumstances will permit.

9. Let new volunteer forces be brought forward as fast as possible, and especially into the camps on the two sides of the river here.

(July 27, 1861.)

When the foregoing shall have been substantially attended to:
1. Let Manassas Junction (or some point on one or other of the railroads near it) and Strasburg be seized and permanently held, with an open line from Washington to Manassas, and an open line from Harper's Ferry to Strasburg—the military men to find the way of doing these.

better still for a year—ought at once to be proposed, with a view to a peaceful adjustment. Then Congress should call a National Convention, to meet at the earliest possible day. And there should be an immediate and mutual exchange or release of prisoners and a disbandment of forces. I do not consider myself at present a judge of anything but the public sentiment. That seems to me everywhere gathering and deepening against a prosecution of the war. The gloom in this city is funereal—for our dead at Bull Run were many, and they lie unburied yet. On every brow sits sullen, scorching, black despair. It would be easy to have Mr. Crittenden move any proposition that ought to be adopted, or to have it come from any proper quarter. The first point is to ascertain what is best that can be done,—which is the measure of our duty,—and do that very thing at the earliest moment.

This letter is written in the strictest confidence, and is for your eye alone. But you are at liberty to say to members of your Cabinet that you know I will second any move you may see fit to make. But do nothing timidly nor by halves. Send me word what to do. I will live till I can hear it at all events. If it is best for the country and for mankind that we make peace with the rebels at once and on their own terms, do not shrink even from that. But bear in mind the greatest truth: "Whoso would lose his life for my sake shall save it." Do the thing that

2. *This done, a joint movement* *is the highest right, and tell me how* *from Cairo on Memphis, and from* *I am to second you.* *Cincinnati on East Tennessee.*[60]

Yours, in the depths of bitterness, HORACE GREELEY[61]

Lincoln preserved the confidence of the agonized and distracted editor. Three years later, Greeley's letter was a subject of discussion between Lincoln and his secretaries. John Hay recites the incident in his diary for April 30, 1864.

The President came loafing in as it grew late and talked about the reception which his Hodges letter has met with. He seemed rather gratified that the Tribune *was in the main inspired by a kindly spirit in its criticism. He thought of & found & gave to me to decipher Greeley's letter to him of the 29th July, 1861. This most remarkable letter still retains for me its wonderful interest as the most insane specimen of pusillanimity that I have ever read. When I had finished reading, Nicolay said, "That wd be nuts to the* Herald. *Bennett wd willingly give $10,000 for that." To which the Prest [President], tying the red tape around the package, answered, "I need $10,000 very much but he could not have it for many times that."*[62]

Lincoln could hold his fire. The red tape around the package was not unfastened until the letter was published in the *Century Magazine* twenty-four years later.[63]

---

[60] Nicolay and Hay, *Complete Works*, VI, 331–33.

[61] Nicolay and Hay, *Abraham Lincoln*, IV, 365–66. Original in Robert Todd Lincoln Collection, Library of Congress, Washington, D.C. (10921).

[62] Tyler Dennett, *Lincoln and the Civil War—In the Diaries and Letters of John Hay*, p. 178.

[63] *Century Magazine*, June, 1888, pp. 290–91.

What I do about slavery, and the colored race, I do because I believe it helps to save the Union; and what I forbear, I forbear because I do not believe it would help to save the Union.

Lincoln[1]

On the face of this wide earth, Mr. President, there is not one disinterested, determined, intelligent champion of the Union cause who does not feel that all attempts to put down the Rebellion, and at the same time uphold its inciting cause, are preposterous and futile.

Greeley[2]

8 Emancipation

Addressing the Republican State Convention at Springfield, Illinois, which had named him as the Republican candidate for United States Senator, Lincoln made his most pregnant and prophetic utterance on the slavery issue. "A house divided against itself cannot stand," he said. "I believe this government cannot endure permanently half slave and half free. I do not expect the Union to be dissolved—I do not expect the house to fall—but I do expect it will cease to be divided. It will become all one thing, or all the other."[3] This portentous declaration was made after mature deliberation and against the advice of his friends. He never departed from that view, nor did he ever explain the process by which he expected the house would cease to be divided. He could hardly have anticipated then that it would fall to his lot to take the first significant step in that direction in the issuance of the Emancipation Proclamation.

He was elected President on a platform which pledged him and the Republican party to maintain and defend the right of each state "to

---

[1] John G. Nicolay and John Hay, eds., *Complete Works of Abraham Lincoln*, VIII, 15–16, Lincoln to Greeley, August 22, 1862.

[2] *Tribune*, August 19, 1862, Greeley to Lincoln.

[3] Nicolay and Hay, *op. cit.*, III, 2.

order and control its own domestic institutions."[4] In his inaugural address on March 4, 1861, Lincoln quoted this plank in the Republican platform and reiterated his support of it. "I have no purpose," he said, "directly or indirectly to interfere with the institution of slavery in the States where it exists. I believe I have no lawful right to do so, and I have no inclination to do so." He went further and assured the South that "the prosperity, peace, and security" of no section of the country would be endangered by the incoming Administration and pledged himself to the faithful support of the provision of the Constitution concerning the delivering up of fugitives from service or labor. At the same time he repeated his often-expressed view that "the Union of these States is perpetual" and that "no State upon its own mere motion can lawfully get out of the Union."[5]

A committee from the Virginia Convention presented a preamble and resolution to the President on April 13, 1861, asking him to communicate to the convention the policy the Federal Executive intended to pursue in regard to the Confederate states. In reply, Lincoln referred the convention to his inaugural address which he reaffirmed in toto.[6] In his proclamation on April 15, 1861, the President indicated the first services assigned to the militia would probably be "to repossess the forts, places, and property" seized from the Union and declared that care would be taken "to avoid any devastation, and destruction of or interference with property."[7] In his first message to the Thirty-seventh Congress on July 4, 1861, the President deemed it proper to say that upon the suppression of the Rebellion it would be his purpose then, as ever, "to be guided by the Constitution and the laws" and that he probably would have no different understanding of the relations of the Federal government and the states "than that expressed in the inaugural address."[8]

The basic policy of the President in adhering strictly to the Constitution and the laws and in avoiding any interference with the right of any state to order and control its own domestic institutions was promptly confirmed by the Thirty-seventh Congress. A resolution to that effect passed the House on July 22 and the Senate on July 25 in substantially identical language. The House resolution read:

---

[4] Horace Greeley and John F. Cleveland, eds., A *Political Text-book*, pp. 26–27.
[5] Nicolay and Hay, *op. cit.*, VI, 169–85.
[6] *Ibid.*, pp. 243–45.
[7] *Ibid.*, pp. 246–48.
[8] *Ibid.*, p. 323.

Resolved by the House of Representatives of the Congress of the United States, That the present deplorable civil war has been forced upon the country by the disunionists of the Southern States, now in arms against the constitutional Government, and in arms around the capital; that in this national emergency, Congress, banishing all feelings of mere passion or resentment, will recollect only its duty to the whole country; and that this war is not waged on their part in any spirit of oppression, or for any purpose of conquest or subjugation, or purpose of overthrowing or interfering with the rights or established institutions of those States, but to defend and maintain the supremacy of the Constitution, and to preserve the Union with all the dignity, equality, and rights of the several States unimpaired; and that as soon as these objects are accomplished the war ought to cease.[9]

Congress was less positive and prompt in its confirmation and support of the emergency war measures employed by the President on his own responsibility. On the third day of the session a Joint Resolution was introduced in the Senate enumerating in the preamble six assumed extra-legal acts of the President: first, the proclamation on April 15 calling for 75,000 militia; second, the blockade on April 19 of the ports in South Carolina, Georgia, Alabama, Florida, Mississippi, Louisiana, and Texas; third, the blockade on April 27 of the ports in Virginia and North Carolina; fourth, the suspension on April 27 of the writ of habeas corpus at any point on or in the vicinity of any military line between the city of Philadelphia and the city of Washington; fifth, the calling into the service of the United States on May 3 of 42,034 volunteers, the increasing of the regular Army by the addition of 22,714 men, and the increasing of the Navy by the addition of 18,000 men; and sixth, the suspension on May 10 of the writ of habeas corpus on the coast of Florida. The resolution was concluded with the declaration that all of these "extraordinary acts, proclamations and orders" were "in all respects legal and valid." The resolution languished from day to day, was at times the subject of extended acrimonious debate, was reconsidered in the Senate in the closing hours of the session, and finally failed of adoption.[10]

Toward the close of the session an act was passed which in part saved the day for the President. A rider was attached to an innocent bill increasing the pay of the privates in the regular Army and the volunteers, which provided that all the "acts, proclamations and orders" of the President after March 4 "respecting the Army and Navy of the United States, and calling out or relating to the militia or volunteers from the

---

[9] *Cong. Globe*, 37th Cong., 1st sess., pp. 223, 265.
[10] *Ibid.*, pp. 16, 393.

States are hereby approved and in all respects legalized and made valid."[11] Congress thus adjourned without formal approval of the President's actions in suspending the writ of habeas corpus and in blockading the Southern ports. In his message the President said these measures were ventured upon under what appeared to be "a popular demand and a public necessity" with the expectation and trust that if necessary Congress would ratify them. He believed that nothing had been done beyond the "constitutional competency of Congress," and "submitted entirely to the better judgment of Congress" the question of any needful legislation.[12]

"By his emergency acts," says J. G. Randall, "and his wide use of executive power in the months just following the outbreak of war, Lincoln set a pattern for his whole administration. It was the pattern of a President who did not as a rule depend upon, or work with the Congress, but hewed out his own path, assumed executive power even when he questioned its legality, reached his own decisions (not without vacillation), and, on rare occasions, turned to Congress for *post facto* approval. Usually he did not even seek this ratification after the fact."[13]

Convinced at last that secession was to be "crushed out in blood and fire if necessary," Greeley wholeheartedly supported the war measures of the President which were the subject of consideration and debate in the Thirty-seventh Congress.[14] "President Lincoln's acts," he said, "need no defense. He would have deserved impeachment and overthrow if he had failed to perform them, constitutional or unconstitutional."[15]

Congress on its own motion passed a far-reaching though not effective measure entitled "An Act to Confiscate Property Used for Insurrectionary Purposes."[16] Lincoln signed the bill with some reluctance, for he was not ready for the hint of emancipation it contained. As originally introduced, the bill provided for the confiscation of property used in aiding, abetting, or promoting the present or any future insurrection. It was understood that the term "property" included slaves. Senator Trumbull of Illinois proposed an amendment which he explained as follows: "The amendment provides that if any person held to service or labor in any State, under the laws thereof (by which, of course, is

---

[11] *Cong. Globe*, 37th Cong., 1st sess., Appendix, pp. 44–45.
[12] Nicolay and Hay, *op. cit.*, VI, 308–10.
[13] J. G. Randall, *Lincoln the President*, I, 373.
[14] *Tribune*, April 26, 1861.
[15] *Ibid.*, July 28, 1861.
[16] *Cong. Globe*, 37th Cong., 1st sess., Appendix, p. 42.

meant a slave in any of these States), if employed in aid of this rebellion, in digging ditches or entrenchments, or in any other way, or if used for carrying guns, or if used to destroy this Government, by the consent of his master, his master shall forfeit all right to him, and he shall be forever discharged."[17] The amendment occasioned extended debate in the House, and a substitute which did not greatly change the import of the original was passed which was acceptable to Senator Trumbull. What it amounted to was that claims to the labor of slaves engaged in hostile military service were forfeited. It paved the way for a second Confiscation Act on July 17, 1862.

In the early period of the conflict, Greeley also strongly supported the basic object of the war as defined by the President and by Congress. He insisted that the struggle for and against the integrity of the Union should not be complicated with questions concerning the perpetuation of slavery. The demands of those who required the war for the Union to be a war for the extinction of slavery, or to be a war for the protection of slavery, were "untimely and unreasonable." "This War," Greeley said, taking his cue from Lincoln, "is in truth a War for the preservation of the Union, and not for the destruction of Slavery." Hedging a bit, with a prophetic eye to the future, he went on, "But if Slavery should insist on making up an issue between itself and the Union, then we are sure it would do so at its peril."[18]

This view was maintained through the months of May, June, and July while the *Tribune* was pressing the Administration for action against the rebels. The relations of slavery to the war called for precise definitions to keep clear that the war was not being waged either to overthrow or to protect slavery. Greeley declared the war to be "the uprising of loyal citizens *en masse* for the maintenance of the Federal Union and the supremacy of the Federal laws in all the States, and not for the enforcement of the peculiar local policy of any single State or class of States. In fine, so far as slavery is concerned it is a war of *nonintervention*."[19] Again, in answer to critics who charged him with having urged forward the war as a means for the abolition of slavery, Greeley declared that the accusation was false and said that he could not ask the President to carry on a war for any object which would involve a violation of his oath of office.[20] In the troubled days in August,

---

[17] *Cong. Globe,* 37th Cong., 1st sess., pp. 218–19.
[18] *Tribune,* May 12, 1861.
[19] *Ibid.,* May 27, 1861.
[20] *Ibid.,* July 21, 1861.

1861, when Greeley was recovering from brain fever and the *Tribune* was still being racked by the Bull Run episode, he reaffirmed his position that the war should not interfere with any of the peculiar institutions of the seceded states "unless those institutions are wantonly thrown across the pathway over which the national cause is moving, when, like other obstacles that interpose between us and the patriotic ends we seek to attain, they will be set aside."[21]

Thus after Bull Run and after the adjournment of the first session of the Thirty-seventh Congress on August 6, it was clear to the North, if not to the South, that the government was engaged in a war for the preservation of the Union and the enforcement of the Federal laws in accordance with the Constitution and not either for or against slavery. This position the President had taken in his inaugural address, in his message to Congress, and upon all occasions when he was called to discuss the issue. Congress by explicit resolution had endorsed and reaffirmed the President's position. And Greeley in this particular was in complete agreement with the President and Congress.

The question of how the President, the Congress, and the editor of the *Tribune* expected to wage a successful war for the Union and blithely ignore slavery was not answered because it was not raised. Congress and Greeley were apparently more concerned, and were certainly more vocal, about the possibility of emancipation than the President was. Lincoln was schooled in keeping his own counsel. If he then nursed the hope that the war would end in the destruction of slavery, he kept that hope in his own breast. It was inevitable—and must have been clear in the minds of intelligent men, North and South—that slavery would be "wantonly thrown across the pathway" over which the national cause was moving. A series of significant incidents led finally to emancipation.

One of the earliest issues had to do with the disposition of slaves of belligerents who had found their way into the Union lines either by running away from their masters or by seizure as property. In May, 1861, prior to the passage of the Confiscation Act, General B. F. Butler, in command of Fort Monroe, initiated the practice of regarding such slaves as contraband of war. This far-reaching practice began in a very simple way, as a result of three Virginia slaves making their way to Fort Monroe to avoid building batteries in North Carolina. Under a flag of truce an agent of their owner demanded their return to their owner under the provisions of the Fugitive Slave Law. General Butler's re-

21 *Ibid.*, August 28, 1861.

sponse was that the law did not operate in Virginia, which claimed to be a foreign country, and that their master might have his property restored to him if he would come to the front and take the oath of allegiance to the United States. Butler's action was in effect ratified by the Confiscation Act and was also directly approved by the War Department. Lincoln maintained his consistent position by instructing the Secretary of War, Simon Cameron, in advising General Butler of the general principles to be followed, to say that, "It is the desire of the President that all existing rights in all the States be respected and maintained."[22]

Greeley, as was to be expected, applauded General Butler's action. He declared that with regard to no feature of the war had there been so universal a concurrence of sentiment in the loyal states as upon the General's determination to detain all Negro slaves entering his camp in the rebel states as contraband of war. "Following the clear indications of public opinion, as well as the sound maxims of law," Greeley said, "we trust the Government will direct all Commanders of our land and naval forces to adopt and carry out this doctrine."[23] He therefore thoroughly approved of the Confiscation Act which shortly followed and commented that it would be as absurd to exclude slaves from the effect of such an act as it would be to exclude horses or cattle or any other property that could be converted into money or made serviceable for any purpose that would advance insurrection. Still following closely Lincoln's line of reasoning on this issue, Greeley made it clear that the property thus confiscated must be used to aid and abet insurrection.[24]

The next significant incident in the emancipation drama came as a jolt to the President and the entire country. On August 30, General John C. Frémont, Commander of the Department of the West with headquarters at St. Louis, issued a proclamation, assuming the administrative powers of the state of Missouri, establishing martial law throughout the state, announcing that all persons taken with arms in their hands within his lines would be tried by court-martial and if found guilty would be shot. Frémont's proclamation also declared that the property, real and personal, of all persons taking up arms against the United States would be confiscated to the public use, and their slaves, if they had any, would be set free.[25]

Lincoln acted promptly. On September 2 he addressed a letter to

---

[22] John G. Nicolay and John Hay, *Abraham Lincoln—A History*, IV, 385-96.
[23] *Tribune*, May 31, 1861.
[24] *Ibid.*, July 30, 1861.
[25] Nicolay and Hay, *Abraham Lincoln*, IV, 416-17.

Frémont, "written in a spirit of caution and not of censure," ordering him to allow no man to be shot under the proclamation without the President's approbation or consent and coming straight to the heart of the matter:

I think there is great danger that the closing paragraph, in relation to the confiscation of property and the liberating of slaves of traitorous owners, will alarm our Southern Union friends and turn them against us; perhaps ruin our rather fair prospect for Kentucky. Allow me, therefore, to ask that you will, as of your own motion, modify that paragraph so as to conform to the first and fourth sections of the act of Congress entitled, "An act to confiscate property used for insurrectionary purposes," approved August 6, 1861, a copy of which act I herewith send you.[26]

Frémont ignored the gracious privilege the President had given him of recalling his ill-timed and wholly unwarranted edict of emancipation, and sent his wife to Washington with a letter declining to retract his words and asking Lincoln openly to direct him to make the correction.[27] The President replied on September 11 and ordered Frémont to modify the clause of his proclamation relating to the liberation of slaves "to conform to, and not to transcend, the provisions in the same subject" in the Confiscation Act.[28]

Frémont's action was popular in many quarters. Orville H. Browning, who succeeded Douglas as senator from Illinois, took the President to task.[29] While Lincoln did not engage in any public defense of his action, he did rebuke Senator Browning in a confidential letter under date of September 22, in which he set forth in characteristic style his position at the time.

Private & confidential

Executive Mansion
Washington Sept 22d 1861.

Hon. O. H. Browning
My dear Sir
    Yours of the 17th is just received; and coming from you, I confess it astonishes me. That you should object to my adhering to a law, which you

---

[26] Nicolay and Hay, *Complete Works*, VI, 350–51, Lincoln to Frémont, September 2, 1861.

[27] Nicolay and Hay, *Abraham Lincoln*, IV, 418–19. See also Allan Nevins, *Frémont, Pathmarker of the West*, pp. 499–507.

[28] Nicolay and Hay, *Complete Works*, VI, 353, Lincoln to Frémont, September 11, 1861.

[29] Robert Todd Lincoln Collection, Library of Congress, Washington, D.C. (11724), Browning to Lincoln, September 17, 1861.

had assisted in making, and presenting to me, less than a month before, is odd enough. But this is a very small part. Genl. Fremont's proclamation, as to confiscation of property, and the liberation of slaves, is purely political, and not within the range of military law, or necessity. If a commanding General finds a necessity to seize the farm of a private owner, for a pasture, an encampment, or a fortification, he has the right to do so, and to so hold it, as long as the necessity lasts; and this is within military law, because within military necessity. But to say the farm shall no longer belong to the owner, or his heirs forever; and this as well when the farm is not needed for military purposes as when it is, is purely political, without the savor of military law about it. And the same is true of slaves. If the General needs them, he can seize them, and use them; but when the need is past, it is not for him to fix their permanent future condition. That must be settled according to laws made by law-makers, and not by military proclamations. The proclamation in the point in question, is simply "dictatorship." It assumes that the general may do anything he pleases—confiscate the lands and free the slaves of loyal people, as well as of disloyal ones. And going the whole figure I have no doubt would be more popular with some thoughtless people, than that which has been done! But I cannot assume this reckless position; nor allow others to assume it on my responsibility. You speak of it as being the only means of saving the government. On the contrary it is itself the surrender of the government. Can it be pretended that it is any longer the government of the U.S.—any government of Constitution and laws,—wherein a General, or a President, may make permanent rules of property by proclamation?

I do not say Congress might not with propriety pass a law, on the point, just such as General Fremont proclaimed. I do not say I might not, as a member of Congress, vote for it. What I object to is, that I as President, shall expressly or impliedly seize and exercise the permanent legislative functions of the government.

So much as to principle. Now as to policy. No doubt the thing was popular in some quarters, and would have been more so if it had been a general declaration of emancipation. The Kentucky Legislature would not budge till that proclamation was modified; and Gen. Anderson telegraphed me that on the news of Gen. Fremont having actually issued deeds of manumission, a whole company of our Volunteers threw down their arms and disbanded. I was so assured, as to think it probable, that the very arms we had furnished Kentucky would be turned against us. I think to lose Kentucky is nearly the same as to lose the whole game. Kentucky gone, we cannot hold Missouri, nor, as I think, Maryland. These all against us, and the job on our hands is too large for us. We would as well consent at once, including the surrender of this capitol. On the contrary, if you will give up your restlessness for new positions, and back me manfully on the grounds upon which you and other kind friends gave me the election, and have approved in my public documents, we shall go through triumphantly.

You must not understand I took my course on the proclamation because of Kentucky. I took the same ground in a private letter to General Fremont before I heard from Kentucky.

You think I am inconsistent because I did not also forbid Gen. Fremont to shoot men under the proclamation. I understand that part to be within military law; but I also think, and so privately wrote Gen. Fremont, that it is impolitic in this, that our adversaries have the power, and will certainly exercise it, to shoot as many of our men as we shoot of theirs. I did not say this in the public letter, because it is a subject I prefer not to discuss in the hearing of our enemies.

There has been no thought of removing Gen. Fremont on any ground connected with his proclamation; and if there has been any wish for his removal on any ground, our mutual friend Sam Glover can probably tell you what it was. I hope no real necessity for it exists on any ground.

Suppose you write to Hurlbut and get him to resign.

Your friend as ever
A. Lincoln[30]

Greeley had decidedly mixed emotions in dealing editorially with the Frémont situation. Lincoln and Greeley had campaigned vigorously for the election of Frémont as President on the Republican ticket in 1856. Greeley idealized Frémont and believed strongly in the integrity of his character and purpose. Before he learned of Lincoln's action he published Frémont's proclamation in the *Tribune* on September 1 and 2 and characterized it as "bold and explicit" and as giving "the slaveholders fair notice that so many of them as aid the Rebels will lose their slaves if the rebellion does not succeed." After Lincoln's order was known, mindful of his "Just Once" assurance to the public, Greeley dealt in gingerly fashion with the issue and grudgingly accepted the President's decision. "We are not censuring the course which the President has seen fit to take," he said, "with regard to Gen. Fremont and his energetic Proclamation. In view of the critical condition of Kentucky and of Maryland, the President has doubtless done what appeared to him not only expedient but urgently necessary. We have no desire to precipitate the march of events. . . . It is our clear conviction, however, that the nation cannot always stand meekly parrying the deadly

---

[30] Illinois State Historical Library, Lincoln to Browning, September 22, 1861. See also Robert Todd Lincoln Collection (11922 and 11926), *op. cit.*; and Harlan Hoyt Horner, "Lincoln Rebukes a Senator," *Journal of the Illinois State Historical Society*, XLIV, No. 2, 103–19.

thrusts of the Slave Power—it will at last be compelled to return them in the very temper in which they are delivered."[31] When shortly thereafter, for accumulated reasons, Frémont was relieved of his command, Greeley acquiesced and expressed the hope that the President would never hesitate to place and displace military officers as he should from time to time deem most conducive to the public good, and never fear that he would not be sustained in so doing, even by those whose judgment might differ from his own. He praised Frémont as a man who could fall with dignity and without losing at the moment of a great and sudden trial "his keen sense of self respect and of his duty to his country."[32]

At about this time it appears that Lincoln entered into a weird arrangement through his friend, Robert J. Walker, former territorial governor of Kansas, then in his confidence at Washington, by which he hoped to bring Greeley more closely into line with the Administration or at least to moderate his future fulminations against it. One James R. Gilmore was the go-between. Walker and Gilmore, interested in establishing a new magazine designated as the *Continental Monthly*, hit upon a plan of furnishing Greeley advance information concerning government policy in return for which the *Tribune* would publicize the new magazine and Greeley would occasionally write for it. It seems very unlike Lincoln to permit himself to become involved in a backdoor undertaking such as this, and the elaborate and graphic details recorded by Gilmore may overstate the attendant circumstances.[33] In any event, Lincoln ratified the arrangement. He wrote the following letter, ostensibly to Walker, which Gilmore was permitted to bring to Greeley's notice.

Washington, November 21, 1861

Dear Governor: I have thought over the interview which Mr. Gilmore has had with Mr. Greeley, and the proposal that Greeley has made to Gilmore, namely that he (Gilmore) shall communicate to him (Greeley) all that he learns from you of the inner workings of the administration, in return for his (Greeley's) giving such aid as he can to the new magazine, and allowing you (Walker) from time to time the use of his (Greeley's) columns when it is desirable to feel of, or forestall, public opinion on important subjects. The arrangement meets my unqualified approval, and I shall further it to the extent of my ability, by opening to you—as I do now—fully the policy

---

[31] *Tribune*, September 19, 1861.

[32] *Ibid.*, October 22 and November 27, 1861.

[33] James R. Gilmore, *Personal Recollections of Abraham Lincoln and the Civil War,* pp. 39–63.

*of the Government,—its present views and future intentions when formed,
—giving you permission to communicate them to Gilmore for Greeley; and
in case you go to Europe I will give these things direct to Gilmore. But all
this must be on the express and explicit understanding that the fact of these
communications coming from me shall be absolutely confidential,—not to
be disclosed by Greeley to his nearest friend, or any of his subordinates.
He will be, in effect, my mouth-piece, but I shall not be known to be the
speaker.*

*I need not tell you that I have the highest confidence in Mr. Greeley.
He is a great power. Having him firmly behind me will be as helpful to me
as an army of one hundred thousand men. That he has ever kicked the
traces has been owing to his not being fully informed. Tell Gilmore to say
to him that, if he ever objects to my policy, I shall be glad to have him state
to me his views frankly and fully. I shall adopt his if I can. If I cannot, I
will at least tell him why. He and I should stand together, and let no minor
differences come between us; for we both seek one end, which is the saving
of our country. Now, Governor, this is a longer letter than I have written
in a month,—longer than I would have written for any other man than
Horace Greeley.*

Your friend, truly
Abraham Lincoln

*P.S.—The sooner Gilmore sees Greeley the better, as you may before long
think it wise to ventilate our policy on the* Trent *affair.*[34]

Gilmore reported that Greeley was delighted with the arrangement.
Some further credence may be given to this un-Lincoln-like procedure
by the fact that Greeley published a two-column homily in the *Tribune*
on November 20 on "The Government and the Press." He insisted that
the government should recognize the ability of the press to serve the
republic by honest and fearless criticism rather than by indiscriminate
laudation. "But let the Government and the Press," he said, "do justice
to each other's motives; let the Press realize that the Government,
though it may err in judgment, cannot possibly be wrong in purpose;
and let the Government feel that the Press, where it ventures to criti-
cise the acts of the Nation's chosen leaders in this struggle, does so only
because the triumph of the Republic is in its view above all personal
considerations, and all will yet be well."

This secret alliance was doomed to failure. Gilmore was a doubtful
quantity and Greeley could not work in harness. When events stirred
him, he shortly fell into his old habits. Lincoln's letter reveals the politician at his slyest and the lawyer at his weakest. It may, indeed, show

---

[34] Nicolay and Hay, *Complete Works*, XI, 120–22, Lincoln to Walker, November 21,
1861.

the depths to which the solitary man in the White House was driven for some kind of anchorage in the storm that constantly surrounded him. One would like to think that Lincoln was not the author of that letter. Although it was signed "Abraham Lincoln," a signature used on public documents, his letters were almost always signed "A. Lincoln"; and rarely, if ever, did he use the superscription, "Your friend, truly."

The next official to jump over the traces was a member of the Cabinet. Without conferring with the President, Secretary of War Cameron incorporated in his annual report for submission to Congress a suggestion, if not a recommendation, that slaves forfeited as property in the course of the war should be employed directly in military service; he made this startling statement in his report: "If it shall be found that the men who have been held by the rebels as slaves are capable of bearing arms and performing efficient military service, it is the right, and may become the duty, of the Government to arm and equip them, and employ their services against the rebels, under proper military regulation, discipline and command." Cameron had even sent advance copies of his report to postmasters in the principal cities for release to the press as soon as the report should be handed down before Congress. Lincoln promptly ordered that the advance copies of the report be recalled by telegraph and that a revised report be prepared omitting all reference to the arming of slaves. Cameron took his medicine.[35]

The telegraphic recall of Cameron's original report did not reach the *Tribune* before Greeley had fully analyzed and approved it.[36] When he learned that the report of the Secretary of War had been modified "*a la* Fremont's Proclamation," he remarked that "it would seem to be more strictly a document emanating *from* the President rather than one addressed to him." Pointing out that the report of the Secretary of the Navy making an almost identical recommendation had not been modified, he quoted an old proverb which affirms that "One may steal a horse with impunity while another shall be hung for merely looking over a hedge."[37]

The President's annual message to Congress on December 3, 1861, was less coherent in form and less felicitous in language than many of his other public documents. Routine affairs were discussed in a colorless way, and the message as a whole gave little evidence of the violence of

---

[35] Nicolay and Hay, *Abraham Lincoln*, V, 126. See also Lee F. Crippen, *Simon Cameron—Ante-Bellum Years*; and A. Howard Meneely, *The War Department—1861*.

[36] *Tribune*, December 4, 1861.

[37] *Ibid.*, December 5, 1861.

the Rebellion or even of the terrific strain under which the President was living from day to day. He pointed out that slaves of rebels forfeited as property under the Confiscation Act of August 6, 1861, were already dependent on the United States and should be provided for. He thought it not unlikely that some of the states might pass similar enactments for their own benefit. He recommended that Congress provide for accepting such persons according to some mode of evaluation, that upon such acceptance they at once be deemed free, and that steps be taken for colonizing them together with those forfeited directly to the government. Schemes of this nature were strongly in his mind. He contented himself with an extremely brief reaffirmation of "the principles or general purposes stated and expressed" in his inaugural address and in his message to the special session of Congress. "The Union must be preserved," he said; "and hence all indispensable means must be employed. We should not be in haste to determine that radical and extreme measures, which may reach the loyal as well as the disloyal, are indispensable."[38] In this latter statement he was undoubtedly thinking of universal emancipation, although still keeping that possibility in the background.

On November 15 the President had received a letter from George Bancroft, the eminent historian, declaring that "Civil war is the instrument of Divine Providence to root out social slavery."[39] In reply Lincoln had said: "The main thought in the closing paragraph of your letter is one which does not escape my attention, and with which I must deal in all due caution, and with the best judgment I can bring to it."[40]

In reviewing the President's annual message to Congress, the editor of the *Tribune* forgot completely his assurance a few months previous of his purpose merely to record passing events and not to indulge in advice or counsel to the government. He also forgot or marked off the stillborn understanding he had had a few weeks previous with Gilmore and Walker. It is true he remarked upon the contrast between the President's message and that "so recently addressed to the rival rebel conclave by Jefferson Davis." Davis was, in Greeley's view, quite commonly assumed as the abler of the two men and certainly the better grammarian, with the ability to use the English language with "decided perspicuity and force." The spirit of Davis' manifesto, however, was "truculent, sanguinary, demoniac," while the President was not moved to

---

[38] Nicolay and Hay, *Complete Works*, VII, 28–60.
[39] *Ibid.*, p. 20.
[40] *Ibid.*, pp. 20–21, Lincoln to Bancroft, November 18, 1861.

"one harsh inculpation." In placing the duty of "preserving the Union above all conflicting considerations," Lincoln was clearly right, but he was "late to realize the necessity of still sterner measures aimed at the source and mainspring of the rebellion." And here Greeley's temperamental fever, which had been slowly rising again since his serious illness after Bull Run, showed signs of coming to the boiling point.

That the integrity of the Union should be the paramount object of loyal Americans in this contest, is on all hands conceded. The practical question is— Can this end be promoted by further deferment to and bolstering up of Slavery? While rebel corsairs are sinking and burning our unarmed merchant vessels on the ocean, shall we recognize and uphold the claim of rebels to property in human beings? We say, No—it is dangerous, fatal to do so: it is giving a factious and unjust strength to the public enemy; it is cherishing the viper which has its fangs now fastened in the National breast. Notify the slaveholders frankly that they may have thirty or sixty days more in which to lay down their arms and return to loyalty; but if they shall continue to defy the National authority and menace the National existence after the expiration of that term, their slaves shall, as a matter of inexorable public policy—nay, as a means of saving the National life at a cost less than ruinous —be proclaimed free, and invited to make their way to the Union lines, and there be recognized and treated as freemen. Such is the policy which we believe most effective and most merciful, and we trust it will yet receive the President's hearty concurrence.[41]

Lincoln did not forget an assurance to Bancroft that he would "deal in all due caution" with the slavery issue. Failing in an exploratory and experimental venture in Delaware, he turned to Congress with a special message on March 6, 1862, recommending the adoption of the following Joint Resolution:

Resolved, *That the United States ought to cooperate with any State which may adopt gradual abolishment of slavery, giving to such State pecuniary aid, to be used by such State, in its discretion, to compensate for the inconveniences, public and private, produced by such change of system.*

In his brief message accompanying the proposed Joint Resolution, Lincoln went a bit further than he had ever done before. Referring to his statement in his annual message to Congress that "all indispensable means" must be employed to preserve the Union, he declared: "I said this not hastily, but deliberately"; and gave clear intimation of his thinking about the steps ahead with the words, "Such [means] as may

---

[41] *Tribune*, December 4, 1861.

seem indispensable, as may obviously promise great efficiency, toward ending the struggle, must and will come."[42]

Lincoln now made deliberate effort to interest the public in his plan for the compensated abolishment of slavery. He invited delegations from Delaware, Kentucky, Maryland, Missouri, and Virginia to meet him at the White House on March 10 to discuss the implications of the Joint Resolution he had submitted to Congress. A memorandum of the interview was prepared by the Hon. J. W. Crisfield, senator from Maryland. The President told the delegation that he "had no designs on this particular subject" beyond the proposed action in the resolution and that in his view "emancipation was a subject exclusively under the control of the States." In the course of the interview the President was informed that the *Tribune* had endorsed the resolution and understood it to mean "gradual emancipation" or "something worse." Lincoln replied that he must not be expected to quarrel with the *Tribune* before the right time and that he hoped never to have to do it.[43] During these days Lincoln wrote to Raymond of the *New York Times*[44] and to Senator James A. McDougall[45] of California pointing out that the cost of eighty-seven days of the war would pay for all the slaves in Delaware, the District of Columbia, Kentucky, Maryland, and Missouri at $400 "per head." The resolution was passed in the House on March 11, in the Senate on April 2, and approved by the President on April 10.[46]

Greeley certainly endorsed the President's recommendation with more than his usual vehemence. He had never printed a state paper with "more satisfaction." It was "an epoch in the history of the country." The 6th of March would yet be celebrated as a day which initiated the nation's deliverance from "the most stupendous wrong, curse and shame of the Nineteenth Century." In his first burst of enthusiasm Greeley noted that his neighbor the *Herald* had lately suggested the re-election of Abraham Lincoln as President of the United States and he heartily seconded the motion.[47]

Greeley did not voice his full feelings in one editorial but discussed the President's action on several occasions.[48] Lincoln was portrayed as one of those minds that work, "not quickly nor brilliantly, but ex-

---

[42] Nicolay and Hay, *Complete Works*, VII, 112–15.
[43] *Ibid.*, pp. 120–28.
[44] *Ibid.*, p. 119, Lincoln to Raymond, March 9, 1862.
[45] *Ibid.*, pp. 132–34, Lincoln to McDougall, March 14, 1862.
[46] *Cong. Globe*, 37th Cong., 2d sess., Appendix, p. 420.
[47] *Tribune*, March 7, 1862.
[48] *Ibid.*, March 8, 11, 1862.

haustively." There was nothing violent about his remedy for the disease, but he saw clearly that the Rebellion could not be suppressed as long as slavery had an assured existence. The proposed resolution with the President's words to Congress accompanying it was the greatest public document since the American Declaration of Independence. The names of two men would remain forever illustrious in the history of the nineteenth century: ALEXANDER II of Russia and ABRAHAM LINCOLN of America. They were the great leaders in "Man's Emancipation" and would be remembered and honored "as long as Freedom is dear to the human heart." "For our part," said Greeley, "we thank God that Abraham Lincoln is President of the United States, and the whole country, we cannot doubt, will be thankful that we have at such a time so wise a ruler."

Following these glowing editorial comments, Greeley wrote to his friend, Schuyler Colfax, then Speaker of the House, asking him to assure the President that the *Tribune* would support him in his emancipation effort if he would advise its editor what to do. In response Lincoln wrote directly to Greeley:

Private

Executive Mansion
Washington, March 24, 1862

Hon. Horace Greeley
My Dear Sir: Your very kind letter of the 16th to Mr. Colfax has been shown me by him. I am grateful for the generous sentiments and purposes expressed toward the administration. Of course I am anxious to see the policy proposed in the late special message go forward, but you have advocated it from the first, so that I need to say little to you on that subject. If I were to suggest anything it would be that as the North is already for the measure, we should urge it persuasively, and not menacingly upon the South. I am a little uneasy about the abolishment of slavery in the District, not but I would be glad to see it abolished, but as to the time and manner of doing it. If some one or more of the border states would move first, I should greatly prefer it; but if this cannot be in a reasonable time, I would like the bill to have the three main features—gradual—compensation—and vote of the people—I do not talk to members of Congress on the subject except when they ask me—I am not prepared to make any suggestion about confiscation —I may drop you a line hereafter.

Yours truly
A. Lincoln[49]

---

[49] Greeley Papers, Pierpont Morgan Library, New York City, Lincoln to Greeley, March 24, 1862.

It will be recalled that Congressman Lincoln had once sent up a "trial balloon" in the House on January 10, 1849, in the form of a bill abolishing slavery in the District of Columbia. That bill, which failed of passage, contained the three features for which he was still contending as President thirteen years later, namely, gradual emancipation, compensation, and vote of the people.[50] The tenacity of his basic views on long-range issues was hardly exceeded by the zeal with which the editor of the *Tribune* stuck to his fundamental convictions. On April 16, less than a month after Lincoln referred to the matter in his letter to Greeley, he signed an act abolishing slavery in the District, which provided for immediate emancipation and for compensation to the owners not to exceed an aggregate of $300 per slave. The act also appropriated $100,000 for the expenses of possible voluntary emigration of slaves to Haiti or Liberia.[51] His pet plan failed in two particulars, gradual emancipation and a favorable vote of the people, but the object he had long sought had been attained. In his brief message to Congress, notifying that body that he had approved the act, he said:

I have never doubted the constitutional authority of Congress to abolish slavery in this District; and I have ever desired to see the national capital freed from the institution in some satisfactory way. Hence there has never been in my mind any question upon the subject except the one of expediency, arising in view of all the circumstances. If there be matters within and about this act which might have taken a course or shape more satisfactory to my judgment, I do not attempt to specify them. I am gratified that the two principles of compensation and colonization are both recognized and practically applied in the act.[52]

Lincoln wanted *his* way as strongly as any man who has ever been President, but he knew how and when to yield. The statesman was bigger than the politician. Greeley was again overjoyed. "The Capital of the American Republic," he editorially shouted, "has ceased to be a slaveholding city! . . . Thank God for one wrong redressed—one burning shame washed away! . . . So events march, God overruling and guiding them to wise and benignant though often inscrutable ends. Live the Republic!"[53]

Generals and Cabinet members had to learn the hard way that the President did not regard it as their function to determine and announce

---

[50] *Cong. Globe*, 30th Cong., 2d sess., p. 212.
[51] *Cong. Globe*, 37th Cong., 2d sess., Appendix, pp. 347–48.
[52] Nicolay and Hay, *Complete Works*, VII, 146–47.
[53] *Tribune*, April 17, 1862.

general policies touching the conduct of the war. In spite of the experience of Butler and Frémont and Cameron in the record, Major General David Hunter, in command of the Department of the South, issued a general order from Port Royal, South Carolina, on May 9, 1862, declaring the persons heretofore held as slaves in Georgia, Florida, and South Carolina "forever free."[54] Hunter's order first came to the attention of the President through dispatches to the press. On May 19 Lincoln issued a proclamation revoking the order and serving fresh notice to all commanders of the limits of their authority and responsibility in the words, "I further make known that, whether it be competent for me, as commander-in-chief of the army and navy, to declare the slaves of any State or States free, and whether, at any time, in any case, it shall have become a necessity indispensable to the maintenance of the government to exercise such supposed power, are questions which, under my responsibility, I reserve to myself, and which I cannot feel justified in leaving to the decision of commanders in the field." The President went on to repeat the Joint Resolution he had submitted to Congress in March touching on the gradual abolishment of slavery in each state through compensation, and, departing from his usual practice in official documents, made a direct appeal to the slave states to employ this method of emancipation. "I do not argue," he said, "I beseech you to make arguments for yourselves. . . . So much good has not been done, by one effort, in all past time, as in the providence of God it is now your high privilege to do."[55]

Greeley dealt with the President's revocation of Hunter's order with more than his customary restraint. Between the lines it could clearly be inferred that Greeley would have sustained Hunter, but he deferred to the judgment of the President in exercising his right and duty in determining what was best not for three states only but to assure the triumph of the Union cause everywhere.[56] Not content with unqualified endorsement, however, he continued:

> But we entreat the President now to consider and act upon the manifest necessity of having a definite, unvarying, clearly understood policy with regard to this subject. On behalf of the whole People we demand an unequivocal answer to these questions—"What shall be the future condition of the slave of a Rebel who escapes from the dominions of Jeff. Davis within the lines of our armies?" "What of those slaves who are abandoned by

[54] Nicolay and Hay, *Complete Works*, VII, 170–71.
[55] *Ibid.*, pp. 171–73.
[56] *Tribune*, May 19, 1862.

*their Rebel masters fleeing before the advancing hosts of the Union?"
"What of the slave whose Rebel master remains with him until both are
enveloped by the Union forces?"*[57]

Later, Greeley deemed the President's proclamation superseding
Hunter's order as one of the most significant documents of the times,
which would bear repeated readings, and the oftener read would be
found the more pregnant with important inferences. It indicated decided progress in the right direction, and its tone made it singularly acceptable with the public.[58]

The Joint Resolution of Congress, passed in April, touching gradual
abolishment of slavery through compensation, and the President's subsequent conferences with representatives of the border states with relation to this issue came to nothing. Lincoln again demonstrated that he
could be quite as persistent as Greeley in the pursuit of his own ideas.
Five days before the second session of the Thirty-seventh Congress was
to adjourn he called the representatives of the border states together
again, on July 12, 1862, and presented another appeal to them to promote compensated emancipation. His mind was already occupied with
a more decisive emancipation measure, but he clung almost desperately
to his hope of favorable action upon his plan by the border states. His
remarks before the conference show only one side of his thinking at
that time and were not unlike the earnest summing up of a hopeless
case by a lawyer before a jury.

GENTLEMEN: *After the adjournment of Congress, now very near, I shall
have no opportunity of seeing you for several months. Believing that you
of the border States hold more power for good than any other equal number of members, I feel it a duty which I cannot justifiably waive to make
this appeal to you. I intend no reproach or complaint when I assure you
that, in my opinion, if you all had voted for the resolution in the gradual-
emancipation message of last March, the war would now be substantially
ended. And the plan therein proposed is yet one of the most potent and
swift means of ending it. Let the States which are in rebellion see definitely
and certainly that in no event will the States you represent ever join their
proposed confederacy, and they cannot much longer maintain the contest.
But you cannot divest them of their hope to ultimately have you with them
so long as you show a determination to perpetuate the institution within
your own States. Beat them at elections, as you have overwhelmingly done,
and, nothing daunted, they still claim you as their own. You and I know*

---

[57] *Ibid.*, May 20, 1862.
[58] *Ibid.*, May 29, 1862.

what the lever of their power is. Break that lever before their faces, and they can shake you no more forever. Most of you have treated me with kindness and consideration, and I trust you will not now think I improperly touch what is exclusively your own, when, for the sake of the whole country, I ask, Can you, for your States, do better than to take the course I urge? Discarding punctilio and maxims adapted to more manageable times, and looking only to the unprecedentedly stern facts of our case, can you do better in any possible event? You prefer that the constitutional relation of the States to the nation shall be practically restored without disturbance of the institution; and if this were done, my whole duty in this respect, under the Constitution and my oath of office, would be performed. But it is not done, and we are trying to accomplish it by war. The incidents of the war cannot be avoided. If the war continues long, as it must if the object be not sooner attained, the institution in your States will be extinguished by mere friction and abrasion—by the mere incidents of the war. It will be gone, and you will have nothing valuable in lieu of it. Much of its value is gone already. How much better for you and for your people to take the step which at once shortens the war and secures substantial compensation for that which is sure to be wholly lost in any other event! How much better to thus save the money which else we sink forever in the war! How much better to do it while we can, lest the war ere long render us pecuniarily unable to do it! How much better for you as seller, and the nation as buyer, to sell out and buy out that without which the war could never have been, than to sink both the things to be sold and the price of it in cutting one another's throats? I do not speak of emancipation at once, but of a decision at once to emancipate gradually. Room in South America for colonization can be obtained cheaply and in abundance, and when numbers shall be large enough to be company and encouragement for one another, the freed people will not be so reluctant to go.

I am pressed with a difficulty not yet mentioned—one which threatens division among those who, united, are none too strong. An instance of it is known to you. General Hunter is an honest man. He was, and I hope still is, my friend. I valued him none the less for his agreeing with me in the general wish that all men everywhere could be free. He proclaimed all men free within certain States, and I repudiated the proclamation. He expected more good and less harm from the measure than I could believe would follow. Yet, in repudiating it, I gave dissatisfaction, if not offense, to many whose support the country cannot afford to lose. And this is not the end of it. The pressure in this direction is still upon me, and is increasing. By conceding what I now ask, you can relieve me, and, much more, can relieve the country, in this important point. Upon these considerations I have again begged your attention to the message of March last. Before leaving the capital, consider and discuss it among yourselves. You are patriots and statesmen, and as such I pray you consider this proposition, and at the least commend it to the consideration of your States and people. As you would perpetuate popular government for the best people in the world, I beseech you that you do in no wise omit this. Our common country is in great peril, demanding the loftiest views and boldest action to bring it speedy relief. Once relieved, its form of government is saved to the world, its beloved history and cherished memories are vindicated, and its happy future fully assured and rendered inconceivably grand. To you, more than to any others, the privilege is given to assure that happiness and swell that grandeur, and to link your own names therewith forever.[59]

Two days after his conference with the border-state representatives, the President sent a message to Congress submitting a draft of a bill to compensate any state which might abolish slavery within its limits and "respectfully and earnestly" recommended its passage. He could hardly have anticipated favorable action in the closing days of the session.

Be it enacted by the Senate and House of Representatives of the United States of America in Congress assembled, That whenever the President of the United States shall be satisfied that any State shall have lawfully abolished slavery within and throughout such State, either immediately or gradually, it shall be the duty of the President, assisted by the Secretary of the Treasury, to prepare and deliver to such State an amount of six per cent. interest-bearing bonds of the United States equal to aggregate value, at — dollars per head, of all the slaves within such State as reported by the census of the year one thousand eight hundred and sixty; the whole amount for any one State to be delivered at once if the abolishment be immediate, or in equal annual instalments if it be gradual, interest to begin running on each bond at the time of its delivery, and not before.

And be it further enacted, That if any State having so received any such bonds, shall at any time afterward by law reintroduce or tolerate slavery within its limits, contrary to the act of abolishment upon which such bonds shall have been received, said bonds so received by said State shall at once be null and void, in whosesoever hands they may be, and such State shall refund to the United States all interest which may have been paid on such bonds.[60]

The second session of the Thirty-seventh Congress adjourned sine die on July 17, 1862. Its action as a whole marked the tightening of the coils around slavery. In addition to the Joint Resolution committing the government to a policy of gradual abolishment of slavery in the

---

[59] Nicolay and Hay, *Complete Works*, VII, 270–74.
[60] *Ibid.*, pp. 276–77.

several states through compensation and to the act abolishing slavery in the District of Columbia, other actions were taken which clearly indicated the trend. An act approved on March 13 forbade all officers or persons in the military and naval service from employing any of their forces for the return of fugitive slaves.[61] An act approved on May 21 provided for the education of colored children in the District of Columbia.[62] An act approved on June 5 authorized the President to appoint diplomatic representatives to Haiti and Liberia.[63] An innocent little act approved on June 19 provided:

That from and after the passage of this act there shall be neither slavery nor involuntary servitude in any of the Territories of the United States now existing, or which may at any time hereafter be formed or acquired by the United States, otherwise than in the punishment of crimes whereof the party shall have been duly convicted.[64]

Lincoln must have mused a bit when he affixed his signature to that measure. The exigencies of war had without great public clamor promptly determined an issue, which, in one way or another, had engaged his attention throughout his political career.

An act approved on July 11 was designed to put into effect the treaty between the United States and Great Britain for the suppression of the African slave trade and authorized the President by and with the advice and consent of the Senate to appoint a judge and an arbitrator on the part of the United States, respectively, at New York, Sierra Leone, and the Cape of Good Hope.[65]

The most outstanding action of the Congress touching the slavery issue and the growing problem of emancipation which had been approved on the last day of the session, July 17, was "An Act to Suppress Insurrection, to punish Treason and Rebellion, to seize and confiscate the Property of Rebels, and for other purposes." This act went much further than the initial measure passed in the special session of Congress. It fixed penalties for treason and for aiding or inciting insurrection and rebellion and declared that persons adjudged guilty of either offense should be disqualified to hold office in the United States and that their slaves should be made free. It authorized and directed the President to seize and use for the benefit of the United States "all the estate and

---

[61] *Cong. Globe*, 37th Cong., 2d sess., Appendix, p. 340.
[62] *Ibid.*, pp. 356–57.
[63] *Ibid.*, p. 361.
[64] *Ibid.*, p. 364.
[65] *Ibid.*, p. 394.

property, money, stocks, credit and effects of officers of the army and navy, administrative officers, national, state or municipal, of the so-called confederate States of America." It also provided for like seizure of the property of persons outside of the Confederacy engaged in aiding or abetting the Rebellion and gave such persons sixty days in which to return to allegiance to the United States. It provided further that all slaves of rebels taking refuge within the lines of the Army, captured by the Army, deserted by their owners, or found within areas occupied by the forces of the United States "should be forever free of their servitude, and not again held as slaves." It forbade the delivering up of any slave escaping into free territory, except upon proof that the owners had not borne arms against the United States or in any way aided the Rebellion. Beyond these provisions, the act authorized the President to employ persons of African descent for the suppression of the Rebellion in such manner as he might judge best for the public welfare and authorized the President further "to make provision for the transportation, colonization, and settlement, in some tropical country beyond the limits of the United States, of such persons of the African race, made free by the provisions of this act, as may be willing to emigrate."[66]

Lincoln approved in desultory fashion of the several provisions of the bill as it came to him. He objected, however, to what he termed "the sum of those provisions" which resulted in "the divesting of title forever," and on this ground held that the act was unconstitutional. It became known in Congress that the President was disposed to veto the measure on constitutional grounds. Advocates of confiscation and emancipation at once introduced a Joint Resolution explanatory of the act and providing that it should "be so construed as not to apply to any act or acts done prior to the passage thereof; nor to include any member of a State Legislature, or judge of any State court, who has not in accepting or entering upon his office, taken an oath to support the constitution of the so-called confederate States of America; nor shall any punishment of proceedings under said act be so construed as to work a forfeiture of the real estate of the offender beyond his natural life." The Joint Resolution was passed on the day before the closing of the session. Before Lincoln learned of the passage of the resolution, he had determined to veto the bill and had prepared a message to the House, in which the bill originated, explaining his veto. When the resolution reached him he approved both the bill and the resolution and in a brief

---

[66] *Ibid.*, pp. 412–13.

message to Congress transmitted the explanation of his contemplated veto.[67]

This act was a war measure broadly designed to aid in the suppression of the Rebellion. Lincoln was in sympathy with the purposes of the act although he was not wholehearted in his support of it. His contemplation of a veto of the act in time of war, because it appeared to him unconstitutional in one particular, was not consistent with his previous action in the prosecution of the war, nor with the action he must even then have known he was soon to take. It almost looked as if he were anxious to get Congress out of the way so that he could go on with his war. The constitutionality of the measure was sharply discussed in Congress as was the Joint Resolution, especially in the Senate. Friends of the measure who did not deem the resolution germane or necessary were willing to vote for it in order to save the act. In the Senate Chamber, Sumner voiced a view which commanded wide respect and which took issue with the President squarely and convincingly in words which Lincoln might consistently have uttered himself:

Of course, sir, I cannot enter into the doubts attributed to the President. To me they seem utterly groundless and fallacious. They proceed on the mistaken idea that we are proceeding by indictment *and not by* war; *and they voluntarily subject the country to all the constraints of a criminal trial when the exigency requires the ample latitude of war. If soldiers are sent forth to battle, if fields are occupied as camps, and houses are occupied as hospitals, without permission of the owners, it is by virtue of the war powers of Congress, or, in other words, the belligerent rights of this Government. And it is by virtue of these same belligerent rights that the property of an enemy may be taken; nor, if he be an enemy, is there any check upon these rights in the Constitution. Whether you choose to take his property for life, or beyond life, the Constitution is indifferent; for all constitutional limitations are entirely inapplicable to belligerent rights. According to express words, you may not abridge the "freedom of speech or the press"; nor "infringe the right of the people to keep and bear arms." Nor can you take "life, liberty, or property without due process of law." And yet, wherever your armies move, and elsewhere, too, you do all these very things in the exercise of acknowledged belligerent rights. But the right of confiscation, whether for life or beyond life, is clear.*[68]

For weeks before the second session of the Thirty-seventh Congress began, and throughout the session, Greeley was impatient with what

---

[67] Nicolay and Hay, *Complete Works,* VII, 280–86.
[68] *Cong. Globe,* 37th Cong., 2d sess., p. 3382.

he deemed tardy prosecution of the war, and he was slowly warming up to a point of explosion in demanding that something should be done about its cause. This warming up process may be illustrated by his progressive references to the possibility and probability of emancipation as a war measure. The editorial columns of the *Tribune* during this period reveal the following comments:

October 17, 1861. It was declared that no American journal pretending to be loyal had intimated that the integrity of the Union should be sacrificed to the preservation of slavery, and that it was tacitly assumed on all sides that when all other means failed it would be "expedient and proper to save the Republic by proclaiming Emancipation."

October 19. It was held that if emancipation was the speediest and most effective way to end the Rebellion, the people would sooner or later find it out.

December 6. It was demanded and insisted on that as the efforts and sacrifices of the nation were not to be diverted to the overthrow of slavery, so they would not be rendered ineffective or fruitless "by anxiety to uphold and perpetuate Slavery."

December 16. The "firm conviction" was voiced that the war for the Union might be triumphantly ended within ninety days if there should be no hesitation as to the use of the readiest and most efficient means. If it should be proclaimed and understood that slaveholding by rebels was not recognized and sustained by the government and armies of the United States, the struggle, though sharp, would be short.

December 20. To end the war leaving slavery its old vantage ground would prove "but a brief and hollow truce."

December 26. It was demanded that the constitutional obligations —actual or assented, expressed or understood—of American citizens to uphold or to defer to slavery be officially recognized as expressly and strictly limited to the claims of *loyal* slaveholders, "to the exclusion of all rebels and traitors."

December 31. The sole choice lay "between a speedy triumph and an inglorious and total defeat."

January 3, 1862. "The Union must be saved soon or never."

January 9. "We do not see how the Union and Slavery can both be upheld."

January 16. "Let none fancy us afraid that Slavery will not fall with the Rebellion."

January 31. "Do you ask how to put down the rebellion? Destroy

Slavery. Do you ask how to prevent European intervention? Destroy Slavery."

February 18. "Let the Rebellion be swept out of existence with fire and sword! No rest for traitors!"

February 22. "We hold that the chief danger of the Nation to-day to be that of shameful and ruinous compromise, whereby the traitor chiefs should regain all they have forfeited by treason."

March 8. The Rebellion "will never be ended so long as Slavery has an assured existence."

April 19. "Let all thought of resentment toward individuals or sections be therefore buried in one unanimous resolve that Slavery shall die and the Nation enduringly live."

May 1. "We ask that the Union shall proclaim freedom to every slave of a rebel upon condition that he come within our lines and does what he can for the Union cause."

May 19. "We shall stand by our Government to the last, let it take whatever course it shall deem best, but we lack faith in its ability at once to uphold Slavery and reconstruct the Union."

May 29. "When the core of the disease is removed, its issues will dry up and disappear."

June 21. "A simple Proclamation by the Federal Executive—'All you able-bodied men who are willing to work or fight for the Union, repair to the most convenient Federal camp, and there grasp the ax, the spade or the rifle as shall be deemed advisable, and your liberty at least shall be assured and protected'—would within two months rally at least One Hundred Thousand new supporters to the National standards."

July 17. "We do not fear that the right thing will not ultimately be done, but that it will be done too late."

July 25. "Now, then, 'what the *Tribune* would have' is a brief, frank, stirring Proclamation from the President recognizing the Confiscation-Emancipation Act as the law of the land and the basis of the new War Policy resolved on by the Nation, requiring all Military and Naval commanders to take notice of the fact and govern themselves accordingly, while exhorting all able-bodied men held in bondage by Rebels to quit serving them at the earliest possible moment and repair to the most accessible Union post, there to enter the service of the United States if required and receive certificates of freedom."

July 26. "We entreat that the President's recognition of the new act as the basis of our future War Policy, be prompt, frank, thorough and decisive."

August 6. "In executing its stern resolves, the Federal Government must show no craven consideration for the local laws of the revolted States."

August 8. "Meantime, the Republic will not die—it was never more tenacious of life than at this moment. It is Slaveholding Treason that is to go by the board: just have faith to work and wait awhile, and you will see!"

August 13. "No foreign country but Dahomey would venture to side with the Davis Confederacy if it were made clear that it was fighting for Slavery while we were fighting against it."

August 16. "It is every day becoming more and more the conviction of our best minds that there can be no permanent settlement with the South short of a general act of emancipation."

Then, dated August 19 and published on the editorial page of the *Tribune* on August 20, came the fulmination, not unexpectedly, however, since according to Gilmore, Lincoln had intimation in advance of Greeley's purpose.[69] On July 18 it appears that Governor Walker and Gilmore had called on the President and discussed with him the desirability of informing Greeley of the contemplated Emancipation Proclamation as a means of warding off his editorial attack. Gilmore was authorized to carry the information to Greeley, but "The Prayer of Twenty Millions" greeted him in the *Tribune* on the morning of his arrival in New York.

The Prayer of Twenty Millions

To ABRAHAM LINCOLN, *president of the United States:*

DEAR SIR: *I do not intrude to tell you—for you must know already—that a great proportion of those who triumphed in your election, and of all who desire the unqualified suppression of the Rebellion now desolating our country, are sorely disappointed and deeply pained by the policy you seem to be pursuing with regard to the slaves of the Rebels. I write only to set succinctly and unmistakably before you what we require, what we think we have a right to expect, and of what we complain.*

I. We require of you, as the first servant of the Republic, charged especially and preëminently with this duty, that you EXECUTE THE LAWS. *Most emphatically do we demand that such laws as have been recently enacted,*

---

[69] Gilmore, *op. cit.,* pp. 75–85.

which therefore may fairly be presumed to embody the present will and to be dictated by the present needs of the Republic, and which, after due consideration have received your personal sanction, shall by you be carried into full effect, and that you publicly and decisively instruct your subordinates that such laws exist, that they are binding on all functionaries and citizens, and that they are to be obeyed to the letter.

II. *We think you are strangely and disastrously remiss in the discharge of your official and imperative duty with regard to the emancipating provisions of the new Confiscation Act. Those provisions were designed to fight Slavery with Liberty. They prescribe that men loyal to the Union, and willing to shed their blood in her behalf, shall no longer be held, with the Nation's consent, in bondage to persistent, malignant traitors, who for twenty years have been plotting and for sixteen months have been fighting to divide and destroy our country. Why these traitors should be treated with tenderness by you, to the prejudice of the dearest rights of loyal men, we cannot conceive.*

III. *We think you are unduly influenced by the counsels, the representations, the menaces, of certain fossil politicians hailing from the Border Slave States. Knowing well that the heartily, unconditionally loyal portion of the White citizens of those States do not expect nor desire that Slavery shall be upheld to the prejudice of the Union—(for the truth of which we appeal not only to every Republican residing in those States, but to such eminent loyalists as H. Winter Davis, Parson Brownlow, the Union Central Committee of Baltimore, and to The Nashville Union)—we ask you to consider that Slavery is everywhere the inciting cause and sustaining base of treason: the most slaveholding sections of Maryland and Delaware being this day, though under the Union flag, in full sympathy with the Rebellion, while the Free-Labor portions of Tennessee and of Texas, though writhing under the bloody heel of Treason, are unconquerably loyal to the Union. So emphatically is this the case, that a most intelligent Union banker of Baltimore recently avowed his confident belief that a majority of the present Legislature of Maryland, though elected as and still professing to be Unionists, are at heart desirous of the triumph of the Jeff. Davis conspiracy; and when asked how they could be won back to loyalty, replied—"Only by the complete Abolition of Slavery." It seems to us the most obvious truth, that whatever strengthens or fortifies Slavery in the Border States strengthens also Treason, and drives home the wedge intended to divide the Union. Had you from the first refused to recognize in those States, as here, any other than unconditional loyalty—that which stands for the Union, whatever may become of Slavery—those States would have been, and would be, far more helpful and less troublesome to the defenders of the Union than they have been, or now are.*

IV. *We think timid counsels in such a crisis calculated to prove perilous,* and probably disastrous. It is the duty of a Government so wantonly, wickedly assailed by Rebellion as ours has been to oppose force to force in a defiant, dauntless spirit. It cannot afford to temporize with traitors nor with semi-traitors. It must not bribe them to behave themselves, nor make them fair promises in the hope of disarming their causeless hostility. Representing a brave and high-spirited people, it can afford to forfeit anything else better than its own self-respect, or their admiring confidence. For our Government even to seek, after war has been made on it, to dispel the affected apprehensions of armed traitors that their cherished privileges may be assailed by it, is to invite insult and encourage hopes of its own downfall. The rush to arms of Ohio, Indiana, Illinois, is the true answer at once to the Rebel raids of John Morgan and the traitorous sophistries of Beriah Magoffin.

V. We complain that the Union cause has suffered, and is now suffering immensely, from mistaken deference to Rebel Slavery. Had you, Sir, in your Inaugural Address, unmistakably given notice that, in case the Rebellion already commenced were persisted in, and your efforts to preserve the Union and enforce the laws should be resisted by armed force, you would recognize no loyal person as rightfully held in Slavery by a traitor, we believe the Rebellion would therein have received a staggering if not fatal blow. At that moment, according to the returns of the most recent elections, the Unionists were a large majority of the voters of the Slave States. But they were composed in good part of the aged, the feeble, the wealthy, the timid—the young, the reckless, the aspiring, the adventurous, had already been largely lured by the gamblers and negro-traders, the politicians by trade and the conspirators by instinct, into the toils of Treason. Had you then proclaimed that Rebellion would strike the shackles from the slaves of every traitor, the wealthy and the cautious would have been supplied with a powerful inducement to remain loyal. As it was, every coward in the South soon became a traitor from fear; for Loyalty was perilous, while Treason seemed comparatively safe. Hence the boasted unanimity of the South—a unanimity based on Rebel terrorism and the fact that immunity and safety were found on that side, danger and probable death on ours. The Rebels from the first have been eager to confiscate, imprison, scourge and kill: we have fought wolves with the devices of sheep. The result is just what might have been expected. Tens of thousands are fighting in the Rebel ranks to-day whose original bias and natural leanings would have led them into ours.

VI. We complain that the Confiscation Act which you approved is habitually disregarded by your Generals, and that no word of rebuke for them from you has yet reached the public ear. Fremont's Proclamation and Hunter's Order favoring Emancipation were promptly annulled by you; while Halleck's No. 3, forbidding fugitives from Slavery to Rebels to come within his lines—an order as unmilitary as inhuman, and which received the hearty approbation of every traitor in America—with scores of like tendency, have never provoked even your own remonstrance. We complain that the officers of your Armies have habitually repelled rather than invited approach of slaves who would have gladly taken the risks of escaping from their Rebel masters to our camps, bringing intelligence often of inestimable value to the Union cause. We complain that those who have thus escaped to us, avowing a willingness to do for us whatever might be required, have been brutally and madly repulsed, and often surrendered to be scourged, maimed and tortured by the ruffian traitors, who pretend to own them. We complain that a large proportion of our regular Army Officers, with many of the Volunteers, evince far more solicitude to uphold Slavery than to put down the Rebellion. And finally, we complain that you, Mr. President, elected as a Republican, knowing well what an abomination Slavery is, and how emphatically it is the core and essence of this atrocious Rebellion, seem never to interfere with these atrocities, and never give a direction to your Military subordinates, which does not appear to have been conceived in the interest of Slavery rather than of Freedom.

VII. Let me call your attention to the recent tragedy in New-Orleans, whereof the facts are obtained entirely through Pro-Slavery channels. A considerable body of resolute, able-bodied men, held in Slavery by two Rebel sugar-planters in defiance of the Confiscation Act which you have approved, left plantations thirty miles distant and made their way to the great mart of the South-West, which they knew to be the indisputed possession of the Union forces. They made their way safely and quietly through thirty miles of Rebel territory, expecting to find freedom under the protection of our flag. Whether they had or had not heard of the passage of the Confiscation Act, they reasoned logically that we could not kill them for deserting the service of their lifelong oppressors, who had through treason become our implacable enemies. They came to us for liberty and protection, for which they were willing to render their best service: they met with hostility, captivity, and murder. The barking of the base curs of Slavery in this quarter deceives no one—not even themselves. They say, indeed, that the negroes had no right to appear in New Orleans armed (with their implements of daily labor in the cane-field); but no one doubts that they would gladly have laid these down if assured that they should be free. They were set upon and maimed, captured and killed, because they sought the benefit of that act of Congress which they may not specifically have heard of, but which was none the less the law of the land—which they had a clear right to the benefit of—which it was somebody's duty to publish far and wide, in order that so many as possible should be impelled to desist from serving Rebels and the Rebellion and come over to the side of the Union. They sought their liberty in strict accordance with the law of the land—they were butchered or reënslaved for so doing by the help of Union soldiers enlisted to fight against

Slaveholding Treason. It was somebody's fault that they were so murdered —if others shall hereafter suffer in like manner, in default of explicit and public directions to your generals that they are to recognize and obey the Confiscation Act, the world will lay the blame on you. Whether you will choose to hear it through future History and at the bar of God, I will not judge. I can only hope.

VIII. On the face of this wide earth, Mr. President, there is not one disinterested, determined, intelligent champion of the Union cause who does not feel that all attempts to put down the Rebellion and at the same time uphold its inciting cause are preposterous and futile—that the Rebellion, if crushed out tomorrow, would be renewed within a year if Slavery were left in full vigor—that Army officers who remain to this day devoted to Slavery can at best be but half-way loyal to the Union—and that every hour of deference to Slavery is an hour of added and deepened peril to the Union. I appeal to the testimony of your Embassadors in Europe. It is freely at your service, not at mine. Ask them to tell you candidly whether the seeming subserviency of your policy to the slaveholding, slavery-upholding interest, is not the perplexity, the despair of statesmen of all parties, and be admonished by the general answer.

IX. I close as I began with the statement that what an immense majority of the Loyal Millions of your countrymen require of you is a frank, declared, unqualified, ungrudging execution of the laws of the land, more especially of the Confiscation Act. That Act gives freedom to the slaves of Rebels coming within our lines, or whom those lines may at any time inclose—we ask you to render it due obedience by publicly requiring all your subordinates to recognize and obey it. The Rebels are everywhere using the late anti-negro riots in the North, as they have long used your officers' treatment of negroes in the South, to convince the slaves that they have nothing to hope from a Union success—that we mean in that case to sell them into a bitter bondage to defray the cost of war. Let them impress this as a truth on the great mass of their ignorant and credulous bondsmen, and the Union will never be restored—never. We cannot conquer Ten Millions of People united in solid phalanx against us, powerfully aided by the Northern sympathizers and European allies. We must have scouts, guides, spies, cooks, teamsters, diggers and choppers from the Blacks of the South, whether we allow them to fight for us or not, or we shall be baffled and repelled. As one of the millions who would gladly have avoided this struggle at any sacrifice but that of Principle and Honor, but who now feel that the triumph of the Union is indispensable not only to the existence of our country but to the well-being of mankind, I entreat you to render a hearty and unequivocal obedience to the law of the land.

Yours,

Horace Greeley.

New York, August 19, 1862.

Before quoting Lincoln's reply, which was immediate, it may be well to present the existing evidence of what was going on in the President's mind during these months of uncertainty. We know that Lincoln had long advocated gradual emancipation through compensation and that he strongly favored colonization. On the question of emancipation by presidential edict as a war measure, he deliberately kept his own counsel and in all his public utterances clung to his view that the war was being prosecuted to preserve the Union and not to interfere with the legal status of slavery. It is true he had more than once spoken in general terms of the employment of all "indispensable means" to suppress the Rebellion.

So far as the record goes it was not until July 13, 1862, that Lincoln broached the subject of emancipation even to the members of his Cabinet. The Secretary of the Navy, Gideon Welles, recorded in his diary what took place on that day. The President had invited Seward and Welles to accompany him in his carriage to attend the funeral of an infant child of Edwin M. Stanton, then Secretary of War. On this occasion Lincoln first mentioned to his associates the subject of emancipating the slaves by proclamation in case the rebels did not cease to persist in their war on the government and the Union. He saw no evidence of any purpose on their part to desist. He had given the subject much thought, realized the importance and delicacy of the movement, and had about come to the conclusion that it was a military necessity for the salvation of the Union. He assured Seward and Welles that this was the first time he had mentioned the subject to anyone. "It was a new departure for the President," wrote Welles, "for until this time, in all our previous interviews, whenever the question of emancipation or the mitigation of slavery had been in any way alluded to, he had been prompt and emphatic in denouncing any interference by the General Government with the subject. This was, I think, the sentiment of every member of the Cabinet, all of whom, including the President, considered it a local, domestic question appertaining to the States respectively, who had never parted with their authority over it."[70]

This discussion of the possibility of emancipation as a necessity of war, it should be kept in mind, occurred on the day after Lincoln had addressed the representatives of the border states on the question of compensated emancipation when he had said: "I do not speak of emancipation at once, but of a decision at once to emancipate grad-

---

[70] Edgar T. Welles, ed., *The Diary of Gideon Welles*, I, 70–71.

ually."[71] It should also be kept in mind that the day after his talk with Seward and Welles, the President submitted to Congress a draft of a bill to compensate any state which might abolish slavery and earnestly recommended its passage.[72]

The testimony of Secretary Welles is confirmed by the diary of the Secretary of the Treasury, Salmon P. Chase, who left a full account of a Cabinet meeting held on July 21. "I went at the appointed hour," said Chase, "and found that the President had been profoundly concerned at the present aspect of affairs, and had determined to take some definite steps in respect to military action and slavery."[73] The Cabinet met again on July 22; Chase recorded the deliberations fully, and touching the main issue said:

The question of arming slaves was then brought up and I advocated it warmly. The President was unwilling to adopt this measure, but proposed to issue a proclamation, on the basis of the Confiscation Bill, calling upon the States to return to their allegiance—warning the rebels the provisions of the Act would have full force at the expiration of sixty days—adding, on his own part, a declaration of his intention to renew, at the next session of Congress, his recommendation of compensation to States adopting the gradual abolishment of slavery—and proclaiming the emancipation of all slaves within States remaining in insurrection on the first of January, 1863.[74]

The proposed proclamation as submitted to the Cabinet on July 22 read as follows:

IN PURSUANCE *of the sixth section of the act of Congress entitled "An act to suppress insurrection and to punish treason and rebellion, to seize and confiscate property of rebels, and for other purposes" approved July 17, 1862, and which act and the joint resolution explanatory thereof are herewith published, I, Abraham Lincoln, President of the United States, do hereby proclaim to and warn all persons within the contemplation of said sixth section to cease participating in, aiding, countenancing, or abetting the existing rebellion, or any rebellion, against the Government of the United States, and to return to their proper allegiance to the United States, on pain of the forfeitures and seizures as within and by said sixth section provided.*

And I hereby make known that it is my purpose, upon the next meeting of Congress, to again recommend the adoption of a practical measure for tendering pecuniary aid to the free choice or rejection of any and all States which may then be recognizing and practically sustaining the authority of

---

[71] Nicolay and Hay, *Complete Works*, VII, 272.
[72] *Ibid.*, pp. 276–77.
[73] Salmon P. Chase, *Diary and Correspondence of Salmon P. Chase*, II, 45–47.
[74] *Ibid.*, p. 48.

the United States, and which may then have voluntarily adopted, or there-
after may voluntarily adopt, gradual abolishment of slavery within such
State or States; that the object is to practically restore, thenceforward to
be maintained, the constitutional relation between the General Government
and each and all the States wherein that relation is now suspended or dis-
turbed; and that for this object the war, as it has been, will be prosecuted.
And as a fit and necessary military measure for effecting this object, I, as
commander-in-chief of the army and navy of the United States, do order
and declare that on the first day of January, in the year of our Lord one
thousand eight hundred and sixty-three, all persons held as slaves within
any State or States wherein the constitutional authority of the United States
shall not then be practically recognized, submitted to, and maintained, shall
then, thenceforward, and forever be free.[75]

The best account of this memorable Cabinet meeting is to be found
in the President's own words as reported by F. B. Carpenter, the artist,
who was commissioned in 1864 to paint a portrait of the Cabinet at
the first reading of the Emancipation Proclamation. Carpenter's account of what Lincoln said fits in closely with such other records as
are available and has been widely accepted:

"It had got to be," said he, "midsummer, 1862. Things had gone on from
bad to worse, until I felt that we had reached the end of our rope on the plan
of operations we had been pursuing; that we had about played our last card,
and must change our tactics, or lose the game! I now determined upon the
adoption of the emancipation policy; and, without consultation with, or the
knowledge of the Cabinet, I prepared the original draft of the proclamation,
and, after much anxious thought, called a Cabinet meeting upon the sub-
ject. This was the last of July, or the first part of the month of August, 1862."
(The exact date he did not remember.) "This Cabinet meeting took place,
I think, upon a Saturday. All were present, excepting Mr. Blair, the
Postmaster-General, who was absent at the opening of the discussion, but
came in subsequently. I said to the Cabinet that I had resolved upon this
step, and had not called them together to ask their advice, but to lay the
subject-matter of a proclamation before them; suggestions as to which would
be in order, after they had heard it read. Mr. Lovejoy," said he, "was in error
when he informed you that it excited no comment, excepting on the part
of Secretary Seward. Various suggestions were offered. Secretary Chase
wished the language stronger in reference to the arming of the blacks. Mr.
Blair, after he came in, deprecated the policy, on the ground that it would
cost the Administration the fall elections. Nothing, however, was offered

---

[75] Nicolay and Hay, *Complete Works,* VII, 289–90.

that I had not already fully anticipated and settled in my own mind, until Secretary Seward spoke. He said in substance: 'Mr. President, I approve of the proclamation, but I question the expediency of its issue at this juncture. The depression of the public mind, consequent upon our repeated reverses, is so great that I fear the effect of so important a step. It may be viewed as the last measure of an exhausted government, a cry for help; the government stretching forth its hands to Ethiopia, instead of Ethiopia stretching forth her hands to the government.' His idea," said the President, "was that it would be considered our last shriek, *on the retreat." (This was his* precise *expression.) " 'Now,' continued Mr. Seward, 'while I approve the measure, I suggest, sir, that you postpone its issue, until you can give it to the country supported by military success, instead of issuing it, as would be the case now, upon the greatest disasters of the war!' " Mr. Lincoln continued: "The wisdom of the view of the Secretary of State struck me with very great force. It was an aspect of the case that, in all my thought upon the subject, I had entirely overlooked. The result was that I put the draft of the proclamation aside, as you do your sketch for a picture, waiting for a victory."*[76]

On the day of this Cabinet meeting the Secretary of War, by order of the President, had issued an order to all commanders in Virginia, North Carolina, Georgia, Florida, Alabama, Mississippi, Louisiana, Texas, and Arkansas directing them to seize and use any property, real or personal, for supplies or other purposes; to employ as laborers as many persons of African descent as could be used advantageously and to give them reasonable wages; to keep accounts both as to property and persons of African descent as a basis upon which compensation could be made in proper cases.[77] On July 25 the President issued a proclamation in connection with the sixth section of the Confiscation Act, approved July 17, warning "all persons within the contemplation of said sixth section to cease participating in, aiding, countenancing, or abetting the existing rebellion, or any rebellion against the Government of the United States, and to return to their proper allegiance to the United States, on pain of the forfeitures and seizures as within and by said sixth section provided."[78]

In private correspondence Lincoln began to hint at something to come. To Reverdy Johnson he wrote on July 26: "I am a patient man —always ready to forgive on the Christian terms of repentance, and also to give ample time for repentance. Still I must save this govern-

---

[76] Francis B. Carpenter, *Six Months at the White House*, pp. 20–22.
[77] Nicolay and Hay, *Complete Works*, VII, 287–88.
[78] *Ibid.*, pp. 291–92.

ment, if possible. What I cannot do, of course I will not do; but it may as well be understood, once for all, that I shall not surrender this game leaving any available card unplayed."[79]

To Cuthbert Bullitt he wrote on July 28: "What would you do in my position? Would you drop the war where it is? Or would you prosecute it in the future with elder-stock squirts charged with rose-water? Would you deal lighter blows rather than heavier ones? Would you give up the contest, leaving any available means unapplied?"[80]

To August Belmont he wrote on August 31: "This government cannot much longer play a game in which it stakes all, and its enemies stake nothing."[81]

On August 14 the President gave an audience to a committee of colored men at the White House and said to them that without the institution of slavery and the colored race as a basis the war could not have an existence. He then made a plea for colonization in Central America and said that he could make a successful commencement if he could have a hundred, fifty, or even twenty-five tolerably intelligent men with their wives and children able to "cut their own fodder."[82]

On August 23 Lincoln's reply to "The Prayer of Twenty Millions" was first published in the *National Intelligencer*. Although addressed to Greeley, it was shrewdly calculated to arrest the attention of the nation and to accustom the public mind to "freeing all the slaves":

Executive Mansion,
Washington, August 22, 1862.

Hon. Horace *Greely* [sic]:
Dear Sir—

I have just read yours of the 19th *addressed to myself through the New-York Tribune— If there be in it any statements, or assumptions of fact, which I may know to be erroneous, I do not, now and here, controvert them. If there be in it any inferences which I may believe to be falsely drawn, I do not now and here, argue against them. If there be perceptable [sic] in it an impatient and dictatorial tone, I waive it in deference to an old friend, whose heart I have always supposed to be right—*

As to the policy I "seem to be pursuing" as you say, I have not meant to leave any one in doubt—

I would save the Union. I would save it the shortest way under the Constitution. The sooner the national authority can be restored, the nearer the

---

[79] *Ibid.*, pp. 292–94, Lincoln to Reverdy Johnson, July 26, 1862.
[80] *Ibid.*, pp. 294–98, Lincoln to Cuthbert Bullitt, July 28, 1862.
[81] *Ibid.*, pp. 299–300, Lincoln to August Belmont, July 31, 1862.
[82] *Ibid.*, VIII, 1–9.

Union will be "the Union as it was." (Broken eggs can never be mended, and the longer the breaking process, the more will be broken—) If there be those who would not save the Union, unless they could at the same time save slavery, I do not agree with them— If there be those who would not save the Union unless they could at the same time destroy slavery, I do not agree with them.

My paramount object in this struggle is to save the Union, and is not either to save or to destroy slavery— If I could save the Union without freeing any slave I would do it, and if I could save it by freeing all the slaves I would do it; and if I could save it by freeing some and leaving others alone I would also do that— What I do about slavery, and the colored race, I do because I believe it helps to save the Union; and what I forbear, I forbear because I do not believe it would help to save the Union— I shall do less whenever I shall believe what I am doing hurts the cause, and I shall do more whenever I shall believe doing more will help the cause— I shall try to correct errors when shown to be errors; and I shall adopt new views so fast as they shall appear to be true views—

I have here stated my purpose according to my view of official duty; and I intend no modification of my oft-expressed personal wish that all men everywhere could be free—

Yours,

A. Lincoln[83]

Never satisfied in any debate without a rejoinder, Greeley published Lincoln's letter on the editorial page of the *Tribune* on August 25 and followed it with further protestations in a letter addressed to the President.

*Dear Sir:— Although I did not anticipate nor seek any reply to my former letter unless through your official acts, I thank you for having accorded one, since it enables me to say explicitly that nothing was further from my thought than to impeach in any manner the sincerity or the intensity of your devotion to the saving of the Union. I never doubted, and have no friend who doubts, that you desire, before and above all else, to re-establish the now derided authority, and vindicate the territorial integrity, of the Republic. I intended to raise only this question,—*Do you propose to do this by recognizing, obeying, and enforcing the laws, or by ignoring, disregarding, and in effect defying them?

I stand upon the law of the land. The humblest has a clear right to invoke its protection and support against even the highest. That law—in strict ac-

---

[83] *Ibid.*, pp. 15–16, Lincoln to Greeley, August 22, 1862. Reproduced with Lincoln's underlining, spelling, and punctuation from the original in the Wadsworth Atheneum, Hartford, Connecticut. The sentence in parentheses about broken eggs was crossed out by Lincoln.

cordance with the law of nations, of Nature, and of God—declares that every traitor now engaged in the infernal work of destroying our country has forfeited thereby all claim or color of right lawfully to hold human beings in slavery. I ask of you a clear and public recognition that this law is to be obeyed wherever the national authority is respected. I cite to you instances wherein men fleeing from bondage to traitors to the protection of our flag have been assaulted, wounded, and murdered by soldiers of the Union, unpunished and unrebuked by your General Commanding,—to prove that it is your duty to take action in the premises,—action that will cause the law to be proclaimed and obeyed wherever your authority or that of the Union is recognized as paramount. The Rebellion is strengthened, the national cause is imperilled, by every hour's delay to strike Treason this staggering blow.

When Fremont proclaimed freedom to the slaves of rebels, you constrained him to modify his proclamation into rigid accordance with the terms of the existing law. It was your clear right to do so. I now ask of you conformity to the principle so sternly enforced upon him. I ask you to instruct your generals and commodores, that no loyal person—certainly none willing to render service to the national cause—is henceforth to be regarded as the slave of any traitor. While no rightful government was ever before assailed by so wanton and wicked a rebellion as that of the slaveholders against our national life, I am sure none ever before hesitated at so simple and primary an act of self-defense, as to relieve those who would serve and save it from chattel servitude to those who are wading through seas of blood to subvert and destroy it. Future generations will with difficulty realize that there could have been hesitation on this point. Sixty years of general and boundless subserviency to the slave power do not adequately explain it.

Mr. President, I beseech you to open your eyes to the fact that the devotees of slavery everywhere—just as much in Maryland as in Mississippi, in Washington as in Richmond—are to-day your enemies, and the implacable foes of every effort to re-establish the national authority by the discomfiture of its assailants. Their President is not Abraham Lincoln, but Jefferson Davis. You may draft them to serve in the war; but they will only fight under the Rebel flag. There is not in New York to-day a man who really believes in slavery, loves it, and desires its perpetuation, who heartily desires the crushing out of the Rebellion. He would much rather save the Republic by buying up and pensioning off its assailants. His "Union as it was" is a Union of which you were not President, and no one who truly wished freedom to all ever could be.

If these are truths, Mr. President, they are surely of the gravest importance. You cannot safely approach the great and good end you so intently meditate by shutting your eyes to them. Your deadly foe is not blinded by any mist in which your eyes may be enveloped. He walks straight to his goal, knowing well his weak point, and most unwillingly betraying his fear that you too *may see and take advantage of it. God grant that his apprehension may prove prophetic!*

That you may not unseasonably perceive these vital truths as they will shine forth on the pages of history,—that they may be read by our children irradiated by the glory of our national salvation, not rendered lurid by the blood-red glow of national conflagration and ruin,—that you may promptly and practically realize that slavery is to be vanquished only by liberty,—is the fervent and anxious prayer of

Yours truly,
Horace Greeley[84]

New York, August 24, 1862.

The *New York Times* printed Lincoln's letter on August 25 on its front page and editorially remarked that he could not have said anything more satisfactory to the country in general. "The letter, like all Mr. Lincoln's literary attempts," the *Times* continued, "exhibits the peculiarities of his mind and style; but the logical sequence and precision, and the grammatical accuracy of this, is greatly in advance of any previous effort. It is in infinitely better taste, too, than the rude epistle to which it is an answer." The *Times* returned to the subject on August 25 and said:

The chief difference between Mr. Lincoln and Mr. Greeley seems to be this: that the former is President and was sworn on his own conscience, and must be governed by his own sense of oath, honor and duty, as to the time and manner of his actions. On the other hand Mr. Greeley having clearer conceptions, it may be, of right, policy and statesmanship, wishes to substitute his conscience for Mr. Lincoln's in the present National perplexity. The President not yet seeing the propriety of abdicating in behalf of our neighbor, consoles him with a letter that assures the country of abundant sanity in the White House.

On August 27 Greeley wrote to George W. Wright: "As to Old Abe's letter, I consider it a sign of progress. I have no doubt the Nation will get on the right ground at last; I only fear it will get *under* the ground previously. It is time to fight with both hands now."[85] Subsequently, more than three years after Lincoln's death, Greeley recorded his belief that Lincoln's letter had been prepared before he ever saw the "Prayer" and that he merely used the occasion for setting his own altered position—"changed not by volition but by circumstances"

---

[84] *Tribune,* August 25, 1862, Greeley to Lincoln.
[85] Greeley Papers, Library of Congress, Washington, D.C., Greeley to George W. Wright, August 27, 1862.

—fairly before the country. Looking back upon the event, Greeley was generous enough, however, to remark that he had no doubt that Lincoln's letter expressed "the exact literal truth, precisely as it lay in his mind."[86]

So far as the President was concerned, this flurry with the editor of the *Tribune* came to an end promptly, and the papers connected with it no doubt went into the pigeonhole labeled "Horace Greeley" with a sigh of relief by the tired man in the White House.

Now privately informed of the President's anticipated Emancipation Proclamation, Greeley continued to hammer along the line he had been pursuing for months. He demanded of the President "obedience to the laws of the land," continued to urge the enforcement of the Confiscation Act in "no grudging, half-way, underhand, equivocating, clandestine deference" but in "an open, loyal, hearty, thorough recognition and execution of it." "Let it be proclaimed tomorrow from the White House," he said, "that *every slave fleeing to us from the Rebels is thenceforth a free man*, and the knell of Treason will have been sounded."[87] He again offered advice to the Administration to "have the patriotism and the fortitude to sacrifice whatever stands in the way" and warned that the people would not tolerate in their rulers "hesitation, timidity, blundering."[88]

During this period while Greeley was demanding, advising, and warning in his accustomed fashion, the President received a committee from the religious denominations of Chicago asking him to issue a proclamation of emancipation. With the tentative copy of such a document in his desk, he said to the committee:

What good would a proclamation of emancipation from me do, especially as we are now situated? I do not want to issue a document that the whole world will see must necessarily be inoperative, like the Pope's bull against the comet. Would my word free the slaves, when I cannot even enforce the Constitution in the rebel States? . . . For instance, when, after the late battles at and near Bull Run, an expedition went out from Washington under a flag of truce to bury the dead and bring in the wounded, and the rebels seized the blacks who went along to help, and sent them into slavery, Horace Greeley said in his paper that the government would probably do nothing about it. What could I do? Now, then, tell me, if you please, what possible result of good would follow the issuing of such a proclamation as

---

[86] MS, Greeley's lecture on "Abraham Lincoln," p. 40, Henry E. Huntington Library, San Marino, California.

[87] *Tribune*, August 22, 1862.

[88] *Ibid.*, September 4, 1862.

you desire? Understand, I raise no objections against it on legal or constitutional grounds; for, as commander-in-chief of the army and navy, in time of war I suppose I have a right to take any measure which may best subdue the enemy. . . . I have not decided against a proclamation of liberty to the slaves, but hold the matter under advisement; and I can assure you that the subject is on my mind, by day and night, more than any other. Whatever shall appear to be God's will, I will do.[89]

The literal "by day and night" deliberation continued until the preliminary Emancipation Proclamation was given to the world on September 22, 1862. Again we must turn to F. B. Carpenter's record for Lincoln's own words:

From time to time I added or changed a line, touching it up here and there, anxiously watching the progress of events. Well, the next news we had was of Pope's disaster at Bull Run. Things looked darker than ever. Finally, came the week of the battle of Antietam. I determined to wait no longer. The news came, I think, on Wednesday, that the advantage was on our side. I was then staying at the Soldiers' Home, (three miles out of Washington.) Here I finished writing the second draft of the preliminary proclamation; came up on Saturday; called the Cabinet together to hear it, and it was published the following Monday.[90]

More than two years later in speaking of the proclamation, Lincoln said to Carpenter: "It is the central act of my administration, and the great event of the nineteenth century."[91]

John Hay missed the opportunity of his life by failing to record in his diary the full circumstances attending the preparation and issuance of what he termed "the momentous document."[92] Not so the more faithful diarists, Chase and Welles. They were in substantial agreement in their accounts of what took place at the Cabinet meeting on Monday, September 22. Lincoln had kept his own counsel on the emancipation issue until he first discussed it with the Cabinet in July; he had then put it aside awaiting a signal Union victory; he waited until he felt it was God's will before determining upon action; and he now submitted the proclamation to the Cabinet for their advice and counsel as to details but with the already settled determination to go forward with its promulgation. They also agreed that after minor

---

[89] Nicolay and Hay, *Complete Works*, VIII, 28–33.

[90] Carpenter, *op. cit.*, pp. 22–23.

[91] *Ibid.*, p. 90. For accounts of Antietam, see Henry Steele Commager, *The Blue and the Gray*, I, 203–27; and Kenneth P. Williams, *Lincoln Finds a General*, II, 445–79.

[92] Tyler Dennett, *Lincoln and the Civil War—In the Diaries and Letters of John Hay*, p. 50.

changes in language all members of the Cabinet, except Secretary Blair, fully approved of the proposed action. Mr. Blair approved in principle but thought the time not propitious.

According to Chase, Lincoln opened the Cabinet meeting by reading a chapter from a book he had just received from Artemas Ward, to the enjoyment of all except Secretary Stanton, and then assuming a graver tone said:

Gentlemen: I have, as you are aware, thought a great deal about the relation of this war to Slavery: and you all remember that, several weeks ago, I read to you an Order I had prepared on this subject, which, on account of objections made by some of you, was not issued. Ever since then, my mind has been much occupied with this subject, and I have thought all along that the time for acting on it might very probably come. I think the time has come now. I wish it were a better time. I wish that we were in better condition. The action of the army against the rebels has not been quite what I should have best liked. But they have been driven out of Maryland, and Pennsylvania is no longer in danger of invasion. When the rebel army was at Frederick, I determined, as soon as it should be driven out of Maryland, to issue a Proclamation of Emancipation such as I thought most likely to be useful. I said nothing to any one; but I made the promise to myself, and (hesitating a little)—to my Maker. The rebel army is now driven out, and I am going to fulfill that promise. I have got you together to hear what I have written down. I do not wish your advice about the main matter—for that I have determined for myself. This I say without intending anything but respect for any one of you. But I already know the views of each on this question. They have been heretofore expressed, and I have considered them as thoroughly and carefully as I can. What I have written is that which my reflections have determined me to say. If there is anything in the expressions I use, or in any other minor matter, which any one of you thinks had best be changed, I shall be glad to receive the suggestions. One other observation I will make. I know very well that many others might, in this matter, as in others, do better than I can; and if I were satisfied that the public confidence was more fully possessed by any one of them than by me, and knew of any Constitutional way in which he could be put in my place, he should have it. I would gladly yield it to him. But though I believe that I have not so much of the confidence of the people as I had some time since, I do not know that, all things considered, any other person has more; and, however this may be, there is no way in which I can have any other man put where I am. I am here. I must do the best I can, and bear the responsibility of taking the course which I feel I ought to take.[93]

---

[93] Chase, *op. cit.*, II, 87–88.

The diary of Gideon Welles touching this Cabinet meeting confirms that of Chase very literally:

The subject was the Proclamation for emancipating the slaves after a certain date, in States that shall then be in rebellion. For several weeks the subject has been suspended, but the President says never lost sight of. When it was submitted, and now in taking up the Proclamation, the President stated that the question was finally decided, the act and the consequences were his, but that he felt it due to us to make us acquainted with the fact and to invite criticism on the paper which he had prepared. There were, he had found, not unexpectedly, some differences in the Cabinet, but he had, after ascertaining in his own way the views of each and all, individually and collectively, formed his own conclusions and made his own decisions. In the course of the discussion on this paper, which was long, earnest, and, on the general principle involved, harmonious, he remarked that he had made a vow, a covenant, that if God gave us the victory in the approaching battle, he would consider it an indication of Divine will, and that it was his duty to move forward in the cause of emancipation. It might be thought strange, he said, that he had in this way submitted the disposal of matters when the way was not clear to his mind what he should do. God had decided this question in favor of the slaves. He was satisfied it was right, was confirmed and strengthened in his action by the vow and the results. His mind was fixed, his decision made, but he wished his paper announcing his course as correct in terms as it could be made without any change in his determination.[94]

These closely related accounts by two responsible members of the Cabinet are in part confirmed in substance by still another diary. James C. Welling, one of the editors of the *National Intelligencer*, recorded in his diary on September 27 a visit he had that day from the Hon. Edward Stanley, military governor of North Carolina. Stanley told Welling that he had had several interviews with the President respecting the "Proclamation of Freedom." The President had told him that the proclamation had become a civil necessity to prevent the radicals from openly embarrassing the government in the conduct of the war. The President further expressed the belief that, without the proclamation for which they had been clamoring, the radicals in Congress would take the extreme step of withdrawing supplies for carrying on the war, leaving the whole land in anarchy. Mr. Lincoln said that he prayed to the Almighty to save him from this necessity, adopting

---

[94] Welles, *op. cit.*, I, 142–45.

the language of our Saviour, "If it be possible, let this cup pass from me," but the prayer had not been answered.[95]

Acting, in his view under Divine guidance, Lincoln announced "the great event of the nineteenth century," including the memorable words, "on the first day of January, in the year of our Lord one thousand eight hundred and sixty-three, all persons held as slaves within any State or designated part of a State the people whereof shall then be in rebellion against the United States, shall be then, thenceforward, and forever free."[96]

In his rejoicing at the preliminary proclamation, Greeley rose to new heights. It seemed almost as if the *editor* had for the time being been swallowed up by the finer instincts of the *man*. The proclamation was published on the editorial page of the *Tribune* on September 23 together with a detailed analysis of its terms ending with the words "GOD BLESS ABRAHAM LINCOLN!"

On the following day, Greeley developed "The Proclamation of Freedom" at length, declaring that "in the lives of nations and of men there comes sometimes a precious moment, a mere point of time, on the proper use of which depends salvation for that life, whether temporal or eternal. That moment has come to us." The proclamation of the President was "one of those stupendous facts in human history which marks not only an era in the progress of the nation, but an epoch in the history of the world." Turning to the man who had been the instrument of this great act, he said:

Let the President know that everywhere throughout the land he is hailed as Wisest and Best, and that by this great deed of enfranchisement to an oppressed people—a deed, the doing whereof was never before vouchsafed to any mortal ruler—he re-creates a nation. . . . But this man, sprung from the people, has gauged the wisdom and the virtue of the commonalty, and speaks with their voice. The sagacity and the integrity which so distinguish him have no more failed him now than heretofore. All good men praise him; all far-seeing men approve his action; all brave men applaud the courage which, unappalled by accumulating danger, never falters, never yields, but puts forth its strength at the right moment, and plants the right blow in the right place. It is the way to conquer; it must conquer; it cannot fail.

During the hundred days between the issuance of the preliminary and final emancipation proclamations, Greeley maintained a kindly, and at least judicial attitude toward the Administration. His optimistic

---

[95] *North American Review*, February, 1880, pp. 171–72.
[96] Nicolay and Hay, *Complete Works*, VIII, 36–41.

viewpoint was maintained in part by the President's action in relieving General McClellan from the command of the Army of the Potomac. Greeley had been among those who hailed McClellan's appointment to this post with "hope and joy." He trusted McClellan as "the predestined right arm of the Republic," and it took many months to cure him of that "fond delusion." McClellan's "chronic incapacity for getting on" had worked the change.[97] Greeley was not alone in his impatience with McClellan. The President no doubt shared Greeley's views long before he acted.

Rothschild sums up the relations between the President and McClellan aptly:

A father, advising, chiding, encouraging, by turns, a wilful son could not have treated this rasping officer with more uniform indulgence. We rise from a reading of their correspondence with a nicer perception of the President's nobility of character—a keener admiration than ever of his rugged strength. Strong enough to hold McClellan where he had put him, in the teeth of perhaps as powerful an opposition as has ever been massed against a commander; strong enough to ignore the signs which foreshadowed McClellan's political rivalry; and strong, above all, in the perfect self-control with which he met McClellan's unmerited reproaches, Lincoln manifested, throughout this trying period, how high he deserves to rank among the masters of men.[98]

In his annual message to Congress on December 1, 1862, Lincoln referred incidentally to his preliminary proclamation of September 22 and then only as a means of paving the way for a discussion of "compensated emancipation." He made no reference whatever to the final proclamation which was to be promulgated on January 1, 1863. Instead, he entered into an extended discussion of the desirability and adaptability of the United States as the home of one national family. "In all its adoptions and aptitudes," he said, "it demands union and abhors separation." To this end he recommended three articles amendatory to the Constitution: first, providing for compensation to every state wherein slavery existed which should "abolish the same therein at any time or times" before January 1, 1900; second, providing that all slaves who enjoyed "actual freedom by the chances of war before the end of the rebellion" should be "forever free," but that the owners of such slaves who were not disloyal should be compensated for

---

[97] *Tribune*, November 10, 1862.
[98] Alonzo Rothschild, *Lincoln, Master of Men*, p. 392. See also Williams, *op. cit.*, II, 475–79.

them; third, authorizing Congress to appropriate money and otherwise provide "for colonizing free colored persons, with their own consent, at any place or places without the United States." He then entered into an elaborate explanation and defense of these proposed amendments to the Constitution and ended his appeal in these memorable words: "In giving freedom to the slave, we assume freedom to the free—honorable alike in what we give and what we preserve. We shall nobly save or meanly lose the last, best hope of earth. Other means may succeed; this could not fail. The way is plain, peaceful, generous, just—a way which, if followed, the world will forever applaud, and God must forever bless."[99]

Greeley's amiable mood was still upon him when he approached the discussion of the President's message on December 2. He was well pleased that the country should have one among its leaders "in whose integrity, patriotism, and uncalculating devotion to the noblest ends, all may and do confide. . . . There lives no loyal American," he said, "who distrusts his earnest desire to serve and save the Union." Greeley interpreted the message to mean the President's full recognition that slavery had become the implacable foe of the American Union and that slavery must die in order that the republic should live. Heartily agreeing with the President on the main question, Greeley differed on subordinate points "without reserve and without feeling." He did not favor "Gradualism" and "Negro Exportation." He was ready, however, to waive all incidentals. "Gradualism, Compensation, Exportation," he said, "if these tubs amuse the whale, let him have them."

The one hundred days approached an end. The final discussion of the Emancipation Proclamation took place at Cabinet meetings on Monday, December 29, and on Wednesday, December 31, 1862.[100] The President accepted minor suggestions in form made by several members of the Cabinet and completed the document which was given to the world on January 1, 1863. It ended with the words: "And upon this act, sincerely believed to be an act of justice, warranted by the Constitution upon military necessity, I invoke the considerate judgment of mankind and the gracious favor of Almighty God."[101]

The climax of Greeley's enthusiasm was apparently reached upon the issuance of the preliminary proclamation. Although the *Tribune* printed the proclamation in full on the editorial page on January 3,

---

[99] Nicolay and Hay, *Complete Works*, VIII, 93–131.
[100] Welles, *op. cit.*, I, 209–11.
[101] Nicolay and Hay, *Complete Works*, VIII, 161–64.

1863, and Greeley hailed it as "a great stride toward the restoration of the Union," he immediately complained because it did not apply to Tennessee and the lower portion of Louisiana which he insisted were in "flagrant rebellion." In this connection he expressed his profound regret that the President had not "hewed up to the line chalked by himself." And then, as if on second thought, he concluded his grumbling editorial with the words: "Let it not be said that we cavil at the Proclamation and seek to undervalue it. It is worth very much, even though it might have been made worth far more. We trust that it will play a great and beneficent part in rescuing our country from anarchy and devastation, and restoring it to unity and peace."

Three days after discussing the proclamation, Greeley wrote one of his few letters to the President on a purely personal matter. Ward H. Lamon, United States Marshal for the District of Columbia, had brought suit against Greeley in the Circuit Court for the District for alleged libel in the *Tribune*. Through Lincoln's intervention the case never came to trial. On January 6, Greeley wrote a kindly note of thanks to Lincoln for his "interposition in the libel case," but he could not refrain from ending the note with his uppermost thought: "Hoping that our sky begins at length to clear, and trusting that an early opportunity will be found for making an honorable peace, I remain, Yours, gratefully, Horace Greeley." Greeley dated the letter incorrectly, "January 6, 1862," instead of January 6, 1863.[102]

In his annual message to Congress on December 8, 1863, Lincoln outlined the part the Emancipation Proclamation had played in restoring the nation to unity and peace in the eleven months since its issuance. The complete opening of the Mississippi had divided the rebel-dominated country into distinct parts, with no practical means of communication between them. Tennessee and Arkansas had been substantially cleared of insurgent control and influential citizens in each state, owners of slaves and advocates of slavery at the beginning of the Rebellion, had now declared openly for emancipation. Of the states not included in the Emancipation Proclamation, Maryland and Missouri, neither of which three years before would tolerate any extension of slavery into new territories, now only disputed as to the best mode of removing it within their own limits. Of those who had been slaves at the beginning of the Rebellion, fully 100,000 were in the United States military service, and 50,000 of these were bearing arms

---

[102] Robert Todd Lincoln Collection (13856), *op. cit.*, Greeley to Lincoln, January 6, 1863.

in the ranks. No servile insurrection, or tendency to violence or cruelty, had marked the measures of emancipation and the arming of the Negroes. The tone of public sentiment in foreign countries concerning emancipation was much improved. At home the annual elections following emancipation were highly encouraging to those whose official duty it was to see the country through its great trial.[103]

In the light of this "new reckoning" the President had thought fit to issue on the day of his annual message to Congress a Proclamation of Amnesty and Reconstruction, a copy of which he now transmitted to the Congress. He believed that nothing had been attempted beyond what was amply justified by the Constitution. Discussing the terms of the proclamation, the President said:

But if it be proper to require, as a test of admission to the political body, an oath of allegiance to the Constitution of the United States, and to the Union under it, why also to the laws and proclamations in regard to slavery? Those laws and proclamations were enacted and put forth for the purpose of aiding in the suppression of the rebellion. To give them their fullest effect, there had to be a pledge for their maintenance. In my judgment they have aided, and will further aid, the cause for which they were intended. To now abandon them would be not only to relinquish a lever of power, but would also be a cruel and an astounding breach of faith. I may add, at this point, that while I remain in my present position I shall not attempt to retract or modify the Emancipation Proclamation; nor shall I return to slavery any person who is free by the terms of that proclamation, or by any of the acts of Congress.[104]

The *Tribune* printed the President's message in full on December 10, 1863, and Greeley gave it his cordial approval. He discussed at length the President's plan "for the restoration of the insurgent States to the authority and rights abdicated by their rebellion" and held that no one who meant to be loyal could object to the conditions prescribed by the President. "Ninety of every hundred Rebels may be restored to every right to-morrow," he said, "without sacrificing or relinquishing any particle of their property; while nine-tenths of the residue are required to relinquish nothing but their right to oppress and sell their fellow men. . . . Thanks, then, to our President, for the wise humanity and generous impulses which prompted the issue of his Proclamation of amnesty! It must be that in this sign we shall conquer!"

The war dragged on for another year. Again, on December 6, 1864,

---

[103] Nicolay and Hay, *Complete Works*, IX, 224–53.
[104] *Ibid.*, pp. 218–23, 249.

the President, now triumphantly re-elected for a second term, gave an account of his stewardship to Congress. Lincoln's discussion of the Rebellion in this annual message, which was to be his last, deserves high rank among his public documents. On the whole, he found the outlook hopeful. At the last session of Congress a proposed amendment to the Constitution abolishing slavery had passed the Senate but had failed in the House. He recommended the passage of the measure at this session and declared that the voice of the people, as expressed in the recent election, now heard for the first time upon the question, was clearly in favor of such constitutional amendment. "In affording the people the fair opportunity of showing one to another and to the world," he said, "this firmness and unanimity of purpose, the election has been of vast value to the national cause." Proceeding in optimistic vein, he produced statistics to show that the election had exhibited the further fact that the nation did "not approach exhaustion in the most important branch of national resources—that of living men." He held also that material resources were "more complete and abundant than ever." The national resources both in man power and in material things were not exhausted and he believed were inexhaustible. Moreover, the election had demonstrated that the public purpose to re-establish and maintain the national authority was unchanged and he believed unchangeable. He again declared that he retracted nothing he had heretofore said as to slavery, that he would not attempt to retract or modify the Emancipation Proclamation, nor return to slavery any person made free by the terms of the proclamation or by any of the acts of Congress. The President then ended this notable document with two significant utterances:

If the people should, by whatever mode or means, make it an executive duty to reënslave such persons, another, and not I, must be their instrument to perform it.

In stating a single condition of peace, I mean simply to say, that the war will cease on the part of the government whenever it shall have ceased on the part of those who began it.[105]

The *Tribune* printed the President's message in full on December 7, 1864, and Greeley said that this "straight-forward and business-like document" was "certain to be universally read and universally understood. . . . Not even the most violent opponent of Mr. Lincoln can complain that his policy has an uncertainty about it, or that it is not as thoroughly radical as his warmest admirer would have it. Peace by

---

[105] *Ibid.*, X, 283–310.

the submission or conquest of Rebels, and the total abolition of Slavery, will be the determined purpose of the new Administration. The Country has sanctioned and will accept the policy."

The Joint Resolution proposing an amendment to the Constitution abolishing slavery had been passed by the Senate on April 8, 1864, by a vote of yeas 38, nays 6.[106] The vote in the House on July 15 resulted after extended debate in yeas 93, nays 65, and absent or not voting, 23.[107] The resolution not having secured a two-thirds vote was thus lost. In the next session, following the President's recommendation, the resolution was brought up for reconsideration in the House and was passed on January 31, 1865, the final vote being yeas 119, nays 56, not voting, 8.[108] By a happy inadvertence the Joint Resolution was sent to the President who formally signed it on February 1.[109] Later the Senate passed a resolution declaring that such approval was unnecessary.[110] Nevertheless, it must have been one of the most satisfying moments in Lincoln's entire career when he affixed his signature to that document. Lincoln was serenaded at the White House and made a brief informal speech in which he said the occasion was one of congratulation to the country and to the whole world. He announced with pride that his home state of Illinois had already ratified the resolution, the first state to take action. He regarded the proposed amendment as a "king's cure-all for all the evils."[111]

Greeley was once more in his element. "A majority of the American People have decided," he said, "that Slavery shall die, because sore experience has taught them that its perpetuation is inconsistent with the integrity and safety of the Republic. They seek for a genuine, lasting Peace; hence they have voted to eradicate that root of bitterness which has distracted and nearly ruined her." And he ended his editorial with the words: "LONG LIVE THE REPUBLIC!"[112]

Lincoln did not live to see the ratification of the Joint Resolution by the requisite three-fourths of the states. It was not until December 18, 1865, that William H. Seward, still Secretary of State under President Johnson, was able to announce the adoption of the Thirteenth Amendment to the Constitution of the United States:

---

[106] *Cong. Globe,* 38th Cong., 1st sess., p. 1490.
[107] *Ibid.,* p. 2995.
[108] *Ibid.,* 2d sess., p. 531.
[109] Nicolay and Hay, *Abraham Lincoln,* X, 86.
[110] *Cong. Globe,* 38th Cong., 2d sess., p. 629.
[111] Nicolay and Hay, *Complete Works,* X, 352–53.
[112] *Tribune,* February 1, 1865.

Section 1. Neither slavery nor involuntary servitude except as punishment for crime whereof the party shall have been duly convicted, shall exist within the United States, or any place subject to their jurisdiction.

Section 2. Congress shall have power to enforce this article by appropriate legislation.[113]

Greeley had the last word. His editorial on December 20, 1865, was entitled "The End of Slavery" and read in part:

The death of Slavery comes well upon the great anniversary of the human soul. If in the supreme thanksgiving of the year Christian men and women rejoice that Christianity lives through the blood of its martyr, let them also thank God that Slavery is dead through the blood of many martyrs. The annulment of our one great legalized tyranny throughout all the land is an occasion of profound and solemn thankfulness; for although the whole country has anticipated it, it was only in view of rejoicing over its downfall. Such an occasion seems one for the race more than for ourselves; but we have especial reason to ask our brethren of the South to join with us in heartiest thanksgiving that their own chains are broken, and that their own hands, though subdued, have approved the act which set them free.

They had much in common when it came to slavery, these two self-willed, deeply determined men. They achieved a passion for freedom early in their careers, believed that slavery was irretrievably wrong, and nurtured the hope for its ultimate extinction. Their differences toward the end of the struggle concerning emancipation were largely of time and method. Greeley was always in a hurry. Before the war began he was willing to let the erring sisters go in peace. After Sumter he put the Union first and preached eloquently that the Union and slavery could not endure side by side. Not deeply concerned about the time, the method, and the result, he urged universal emancipation as a war measure.

Lincoln would not be hurried. His oath of office was always in his mind and his fundamental object, the preservation of the Union. Almost to the very last, he nursed the delusion that the slavery issue might be settled by gradualism, compensation, vote of the people, and colonization. He was singularly unable to win enthusiastic and widespread support for any one of his proposed methods. And his final resort to emancipation as a necessity of war related only to the slaves in disloyal states.

Greeley was quicker than Lincoln to see that a long-protracted,

[113] J. G. Randall, *Constitutional Problems Under Lincoln*, pp. 396–401.

gradual emancipation would only aggravate the trouble; that the North would never buy victory by paying for the slaves; that the vote of the people to abolish slavery would never come while the Rebellion continued; and that colonization simply would not work.

In the end, their joint hopes were realized. Slavery was abolished throughout the nation and by due process of law. They had a righteous stubbornness and a tenacious belief in the essential rightness of their individual processes of reasoning. Lincoln said that Greeley's support was worth a hundred thousand men in the field.[114] Greeley said, in reflection, that "the one providential leader, the indispensable hero of the great drama, was Abraham Lincoln."[115] The calm wisdom of the President and the impetuous temper of the editor made immeasurable contribution to the death of slavery.

---

[114] Nicolay and Hay, *Complete Works*, XI, 120–22, Lincoln to Walker, November 21, 1861.

[115] MS, Greeley's Lecture on "Abraham Lincoln," *op. cit.*, p. 50.

I not only intend a sincere effort for peace, but I intend that you shall be a personal witness that it is made.

Lincoln[1]

Mr. President, I fear you do not realize how intently the people desire any peace consistent with the national integrity and honor, and how joyously they would hail its achievement, and bless its authors.

Greeley[2]

9 Peace overtures

Greeley labored under the hallucination that the slave states in revolt might be allowed to go in peace. From the time of Lincoln's election until after Fort Sumter was fired upon he talked repeatedly about a national convention which he blithely assumed would reach agreement on perfectly friendly terms. Even after the total collapse of the Peace Congress held in early February, 1861, upon the invitation of the Legislature of Virginia, he continued in this vein and insisted that the Union could not and should not be held together by force. Typical of his editorials in November and December, 1860, and in January, February, March, and early April, 1861, is this summing up which appeared in the *Tribune* on January 14 under the heading "Peaceful Separation":

As to Secession, I have said repeatedly and here repeat, that, if the People of the Slave States, or of the Cotton States alone, really wish to get out of the Union, I am in favor of letting them out as soon as that result can be peacefully and constitutionally attained. . . . I want no States kept in the Union by coercion. . . . Let there be an open and full canvass—let the champions of the Union have a fair opportunity to present and argue the matter to the People, secure against violence and outrage—let the vote be

---

[1] John G. Nicolay and John Hay, eds., *Complete Works of Abraham Lincoln*, X, 159, Lincoln to Greeley, July 15, 1864.

[2] Robert Todd Lincoln Collection (34316), Library of Congress, Washington, D.C., Greeley to Lincoln, July 7, 1864.

so taken that quiet, peaceful, Union-loving men may vote as they think, without apprehension or insult—and if the South declares for Disunion, I will join you in urging the requisite change in the Constitution to let them out.

After the attack on Fort Sumter Greeley no longer talked about peaceful separation. The day after the Fort was surrendered he declared, "There is no more thought of bribing or coaxing the traitors who have dared to aim their cannon balls at the flag of the Union."[3] And on April 27 he dismissed disunion and peace by negotiation with the forcible utterance: "No, the American people have not hastily or recklessly been driven into this war; but finding it forced upon them, they mean so to wage it that the National Integrity shall receive no detriment, and that, while the Republic is preserved with undiminished boundaries, there will remain an awful warning to all who shall ever hereafter entertain the idea of destroying the American government or dismembering the American nation."

Greeley could not resist the temptation, however, "to say a few words" to the President about possible terms of peace. Feeling that the rebels were anxious to end the war, he wrote Lincoln this letter of advice:

> *Office of the Tribune*
> *Dec. 12, 1862*
>
> *Dear Sir:*
> *I wish to say a few words to you respecting the prospect and the conditions of Peace.*
> *That the Rebels are deathly sick of their job, and anxious to get out of it, I have so much testimony that I cannot doubt. I presume you have still more.*
> *To ensure an early and honorable Peace, a vigorous prosecution of the War, under able and careful Generals of unquestioned and undeviating loyalty, with the decided and thorough enforcement of the Emancipation policy, seem to me all-sufficient. Ensure us these, and the War will surely end before June.*
> *I believe Peace might very soon be made on these terms:*
> *1. A General Amnesty to all who will return to Loyalty.*
> *2. General Emancipation on or before the 4th day of July next.*
> *3. The Public debt of the Confederacy not to exceed $400,000,000 to be assumed by the Union.*
> *4. $100,000,000 to be divided among the loyal Slave States and districts for the entire destruction of their Slavery on or before the 4th of July next.*

---

[3] *Tribune,* April 15, 1861.

All this will cost less than to prosecute the War through 1863. And on this basis peace may be made before March. At least, I feel sure that the right man could do it.

I write, then, to pray you not to hesitate, nor qualify, but issue your second Emancipation Proclamation, declaring all Slaves in Rebel districts free on the 1st of January next, but add to it (or precede it with) an offer of complete amnesty to all persons now in rebellion who shall return to loyalty publicly and unequivocally before the 1st of February. If with this could in due time be associated the other features of a General Pacification already intimated, I feel sure that we may have a lasting and glorious peace by March.

Yours,

Horace Greeley[4]

Hon. A. Lincoln
    Washington

P.S. I pray you give Fremont a chance.

Although he consistently urged vigorous prosecution of the war, Greeley watched keenly for any overtures from the South toward peace. He lent a ready ear to anyone who came to him with peace proposals. Shortly after he had written to Lincoln, he was approached by a self-appointed peacemonger by the name of Jewett. Greeley characterized him as "the most active agitator for Peace" and cautioned him in terms which might have been written by Lincoln himself:

New York, Jan. 2, 1863

W. C. Jewett, esq., Washington, D.C.

Dear Sir: In whatever you may do to restore peace to our distracted country, bear these things in mind:

1. Whatever action is taken must be between the Government of the United States and the accredited authorities of the Confederates. There must be no negotiations or conditions between unofficial persons. All you can do is to render authorized negotiations possible by opening a way for them.

2. In such negotiations, our Government cannot act without a trusted though informal assurance that the Confederates have taken the initiative. The rupture originated with them; they must evince a preliminary willingness to make peace; and, on being assured that this is reciprocated, they must initiate the formal proposition.

3. If arbitration shall be resorted to, these conditions must be respected: First—The arbiter must be a Power which has evinced no partiality or unfriendliness to either party. Second—One that has no interest in the partition or downfall of our country. Third—One that does not desire the failure

---

[4] Robert Todd Lincoln Collection (20115), *op. cit.*, Greeley to Lincoln, December 12, 1862.

of the republican principle in government. Great Britain and France are necessarily excluded by their having virtually confessed their wishes that we should be divided; and Louis Napoleon has an especial interest in proving republics impracticable. For if the republican is a legitimate, beneficent form of government, what must be the verdict of history on the destroyer of the French Republic?

You will find, I think, no hearty supporter of the Union who will agree that our Government shall act in the premises, except on a frank, open proposition from the Confederates, proposing arbitration by a friendly Power or Powers. I can consider no man a friend of the Union who makes a parade of Peace propositions or Peace agitation prior to such action.

Yours,

HORACE   GREELEY[5]

Jewett who had business interests in Colorado and who made several trips to Europe in the vain hope of enlisting the mediation of foreign powers came to be known as "Colorado" Jewett. In this particular venture the only word he brought back to Greeley was that no word of conciliation or arbitration could be evoked from the Confederate government. After weeks of "earnest pursuit of some endurable Peace proposition from the Rebels," during which Greeley was apparently in frequent touch with Jewett, he gave "it up without having come in sight of any Rebel proposition at all."

Early in May, 1863, the *New York Express*, edited by James Brooks who had recently been chosen to represent a portion of New York City in Congress, made a bitter attack on Lincoln, charging that he was hostile to any other than a disunion peace.

The Proclamation of January 1 [Brooks declared] put an end to all hope of peace from this Administration. The acts of Congress then slammed to every door for peace, and opened wide the gates of Janus. The War Administration has since been so conducted, as if purposely, to strengthen the South and to weaken the North, thereby increasing and exalting the hopes of Independence on the part of Southern Secessionists, and weakening the ardent expectations of both Conservative Republicans as well as of Democrats for the early restoration of the Union, upon the principle of compromise and concession— Purposely, we say, because soldiers seem ever so handled, so maneuvered in Washington, as if designedly to be in the wrong place at the right time.[6]

---

[5] *Tribune,* May 11, 1863.
[6] *New York Express,* May 9, 1863.

Greeley had more than once used almost this language in criticizing McClellan, but in this instance he came valiantly to the defense of the President and proposed to show by reference to conspicuous facts and unquestioned documents "the utter, inexcusable untruth of this assault." He held that Lincoln's inaugural address "was one continuous, beseeching appeal for Peace—Peace." Never before had an Executive of any nation so pleaded and entreated that the country be spared the horrors of civil war. "From that hour to the present," he said, "every Message, every utterance of President Lincoln has attested his anxiety for the earliest possible restoration of Peace."[7]

Greeley sustained and voiced this view at intervals throughout the remainder of 1863. He deemed it essential that the people of the loyal states should stand by their government and have faith in its doing whatever was for the best. In July he declared that there was not in all America another man who would more gladly and gratefully see the war brought to an early and honorable peace than the President.[8] Again, he proposed to leave the arrangements of conditions of peace to the President and his constitutional advisers, and urged that loyal citizens could make their greatest contribution "toward securing an early and fit pacification of the country by swelling the ranks of the Union armies."[9]

Lincoln was invited to attend a mass meeting of unconditional Union men to be held in Springfield, Illinois, on September 3, 1863. Unable to accept the invitation he sent a lengthy letter to James C. Conkling and suggested that "he read it very slowly" to the meeting. It was adroitly directed to the nation and especially to the critics of the Administration. Touching the prospect of peace, he said:

There are those who are dissatisfied with me. To such I would say: You desire peace, and you blame me that we do not have it. But how can we attain it? There are but three conceivable ways: First, to suppress the rebellion by force of arms. This I am trying to do. Are you for it? If you are, so far we are agreed. If you are not for it, a second way is to give up the Union. I am against this. Are you for it? If you are, you should say so plainly. If you are not for force, nor yet for dissolution, there only remains some imaginable compromise. I do not believe any compromise embracing the maintenance of the Union is now possible. All I learn leads to a directly opposite belief.

---

[7] *Tribune*, May 11, 1863.

[8] *Ibid.*, July 10, 1863.

[9] *Ibid.*, July 27, 1863.

The strength of the rebellion is its military, its army. That army dominates all the country and all the people within its range. Any offer of terms made by any man or men within that range, in opposition to that army, is simply nothing for the present, because such man or men have no power whatever to enforce their side of a compromise, if one were made to them.

To illustrate: Suppose refugees from the South and peace men of the North get together in convention, and frame and proclaim a compromise embracing a restoration of the Union. In what way can that compromise be used to keep Lee's army out of Pennsylvania. Mead's army can keep Lee's army out of Pennsylvania, and, I think, can ultimately drive it out of existence. But no paper compromise to which the controllers of Lee's army are not agreed can at all affect that army. In an effort at such compromise we should waste time which the enemy would improve to our disadvantage; and that would be all. A compromise, to be effective, must be made either with those who control the rebel army, or with the people first liberated from the domination of that army by the success of our own army. Now, allow me to assure you that no word or intimation from that rebel army, or from any of the men controlling it, in relation to any peace compromise, has ever come to my knowledge or belief. All charges and insinuations to the contrary are deceptive and groundless. And I promise you that if any such proposition shall hereafter come, it shall not be rejected and kept a secret from you. I freely acknowledge myself the servant of the people, according to the bond of service—the United States Constitution—and that, as such, I am responsible to them.

Lincoln went on in this remarkable letter addressing himself directly to those who were dissatisfied with him about the status of the Negro. He reiterated his position that the Emancipation Proclamation as a war measure was warranted and justified under the Constitution because he believed it invested him as commander-in-chief "with the law of war in time of war." He insisted that the promise of freedom must be kept. "The signs look better," he said. "The Father of Waters again goes unvexed to the sea."[10]

The *Tribune* published Lincoln's letter in full on September 3 and analyzed it in detail in an editorial which perhaps gave the President the most unqualified endorsement he had received throughout his Administration. Greeley, if he penned it—and it bears marks of his hand —outdid himself in frankness, candor, and praise. The President's language was "plain, forcible and eminently direct." The time was "well chosen." The letter contained "words of wisdom" and exhibited "the

---

[10] Nicolay and Hay, *op. cit.*, IX, 95–102, Lincoln to James C. Conkling, August 26, 1863.

wide grasp of a statesman" and "the firm demeanor of a ruler." It was marked by "honesty of purpose" and "a most vigorous common-sense. . . . He meets the question of peace fairly, and he means to gain it by force of arms because there is no other way. There is no other way, because he will not, as he knows the people will not, consent to a dissolution of the Union, and because no compromise is possible save with the army, or those who control the armies of the Rebels." This unusual tribute ended with the words, "Again we say: God Bless Abraham Lincoln! 'THE PROMISE MUST BE KEPT.'"

With his annual message to Congress on December 8, 1863, Lincoln also transmitted a Proclamation of Amnesty and Reconstruction. In summing up the terms in the proclamation and the message, on which the President appeared to be willing and anxious to restore peace, Greeley said:

No vengeance—no military execution—no confiscation—no more devastation—let us all be friends, equals, brothers, once more. But Slavery, the wicked, wanton fomenter of this horrible strife, must die, or the Peace will be a hollow delusive truce, to be soon followed by another desolating war. Slavery dead, there is nothing left to quarrel about; and it will never again be possible to raise an army in this country to fire at the American flag and fight to destroy the Great Republic. Simply because every persistent slaveholder is at heart a partisan of the Rebellion, and, so long as he wants Slavery perpetuated, can be nothing else, it is essential that Slavery should die to the end that the Republic may surely live. Such is our President's programme, and we endorse every word of it. It is not merely wise and just—it is humane and beneficent. It is the true programme for saving life and stanching the wounds of our country.[11]

Greeley continued in the early months of 1864, at least until the political pot began to boil, to consider himself an "unconditional loyalist"; that is, one who stood by the government even when its policies ran counter to his convictions. He urged from time to time that those who meant to see the country through its perils could not afford "to wrangle and split up into cliques and petty factions."[12] Even as he began quietly to lay plans to see someone more to his liking succeed Lincoln, he counseled that nothing should be said or done to render cooperation impracticable or to prevent Unionists from rallying around the "good and true men" who might be nominated.[13] "To assail those

---

[11] *Tribune,* December 16, 1863.
[12] *Ibid.,* February 1, 1864.
[13] *Ibid.,* February 23, 1864.

whom the People have duly invested with authority," he, said, "is to weaken and endanger the authority as well as those to whom it has been temporarily intrusted. Hence, many things that might be truly said, and in quiet times would be properly said, are now forborne by considerate, devoted patriots."[14]

The *Tribune* editorial rooms were not free from the gloom which pervaded the North in the dismal summer of 1864. Greeley was unusually restive. The Baltimore Convention had been held in May, contrary to Greeley's advice; and Lincoln had been nominated for a second term, contrary to Greeley's wishes. Throughout the summer he was conniving with a group of discontented Republicans to bring about Lincoln's withdrawal or to put a second ticket in the field. He sensed and shared the general weariness of war, the dissatisfaction with Lincoln's tedious policies, and the urgent desire of the people for peace. Forgetting his frequent assurances to his constituency that he would not interfere with the prosecution of the war and that he would support the Administration in its efforts to restore the Union and to establish an honorable peace, he temporized with self-appointed peacemakers and lost his head in an unfortunate episode.

Emissaries of the Confederacy were floating about in Canada and making questionable contacts across the border with Peace Democrats and radical Republicans, ostensibly with a view to peace but more directly with the hope of defeating Lincoln in the coming election. Among these agents of Jefferson Davis were James P. Holcombe, sometime professor at the University of Virginia and a Representative in the Confederate Congress; Clement C. Clay, formerly United States senator from Alabama; Jacob Thompson, who had been Secretary of the Interior in Buchanan's Cabinet; and George N. Sanders, a political adventurer from Kentucky. Sanders was a man of the type of "Colorado" Jewett, and eventually these two worthies got together in Canada as go-betweens.

The record does not indicate just how and when Greeley became involved, but Jewett was delegated to contact Greeley, and the record begins with this letter:

Niagara Falls, July 5, 1864.

My Dear Mr. Greeley:—In reply to your note, I have to advise having just left Hon. George N. Sanders, of Kentucky, on the Canada side. I am authorized to state to you, for your use only, not the public, that two am-

---

[14] *Ibid.*, March 1, 1864.

bassadors of Davis & Co. are now in Canada, with full and complete powers for a peace, *and Mr. Sanders requests that you come on immediately to me, at Cataract House, to have a private interview, or if you will send the President's protection for him and two friends, they will come on and meet you. He says the whole matter can be consummated by me, you, them, and President Lincoln. Telegraph me in such form that I may know if you come here, or they to come on with me.*

Yours,

W. C. Jewett.[15]

This letter shows that Greeley had already been in touch with Jewett, but the record does not indicate who initiated their correspondence.

Jewett was impatient. The next day he sent this telegram to Greeley:

H. Greeley, Tribune:
Will you come here? Parties have full power. Wrote you yesterday.

Jewett[16]

Jewett was wholly in error in advising Greeley that the Confederate agents had full power to offer terms of peace. Greeley, none too sure of Jewett, was cautious. He sent Jewett's letter to Lincoln with a long screed of his own:

New York, July 7, 1864.

My Dear Sir:—I venture to enclose you a letter and telegraphic dispatch that I received yesterday from our irrepressible friend, Colorado Jewett, at Niagara Falls. I think they deserve attention. Of course I do not indorse Jewett's positive averment that his friends at the Falls have "full powers" from J. D., though I do not doubt that he thinks they have. I let that statement stand as simply evidencing the anxiety of the Confederates everywhere for peace. So much is beyond doubt.

And therefore I venture to remind you that our bleeding, bankrupt, almost dying country also longs for peace—shudders at the prospect of fresh conscriptions, of further wholesale devastations, and of new rivers of human blood; and a widespread conviction that the Government and its prominent supporters are not anxious for peace, and do not improve proffered opportunities to achieve it, is doing great harm now, and is morally certain, unless removed, to do far greater in the approaching elections.

It is not enough that we anxiously desire a true and lasting peace; we ought to demonstrate and establish the truth beyond cavil. The fact that A. H. Stephens was not permitted a year ago to visit and confer with the authorities

---

[15] Henry J. Raymond, *The Life, Public Services and State Papers of Abraham Lincoln*, p. 571.
[16] *Ibid.*

at Washington has done harm; which the tone at the late National Convention at Baltimore is not calculated to counteract.

I entreat you, in your own time and manner, to submit overtures for pacification to the Southern insurgents, which the impartial must pronounce frank and generous. If only with a view to the momentous election soon to occur in North Carolina, and of the draft to be enforced in the Free States, this should be done at once. I would give the safe-conduct required by the rebel envoys at Niagara, upon their parole to avoid observation and to refrain from all communication with their sympathizers in the loyal States; but you may see reasons for declining it. But whether through them or otherwise, do not, I entreat you, fail to make the Southern people comprehend that you, and all of us, are anxious for peace, and prepared to grant liberal terms. I venture to suggest the following

PLAN OF ADJUSTMENT.

1. *The Union is restored and declared perpetual.*
2. *Slavery is utterly and forever abolished throughout the same.*
3. *A complete amnesty for all political offences, with a restoration of all the inhabitants of each State to all the privileges of citizens of the United States.*
4. *The Union to pay four hundred million dollars ($400,000,000) in five per cent. United States stock to the late Slave States, loyal and secession alike, to be apportioned pro rata, according to their slave population respectively, by the census of 1860, in compensation for the losses of their loyal citizens by the abolition of slavery. Each State to be entitled to its quota upon the ratification by its legislature of this adjustment. The bonds to be at the absolute disposal of the legislature aforesaid.*
5. *The said Slave States to be entitled henceforth to representation in the House on the basis of their total, instead of their federal population, the whole now being free.*
6. *A national convention, to be assembled so soon as may be, to ratify this adjustment, and make such changes in the Constitution as may be deemed advisable.*

Mr. President, I fear you do not realize how intently the people desire any peace consistent with the national integrity and honor, and how joyously they would hail its achievement, and bless its authors. With United States stocks worth but forty cents in gold per dollar, and drafting about to commence on the third million of Union soldiers, can this be wondered at?

I do not say that a just peace is now attainable, though I believe it to be so. But I do say that a frank offer by you to the insurgents of terms which the impartial say ought to be accepted will, at the worst, prove an immense and sorely needed advantage to the national cause. It may save us from a Northern insurrection.

Yours, truly,

Horace Greeley.

Hon. A. Lincoln, President, Washington, D.C.

P.S.—Even though it should be deemed unadvisable to make an offer of terms to the rebels, I insist that, in any possible case, it is desirable that any offer they may be disposed to make should be received, and either accepted or rejected. I beg you to invite those now at Niagara to exhibit their credentials and submit their ultimatum.

H.G.[17]

The irrelevant matters in Greeley's letter call for explanation. Alexander H. Stephens, Vice-President of the Confederacy, had sought in the summer of 1863 to confer with Lincoln with relation to possible terms of peace. He had communicated through naval authorities that he was the "bearer of a communication in writing from Jefferson Davis, Commander-in-Chief of the land and naval forces of the Confederate States, to Abraham Lincoln, Commander-in-Chief of the land and naval forces of the United States," and that he desired to proceed directly to Washington in his own steamer, the "Torpedo." Lincoln had declined the request largely because the communication assumed the independence of the so-called Confederate states and had sent the following reply: "The request of A. H. Stephens is inadmissable. The customary agents and channels are adequate for all needful communication and conference between the United States forces and the insurgents."[18] Greeley had apparently forgotten that the week after Lincoln had declined to see Stephens the *Tribune* had said: "We say to those who honestly desire an early and honorable Peace, Confide in your Government, and do not embarrass it by factious or weakening demonstrations," and that the *Tribune* had deliberately endorsed Lincoln's refusal to receive Stephens.[19]

Greeley also went far afield in referring to "the tone at the late National Convention at Baltimore." With the possible exception of the plank endorsing Lincoln, Greeley could have written the Baltimore platform. The fundamental positions expressed in it were in close ac-

---

[17] Robert Todd Lincoln Collection (34316), *op. cit.*, Greeley to Lincoln, July 7, 1864.
[18] John G. Nicolay and John Hay, *Abraham Lincoln—A History*, VII, 372–74. See also Edgar T. Welles, ed., *The Diary of Gideon Welles*, I, 359–63.
[19] *Tribune*, July 13, 1863.

cord with his repeated preachments. The other references in the letter, to the draft and to the situation in North Carolina, were also wholly beside the point. Greeley was struggling to find something on which to base complaint.

It called for nothing short of effrontery for the editor to submit an unsolicited "Plan of Adjustment" with the specific terms of peace which the President should name. By a singular coincidence, however, Greeley's proposals, submitted July 7, were almost identical with the informal terms which had been dictated by Lincoln to Gilmore on July 6 for possible use in a contemplated conference with Jefferson Davis.

Lincoln replied promptly to Greeley's letter. A moment of relaxation must have come to the harassed President when he committed the task to Greeley. His letter reveals the shrewd politician and the clever lawyer getting a little fun out of a serious situation:

Washington, D.C., July 9, 1864.

Hon. Horace Greeley:

Dear Sir:—Your letter of the 7th, with enclosures, received. If you can find any person anywhere professing to have any proposition of Jefferson Davis, in writing, for peace, embracing the restoration of the Union and abandonment of slavery, whatever else it embraces, say to him he may come to me with you; and that if he really brings such proposition, he shall, at the least, have safe conduct with the paper (and without publicity, if he chooses) to the point where you shall have met him. The same if there be two or more persons.

Yours truly,
A. Lincoln[20]

Greeley was neatly trapped, he had not expected to have the tables turned on him. After petulantly dragging in the proposed Stephens peace mission again and offering the President further advice upon his dealings with North Carolina, he reluctantly agreed "to look into the hand of whomsoever may be at Niagara," though the project he wanted the President to undertake he now regarded as "manifestly hopeless."

Office of The Tribune, New York, July 10, 1864.

My Dear Sir:—I have yours of yesterday. Whether there be persons at Niagara (or elsewhere) who are empowered to commit the rebels by negotiation, is a question; but if there be such, there is no question at all that they would decline to exhibit their credentials to me, much more to open their budget and give me their best terms. Green as I may be, I am not quite so

---

[20] Nicolay and Hay, *Complete Works*, X, 154, Lincoln to Greeley, July 9, 1864.

verdant as to imagine anything of the sort. I have neither purpose nor desire to be made a confidant, far less an agent, in such negotiations. But I do deeply realize that the rebel chiefs achieved a most decided advantage in proposing or pretending to propose to have A. H. Stephens visit Washington as a peacemaker, and being rudely repulsed; and I am anxious that the ground lost to the national cause by that mistake shall somehow be regained in season for effect on the approaching North Carolina election. I will see if I can get a look into the hand of whomsoever may be at Niagara; though that is a project so manifestly hopeless that I have little heart for it, still I shall try.

Meantime I wish you would consider the propriety of somehow apprising the people of the South, especially those of North Carolina, that no overture or advance looking to peace and reunion has ever been repelled by you, but that such a one would at any time have been cordially received and favorably regarded, and would still be.

Yours,
Horace Greeley.[21]

Hon. A. Lincoln

This letter was delayed and did not reach Lincoln until after he had received another letter under date of July 13. The letter of July 10 was therefore never specifically answered. Between his letters of July 10 and 13 to Lincoln, Greeley had a brief note from Sanders which, it appears, he did not send to Lincoln:

Clifton House, Niagara Falls,
Canada West, July 12, 1864.

Dear Sir:—I am authorized to say that Honorable Clement C. Clay, of Alabama, Professor James P. Holcombe, of Virginia, and George N. Sanders, of Dixie, are ready and willing to go at once to Washington, upon complete and unqualified protection being given either by the President or Secretary of War. Let the permission include the three names and one other. Very respectfully,

George N. Sanders.[22]

To Hon. Horace Greeley

In his letter of July 13, Greeley was still hopeful that he might shift the undertaking directly to Lincoln's shoulders:

Office of The Tribune, New York, July 13, 1864.

My Dear Sir:—I have now information on which I can rely that two persons duly commissioned and empowered to negotiate for peace are at this

---

[21] Robert Todd Lincoln Collection (34403), *op. cit.*, Greeley to Lincoln, July 10, 1864.
[22] Raymond, *op. cit.*, p. 575, George N. Sanders to Greeley, July 12, 1864.

moment not far from Niagara Falls, in Canada, and are desirous of conferring with yourself, or with such persons as you may appoint and empower to treat with them. Their names (only given in confidence) are Hon. Clement C. Clay, of Alabama, and Hon. Jacob Thompson, of Mississippi. If you should prefer to meet them in person, they require safe-conducts for themselves, and for George N. Sanders, who will accompany them. Should you choose to empower one or more persons to treat with them in Canada, they will of course need no safe-conduct; but they cannot be expected to exhibit credentials save to commissioners empowered as they are. In negotiating directly with yourself, all grounds of cavil would be avoided, and you would be enabled at all times to act upon the freshest advices of the military situation. You will of course understand that I know nothing and have proposed nothing as to terms, and that nothing is conceded or taken for granted by the meeting of persons empowered to negotiate for peace. All that is assumed is a mutual desire to terminate this wholesale slaughter, if a basis of adjustment can be mutually agreed on, and it seems to me high time that an effort to this end should be made. I am of course quite other than sanguine that a peace can now be made, but I am quite sure that a frank, earnest, anxious effort to terminate the war on honorable terms would immensely strengthen the Government in case of its failure, and would help us in the eyes of the civilized world, which now accuses us of obstinacy, and indisposition even to seek a peaceful solution of our sanguinary, devastating conflict. Hoping to hear that you have resolved to act in the premises, and to act so promptly that a good influence may even yet be exerted on the North Carolina election next month,

I remain yours,
Horace Greeley.[23]

Hon. A. Lincoln, Washington.

It will be noted from this letter that Greeley had apparently received additional information from some source which he relied upon and which convinced him that at least two persons representing the Confederacy were "duly commissioned and empowered to negotiate for peace." What the source of his fresh information was, does not appear. It could hardly have been the note from Sanders, for there the three persons mentioned as merely "ready and willing" to go to Washington were Clay, Holcombe, and Sanders. In the letter of July 13, Greeley refers to Clay and Thompson as the emissaries who were to be accompanied by Sanders. In the light of subsequent happenings, it is difficult to understand how any agency could have afforded Greeley convincing evidence that the Confederate agents were "commissioned and em-

---

[23] Robert Todd Lincoln Collection (34458), *op. cit.*, Greeley to Lincoln, July 13, 1864.

powered to negotiate for peace." The impetuous and undependable "Colorado" Jewett may have stepped in at this juncture, but there is no documentary evidence of new information. Greeley's conclusions must be set down as the product of his own imagination.

By this time Lincoln was beginning to lose his patience. He answered Greeley's letter with a telegram:

> Executive Mansion, Washington, July 15, 1864.
>
> Hon. Horace Greeley, New York:—I suppose you received my letter of the 9th. I have just received yours of the 13th, and am disappointed by it. I was not expecting you to send me a letter, but to bring me a man, or men. Mr. Hay goes to you with my answer to yours of the 13th.
>
> A. Lincoln.[24]

The letter from the President which Major Hay carried to Greeley read as follows:

> Executive Mansion, Washington, July 15, 1864.
>
> Hon. HORACE GREELEY:
>
> My Dear Sir:—Yours of the 13th is just received, and I am disappointed that you have not already reached here with those commissioners. If they would consent to come, on being shown my letter to you of the 9th instant, show that and this to them, and if they will come on the terms stated in the former, bring them. I not only intend a sincere effort for peace, but I intend that you shall be a personal witness that it is made.
>
> Yours truly
> A. Lincoln.[25]

In view of Greeley's subsequent action, this letter calls for careful scrutiny. In his letter of July 9 to Greeley, to which he refers, Lincoln had specifically advised Greeley that he might bring to Washington with safe-conduct "*any person anywhere professing to have any proposition of Jefferson Davis, in writing, for peace, embracing the restoration of the Union and abandonment of slavery.*" The terms on which Lincoln was willing to receive the Confederate emissaries could not have been misunderstood even by a schoolboy. In his letter of July 15 Lincoln expressly directed Greeley to show the "commissioners this letter" as well as the letter of July 9, and authorized him to bring them to Washington "*if they will come on the terms stated.*"

---

[24] Nicolay and Hay, *Complete Works*, X, 158–59, Lincoln to Greeley, July 15, 1864.
[25] *Ibid.*, p. 159.

Upon his arrival in New York, after Major Hay had delivered Lincoln's letter to Greeley, he telegraphed the results to the President.

United States Military Telegraph,
War Department, New York, 9 a.m., July 16, 1864.

His Excellency A. Lincoln,
President of the United States:

Arrived this morning at 6 a.m., and delivered your letter few minutes after. Although he thinks some one less known would create less excitement and be less embarrassed by public curiosity, still he will start immediately if he can have an absolute safe-conduct for four persons to be named by him. Your letter he does not think will guard them from arrest, and with only those letters he would have to explain the whole matter to any officer who might choose to hinder them. If this meets with your approbation, I can write the order in your name as A.A.–G., or you can send it by mail. Please answer me at Astor House.

John Hay, A. A.–G.[26]

The President answered Major Hay at once by telegraph as follows:

Executive Mansion, Washington, July 16, 1864.

John Hay, Astor House, New York:

Yours received. Write the safe-conduct as you propose, without waiting for one by mail from me. If there is or is not any thing in the affair, I wish to know it without unnecessary delay.

A. Lincoln.[27]

Following instructions Major Hay provided Greeley with safe-conduct reading:

Executive Mansion, Washington, D.C.

The President of the United States directs that the four persons whose names follow, to wit:

> *Hon. Clement C. Clay,*
> *Hon. Jacob Thompson,*
> *Prof. James P. Holcombe,*
> *George N. Sanders,*

shall have safe-conduct to the City of Washington in company with the Hon. Horace Greeley, and shall be exempt from arrest or annoyance of any

---

[26] Raymond, *op. cit.*, p. 576, John Hay to Lincoln, July 16, 1864.
[27] Nicolay and Hay, *Complete Works*, X, 159, Lincoln to John Hay, July 16, 1864.

kind from any officer of the United States during their journey to the said
City of Washington.

By order of the President:
John Hay, Major and A. A.–G.[28]

Armed with this safe-conduct and certainly having Lincoln's letters
clearly in mind, if not in his immediate possession, Greeley proceeded
to Niagara Falls. On his arrival, employing "Colorado" Jewett as messenger, he addressed the following letter to Clay, Thompson, and Holcombe:

Niagara Falls, N.Y., July 17, 1864.

Gentlemen:—I am informed that you are duly accredited from Richmond
as the bearers of propositions looking to the establishment of peace; that you
desire to visit Washington in the fulfilment of your mission; and that you
further desire that Mr. George N. Sanders shall accompany you. If my in-
formation be thus far substantially correct, I am authorized by the President
of the United States to tender you his safe-conduct on the journey proposed,
and to accompany you at the earliest time that will be agreeable to you. I
have the honor to be, gentlemen,

Yours,
Horace Greeley.[29]
To Messrs, Clement C. Clay, Jacob Thompson, James P. Holcombe,
Clifton House, C.W.

This letter marks the real beginning of Greeley's egregious blunder
in this episode. He told the Confederate agents that he was informed
that they were "duly accredited from Richmond as the bearers of propositions looking to the establishment of peace." At no time did he produce the source of this alleged information. He told them that he was
authorized to conduct them to Washington. That was correct, but he
failed to bring to their attention the terms on which he was authorized
to conduct them to Washington as he had been specifically instructed
by the President in two communications to do. His subsequent explanation of this failure was that the safe-conduct, which did not mention
terms, waived all previous instructions.[30] But Major Hay understood
clearly that the safe-conduct merely expedited the previous instructions

---

[28] *Ibid.*, pp. 159–60, John Hay to Greeley, July 16, 1864.
[29] Raymond, *op. cit.*, p. 577, Greeley to Clement C. Clay, Jacob Thompson, and
James P. Holcombe, July 17, 1864.
[30] *Tribune*, August 5, 1864.

given.[31] The response to Greeley's letter was signed by Clay and Holcombe and wound the coils around the unhappy peacemaker:

Clifton House, Niagara Falls, July 18, 1864.

Sir:—We have the honor to acknowledge your favor of the 17th inst., which would have been answered on yesterday, but for the absence of Mr. Clay. The safe-conduct of the President of the United States has been tendered us, we regret to state, under some misapprehension of facts. We have not been accredited to him from Richmond, as the bearers of propositions looking to the establishment of peace.[32] *We are, however, in the confidential employment of our Government, and are entirely familiar with its wishes and opinions on that subject; and we feel authorized to declare, that if the circumstances disclosed in this correspondence were communicated to Richmond, we would be at once invested with the authority to which your letter refers, or other gentlemen, clothed with full powers, would be immediately sent to Washington with a view of hastening a consummation so much to be desired, and terminating at the earliest possible moment the calamities of the war. We respectfully solicit, through your intervention, a safe-conduct to Washington, and thence by any route which may be designated through your lines to Richmond. We would be gratified if Mr. George Sanders was embraced in this privilege. Permit us, in conclusion, to acknowledge our obligations to you for the interest you have manifested in the furtherance of our wishes, and to express the hope that, in any event, you will afford us the opportunity of tendering them in person before you leave the Falls.*

We remain, very respectfully, &c.,

C. C. CLAY, JR.

J. P. HOLCOMBE.

P.S.—It is proper to state that Mr. Thompson is not here, and has not been staying with us since our sojourn in Canada.[33]

Greeley had the common sense to see that he must now go back to the President and confess that he had been misinformed. He therefore informed Clay and Holcombe that he was obliged to "solicit fresh instructions," blithely unmindful that he had not obeyed the principal instructions already given him:

---

[31] Nicolay and Hay, *Abraham Lincoln,* IX, 190.

[32] Emphasis on the matter in roman type is by the present author.

[33] Raymond, *op. cit.,* pp. 577–78, Clement C. Clay and James P. Holcombe to Greeley, July 18, 1864.

International Hotel, Niagara Falls, N.Y.,
July 18, 1864.

Gentlemen:—I have the honor to acknowledge the receipt of yours of this date by the hand of Mr. W. C. Jewett. The state of facts therein presented being materially different from that which was understood to exist by the President when he intrusted me with the safe-conduct required, it seems to me on every account advisable that I should communicate with him by telegraph, and solicit fresh instructions, which I shall at once proceed to do.

I hope to be able to transmit the result this afternoon, and at all events I shall do so at the earliest moment.

Yours truly,
HORACE GREELEY.[34]

To Messrs, CLEMENT C. CLAY *and* JAMES P. HOLCOMBE, *Clifton House, C.W.*

Clay and Holcombe promptly acknowledged Greeley's note, Jewett still being the go-between:

Clifton House, Niagara Falls, July 18, 1864.

To Hon. H. GREELEY, *Niagara Falls, N.Y.:*

Sir:—We have the honor to acknowledge the receipt of your note of this date by the hands of Colonel Jewett, and will await the further answer which you propose to send to us.

We are, very respectfully, &c.
C. C. CLAY, JR.
JAMES P. HOLCOMBE.[35]

On the same day Greeley sent a telegram to Lincoln quoting a part of the letter of July 18 which he had received from Clay and Holcombe, leaving out their express declaration that they were not accredited from Richmond, and merely saying that he did not find them "empowered" as he had been "previously assured." This time he had no advice to give, and was again ready to shift all responsibility to the President:

Independent Telegraph Line, Niagara Falls, July 18, 1864.

Hon. ABRAHAM LINCOLN, *President:*

I have communicated with the gentlemen in question, and do not find them so empowered as I was previously assured. They say that "we are, however, in the confidential employment of our Government, and entirely familiar with its wishes and opinions on that subject, and we feel authorized

---

[34] *Ibid.,* p. 578, Greeley to Clement C. Clay and James P. Holcombe, July 18, 1864.
[35] *Ibid.,* Clement C. Clay and James P. Holcombe to Greeley, July 18, 1864.

to declare that, if the circumstances disclosed in this correspondence were communicated to Richmond, we would at once be invested with the authority to which your letter refers, or other gentlemen clothed with full power would immediately be sent to Washington with a view of hastening a consummation so much to be desired, and terminating at the earliest possible moment the calamities of war. We respectfully solicit, through your intervention, a safe-conduct to Washington, and thence by any route which may be designated to Richmond." Such is the more material portion of the gentlemen's letter. I will transmit the entire correspondence, if desired. Awaiting your further instructions,

> I remain yours,
> HORACE GREELEY.[36]

Lincoln could hardly have been surprised to discover that Greeley had been misinformed. Determined to find whether there was anything in the affair worthy of consideration, he telegraphed Greeley that he was sending Major Hay to Niagara Falls with a further statement.[37] On receipt of the telegram Greeley sent a note by Jewett to Clay and Holcombe explaining the delay.

> *International Hotel, Niagara Falls, New York, July 19, 1864.*

Gentlemen:—At a late hour last evening (too late for communication with you) I received a dispatch informing me that further instructions left Washington last evening, which must reach me, if there be no interruption, at noon to-morrow. Should you decide to await their arrival, I feel confident that they will enable me to answer definitely your note of yesterday morning. Regretting a delay which I am sure you will regard as unavoidable on my part,

> I remain yours truly,
> HORACE GREELEY.[38]

To Hon. Messrs. C. C. CLAY, JR., *and* J. P. HOLCOMBE, *Clifton House, C.W.*

The meticulous observance of formalities was kept up by an immediate acknowledgment from Clay and Holcombe:

> *Clifton House, Niagara Falls, July 19, 1864.*

Sir:—Colonel Jewett has just handed us your note of this date, in which you state that further instructions from Washington will reach you by noon to-morrow, if there be no interruption. One, or possibly both of us, may be

---

[36] Robert Todd Lincoln Collection (34552), *op. cit.*, Greeley to Lincoln, July 18, 1864.
[37] Nicolay and Hay, *Abraham Lincoln*, IX, 192.
[38] Raymond, *op. cit.*, p. 579, Greeley to Clement C. Clay and James P. Holcombe, July 19, 1864.

obliged to leave the Falls to-day, but will return in time to receive the communication which you promise to-morrow.

We remain truly yours, &c.

JAMES P. HOLCOMBE.

C. C. CLAY, JR.[39]

To the Hon. HORACE GREELEY, *now at the International Hotel.*

Major Hay arrived at Niagara Falls on July 20 and delivered a brief paper in the President's handwriting to the worried and nonplused editor. This significant document read:

Executive Mansion, Washington, July 18, 1864.

TO WHOM IT MAY CONCERN:

Any proposition which embraces the restoration of peace, the integrity of the whole Union, and the abandonment of slavery, and which comes by and with an authority that can control the armies now at war against the United States, will be received and considered by the executive government of the United States, and will be met by liberal terms on substantial and collateral points, and the bearer or bearers thereof shall have safe conduct both ways.

ABRAHAM LINCOLN[40]

Greeley wriggled on the hook. He proposed to bring Jewett into the conference, but Major Hay declined to have anything to do with Jewett; and Greeley, duly delegated by the President of the United States, balked and refused to cross the river to the Clifton House on the Canadian side unless Major Hay would go with him and himself deliver Lincoln's message to the Confederate emissaries.[41] Major Hay agreed, and they were met at the Clifton House by Sanders, who was described by Hay as "a seedy-looking Rebel, with grizzled whiskers and a flavor of old clo'." Sanders conducted them to Professor Holcombe's room where they found him "breakfasting or lunching." Hay described Holcombe as a "tall, solemn, spare, false-looking man, with false teeth, false eyes, and false hair." The note was duly delivered, and Hay informed Holcombe that he would be the bearer of any message Holcombe and his associates might wish to send to Washington. Clay was absent, and nothing was said about Thompson. Holcombe said he could get in touch with Clay by telegraph and would make some response to the note the next day. The interview was brief. As they parted, Hol-

---

[39] *Ibid.*, Clay and Holcombe to Greeley, July 19, 1864.

[40] Nicolay and Hay, *Complete Works*, X, 161.

[41] William Roscoe Thayer, *The Life and Letters of John Hay*, I, 173–83; and Tyler Dennett, *John Hay—From Poetry to Politics*, pp. 45–46.

combe remarked that he had "wanted old Bennett to come up, but he was afraid to come." Greeley replied: "I expect to be blackguarded for what I have done, and I am not allowed to explain. But all I have done has been done under instructions." Anxious to terminate the errand which he now saw was fruitless and fraught with embarrassment for him, Greeley departed posthaste for New York City.

Before leaving Niagara Falls, however, unknown to Major Hay, Greeley had a conference with Jewett and gave him the following certificate:

> *International Hotel, Niagara Falls, July 20, 1864.*
>
> *In leaving the Falls, I feel bound to state that I have had no intercourse with the Confederate gentlemen at the Clifton House, but such as I was fully authorized to hold by the President of the United States, and that I have done nothing in the premises but in fulfilment of his injunctions. The notes, therefore, which you have interchanged between those gentlemen and myself, can in no case subject you to the imputation of unauthorized dealing with public enemies.*
>
> HORACE GREELEY.[42]
>
> *To* w. c. JEWETT, *Esq.*

Hay remained in Niagara Falls, expecting to receive the response of the Confederate emissaries. The day after Greeley's departure, uncertain of what the next step was to be, Major Hay addressed a formal note of inquiry to Professor Holcombe:

> *Major Hay would respectfully inquire whether Professor Holcombe and the gentlemen associated with him desire to send to Washington by Major Hay any messages in reference to the communication delivered to him on yesterday, and in that case when he may expect to be favored with such messages.[43]*

Following the formal style adopted by Major Hay, Professor Holcombe sent this reply:

> *Mr. Holcombe presents his compliments to Major Hay, and greatly regrets if his return to Washington has been delayed by any expectation of an answer to the communication which Mr. Holcombe received from him yesterday, to be delivered to the President of the United States. That communication was accepted as the response to a letter of Messrs. Clay and*

---

[42] Raymond, *op. cit.*, p. 583, Greeley to W. C. Jewett, July 20, 1864.
[43] Don C. Seitz, *Horace Greeley*, p. 258.

Holcombe to the Honorable H. Greeley, and to that gentleman an answer has been transmitted.[44]

The answer to the President's "To Whom It May Concern" statement was transmitted by Clay and Holcombe through Jewett to Greeley. Here again Greeley's procedure is hard to explain. He insisted that the President's declaration should be presented to Professor Holcombe by Major Hay. He certainly knew, that being done, that Major Hay expected the formal reply to be given to him to carry to Washington. Apparently, however, Greeley no sooner parted with Hay than he contacted Jewett and instructed him to inform Clay and Holcombe that he would be pleased to receive any answer they wished to make through Jewett. He went further and authorized Jewett to express his regrets to Clay and Holcombe at *"the sad termination of the initiatory steps for peace, in consequence of the changes made by the President in his instructions to convey commissioners to Washington for negotiations, unconditionally."* All this clearly appears in the letter Clay and Holcombe promptly addressed to Jewett with which they transmitted their answer to the President's formal declaration in a political document, designed for the public and addressed to Greeley. The letter of transmittal to Jewett read:

Clifton House, Niagara Falls, July 20, 1864.

Col. W. C. JEWETT, *Cataract House, Niagara Falls:*

We are in receipt of your note admonishing us of the departure of Hon. Horace Greeley from the Falls, that he regrets the sad termination of the initiatory steps taken for peace, in consequence of the change made by the President in his instructions to convey commissioners to Washington for negotiations, unconditionally, and that Mr. Greeley will be pleased to receive any answer we may have to make through you. We avail ourselves of this offer to enclose a letter to Mr. Greeley, which you will oblige us by delivering. We cannot take leave of you without expressing our thanks for your courtesy and kind offices as the intermediary through whom our correspondence with Mr. Greeley has been conducted, and assuring you that we are, very respectfully,

Your obedient servants,
C. C. CLAY, JR.
JAMES P. HOLCOMBE.[45]

---

[44] *Ibid.*, pp. 258–59.
[45] Raymond, *op. cit.*, pp. 582–83, Clement C. Clay and James P. Holcombe to W. C. Jewett, July 20, 1864.

The long letter addressed to Greeley and sent to him through Jewett, while Major Hay cooled his heels at the Clifton House in Niagara Falls, should be considered with all the previous steps clearly in mind:

Niagara Falls, Clifton House, July 21.

To Hon. HORACE GREELEY:

Sir:—The paper handed to Mr. Holcombe on yesterday, in your presence, by Major Hay, A.A.–G., as an answer to the application in our note of the 18th inst., is couched in the following terms:—

"Executive Mansion, Washington, D.C., July 18, 1864.

"TO WHOM IT MAY CONCERN:

"Any proposition which embraces the restoration of peace, the integrity of the whole Union, and the abandonment of slavery, and which comes by and with an authority that can control the armies now at war against the United States, will be received and considered by the Executive Government of the United States, and will be met by liberal terms on other substantial and collateral points, and the bearer or bearers thereof shall have safe-conduct both ways.

ABRAHAM LINCOLN."

The application to which we refer was elicited by your letter of the 17th inst., in which you inform Mr. Jacob Thompson and ourselves, that you were authorized by the President of the United States to tender us his safe-conduct on the hypothesis that we were "duly accredited from Richmond, as bearers of propositions looking to the establishment of peace," and desired a visit to Washington in the fulfilment of this mission. This assertion, to which we then gave, and still do, entire credence, was accepted by us as the evidence of an unexpected but most gratifying change in the policy of the President—a change which we felt authorized to hope might terminate in the conclusion of a peace, mutually just, honorable, and advantageous to the North and to the South exacting no condition, but that we should be "duly accredited from Richmond as bearers of propositions looking to the establishment of peace," thus proffering a basis for conference as comprehensive as we could desire. It seemed to us that the President opened a door, which had previously been closed against the Confederate States for a full interchange of sentiments, free discussion of conflicting opinions, and untrammelled effort to remove all causes of controversy by liberal negotiations. We indeed could not claim the benefit of a safe-conduct which had been extended to us in a character we had no right to assume, and had never affected to possess; but the uniform declaration of our Executive and Congress, and their thrice repeated and as often repulsed attempts to open negotiations, furnish a sufficient pledge to assure us that this conciliatory manifestation on the part of the President of the United States would be met by them in a temper of equal magnanimity. We had therefore no hesitation in declaring that if this correspondence was communicated to the President of the Confederate States, he would promptly embrace the opportunity presented for seeking a peaceful solution of this unhappy strife. We feel confident that you must share our profound regret that the spirit which dictated the first step towards peace had not continued to animate the counsels of your President.

Had the representatives of the two Governments met to consider this question, the most momentous ever submitted to human statesmanship, in a temper of becoming moderation and equity, followed as their deliberations would have been by the prayers and benedictions of every patriot and Christian on the habitable globe, who is there so bold as to pronounce that the frightful waste of individual happiness and public prosperity, which is daily saddening the universal heart, might not have been terminated, or if the desolation and carnage of war must still be endured through weary years of blood and suffering, that there might not at least have been infused into its conduct something more of the spirit which softens and partially redeems its brutalities? Instead of the safe-conduct which we solicited, and which your first letter gave us every reason to suppose would be extended for the purpose of initiating a negotiation in which neither Government would compromise its rights or its dignity, a document has been presented which provokes as much indignation as surprise. It bears no feature of resemblance to that which was originally offered, and is unlike any paper which ever before emanated from the constitutional Executive of a free people. Addressed "to whom it may concern," it precludes negotiation, and prescribes in advance the terms and conditions of peace. It returns to the original policy of "no bargaining, no negotiations, no truces with rebels, except to bury their dead, until every man shall have laid down his arms, submitted to the Government, and sued for mercy." What may be the explanation of this sudden and entire change in the views of the President, of this rude withdrawal of a courteous overture for negotiation at the moment it was likely to be accepted, of this emphatic recall of words of peace just uttered, and fresh blasts of war to the bitter end, we leave for the speculation of those who have the means or inclination to penetrate the mysteries of his cabinet, or fathom the caprice of his imperial will. It is enough for us to say that we have no use whatever for the paper which has been placed in our hands. We could not transmit it to the President of the Confederate States without offering him an indignity, dishonoring ourselves, and incurring the well-merited scorn of our countrymen.

Whilst an ardent desire for peace pervades the people of the Confederate States, we rejoice to believe that there are few, if any, among them, who would purchase it at the expense of liberty, honor, and self-respect. If it can be secured only by their submission to terms of conquest, the generation is yet unborn which will witness its restitution. If there be any military autocrat in the North, who is entitled to proffer the conditions of this manifesto, there is none in the South authorized to entertain them. Those who control our armies are the servants of the people, not their masters, and they have no more inclination than they have right to subvert the social institutions of the sovereign States, to overthrow their established constitutions, and to barter away their priceless heritage of self-government.

This correspondence will not, however, we trust, prove wholly barren of good results.

If there is any citizen of the Confederate States who has clung to a hope that peace was possible with this Administration of the Federal Government, it will strip from his eyes the last film of such a delusion; or if there be any whose hearts have grown faint under the suffering and agony of this bloody struggle, it will inspire them with fresh energy to endure and brave whatever may yet be requisite to preserve to themselves and their children all that gives dignity and value to life, or hope and consolation to death. And if there be any patriots or Christians in your land, who shrink appalled from the illimitable vista of private misery and public calamity which stretches before them, we pray that in their bosoms a resolution may be quickened to recall the abused authority and vindicate the outraged civilization of their country. For the solicitude you have manifested to inaugurate a movement which contemplates results the most noble and humane, we return our sincere thanks, and are most respectfully and truly

Your obedient servants,
C. C. CLAY, JR.
JAMES P. HOLCOMBE.[46]

Jewett immediately gave a copy of this letter to the press. He was no doubt affronted at Major Hay's unwillingness to have anything to do with him and well he might have been. By July 21 he must have had the note which had been addressed to him on July 18 by Major Hay in which his lack of standing at the White House was clearly indicated. On July 29 the *Tribune* published a clipping from the *Washington Chronicle* which read:

Jewett Repudiated

As an irresponsible person named Jewett, who has recently been acting as an agent and messenger for the Rebel emissaries in Canada, is assiduously laboring, and apparently with some success, to create the impression that he acts by virtue of a certain implied understanding or connection with the Executive Mansion we deem it not improper to state that he has never re-

---

[46] *Ibid.*, pp. 580–82, Clement C. Clay and James P. Holcombe to Greeley, July 21, 1864.

ceived from the President the slightest recognition; and that Maj. Hay, at Niagara, expressly declined to meet him, and that the only letter he has ever received from the Executive Office in answer to his voluminous communications is the following:

Executive Mansion, Washington, July 18, 1864.

Sir: In the exercise of my duty as Secretary in charge of the President's correspondence, it is necessary for me to use a certain discretion in the choice of letters to be submitted to the personal attention of the President. In order to avoid a further waste of time on your part, I have to inform you that your letters are never so submitted. My proceeding in this matter has the sanction of the President.

I am, Sir, very truly, your obedient servant,

JOHN HAY

Wm. Cornell Jewett, Etc, Etc, Etc,

Clay and Holcombe were at least candid in their letter to Greeley. They made no claim to being accredited by the Confederacy. They were naturally surprised at the "To Whom It May Concern" declaration because it brought them the first intimation that there were additional terms upon which the President would be willing to see them. Since his explicit instructions to Greeley had not been brought to their attention, they naturally thought that Lincoln had completely reversed his position. They were perhaps just as well pleased at the turn of events. It gave them opportunity publicly to accuse the President of a breach of faith and to issue a manifesto which they hoped would promote discord in the North and have a bearing on the forthcoming presidential election.

The "unconditional loyalist" in the *Tribune* office now found himself in a most unhappy situation. He was provoked by his neighbors into labored attempts to justify himself. Raymond of the *Times* could not resist the temptation to goad Greeley and slyly remarked that "Mr. Greeley's part in this transaction was more important than he is inclined to represent it." With extreme politeness, but with deadly accuracy, Raymond held the whole proceeding up to the light and innocently suggested the propriety of the publication of all the correspondence.[47]

Greeley published Raymond's analysis of the situation in the *Tribune* on August 5 and added "Comments on the Above" signed "H.G." After reciting the circumstances which led to his going to Niagara

---

[47] *New York Times*, August 4, 1864.

Falls, Greeley pressed the guileless view, from which he never departed, that the President was the one who had blundered. Well aware that he was being laughed at throughout the country, and nursing his discomfiture, he nevertheless persisted:

> But I am not mistaken on the vital point above set forth—that the President finally acquiesced in my views of the matter, so far as to consent to receive whatever proposition agents duly accredited from Richmond might see fit to offer, and that I went to Niagara fully authorized to proffer a Safe-Conduct and accompany to Washington the persons specified, on the understanding that they were empowered to submit and would submit, terms of pacification; and that there were no conditions beyond these. Of course, the missive "To Whom It May Concern," brought to Niagara by Maj. Hay, changed all this. With due submission, I deem this change a mistake—a very grave mistake. . . . I am quite sure the mistake was not originally the President's, but that of some one or more of the gentlemen who are paid $8000 a year from the Treasury for giving him bad advice. . . . I conclude by asking The Times should it recur to this subject, to keep the main point steadily in view. I deny that the overture submitted through Major Hay was the "same offer" that I had been authorized to make; I deny that I was ever required to impose any such "conditions" as those embodied in Major Hay's rescript.

Greeley continued to talk and write in this vein for the remainder of the summer. After the *Tribune* was committed to the support of Lincoln and Johnson early in September, other issues absorbed his energies and served also, to his immense relief, to quiet his critics. Writing the history of this period two years later, Greeley said: "And there was a very wide-spread impression that the overture of the Confederates had not been met in the manner best calculated to strengthen the National cause and invigorate the arm of its supporters. In other words, it was felt that—since the overture originated with them—they should have been allowed to make their own proposition, and not required in effect to make one dictated to them from our side, however inherently reasonable."[48] Thus Greeley, the author, reported as "a wide-spread impression" the views that Greeley, the editor, had urged two years earlier in a vain effort to justify himself. And this latter judgment was rendered only after it was generally known that the Confederate government was without knowledge of the undertaking

---

[48] Horace Greeley, *The American Conflict*, II, 665.

of its loosely instructed emissaries at Niagara and that they were without authority from the Confederacy to treat with the United States on any subject whatever.[49]

Lincoln did not emerge from this episode unscathed. He was criticized for having given any consideration to the initial proposal which came to him through the hands of Jewett, whom even the *World* called "a dancing windbag of popinjay conceit,"[50] and the volatile, excitable Greeley who had a rare capacity for muddling affairs when under tension. The radical Republicans, who were out to defeat him for re-election and not possessed of all the facts, charged him with indecision. The Peace Democrats belabored him for linking the restoration of the Union with the abandonment of slavery. And the Confederate emissaries spread disaffection wherever they could find an opening. In the beginning Lincoln had not anticipated that the Confederates would be found to be accredited; and yet when he learned positively that they were not, he still pursued the matter. His "To Whom It May Concern" declaration was meant for public consumption.

After the episode had been dropped from public consideration, Senator Harlan of Iowa is reported to have said to Lincoln: "Some of us think, Mr. Lincoln, that you didn't send a very good ambassador to Niagara." "Well, I'll tell you about that, Harlan," replied the President. "Greeley kept abusing me for not entering into peace negotiations. He said he believed we could have peace if I would do my part and when he began to urge that I send an ambassador to Niagara to meet Confederate emissaries, I just thought I would let him go up and crack that nut for himself."[51] Reviewing the record, we cannot escape the conviction that Lincoln's chief object was to give the troublesome editor an opportunity to make a fool of himself. If that be the fact, it is comforting evidence, despite the myths surrounding his memory, that Lincoln was not infallible.

A private letter to Abram Wakeman, postmaster of New York, written a few days after the Niagara negotiations were ended shows that Lincoln looked upon the maneuvers of Clay, Holcombe, *et al* as having political implications:

---

[49] Frank H. Severance, *Buffalo Historical Society Publications*, XVIII, 86–87.
[50] *New York World*, July 22, 1864.
[51] Ida M. Tarbell, *The Life of Abraham Lincoln*, II, 198.

(Private)
Executive Mansion, July 25, 1864.

My dear Sir: I feel that the subject which you pressed upon my attention in our recent conversation is an important one. The men of the South recently (and perhaps still) at Niagara Falls tell us distinctly that they are in the confidential employment of the rebellion; and they tell us as distinctly that they are not empowered to offer terms of peace. Does anyone doubt that what they are empowered to do is to assist in selecting and arranging a candidate and a platform for the Chicago convention? Who could have given them this confidential employment but he who, only a week since, declared to Jaquess and Gilmore, that he had no terms of peace but the independence of the South—the dissolution of the Union? Thus, the present presidential contest will almost certainly be no other than a contest between a union and a disunion candidate, disunion certainly following the success of the latter. The issue is a mighty one, for all people, and all times; and whoever aids the right will be appreciated and remembered.

Yours truly,
A. LINCOLN[52]

Feeling strongly that he was being misrepresented before the public, Lincoln wished to have the entire Niagara correspondence published. Greeley had said on August 5 in his comments on the criticism of his action by Raymond in the *Times* that he was willing to publish *all* the correspondence provided he had assurance that such a course would be acceptable to the President. Greeley contacted Major Hay with reference to the matter. The day after Greeley's "comments" in the *Tribune*, Lincoln telegraphed him:

Executive Mansion, August 6, 1864.

Hon. Horace Greeley, New York: Yours to Major Hay about publication of our correspondence received. With the suppression of a few passages in your letters in regard to which I think you and I would not disagree, I should be glad of the publication. Please come over and see me.

A. LINCOLN[53]

Greeley was sulky. He did not respond at once to the President's telegram. Lincoln had the matter strongly on his mind, and two days later he sent a second telegram:

---

[52] Nicolay and Hay, *Complete Works*, X, 170–71, Lincoln to Abram Wakeman, July 25, 1864.

[53] *Ibid.*, p. 182, Lincoln to Greeley, August 6, 1864. See also Robert Todd Lincoln Collection (35055), *op. cit.*, Greeley to John Hay, August 4, 1864.

Executive Mansion, August 8, 1864.

Hon. Horace Greeley, New York: I telegraphed you Saturday. Did you receive the dispatch? Please answer.

A. LINCOLN[54]

Greeley finally responded on August 8, apparently before he had received the second telegram. He left the question of the publication of the correspondence open but declined to go to Washington. The President was surrounded by his "bitterest personal enemies" and a trip to Washington would only result in further mischief. "I will gladly go," he said, "whenever I feel a hope that their influence has waned." He then launched into further criticism of the President and renewed his insistence that an immediate effort should be made for peace.[55]

After receiving Lincoln's second telegram Greeley wrote again on August 9, declining to telegraph, because he had learned from sad experience at Niagara that "my dispatches go to the War Department before reaching you." Then he boiled over in his characteristic fashion:

I fear that my chance for usefulness has passed. I know that nine-tenths of the whole American people, North and South, are anxious for peace— peace on almost any terms—and utterly sick of human slaughter and devastation. I know that, to the general eye, it now seems that the rebels are anxious to negotiate and that we repulse their advances. I know that if this impression be not removed we shall be beaten out of sight next November. I firmly believe that, were the election to take place tomorrow, the Democratic majority in this State and Pennsylvania would amount to 100,000, and that we should lose Connecticut also. Now if the Rebellion can be crushed before November it will do to go on; if not, we are rushing on certain ruin.

What, then, can I do in Washington? Your trusted advisers all think that I ought to go to Fort Lafayette for what I have done already. Seward wanted me sent there for my brief conference with M. Mercier. The cry has steadily been, No truce! No armistice! No negotiation! No mediation! Nothing but surrender at discretion! I never heard of such fatuity before. There is nothing like it in history. It must result in disaster, or all experience is delusive.

Now I do not know that a tolerable peace could be had, but I believe it might have been last month; and, at all events, I know that an honest, sincere

---

[54] Nicolay and Hay, *Complete Works*, X, 183, Lincoln to Greeley, August 8, 1864.
[55] Robert Todd Lincoln Collection (35139), *op. cit.*, Greeley to Lincoln, August 8, 1864.

effort for it would have done us immense good. And I think no Government fighting a rebellion should ever close its ears to any proposition the rebels may make.

I beg you, implore you, to inaugurate or invite proposals for peace forthwith. And in case peace cannot now be made, consent to an armistice for one year, each party to retain unmolested, all it now holds, but the rebel ports to be opened. Meantime let a national convention be held, and there will surely be no more war at all events.[56]

Although his provocation must have been great, Lincoln kept his patience and wrote Greeley on August 9 sending him a full copy of the correspondence and suggesting the parts of Greeley's letters which he deemed it unwise to publish. His letter read:

(Private)

Executive Mansion, August 9, 1864.

Dear Sir: Herewith is a full copy of the correspondence, and which I have had privately printed, but not made public. The parts of your letters which I wish suppressed are only those which, as I think, give too gloomy an aspect to our cause, and those which present the carrying of elections as a motive of action. I have, as you see, drawn a red pencil over the parts I wish suppressed.

As to the Alexander H. Stephens matter, so much pressed by you, I can only say that he sought to come to Washington in the name of the "Confederate States," in a vessel of "the Confederate States navy," and with no pretense even that he would bear any proposal for peace; but with language showing that his mission would be military, and not civil or diplomatic. Nor has he at any time since pretended that he had terms of peace, so far as I know or believe. On the contrary, Jefferson Davis has, in the most formal manner, declared that Stephens had no terms of peace. I thought we could not afford to give this quasi-acknowledgement of the independence of the Confederacy, in a case where there was not even an intimation of anything for our good. Still, as the parts of your letters relating to Stephens contain nothing worse than a questioning of my action, I do not ask a suppression of those parts.

Yours truly,

A. LINCOLN[57]

The parts of Greeley's letters, which Lincoln desired to have omitted, in the event that the correspondence was to be made public, were as follows:

---

[56] *Ibid.* (35171), Greeley to Lincoln, August 8, 1864.

[57] Nicolay and Hay, *Complete Works*, X, 184–85, Lincoln to Greeley, August 9, 1864.

In the letter of July 7, second paragraph, the words "and therefore I venture to remind you that our bleeding, bankrupt, almost dying country also longs for peace, shudders at the prospect of fresh conscriptions, of further wholesale devastations, and of new rivers of human blood, and:" also the words "now, and is morally certain, unless removed, to do far greater in the approaching elections."

In the fourth paragraph, the words "if only with a view to the momentous election soon to occur in North Carolina and of the draft to be enforced in the Free States, this should be done."

In the last paragraph, the words "It may save us from a Northern insurrection."

In the letter of July 10, second paragraph, the words "in season for effect on the approaching North Carolina elections"; and in the last paragraph, the words "especially those of North Carolina."

And in the letter of July 13, last paragraph, the words "that a good influence may even yet be exerted on the North Carolina election next month."[58]

Greeley replied that if his letters were to be published they should be printed as written, and he again charged Lincoln with having changed his ground during the course of the correspondence.[59] Fearful of the effect of a wide dissemination of Greeley's gloomy views, Lincoln dropped the matter and submitted in silence to the misrepresentations which had already reached the public. The full correspondence preceding the conference was not published until after the President's death.

The disinterested observer finds little justification for the persistence with which Lincoln urged certain eliminations and the stubbornness with which Greeley insisted that not a word should be changed. The public was accustomed to Greeley's outbursts. Lincoln overestimated the possible harmful influence of the few utterances he wished to suppress. Greeley had nothing to lose by the eliminations proposed. If they had been made and the correspondence published, the record would still have left him in an untenable position.

Nothing daunted, Greeley continued to write letters of introduction and recommendation to the President as if nothing had happened between them, and got in a word from time to time with reference to the possibility of peace. Thus on August 29 he wrote Lincoln: "What I absorbingly desire is, that the Government shall offer to the revolted States conditions which they *ought* to accept, which the civilized world

---

[58] Raymond, *op. cit.*, p. 587.

[59] Robert Todd Lincoln Collection (35228), *op. cit.*, Greeley to Lincoln, August 11, 1864.

will approve, and which will tend to develop and embolden whatever Union feelings may be latent among them." Again on September 16: "I do not urge you to do anything. I will not even advise. But so anxious am I that not one day of needless blood should be shed in this terrible struggle that I venture to commend," etc. And again on November 23: "I pray that you may so temper your Message as to disarm the Rebellion and pave the way to an early restoration of Peace. I am firm as ever in the faith that Peace may be made soon if the right means are employed in the quest for it."[60]

Lincoln had an eye to history. Although the Niagara incident was closed for the time being, he gathered the papers together and sent them to Raymond of the *Times* as he had sent them to Greeley:

Executive Mansion, August 15, 1864.

My dear Sir: I have proposed to Mr. Greeley that the Niagara correspondence be published, suppressing only the parts of his letters over which the red pencil is drawn in the copy which I herewith send. He declines giving his consent to the publication of his letters unless these parts be published with the rest. I have concluded that it is better for me to submit for the time to the consequences of the false position in which I consider he has placed me than to subject the country to the consequences of publishing their discouraging and injurious parts. I send you this and the accompanying copy, not for publication, but merely to explain to you, and that you may preserve them until their proper time shall come.

Yours truly,

A. LINCOLN[61]

According to Secretary Welles, Lincoln did not consult the Cabinet about the Niagara episode but merely informed the Cabinet from time to time of the steps he had taken. Welles was sorry that the President had permitted himself, "in this irregular way, to be induced to engage in correspondence with irresponsible parties like Sanders and Clay or scheming busybodies like Greeley." Welles was a bit piqued because Lincoln had apparently conferred only with Seward before taking action in this matter.[62] Welles recorded in his diary this appraisal of Greeley:

---

[60] *Ibid.* (35657), Greeley to Lincoln, August 29, 1864; (36369), September 16; (36522), September 21; (38394), November 16; (38623), November 23; (40478), February 6, 1865.

[61] Nicolay and Hay, *Complete Works*, X, 191–92, Lincoln to Henry J. Raymond, August 17, 1864.

[62] Welles, *op. cit.*, II, 83–85, 110.

The Tribune is owned by a company which really desired to give a fair support to the Administration, but Greeley, the editor, is erratic, unreliable, without stability, an enemy of the Administration because he hates Seward, a creature of sentiment or impulse, not of reason nor professed principle. Having gone to extremes in the measures that fomented and brought on this war, he would now go to extremes to quell it. I am prepared to see him acquiesce in a division of the Union, or the continuance of slavery, to accomplish his party schemes. There are no men or measures to which he will adhere faithfully. He is ambitious, talented, but not considerate, persistent, or profound.[63]

The Niagara question came up in the Cabinet meeting informally after Lincoln had sent all the correspondence to Greeley and to Raymond, and after he had considered the incident closed. Welles recorded the President's estimate of Greeley at that time:

Concerning Greeley, to whom the President has clung too long and confidingly, he said to-day that Greeley is an old shoe—good for nothing now, whatever he has been. "In early life, and with few mechanics and but little means in the West, we used," said he, "to make our shoes last a great while with much mending, and sometimes, when far gone, we found the leather so rotten the stitches would not hold. Greeley is so rotten that nothing can be done with him. He is not truthful; the stitches all tear out."[64]

It was a hard summer. August, 1864, was the darkest month of the war and the most uncertain politically. President and editor lived under great stress, and were moved by changing events to varying emotions. Inherently, loving the Union and hating slavery, they were not as far apart as they may at times have imagined. Perhaps unconsciously they summed up where they stood as the Niagara debacle ended in these parallel statements:

Lincoln	Greeley
There have been men base enough to propose to me to return to slavery the black warriors of Port Hudson and Olustee, and thus win the respect of the masters they fought. Should I do so, I should deserve to be damned in time and eternity. Come what will, I will keep my faith with friend and foe. My ene-	*Now we do not contend—though the contrary has been a thousand times asserted—that reunion is possible or endurable only on the basis of Universal Freedom. While we most undoubtedly believe that the best possible basis, and the only one that affords any guarantee against future conspiracies and bloody re-*

[63] *Ibid.*, p. 104.
[64] *Ibid.*, pp. 111–12.

Lincoln

mies pretend that I am now carrying on this war for the sole purpose of abolition. So long as I am President, it shall be carried on for the sole purpose of restoring the Union. But no human power can subdue this rebellion without the use of the emancipation policy, and every other policy calculated to weaken the moral and physical forces of the rebellion. . . . Let my enemies prove to the country that the destruction of slavery is not necessary to a restoration of the Union. I will abide the issue.[65]

Greeley

bellions, we would leave our Government entirely free to do whatever may at any time seem desirable. War has its exigencies which cannot be foreseen and which make their own laws; and Peace is often desirable on other terms than those of our choice. We indicate no inflexible demand when we call attention to the fact that a Pro-Slavery reunion under Democratic auspices must inevitably roll back upon the Free States a tide of intolerant, persecuting, fanatical devotion to slavery, such as was never yet experienced in any country.[66]

The central figure in an almost simultaneous abortive peace effort was Colonel James F. Jaquess, a Methodist minister from Illinois. He was commissioned by Governor Yates to raise and lead to the field the 73d Regiment of Illinois Volunteers. In the spring of 1863 he was serving with the army of General Rosecrans in Tennessee. He had distinguished himself in the service, but he was obsessed with the idea that he could bring about peace through appeals to his fellow churchmen in the South. In May he sought permission through General James A. Garfield, then chief-of-staff to General Rosecrans, to undertake a peace mission and with unbounded assurance declared: "I will go into the Southern Confederacy and return within ninety days with terms of peace that the Government will accept. . . . I propose no compromise with traitors. . . . I propose to do it in the name of the Lord."[67]

Impressed by his earnestness and by his honest zeal, though not anticipating the results he promised, General Rosecrans commissioned James R. Gilmore to carry Jaquess' request to President Lincoln with his endorsement. Lincoln was also apparently moved by the fervor of the appeal and consented in a cautious letter to General Rosecrans that Colonel Jaquess might be granted a furlough.

---

[65] Nicolay and Hay, *Complete Works*, X, 191, August 15, 1864.
[66] *Tribune*, July 28, 1864.
[67] Nicolay and Hay, *Abraham Lincoln*, IX, 202.

Executive Mansion, May 28, 1863.

My dear Sir: *I have but slight personal acquaintance with Colonel Jaquess, though I know him very well by character.*

Such a mission as he proposes I think promises good, if it were free from difficulties, which I fear it cannot be.

First. He cannot go with any government authority whatever. This is absolute and imperative.

Secondly. If he goes without authority, he takes a great deal of personal risk—he may be condemned and executed as a spy.

If, for any reason, you think fit to give Colonel Jacquess a furlough, and any authority from me for that object is necessary, you hereby have it for any length of time you see fit.

Yours truly,

A. LINCOLN.[68]

In due time Colonel Jaquess made his way into the Confederate lines. Gilmore recites with almost too much exactness the experience the Colonel had in talking with Confederate leaders. According to Gilmore, Jaquess said to all and sundry: "Lay down your arms, go back to your allegiance, and the country will deal kindly and generously by you." And the common reply of the Confederates was: "We are tired of war. We are willing to give up slavery. We know it is gone; but so long as our Government holds out, we must stand by it. We cannot betray it and each other." Colonel Jaquess attempted to gain an audience with Jefferson Davis but was unable to do so because he did not bear credentials from Lincoln. This mission, as was to be expected, came to naught.[69]

In the spring of 1864, these would-be peacemakers, Jaquess and Gilmore, got together again. This time Gilmore took the lead. He reported a conference with Lincoln, at which Chase was present, in which the President consented that Jaquess and Gilmore might go on their proposed mission with the express understanding that he had neither suggested, nor requested, nor directed that the journey should be undertaken. Their ostensible purpose was to sound out Jefferson Davis, if possible, on terms of peace. With this understanding Lincoln issued passes for them.[70]

---

[68] Nicolay and Hay, *Complete Works*, VIII, 285, Lincoln to General Rosecrans, May 28, 1863.

[69] James R. Gilmore, *Personal Recollections of Abraham Lincoln and the Civil War*, pp. 137–41, 156–66.

[70] *Ibid.*, pp. 230–93; Nicolay and Hay, *Abraham Lincoln*, IX, 201–21; and Edward Chase Kirkland, *The Peacemakers of 1864*, pp. 86–96.

While Lincoln was extremely careful to make sure that these emissaries went without credentials and with the understanding that it was at the risk of their own necks, he nevertheless indoctrinated Gilmore with the terms of peace which he might lay before Davis, if opportunity offered, on his own account. After extended discussion, in which Chase participated, these terms were recorded by Gilmore as follows:

First. The immediate dissolution of the Southern Government, and disbandment of its armies; and the acknowledgement by all the States in rebellion of the supremacy of the Union.

Second. The total and absolute abolition of slavery in every one of the late Slave States and throughout the Union. This to be perpetual.

Third. Full amnesty to all who have been in any way engaged in the rebellion, and their restoration to all the rights of citizenship.

Fourth. All acts of secession to be regarded as nullities; and the late rebellious States to be, and be regarded, as if they had never attempted to secede from the Union. Representation in the House from the recent Slave States to be on the basis of their voting population.

Fifth. The sum of five hundred millions, in United States stock, to be issued and divided between the late Slave States, to be used by them in payment to slave-owners, loyal and disloyal, for the slaves emancipated by my proclamation. This sum to be divided among the late slave-owners equally and equitably, at the rate of one-half the value of the slaves in the year 1860; and if any surplus should remain, it is to be returned to the United States Treasury. [This clause was finally modified by restricting payment to owners of fifty slaves and under, and reducing the amount named to an absolute sum of four hundred millions.]

Sixth. A national convention to be convened as soon as practicable, to ratify this settlement, and make such changes in the Constitution as may be in accord with the new order of things.

Seventh. The intent and meaning of the foregoing is that the Union shall be fully restored, as it was before the Rebellion, with the exception that all slaves within its borders are, and shall forever be, free men.[71]

It will be noted that the terms dictated to Gilmore by Lincoln were very similar to the "Plan of Adjustment" submitted by Greeley to Lincoln with his letter of July 7 with relation to the Niagara overtures. Jaquess, trusting in the Lord, and Gilmore, trusting in his own conceit, reached Richmond safely and on July 17, 1864, addressed a joint communication to the Confederate Secretary of State reading:

---

[71] Gilmore, *op. cit.*, pp. 243–45.

> *Spotswood House, Richmond, Va.*
> *July 17, 1864.*
>
> *Hon. J. P. Benjamin, Secretary of State, etc.*
>
> Dear Sir:—*The undersigned respectfully solicit an interview with President Davis.*
>
> *They visit Richmond only as private citizens, and have no official charac- ter or authority; but they are acquainted with the views of the United States Government, and with the sentiments of the Northern people, relative to an adjustment of the differences existing between the North and the South, and earnestly hope that a free interchange of views between President Davis and themselves may open the way to such official negotiations as will result in restoring* PEACE *to the two sections of our distracted country.*
>
> *They therefore ask an interview with the President, and, awaiting your reply, are*
>
>

Truly and respectfully yours,
Jaquess and Gilmore[72]

Perhaps to their surprise, Secretary Benjamin sent for them promptly, received them courteously, and arranged during the day for them to meet Davis at the State Department at nine o'clock that evening. At the appointed time they found President Davis and Sec- retary Benjamin awaiting them. Davis talked with them in cordial, informal fashion. In the course of the extended colloquy, Gilmore tried out Lincoln's formula. The general response of Davis to all the proposals advanced by the visitors was: "The North was mad and blind; it would not let us govern ourselves, and so the war came, and now it must go on till the last man of this generation falls in his tracks, and his children seize his musket and fight our battle, unless you acknowledge our right of self-government. We are not fighting for slavery. We are fighting for independence, and that, or extermination, we will have."

Jacquess and Gilmore found their way safely back to the Northern lines, and Gilmore hastened to Washington to report to Lincoln. Senator Sumner was closeted with the President when Gilmore arrived and remained through the conference. There was some talk about submitting Gilmore's report to the *Tribune* for publication, but it was finally decided that the ultimatum Davis had declared should be briefly released by Gilmore under his pen name, Edmund Kirke, in the *Boston Evening Transcript.* That was done on July 22, 1864, and

---

[72] *Ibid.*, pp. 258–59.

Gilmore later published two articles in the *Atlantic Monthly*, "Our Visit to Richmond" and "Our Last Day in Dixie."[73]

Greeley was not the only editor who harassed the President in the troubled summer of 1864. The editor of the *Times*, Henry J. Raymond, in his capacity as chairman, called the Republican National Executive Committee together in the middle of August to take stock on the chances of Lincoln's re-election in November. The prospect seemed most dismal to them. On August 22, voicing the views of the committee, Raymond wrote Lincoln a very discouraging letter in which he made extraordinary proposals.

He had been in active correspondence with the President's "stanchest friends in every State" and found that "the tide is setting strongly against us." Illinois, Indiana, and Pennsylvania were already as good as lost to the Administration and generally "so of the rest." The reasons for this disaffection Raymond ascribed to "the want of military successes" and "the impression in some minds, the fear and suspicion in others, that we are not to have peace in any event under this Administration until slavery is abandoned." There was also the widespread suspicion that peace with Union was impossible.

Having recounted these dire circumstances, Raymond proposed the appointment of a commission to make proffers of peace to Jefferson Davis "on the sole condition of acknowledging the supremacy of the Constitution—all other questions to be settled in a convention of the people of all the States." He could not conceive of any answer which Davis could give to such a proposal which would not strengthen the President and the Union cause everywhere. He closed this remarkable proposal in an earnest but kindly tone:

> *I beg you to excuse the earnestness with which I have pressed this matter upon your attention. It seems to me calculated to do good—and incapable of doing harm. It will turn the tide of public sentiment and avert impending evils of the gravest character. It will arouse and concentrate the loyalty of the country and unless I am greatly mistaken give us an easy and fruitful victory. Permit me to add that if done at all I think this should be done at once,— as your own spontaneous act. In advance of the Chicago Convention it might render the action of that body of very little consequence.*[74]

---

[73] *Atlantic Monthly*, IX, 372, 725.
[74] Nicolay and Hay, *Abraham Lincoln*, IX, 218–19. See also Francis Brown, *Raymond of The Times*, pp. 259–61.

For once it appeared that Greeley and Raymond were almost in collusion. Growing more restless, Raymond and his committee came to Washington on August 25 and, betraying evidence of panic, urged their views on the President. Lincoln was depressed but not disconcerted. It was a tight spot, but Lincoln, the lawyer and politician, came to the rescue of Lincoln, the President. He was the presidential candidate and here was the National Committee and its chairman, the editor of the one paper in New York City which had stoutly supported the Administration, urging a course of action upon him which, in the light of his recent "To Whom It May Concern" declaration, was clearly inadmissible. Lincoln did not lay the proposal before the entire Cabinet but, according to Welles, did discuss it with Seward, Fessenden, and Stanton.[75] Lincoln's lifelong habit, when confronted with a serious issue, was to put his thoughts down on paper. If he should be obliged to accede to this scheme he would "make the proposer of the project the witness of its absurdity." Accordingly, he drafted experimental instructions to Raymond and directed him to seek a conference with Jefferson Davis. He was ready with this document when Raymond and the committee arrived:

Executive Mansion, August 24, 1864.

Sir: You will proceed forthwith and obtain, if possible a conference for peace with Honorable Jefferson Davis, or any person by him authorized for that purpose. You will address him in entirely respectful terms, at all events, and in any that may be indispensable to secure the conference. At said conference you will propose, on behalf of this government, that upon the restoration of the Union and the national authority, the war shall cease at once, all remaining questions to be left for adjustment by peaceful modes. If this be accepted, hostilities to cease at once. If it be not accepted, you will then request to be informed what terms, if any, embracing the restoration of the Union would be accepted. If any such be presented you in answer, you will forthwith report the same to this Government, and await further instructions. If the presentation of any terms embracing the restoration of the Union be declined, you will then request to be informed what terms of peace would be accepted; and, on receiving any answer, report the same to this Government, and await further instructions.[76]

Lincoln's belief that an absurdity could best be exploded by putting it down in writing was again justified. Raymond and his committee

---

[75] Welles, *op. cit.*, II, 119.
[76] Nicolay and Hay, *Abraham Lincoln*, IX, 220–21.

were convinced before they left Washington that the plan of sending a commission to Richmond "would be ignominiously surrendering in advance."[77]

Raymond, unlike Greeley, knew when he had met his master. On August 26, the *Times* published on its editorial page a dispatch from Washington dated August 25 which Raymond himself may have sent to his paper. It indicated a complete reversal of the plan for which Raymond and his associates had gone to Washington to urge upon the President. It read in part:

You may rest assured that all the reports attributing to the Government any movement looking toward negotiations for peace at present are utterly without foundation. . . . The Government has not entertained or discussed the project of proposing an armistice with the rebels; nor has it any intention of sending commissioners to Richmond for the purpose of offering or soliciting terms of peace, or of negotiating with the rebel authorities on that or any other subject. Its sole and undivided purpose is to prosecute the war until the rebellion is quelled.

Raymond had already said in a book published in 1864 that

No one can read Mr. Lincoln's state papers without perceiving in them a most remarkable faculty of "putting things" so as to command the attention and assent of the common people. His style of thought as well as of expression is thoroughly in harmony with their habitual modes of thinking and speaking. His intellect is keen, emphatically logical in its action, and capable of the closest and most subtle analysis: and he uses language for the sole purpose of stating, in the clearest and simplest possible form, the precise idea he wishes to convey. He has no pride of intellect—not the slightest desire for display—no thought or purpose but that of making everybody understand precisely what he believes and means to utter. And while this sacrifices the graces of style, it gains immeasurably in practical force and effect. It gives to his public papers a weight and influence with the mass of the people, which no public man of this country has ever before attained.[78]

The "precise idea" Lincoln wished to convey to Raymond and his committee had been well understood. The document of August 24, stated "in the clearest and simplest possible form," put an end to ill-conceived overtures for peace in the summer of 1864; and the policy expressed, also with clarity and simplicity, in "To Whom It May Concern" stood until Appomattox.

[77] *Ibid.*, p. 221.
[78] Henry J. Raymond, *History of the Administration of President Lincoln*, p. 479.

A second term would be a great honor and a great labor, which, together, perhaps I would not decline if tendered.

Lincoln[1]

Mr. A. Lincoln is a gentleman with whom I hope to be always on terms of civility but not of cordiality. I opposed his renomination for the simple reason that I did not deem him the man for the place. I finally supported his re-election for the country's sake, not his.

Greeley[2]

10   Politics again

Greeley never failed to express his confidence in Lincoln's integrity, patriotism, and desire to preserve the Union. He could not convince himself, however, that Lincoln was really big enough to be President, and especially to direct the affairs of the nation in time of Rebellion. He had not wanted him in the first place and came to his support reluctantly in the campaign of 1860. When Lincoln appeared to agree with him on an important issue, he was lavish in his praise; but he had no conception of the stature of Lincoln among the leading men of his time and no vision of the place he would occupy in history. In this view, to be sure, Greeley was by no means alone. His hesitation about the President's ability to suppress the Rebellion, to eradicate slavery, and to face effectively the problems of reconstruction was augmented by his evaluation of the first two years of the Administration. He began early to think of a successor to Lincoln. In one way or another, he was associated with all of the deliberate movements to choose someone other than Lincoln to lead the Republican party in the campaign of 1864. Count Adam Gurowski recorded in his diary on December 6,

---

[1] John G. Nicolay and John Hay, eds., *Complete Works of Abraham Lincoln*, IX, 183, Lincoln to E. B. Washburne, October 26, 1863.

[2] Edwin D. Morgan Papers, New York State Library, Albany, N.Y., Greeley to Rev. A. Brown, February 26, 1865.

331

1863: "Greeley against reelection—so he told me himself. I record, and we shall see if he holds out."[3]

As early as the spring of 1863 Greeley and other malcontents, especially radicals in Congress, began, quietly at first, to look about for a likely candidate. Largely at Greeley's suggestion they hit upon General William Starke Rosecrans. Greeley arranged to have James R. Gilmore, then on the *Tribune* staff, visit Rosecrans at his headquarters at Murfreesborough, Tennessee, to tell him that his friends were thinking of him as the Republican candidate for the presidency in 1864 and to sound him out on his disposition to enter the campaign. Gilmore made this journey in May, 1863, spent some time with Rosecrans, decided that he would be an eligible candidate, and finally opened up the question with him. As near as he could recall the exact words of Rosecrans half an hour after they were spoken, Gilmore recorded:

The good opinion of those gentlemen is exceedingly gratifying to me, and so is yours, but I assure you that I have not had the remotest suspicion that you were here for any such purpose. I have supposed you were merely gathering literary material; but, my good friend, it cannot be. My place is here. The country gave me my education, and so has a right to my military services; and it educated me for precisely this emergency. So this, and not the presidency, is my post of duty, and I cannot, without violating my conscience, leave it. But let me tell you, and I wish you would tell your friends who are moving in this matter, that you are mistaken about Mr. Lincoln. He is in his right place. I am in a position to know, and if you live you will see that I am right about him.[4]

General James A. Garfield, later President of the United States, was a member of Rosecrans' staff at the time of Gilmore's visit. Garfield's biographer claimed that Rosecrans, on the advice of Garfield, declined the invitation to be a candidate.[5] Many years after the event, Gilmore insisted that Rosecrans had reached his own decision.

Salmon Portland Chase, unlike General Rosecrans, had long been grooming himself for the presidency. His lightning rod was up at the first Republican Convention in 1856, but he withdrew his name before the balloting began; and he was one of the prominent, disappointed candidates at the Wigwam Convention in Chicago in May, 1860. Summoned to Springfield after the election in 1860, he was disap-

---

[3] Adam Gurowski, *Diary*, III, 35.

[4] James R. Gilmore, *Personal Recollections of Abraham Lincoln and the Civil War*, pp. 134–47.

[5] Albert G. Riddle, *The Life, Character and Public Services of J. A. Garfield*, pp. 70–71.

pointed to find that Lincoln proposed to make him Secretary of the Treasury.[6] Always confident of his own ability and anxious to be at the top, he had hoped that the President would proffer him the portfolio of Secretary of State. He finally accepted the post of Secretary of the Treasury, after hesitation up to the last minute, with the firm conviction that he would find ways to outshine the President for whose ability and statesmanship he did not have great respect. There is no doubt that he entered the Cabinet with the definite purpose of building his political fences so as to succeed Lincoln in the 1864 election.[7]

Chase was a voluminous letter writer. He was very discreet in offering direct criticism of his chief, but his letters often indicated the need of a type of leadership at Washington which, it could be readily inferred, he was able to supply. Thus in expressing his regret to the chairman of a committee in New York that he would be unable to attend a celebration of the birthday of Washington in February, 1862, he seized upon the occasion to say: "We need, for the trials of these days, his firmness, his patience, his disinterestedness, his true courage, his lofty sense of justice, his enlightened zeal for impartial freedom. These are the virtues, which exercised in such degree as men are capable of, will not only restore the Union, but will reestablish it in more than its pristine vigor, compactness, and beneficence."[8] Again, in April, he was of the opinion that "There have been other occasions in the course of the struggle in which it seemed to me that a different course from that actually adopted would be better. This is especially true in relation to slavery. It has seemed to me from the early days of the conflict that it was bad policy as well as bad principle to give any support to the institution."[9] And again, in June, to Major General Butler, he wrote: "In my judgment, the military order of General Hunter should have been sustained. The President, who is as sound in head as he is excellent in heart, thought otherwise; and I, as in duty bound, submit my judgment to his."[10]

This vein of semi-concealed criticism of the President, and reference to unsatisfied needs in the conduct of the government, continued until the campaign began in earnest in 1864. He came out directly, how-

---

[6] J. W. Schuckers, *The Life and Public Services of Salmon Portland Chase*, pp. 195–208.

[7] T. Harry Williams, *Lincoln and the Radicals*, p. 307; Albert Bushnell Hart, *Salmon Portland Chase*, p. 309; and Burton J. Hendrick, *Lincoln's War Cabinet*, pp. 371–72.

[8] Schuckers, *op. cit.*, pp. 363–64, Chase to Elliott C. Cowdin, February 20. 1862.

[9] *Ibid.*, pp. 365–66, Chase to Bradford R. Wood, April 2, 1862.

[10] *Ibid.*, pp. 375–76, Chase to Major General Butler, June 24, 1862.

ever, in letting his friends know where he stood. In October, 1863, Chase wrote to one of the editors of the *Independent*, a paper which advocated him as Lincoln's successor:

And do not mistake me. If I know my own heart, a judicial would be more agreeable to my personal feelings than any political position. So I have felt for years, but Providence has kept me hitherto in political positions, and now I think I have done more good in them than I could have effected on the bench. And so I think also concerning the future. Perhaps I am over-confident; but I really feel as if, with God's blessing, I could administer the Government of this country so as to secure and imperilibilize our institutions: and create a party, fundamentally and thoroughly democratic, which would guarantee a succession of successful administrations. I may be over-confident, I say; and I shall take it as a sign that I am, if the people do not call me, and shall be content. . . . I know that many good and true men desire that my services may be required in the highest sphere of administration, and perhaps there is enough of popular confidence in me to warrant their belief that their desires might be realized without extraordinary exertions.[11]

Two days later, Chase apologized to none other than Horace Greeley for his failure to reply more promptly to his "last letters," and assured him that no other man had "so powerfully promoted the increase of just sentiments concerning political rights and duties" through speech and press as he had done. "Because of this," Chase continued, "I greatly value your approval and that confidence which induces you to express a preference for me as the next Union candidate for the chief magistracy. Should circumstances justify your final action in accordance with this preference, and should it be my lot (which does not now seem probable enough to affect me much) to be called to that responsible position, I shall take to it whatever capacity God has given me, and just the same spirit and industry which I have brought to other public duties."[12]

Members of the Cabinet watched with interest Chase's campaign in Ohio during the latter part of October, ostensibly to oppose the election of Vallandigham, representing the Peace Democrats, as governor. Blair declared that this stumping tour was an open declaration of war on the President.[13] Welles slyly remarked that "Chase is understood to have special interest in this election."[14] Bates was afraid

---

[11] *Ibid.*, pp. 393–94, Chase to Rev. Joshua Leavitt, October 7, 1863.
[12] *Ibid.*, pp. 394–95, Chase to Greeley, October 9, 1863.
[13] Hendrick, *op. cit.*, p. 401.
[14] Edgar T. Welles, ed., *The Diary of Gideon Welles*, I, 469.

Chase's head was turned by his eagerness in pursuit of the presidency. "For a long time back," Bates wrote, "he has been filling all the offices in his own vast patronage with extreme partizans, and contrives also to fill many vacancies properly belonging to other departments." Commenting on Chase's speeches Bates remarked further that "Mr. C. attributes the salvation of the country to his own *admirable financial system*" and that Chase's visit to the West was generally understood as "the opening of his campaign for the Presidency."[15]

The "good and true men" on whom Chase relied were not numerous if the outstanding leaders in political life were to be taken into account. Even the Congressional Committee on the Conduct of the War dominated by Benjamin F. Wade, senator from Ohio, and Zachariah Chandler, senator from Michigan, who bitterly opposed Lincoln, did not espouse Chase's cause. On December 9, 1863, a group of lesser lights perfected an "Organization to make S. P. Chase President,"[16] and Chase "consented to their wishes."[17] As his biographer recorded, "The movement fell, however, into bad hands; it was badly officered and was badly managed."[18] This was a mild and conservative statement. It would be hard to find in American political history a more stupid and inept attempt to promote the nomination of a candidate for the presidency.

The committee distributed in February, 1864, a pamphlet entitled "The Next Presidential Election."[19] Allegedly confidential, it was widely circulated, especially in Ohio, under the frank of Senator John Sherman. It avoided all reference to Chase and took the high ground that "In time of civil war with all its attendant calamities, the attempt to advance the personal interest and ambition of any one man, or number of men, without regard to the public good, deserves and should receive universal condemnation." It was deemed to be too early to commit the people to the fortunes of any presidential aspirant, but it appeared to be not improper to make a direct attack on the incumbent of that high office. The pamphlet insisted that the people had lost all confidence in Lincoln's ability to suppress the Rebellion and restore the Union; and Lincoln was variously characterized as "weak and vacillating," as having "feebleness of will," as wanting "intellectual

---

[15] Howard K. Beale, ed., *The Diary of Edward Bates*, pp. 310–11.

[16] Charles R. Wilson, "The Original Chase Organization Meeting and the Next Presidential Election," *Mississippi Valley Historical Review*, XXIII, 61–79.

[17] Schuckers, *op. cit.*, p. 497, Chase to James C. Hall, January 18, 1864.

[18] *Ibid.*, p. 476.

[19] Wilson, *op. cit.*, XXIII, 61–79.

grasp" and "political principle," and as being "indifferent to truth."
"We want in our incoming President," these sly promoters went on,
"an advanced thinker; a statesman profoundly versed in political and
economic science, one who fully comprehends the spirit of the age in
which we live." It was easy to see that this declaration was the ground-
work for the discovery of the man who possessed all the desirable
qualities.

Samuel G. Pomeroy, senator from Kansas, now came into the
picture as head and shoulders of the movement against Lincoln and
for Chase. The famous "Pomeroy Circular" followed soon after the
initial pamphlet. This time the committee to make Chase President
did not hide its purpose in political double-talk, it showed all its true
colors:

*Those in behalf of whom this communication is made have thoroughly
surveyed the political field, and have arrived at the following conclusions:*

*First, that even were the reelection of Mr. Lincoln desirable, it is practi-
cally impossible against the union of influences which will oppose him.*

*Second, that should he be reelected, his manifest tendency towards com-
promises and temporary expedients of policy will become stronger during a
second term than it has been in the first, and the cause of human liberty,
and the dignity and honor of the nation, suffer proportionately, while the
war may continue to languish during his whole Administration, till the
public debt shall become a burden too great to be borne.*

*Third, that the patronage of the Government through the necessities of
the war has been so rapidly increased, and to such an enormous extent, and
so loosely placed, as to render the "one-term principle" absolutely essential
to the certain safety of our republican institutions.*

*Fourth, that we find united in Hon. Salmon P. Chase more of the quali-
ties needed in a President during the next four years than are combined in
any other available candidate; his record, clear and unimpeachable, showing
him to be a statesman of rare ability and an administrator of the very highest
order, while his private character furnishes the surest obtainable guarantee
of economy and purity in the management of public affairs.*

*Fifth, that the discussion of the Presidential question, already commenced
by the friends of Mr. Lincoln, has developed a popularity and strength in
Mr. Chase unexpected even to his warmest admirers; and while we are aware
that this strength is at present unorganized, and in no condition to manifest
its real magnitude, we are satisfied that it only needs systematic and faithful
effort to develop it to an extent sufficient to overcome all opposing obstacles.
For these reasons the friends of Mr. Chase have determined on measures
which shall present his claims fairly and at once to the country. . . .*[20]

---

[20] John G. Nicolay and John Hay, *Abraham Lincoln—A History*, VIII, 319–20.

The public reaction to these pamphlets was most unfortunate for Chase's interests. He was himself quick to see that his friends had over-stepped themselves, and that he was left in an embarrassing position before the public and before the President. He hastened to try to set himself right with Lincoln. In a labored letter, dated February 2, 1864, he explained that he had consented that his name might be used, that he had informed the committee that he "could render them no help," and that he had not been consulted about the committee's organiza-tion and activities. He professed his "respect and esteem" and even "affection" for the President and asked to be informed if there was anything in his action or position prejudicial to the public interest. He did not wish to administer the Treasury Department "one day" with-out the President's "entire confidence."[21]

Lincoln acknowledged receipt of Chase's letter on February 23[22] and wrote him more fully on February 29:

Executive Mansion, February 29, 1864

My dear Sir: I would have taken time to answer yours of the 22d sooner, only that I did not suppose any evil could result from the delay, especially as, by a note, I promptly acknowledged receipt of yours, and promised a fuller answer. Now, on consideration, I find there is really very little to say. My knowledge of Mr. Pomeroy's letter having been made public came to me only the day you wrote but I had, in spite of myself, known of its existence several days before. I have not yet read it, and I think I shall not. I was not shocked or surprised by the appearance of the letter, because I had had knowledge of Mr. Pomeroy's committee, and of secret issues which I sup-posed came from it, and of secret agents who I supposed were sent out by it, for several weeks. I have known just as little of these things as my friends have allowed me to know. They bring the documents to me, but I do not read them; they tell me what they think fit to tell me, but I do not inquire for more. I fully concur with you that neither of us can be justly held re-sponsible for what our respective friends may do without our instigation or countenance; and I assure you, as you have assured me, that no assault has been made upon you by my instigation or with my countenance. Whether you shall remain at the head of the Treasury Department is a question which I shall not allow myself to consider from any standpoint other than my judg-ment of the public service, and, in that view, I do not perceive occasion for a change.

Yours truly,
A. Lincoln[23]

---

[21] Schuckers, *op. cit.*, pp. 500–01, Chase to Lincoln, February 22, 1864.
[22] Nicolay and Hay, *Complete Works*, X, 19, Lincoln to Chase, February 23, 1864.
[23] *Ibid.*, pp. 25–26, Lincoln to Chase, February 29, 1864.

That the editor of the *Tribune*, with his vast news-gathering machine, was privy to all these maneuvers of Chase and his friends from the beginning to the end goes without saying. Finding Rosecrans unwilling to be considered, Greeley had promptly transferred his temporary affections to Chase. When the "Pomeroy Circular" became common property, Greeley was obliged to notice it. He blandly indicated that he did not approve of any "invidious comparisons" which might seem to appear in the circular; but he held that the views of those who had struggled with Chase "to uphold and preserve the just authority of the Union" were entitled to respectful and generous consideration. He regarded Chase's successful discharge of the high trust of Secretary of the Treasury as the marvel of recent history and as "the most difficult achievement of the century." "No other man now in the service of the Republic," he said, "fills a post under the President more important or unenviable than that of the Secretary of the Treasury and no other has been filled with more signal ability or more tireless energy and zeal."[24]

One could almost produce the adjectives which Greeley would have used in characterizing the initial pamphlet and the Pomeroy sequel to it if these documents had been promulgated in the interest of a candidate to whom he was opposed. "Scurrilous," they were, but Greeley would have found more descriptive terms. He was fully aware, too, of Chase's extended and benign correspondence in his own behalf and of the partisan machine he had built up in the Treasury Department. The *Tribune*, ordinarily voicing righteous wrath at such procedures, was silent.

On the contrary, when Chase saw that he had worked himself into an impossible position and had the good sense to withdraw his name from consideration, Greeley regretted his decision and counted himself among those who regarded Chase as eminently qualified for the presidency and who had ardently hoped "to see him called to that exalted station." He let Chase down easily by attributing his withdrawal to his noble conviction that his usefulness as head of the Treasury Department might be impaired if he remained as a candidate for President in rivalry with his official chief. Strange that Chase did not think of that excuse sooner. The blunt truth was—and Greeley knew it as well as Chase—the whole undertaking had evaporated, and Lincoln's nomination was widely anticipated. Greeley intended "no disparagement of others" when he said, "since Henry Clay, we have

---

[24] *Tribune*, February 24, 1864.

known no man better fitted for President, by natural ability, by study and reflection, by training and experience, by integrity and patriotism, by soundness of principle and greatness of soul than is Salmon P. Chase."[25]

A week after receiving Lincoln's letter of February 23, Chase wrote to James C. Hall asking that no further consideration be given to his name.[26] On May 25 he wrote to L. D. Stickney, "Since my letter to Senator Hall, or rather through him to my friends in Ohio and else-where, was written, I had neither asked, nor thought, nor expected to be nominated for President. I would not take the nomination of the Baltimore Convention if it were tendered to me. The delegates have been almost all elected under pledge, express or implied, that they will vote for the nomination of Mr. Lincoln. The nomination of any other man would be justly regarded as a fraud upon the people; and I value conscious integrity of purpose far more than office, even the high-est."[27]

Bates was scornful. "This forced declention [sic] of Mr. Chase," he wrote in his diary on March 9, "is really not worth much. It proves only that the *present* prospects of Mr. Lincoln are too good to be openly resisted, at least, by men within the party. The extreme men who urged Mr. Chase, afraid to array themselves in open opposition to Mr. L[incoln] will act more guardedly—get up as many candidates as they can, *privily*, with the hope of bringing in Mr. C[hase], at last as a com-promise candidate."[28] David Davis, Lincoln's campaign manager in 1860, now a Justice of the Supreme Court, took the same view and wrote Thurlow Weed on March 21, "Mr. Chase's declination is a mere sham, and very ungraceful at that"; and E. D. Morgan wrote Weed on May 29, "Mr. Chase will subside as a presidential candidate after the nomination is made,—not before."[29]

Whatever may have been in the back of Chase's mind, the public accepted him at his word and there was no more campaigning in his behalf. The whole circumstance was naturally embarrassing both for President and Secretary. One thing led to another and differences of view touching appointments in the Treasury Department resulted in Chase's resignation on June 29, 1864. He went into retirement for

---

[25] *Ibid.*, March 11, 1864.

[26] Schuckers, *op. cit.*, pp. 502–03, Chase to James C. Hall, March 5, 1864.

[27] *Ibid.*, pp. 503–04, Chase to the Hon. L. D. Stickney, May 25, 1864.

[28] Beale, *op. cit.*, p. 345.

[29] Harriet A. Weed and Thurlow Weed Barnes, eds., *The Life of Thurlow Weed*, II, Memoir, 445.

the summer "wounded and hurt" by the circumstances which had preceded and attended his resignation.[30] Chief Justice Taney passed away on October 12, 1864, but Lincoln kept "shut-pan"[31] about appointing a successor until after the election. It was well known that Chase inclined toward judicial rather than administrative duties. How far the death of Taney prompted Chase to enter into the campaign for Lincoln's re-election, it is perhaps unseemly to inquire. But Chase, with assurances from Charles Sumner and W. P. Fessenden that he would be appointed Chief Justice, took an active part in the presidential canvass, his speaking tour following close upon the death of Justice Taney.[32] On December 6 the President nominated Salmon P. Chase to be Chief Justice of the Supreme Court of the United States, and the Senate at once, and without a reference, unanimously confirmed the nomination.[33]

Apart from Greeley's busybody efforts to find a candidate to displace Lincoln, his general approach to the campaign of 1864 was markedly disingenuous. As early as August, 1863, in discussing a call for a meeting of the National Democratic Committee to be held on September 7, he deprecated the "oiling up" of party machinery to prepare at that time for a new presidential campaign. The committee was guilty of "a dreary impertinence, a stupid anachronism,"[34] although three months before he himself had dispatched Gilmore to Tennessee to sound out Rosecrans.

In September, Greeley voiced again the view he was frequently to express up to the time the national political conventions were held in 1864. Pursuing his habit of fixing deadlines for the suppression of the Rebellion, contingent upon certain specified accomplishments in the meantime, he now looked forward to the end of the war by July 4, 1864, and urged that all political considerations should be put aside until the victory was won. A few more blows such as were dealt the enemy at Gettysburg and Vicksburg would suffice; and then the people would be ready to discuss the propriety of supporting A, B, or C for next President. Until that time all earnest patriots should quietly ignore the subject.

---

[30] Schuckers, *op. cit.*, p. 511.

[31] Tyler Dennett, *Lincoln and the Civil War—In the Diaries and Letters of John Hay*, p. 231.

[32] Schuckers, *op. cit.*, pp. 509–12.

[33] *Ibid.*, pp. 512–13.

[34] *Tribune*, August 18, 1863.

It will be high time [he said] to plunge into a Presidential contest, on the back of our present National convulsions, when it is settled that this is indispensable. Meantime, if you vaguely hear that this or that eminent civilian or successful General is intriguing for the Presidency, set it down as calumny. Idlers, babblers and self seekers of low degree may inaugurate Presidential intrigues in order to amuse their leisure or increase their consequence; but those who are from day to day paraded as seeking the post are often if not always innocent of even aspiring to it. Let us unite in the resolve to save the Nation first, if possible, and make the next President afterward.[35]

This sage advice was offered publicly by the editor to the American people at the very time that he was in frequent touch with Chase and privately expressing a preference for Chase "as the next Union candidate for the chief magistracy." Two weeks before Chase asked his friends to withdraw his name from consideration, the editor of the *Tribune* was again heartily wishing that the impending presidential contest could be banished from every loyal mind until after July 4, "while every energy, every effort should be devoted to the one paramount object of suppressing the Rebellion and restoring Peace to our distracted country."[36] Since the Republican National Committee had already fixed the date for its convention as June 7 at Baltimore, and since the Democratic National Committee had also fixed the date of its convention as July 4 at Chicago, the canvass was therefore fairly opened, Greeley said, "in defiance of our wishes."

Then it became apparent that the editor had been doing what he had counseled the public not to do. Admitting that Lincoln had "well discharged the responsibilities of his exalted station" and that he was the "first choice" of a large majority of those who had thus far supported the Administration, he nevertheless thought that Lincoln had not proved "so transcendently able" that consideration of other candidates should be forborne. It had not been demonstrated that Chase, Frémont, Butler, or Grant could not do as well. The call from state legislatures and state conventions for Lincoln to run again was not a decisive indication of an "unbiased choice," and the "loyal masses," disposed in Lincoln's favor, had not yet begun to think of the prospective presidential contest.

We freely admit Mr. Lincoln's merits [the editor went on], but we insist that they are not such as to eclipse and obscure those of all the statesmen and soldiers who have aided in the great work of saving the country from

---

[35] *Ibid.*, September 26, 1863.
[36] *Ibid.*, February 23, 1864.

disruption and overthrow. And if others have done as well in their respective spheres, then we hold that the genius of our institutions, the salutary One-Term principle, which has been established by the concurrence of each of our great parties, and by the action of the people, overruling either in turn, counsels the choice of another from among our eminent Unionists for President from and after March 4, 1865.

Greeley had at last come out in the open. He had not made a choice, but he was against Lincoln.

Rosecrans and Chase having been eliminated by time and circumstance, Greeley's choice fell upon his old favorite, Frémont. On the evening of March 18 the Frémont Campaign Club of New York held a meeting at Cooper Institute. The meeting was made up quite as much of anti-Lincolnites as of pro-Frémonters. Speeches were made criticizing Lincoln and praising Frémont. A platform was adopted, and the preamble read in part: "We, the members of the Fremont Campaign Club, being impressed with the increasing dangers of the country, and foreseeing the necessity of placing the Government in the hands of men of firm nature, of fixed principles, and uncompromising patriotism: and being opposed, moreover, to a continuance of the present irresolute and feeble National policy (both foreign and domestic) do hereby nominate Maj.-Gen. John C. Fremont as our candidate for the next Presidency of the United States."

In the midst of the proceedings, in walked Horace Greeley. He was received cordially and was promptly called upon. He said that he had come to the meeting at the invitation of friends, and that while he was friendly to all the gentlemen whose names had been mentioned, he nevertheless believed in the one-term principle. He took occasion again to deplore premature discussions of the presidential contest. For himself, he would give his "enthusiastic and hearty support" to the candidate named by the National Convention. The people of the great state of New York were in favor of putting down the rebellion and its cause; and he "believed that John C. Fremont would carry out such views."[37]

The activities of the Frémont Campaign Club of New York, the People's Committee of St. Louis, and similar agencies in various parts of the country opposed to Lincoln, led a group of radical Republicans to issue on May 4, 1864, "To the Radical Men of the Nation," a call for a mass convention to meet at Cleveland, Ohio, on May 31, in

---

[37] *Ibid.*, March 19, 1864.

advance of the Baltimore Convention scheduled for June 7. Accounts differ, but perhaps four hundred "Radicals, Germans and War Democrats" assembled at Cleveland at the appointed time, some for General Grant and some for Frémont, and mainly without formal credentials.[38] Greeley was expected, but wise excess of caution kept him away. At about that time he was craftily saying: "The Convention which seems to us of absorbing interest is that which Gen. Grant is now holding on the banks of the Chickahominy; next to this, we place that which Gen. Sherman is reassembling around the ramparts of Atlanta."[39] He was too shrewd a poll-taker not to know that Lincoln would be nominated at Baltimore and that all talk of Frémont was wasted gesture. Indeed, the *Tribune* gave scant notice to the Cleveland meeting either before or after it took place.

Frémont was nominated by acclamation and General John Cochrane of New York was named for Vice-President. The platform adopted by the convention was not unique, except that it called for a one-term presidency, for leaving reconstruction exclusively to Congress, and for the confiscation of rebel lands to be divided among soldiers and actual settlers.[40] Frémont dissented from the plank on the confiscation of rebel property but accepted the nomination and took a fling at Lincoln: "The ordinary rights secured under the Constitution and extraordinary powers have been usurped by the Executive." Intimating the possibility of withdrawal should the Baltimore Convention nominate "any man whose past life justifies a well-grounded confidence in his fidelity to our cardinal principles," he concluded his acceptance—"But if Mr. Lincoln should be nominated—as I believe it would be fatal to the country to indorse a policy and renew a power which has cost us the lives of thousands of men, and needlessly put the country on the road to bankruptcy—there will remain no other alternative but to organize against him every element of conscientious opposition with the view to prevent the misfortune of his reelection." Convinced after a few weeks that their candidacy was futile, Frémont and Cochrane withdrew their names on September 21. But, persisting in his animosity toward Lincoln, Frémont wrote to his committee, "In respect to Mr. Lincoln, I continue to hold exactly the sentiments contained in my letter of acceptance. I consider that his Administration has been politically,

---

[38] Nicolay and Hay, *Abraham Lincoln*, IX, 29–51; and Allan Nevins, *Frémont, Pathmarker of the West*, pp. 573–74.

[39] *Tribune*, June 6, 1864.

[40] Nicolay and Hay, *Abraham Lincoln*, IX, 29–51.

militarily, and financially a failure, and that its necessary continuance is a cause of regret for the country." By the time of the withdrawal, Greeley had worked himself around to the point where he was able to say that the discontinuance of the Frémont ticket was "wise, timely and auspicious."[41]

Lincoln was not greatly disturbed by the Cleveland Convention, which Welles called "a meeting of strange odds and ends of parties, and factions, and disappointed and aspiring individuals."[42] Upon hearing from a caller that there were not more than four hundred in the motley crowd which assembled at Cleveland, Lincoln turned to I Samuel, 22:2 and read aloud: "And every one that was in distress, and every one that was in debt, and every one that was discontented, gathered themselves unto him; and he became a captain over them: and there were with him about four hundred men."[43]

In his famous letter to A. G. Hodges on April 4, 1864, Lincoln reviewed briefly and tersely the philosophy and procedure of his Administration in dealing with the Rebellion and with slavery.[44] In this letter he made the often-quoted statement: "I claim not to have controlled events, but confess plainly that events have controlled me." This declaration may be applied literally to his personal relationship to the 1864 campaign. He wanted to serve a second term as President; but he was not as direct in seeking support from his friends as he had been when he wanted to go to Congress. He wrote very few letters making any reference to his ambitions. One letter stood out in the record because it was almost alone. He wrote to E. B. Washburne:

(Private and Confidential)

Executive Mansion, October 26, 1863

My dear Sir: *Yours of the 12th has been in my hands several days. Inclosed I send the leave of absence for your brother, in as good form as I think I can safely put it. Without knowing whether he would accept it, I have tendered the collectorship at Portland, Maine, to your other brother, the governor.*

Thanks to both you and our friend Campbell for your kind words and intentions. A second term would be a great honor and a great labor, which, together, perhaps I would not decline if tendered.

Yours truly,
A. Lincoln[45]

---

[41] *Tribune*, September 23, 1864.
[42] Welles, *op. cit.*, II, 41.
[43] Nicolay and Hay, *Abraham Lincoln*, IX, 40–41.
[44] Nicolay and Hay, *Complete Works*, X, 65–68, Lincoln to A. G. Hodges, April 4, 1864.
[45] *Ibid.*, IX, 182–83, Lincoln to Washburne, October 26, 1863.

From all the reports that came to the White House, Lincoln was politically justified in letting events control him. The *Philadelphia Press*, edited by John W. Forney, voiced the common view the day before the convention assembled: "Nor has the Convention a candidate to choose. Choice is forbidden it by the previous action of the people. It is a body which almost beyond parallel is directly responsible to the people and little more than the instrument of their will. Mr. Lincoln is already renominated, and the Convention will but formally announce the decision to the people."

"The President positively refuses," wrote John Hay in his diary on June 6, "to give even a confidential suggestion in regard to Vice Prest, platform or organization."[46]

The day before the long-heralded Baltimore Convention assembled, Greeley was still wishing that the presidency could be "utterly forgotten or ignored for the next two months." Again he went on record as purposing to act with the great body of his fellow Unionists in the approaching canvass, but he was in no hurry to enter it. His prediction that Abraham Lincoln would be nominated for re-election at Baltimore proved true.

The convention was called to order at noon on Tuesday, June 7, by the Hon. Edwin D. Morgan, senator from New York, chairman of the National Committee.[47] The afternoon and evening sessions were given over to organization and speechmaking. The platform was unanimously adopted on the second day. Henry J. Raymond, editor of the *New York Times*, called for the preservation of the "integrity of the Union," approved the determination of the government of the United States "not to compromise with Rebels," demanded "utter and complete extirpation" of slavery "from the soil of the Republic," forcefully endorsed the Lincoln Administration, and took a fling at European powers in the following resolutions:

Resolved, *That we approve and applaud the practical wisdom, the unselfish patriotism and unswerving fidelity to the Constitution and the principles of American Liberty, with which Abraham Lincoln has discharged, under circumstances of unparalleled difficulty the great duties and responsibilities of the Presidential office; that we approve and indorse, as demanded by the emergency and essential to the preservation of the nation, and as within the Constitution, the measures and acts which he has adopted to defend the nation against its open and secret foes; that we approve especially*

---

[46] Dennett, *op. cit.*, p. 186.

[47] John Tweedy, *A History of the Republican National Conventions, 1856–1908*, pp. 58–79.

the Proclamation of Emancipation, and the employment as Union soldiers of men heretofore held in slavery; and that we have full confidence in his determination to carry out these and all other constitutional measures essential to the salvation of the country into full and complete effect.

Resolved, That we approve the position taken by the Government, that the people of the United States can never regard with indifference the attempt of any European power to overthrow by force or to supplant by fraud the institutions of any republican government on the Western Continent, and that they will view with extreme jealousy, as menacing to the peace and independence of this country, the efforts of any such power to obtain new footholds for monarchial governments, sustained by a foreign military force in near proximity to the United States.

When it came to the nominations, Lincoln had 484 votes and Grant had 22 on the first ballot. Under instructions, the delegates from Missouri had voted for Grant. Missouri then changed its vote, and Lincoln was chosen unanimously. The contest for the nomination for Vice-President mainly centered in Andrew Johnson, Hannibal Hamlin, and Daniel S. Dickinson. Before the first ballot was counted, votes were switched to Johnson and he was declared the unanimous choice.

On Thursday, June 9, a committee waited upon the President at the White House to notify him of his nomination. Lincoln made a brief response:

Mr. Chairman and Gentlemen of the Committee:

I will neither conceal my gratification nor restrain the expression of my gratitude that the Union people, through their convention, in their continued effort to save and advance the nation, have deemed me not unworthy to remain in my present position. I know no reason to doubt that I shall accept the nomination tendered; and yet perhaps I should not declare definitely before reading and considering what is called the platform. I will say now, however, I approve the declaration in favor of so amending the Constitution as to prohibit slavery throughout the nation. When the people in revolt, with a hundred days of explicit notice that they could within those days resume their allegiance without the overthrow of their institution, and that they could not so resume it afterward, elected to stand out, such amendment of the Constitution as now proposed became a fitting and necessary conclusion to the final success of the Union cause. Such alone can meet and cover all cavils. Now the unconditional Union men, North and South, perceive its importance and embrace it. In the joint names of Liberty and Union, let us labor to give it legal form and practical effect.[48]

---

[48] Nicolay and Hay, *Complete Works*, X, 116–17.

The President responded to the formal written notice of his nomination in a letter addressed to the committee:

Executive Mansion, June 27, 1864

Gentlemen: Your letter of 14th instant formally notifying me that I have been nominated by the convention you represent for the Presidency of the United States for four years from the fourth of March next has been received. The nomination is gratefully accepted, as the resolutions of the convention, called the platform, are heartily approved. While the resolution in regard to the supplanting of republican government upon the western continent is fully concurred in, there might be misunderstanding were I not to say that the position of the government in relation to the action of France in Mexico, as assumed through the State Department and approved and indorsed by the convention among the measures and acts of the executive, will be faithfully maintained so long as the state of facts shall leave that position pertinent and applicable. I am especially gratified that the soldier and the seaman were not forgotten by the convention, as they forever must and will be remembered by the grateful country for whose salvation they devote their lives.

Thanking you for the kind and complimentary terms in which you have communicated the nomination and other proceedings of the convention, I subscribe myself,

Your obedient servant,
Abraham Lincoln[49]

The day before the Baltimore Convention assembled, Greeley had announced the purpose of the *Tribune* to stand by the ticket; and the proceedings of the convention were reported fully in its news columns. The occasion was momentous. Great issues were at stake even if peace were promptly to come. The stage was set for Greeley's editorial comments on the Administration and on Lincoln's fitness to carry on. But he lacked the necessary objective viewpoint. He did not want Lincoln, and his acceptance of the nomination was lukewarm and half-hearted. "We cannot but feel," he said, "that it would have been wiser and safer to spike the most serviceable guns of our adversaries by nominating another for President, and thus dispelling all motive, save that of naked disloyalty, for further warfare upon this Administration. . . . All this is of the past. The will of a great majority of the Unionists has been heard and it says, 'Let us have Abraham Lincoln as our President for another term.' We bow to their decision and ardently hope that the result may vindicate their sagacity and prove our apprehensions

---

[49] *Ibid.*, pp. 136–37.

unfounded."[50] Ordinarily, the *Tribune* would have hoisted the names
of the candidates to its masthead. During June, July, and August there
was no daily announcement of the choice of the Baltimore Convention
for President and Vice-President. On only a few occasions during
these months was the reader able to discover who the candidates were
and the attitude of the paper toward them. The wrath of Greeley was
temporarily stirred when the editor of the *Richmond Examiner* characterized Lincoln and Johnson as "A rail-splitting buffoon and a
boorish tailor, both from the backwoods, both growing up in uncouth
ignorance." Greeley disposed of this charge handsomely, as he was
qualified to do, and gave a fair, judicial account of Lincoln's career,
concluding a long editorial in this Greeley-like language:

*Mr. Lincoln, if you will, is not a hero—not a genius—not a man of the
very highest order of intellect. He has made mistakes as President, some of
which it is quite possible that another might have avoided. But is the God-
forsaken traitor who reviles him as an ape, a hyena, as a jackass, one whit
more absurd than the feeble Northern imitator who prates of him as "a rail-
splitting buffoon," who has "grown up in uncouth ignorance" &c., &c.? If
that is a true characterization of one who has stood such tests, overcome
such impediments, and achieved such successes as Abraham Lincoln, then
a democracy based on popular suffrage is an impudent fraud—a stupendous
hoax—and we ought at once to burn our constitutions, close our school-
houses, prohibit all future elections, and dispatch a deputation of notables
to Louis Napoleon to beg him to send us an Emperor. That's all.*[51]

Lincoln made no political speeches either before or after the nomination and deliberately declined to write letters for presentation at
political meetings.[52] He also admonished Federal officials against
undertaking to use official power for or against any candidate. "My
wish, therefore is," he wrote in one instance, "that you will do just as
you think fit with your own suffrage in the case, and not constrain any
of your subordinates to do other than as he thinks fit with his. This is
precisely the rule I inculcated and adhered to on my part, when a
certain other nomination, now recently made was being canvassed
for."[53] The President's public appearances throughout 1864 were
mainly at Sanitary Fairs and serenades.

Shortly after the nomination, however, Lincoln was moved, behind

---

[50] *Tribune*, June 9, 1864.

[51] *Ibid.*, June 24, 1864.

[52] Nicolay and Hay, *Complete Works*, X, 222–23, Lincoln to Isaac M. Schermerhorn,
September 12, 1864.

[53] *Ibid.*, pp. 141–42, Lincoln to John L. Scripps, July 4, 1864.

the scenes at least, to undertake to control events. His refusal to sign the reconstruction bill on the closing day of Congress, July 4, 1864, and his proclamation on July 8, in effect subscribing to its provisions,[54] prompted the Wade-Davis Manifesto, which stirred the radicals to renewed opposition. His call on July 18 for 500,000 volunteers following upon the great losses in the operation against Richmond and the fright from General Early's unsuccessful raid on Washington resulted in widespread dissatisfaction.[55] Greeley and Raymond were goading the President with proposals for peace; and early in August, Thurlow Weed told Lincoln that his re-election was an impossibility. August was the darkest month of the war for the nation and the President. It looked as if events were not going to turn out in his favor.

Anticipating his defeat and contemplating what his course should be between election day and the inauguration of his successor, Lincoln recorded his views; and at a Cabinet meeting on August 23 asked the members to affix their names to a note which he had folded so that its contents could not be seen. The Cabinet did not learn until after the election what the note contained. John Hay recorded the note and the circumstances attending it.

November 11, 1864. . . .

At the meeting of the Cabinet today, the President took out a paper from his desk and said, "Gentlemen, do you remember last summer I asked you all to sign your names to the back of a paper of which I did not show you the inside? This is it. Now, Mr. Hay, see if you can get this open without tearing it?" He had pasted it up in so singular style that it required some cutting to get it open. He then read as follows:

"Executive Mansion
Washington, Aug. 23, 1864

"*This morning, as for some days past, it seems exceedingly probable that this Administration will not be reelected. Then it will be my duty to so cooperate with the President elect, as to save the Union between the election and the inauguration; as he will have secured his election on such ground that he cannot possibly save it afterwards.*

A. Lincoln

[*This was endorsed:*]

*William H. Seward
W. P. Fessenden*

---

[54] *Ibid.*, X, 152–54.
[55] *Ibid.*, pp. 164–66.

Edwin M. Stanton
Gideon Welles
Edwd Bates
M. Blair
J. P. Usher

August 23, 1864"

The President said, "You will remember that this was written at a time [six days before the Chicago nominating Convention] when as yet we had no adversary, and seemed to have no friends. I then solemnly resolved on the course of action indicated above. I resolved, in case of the election of General McClellan, being certain that he would be the candidate, that I would see him and talk matters over with him. I would say, "General, the election has demonstrated that you are stronger, have more influence with the American people than I. Now let us together, you with your influence and I with all the executive power of the Government, try to save the country. You raise as many troops as you possibly can for this final trial, and I will devote all my energies to assisting and finishing the war."

Seward said, "And the General would answer you 'Yes, Yes'; and the next day when you saw him again and pressed these views upon him, he would say, 'Yes, Yes'; & so on forever, and would have done nothing at all."

"At least," added Lincoln, "I should have done my duty and have stood clear before my own conscience."[56]

Throughout the summer, Greeley had continued to nurse the idea that Lincoln might in some way be supplanted by another candidate. In the middle of July he was still unwilling to embark upon "a vehement canvass for the Presidency," believing "matters of graver and more pressing moment" should engage the attention of the American people.[57] By the middle of August he was openly suggesting his pet scheme of two sets of candidates under one electoral ticket with the continued hope of discovering a candidate who would outdistance Lincoln. "Let those Unionists who dislike Mr. Lincoln hold their Convention," he said; "let them name their candidates; but let there be but one Electoral ticket on our side; and let the People severally vote their choice for President; and let the choice of a majority be respected by all the Electors chosen by the Union party."[58]

Behind the scenes Greeley, as a private citizen, was secretly conniving with a group of radicals to call a second Union Convention opposed to Lincoln. Secret meetings of this group were held in New

---

[56] Dennett, *op. cit.*, pp. 237–38.
[57] *Tribune*, July 15, 1864.
[58] *Ibid.*, August 15, 1864.

York the latter part of August, and a call for a convention to be held on September 28 was prepared. Unable to attend one of these meetings, or perhaps warily staying away, Greeley wrote the committee: "Mr. Lincoln is already beaten. He cannot be elected. And we must have another ticket to save us from utter overthrow. If we had such a ticket as could be made by naming Grant, Butler or Sherman for President, we could make a fight yet. And such a ticket we ought to have anyhow, with or without a convention."[59]

Matters stood in this wise when the Democratic National Convention, originally scheduled for July 4, finally assembled in Chicago on August 29, 1864. As had been long anticipated, General George B. McClellan was the choice of the convention for President. George H. Pendleton was named for Vice-President. Nicolay and Hay years later took the view that the platform adopted by the convention was not worth quoting except for the resolution which had been written by Clement L. Vallandigham. It is true that the other provisions of the platform were largely commonplaces upon which no significant campaign issue could be based. The Vallandigham resolution read:

Resolved, *That this Convention does explicitly declare, as the sense of the American people, that after four years of failure to restore the Union by the experiment of war, during which, under the pretense of a military necessity, a war power higher than the Constitution, the Constitution itself has been disregarded in every part, and public liberty and private right alike trodden down and the material prosperity of the country essentially impaired, justice, humanity, liberty, and the public welfare demand that immediate efforts be made for cessation of hostilities, with a view to an ultimate convention of the States, or other peaceable means, to the end that at the earliest practicable moment peace may be restored on the basis of the Federal Union of the States.*

McClellan accepted the nomination but repudiated Vallandigham's resolution in the platform. "The reestablishment of the Union," he said, "in all its integrity is, and must continue to be, the indispensable condition in any settlement. . . . The Union is the one condition of peace. We ask no more." Nicolay and Hay remarked: "Upon this contradictory body of doctrine McClellan began his campaign. The platform of the convention was the law, his letter was the gospel, and the orators of the party might reconcile the two according to their sympathies or their ingenuity."[60]

---

[59] *New York Sun*, June 30, 1889.
[60] Nicolay and Hay, *Abraham Lincoln*, IX, 244–62.

The issue was now joined. Lincoln was committed by the Baltimore platform and by his own indubitable declarations to the preservation of the Union by force and to a constitutional amendment abolishing slavery forever. The Democratic party was pledged to peace at any price, and McClellan had declared himself for peace with the restoration of the Union; but neither the party nor its candidate had said anything about slavery.

With the Democratic platform pulling one way and the candidate another, the result was well nigh assured. And other events promptly dispelled Lincoln's period of gloom. Farragut had won a naval battle at Mobile Bay, and on September 3, close on the heels of the declaration of the National Democratic Convention at Chicago that the war was a failure, Major General William Tecumseh Sherman telegraphed to Washington: "Atlanta is ours, and fairly won."[61] The President immediately issued a Proclamation of Thanksgiving and requested that on the following Sunday all places of worship in the United States should offer thanksgivings to the Supreme Being "for his mercy in preserving our national existence against the insurgent rebels." The President also issued special orders of thanks to Major General Sherman, Admiral Farragut, Major General Granger, and Major General Canby for "the skill and harmony with which the recent operations in Mobile Harbor, and against Fort Powell, Fort Gaines, and Fort Morgan were planned and carried into execution." He also issued orders that on Monday, September 5, in honor of "the recent brilliant achievements of the fleet and land forces" in the Mobile operations a salute of one hundred guns should be given at the arsenal and navy yard in Washington and a similar salute on the following day in each arsenal and navy yard in the United States; and that on Wednesday, September 7, in honor of "the brilliant achievements of the army under command of Major-General Sherman" a salute of one hundred guns should be given at the arsenals at Washington, New York, Boston, Philadelphia, Baltimore, Pittsburgh, Newport (Ky.), St. Louis, New Orleans, Mobile, Pensacola, Hilton Head, and Newbern.[62]

The half-secret plans of the coterie of radicals, who had hoped to force Lincoln from the field, rapidly evaporated. The inept deliberations of the Democratic Convention, Sherman's capture of Atlanta, and the President's proclamation and orders caused the editor of the *Tribune* to take account of stock. He must have pondered long upon

---

[61] *Ibid.*, p. 289.
[62] Nicolay and Hay, *Complete Works*, X, 212–14.

the question of "where are we?" for he came out in a long editorial on September 6, entitled "Where We Are." He labored at length to justify his earlier recommendations that the Union Convention should have been delayed, that the presidential nomination in June was carried under a "popular delusion," and that the past record did not justify the energy and judgment attributed to the Lincoln Administration. Upon this sour note the editor reasoned himself around to the declaration that "Our cause to-day is stronger than ever before." It was not too late to take a new tack. If the Administration lacked vigor, earnestness, understanding, it should be given these qualities by the people and infused with their will, invigorated with their courage, reinforced with their confidence, and overwhelmed by their determination that treason and slavery should not prevail against them. The Administration should not be deserted. "Never let its short-comings, its weaknesses, its short-sightedness, and its delays defeat us," he thundered. "God knows it might have done better; God alone knows how much worse it might have done." He concluded his grudging surrender with the words:

Choose ye! For our part, we have chosen. Better a perpetual dinner of herbs, than the stalled ox in such company—though, for that matter, but little of the stalled ox would fall to the share of those who believed in fighting for the Union. Henceforth, we fly the banner of ABRAHAM LINCOLN *for the next Presidency, choosing that far rather than the Disunion and a quarter of a century of wars, or the Union and political servitude which our opponents would give us. Let the country shake off its apathy; let it realize what is the price of defeat—a price neither we nor the world can afford; let it be understood how near we are to the end of the Rebellion, and that no choice is left us now but the instrument put into our hands, and with that we can and must finish it. We grant, from our own convictions, much that can be said in criticism of the present Administration; for the sake of argument, we will grant anything that any honest and loyal men can say. And then this is our rejoinder—Mr. Lincoln has done seven-eighths of the work after his fashion; there must be vigor and virtue enough left in him to do the other fraction. The work is in his hands; if it passes out of them, it will be, as there are no better, but far worse, to receive it, to our utter ruin. We must re-elect him, and God helping us, we will.*

Thus the *Tribune* lined up to go forward with "the instrument put into our hands." It kept the faith it professed. A series of pamphlets and broadsides, supporting the Union ticket was promptly prepared and advertised from day to day for sale at one dollar per hundred. On

September 14 the New York Union ticket was emblazoned at the masthead and appeared there daily until the election. The names of thirty-three electors for the state of New York appeared on the ticket, two at large and thirty-one from designated districts. The two at large were Horace Greeley and Preston King. Greeley made several campaign speeches, but, except on one or two occasions, the editorial columns of the *Tribune* made little direct reference to Lincoln. Greeley's strategy was to hammer away at McClellan. There was hardly a day in the ensuing campaign when he did not hold McClellan up to the light. All of his rare ability in picking out the faults of an opponent was brought into play. All of his extraordinary power of invective was employed. Here is a typical example:

> *He has never faltered in his devotion to the Slave Power; and that is the real touchstone of Democratic orthodoxy. True, he volunteered for the War; but he did so to save Slavery from the effects of its own suicidal madness, not to punish it for its treason. True, he commanded for a time the Grand Union Army, but no Rebel slaveholder ever justly complained that his chattel was invited by this General to exchange the service of treason for that of his country; and no outnumbered Rebel force ever justly complained that its retreat was hurried or seriously annoyed by McClellan or anyone under his command. True, he made war on the Rebels; but he made it so gently, so considerately, so languidly, that they habitually praised his generalship while it lasted, and regretted it when it was no more.*[63]

In a milder tone, upon another occasion, Greeley clearly set forth the basic issues of the campaign:

> *We oppose Gen. McClellan because of our conviction that he does not want the Rebellion put square down, and never did, even when he was in command of the Union armies. We oppose Mr. Pendleton because he has at all times and under all circumstances maintained a position of courteous and dignified, statesmanlike and manly, but most determined and effective opposition to the War for the Union. We infer from his public career that he esteems Slavery righteous, natural, beneficent, and is doing his best to strengthen and perpetuate it. . . .*
>
> *Abraham Lincoln and Andrew Johnson embody and represent the spirit of unflinching antagonism to the Rebellion—to its spirit, incitements and aims—and they are supported for this reason.*[64]

During the campaign Greeley published in the news columns of the *Tribune* three letters from foreigners which were indicative of the

---

[63] *Tribune*, August 30, 1864.
[64] *Ibid.*, September 30, 1864.

standing of the editor and his paper abroad and which presented significant arguments in support of the Union cause. A letter from John Bright, English orator and statesman, was published on October 17 which read in part:

All those of my countrymen who have wished well to the Rebellion, who have hoped for the break-up of your Union, who have preferred to see a Southern Slave Empire rather than a restored and free Republic, so far as I can observe, are now in favor of the election of Gen. McClellan.

All those who have deplored the calamities which the leaders of the Secession have brought upon your country, who believe that Slavery weakens your power and tarnishes your good name throughout the world, and who regard the restoration of your Union as a thing to be desired and prayed for by all good men, so far as I can judge, are heartily longing for the reelection of Mr. Lincoln.

On October 24 the *Tribune* was able to present a discriminating four-column letter from the Frenchman Count de Gasparin in the course of which he said:

The election of Mr. Lincoln will have a meaning which no one will fail to understand. Every one will know that the war is to be energetically continued to the end; that the war which aims neither at oppression nor conquest will succeed in reestablishing the empire of the Constitution, and in destroying Slavery.

The election of a Democratic candidate, whether it is wished or not, will have a very different signification. It will mean at least an armistice and the raising of the siege of Richmond. It will open to the hopes of the South chances ill-defined and therefore the more perilous.

And again on October 25 the *Tribune* published a four-column letter from Edouard Laboulaye from Paris in which he said:

This is why we await with impatience the Presidential election, praying God that the name that shall be drawn from the urn may be that of the honest and upright Abraham Lincoln, for this name will be a presage of victory, the triumph of justice and right. To vote for McClellan is to vote for the humiliation of the North, the perpetual maintenance of Slavery and the disruption of the great Republic. To vote for Lincoln is to vote for Union and Liberty.

The story persists that Lincoln brought Greeley and the *Tribune* to his active support through the hint that Greeley would be made Postmaster General under the next Administration. It is alleged that this plan was cooked up between Lincoln and Congressman Reuben E. Fenton of New York. One George G. Hoskins, on behalf of Fenton, contacted Greeley. Whatever the circumstances were, it appears that Greeley came out in flying colors for the Republican ticket on the day after Hoskins is said to have laid the plan before him.[65] Such a proposal would have been a consistent part of the pattern he was then following.

More credence is given to the claim that Lincoln won the support of the *New York Herald* late in the campaign by proffering the mission to France to its editor, James Gordon Bennett. Hay records that Senator Harlan of Iowa suggested such action on September 23,[66] and according to A. K. McClure the proffer was made.[67] Bennett declined but was deeply appreciative of the offer and came to the support of Lincoln in his editorial columns.

Frémont's withdrawal of his candidacy for President and the resignation of Montgomery Blair from the portfolio of Postmaster General were not mere coincidences. Frémont withdrew on September 22, and Lincoln called for Blair's resignation on September 23. Frémont was a threat, and Blair had long been a liability to the President. The radicals wanted Blair's scalp. Frémont was not in on the deal; it was clearly between Abraham Lincoln and Zachariah Chandler, who carried on the negotiations, and the hosts of Blair's enemies he represented. Blair withdrew, he claimed, as an act of pure patriotism. "Offered patronage to my friends and disfavor to my enemies," he said, "I refused both. My only consideration was the welfare of the Republican party."[68]

There is abundant evidence that Lincoln countenanced, if he did not direct, the employment of Federal patronage both to secure his renomination and his re-election.[69] As has been indicated, beginning early in January, 1864, all the Union state conventions, save that of Missouri, urged his renomination. Federal and state officeholders and those hoping for office were prominent in these conventions. The typical state convention was accurately described by the *Albany Atlas and Argus,* a Democratic paper, on May 27, 1864, following the Republican meeting at Syracuse on May 25 to select delegates to the Baltimore Convention. This paper said in part: "A glance at the list of delegates to the Republican state convention will satisfy anyone that the people

---

[65] Don C. Seitz, *Horace Greeley,* pp. 267–70.

[66] Dennett, *op. cit.,* p. 215.

[67] A. K. McClure, *Lincoln and Men of War-Times,* pp. 80–82. See also Weed and Barnes, *op. cit.,* I, 619.

[68] Nevins, *op. cit.,* pp. 564–82. See also Williams, *op. cit.,* p. 330; and Harry J. Carman and Reinhard H. Luthin, *Lincoln and the Patronage,* p. 276.

[69] Carman and Luthin, *op. cit.,* pp. 228–99.

have had nothing to do with their selection, and that they represent only the great army of officeholders in our state. From every county comes the internal revenue collector, the assessor, the sub-collectors, the provost marshal or his deputy, and the city and village postmasters."

Throughout the campaigns for the nomination and the election there were two Lincolns in evidence. The President carried on, in all the public documents and official and personal correspondence which have come to light, largely as if there were no political controversies in progress. In a very few instances only did he permit political implications to go into the record. In a sense Lincoln was hardly frank with the people. His public indifference and unconcern did not comport with his intense desire to remain in office, for he was adroitly building fences day by day and marshaling his forces in every section of the country to assure his re-election. Myths about Lincoln as being different from other men are dispelled by the record of Lincoln, the consummate politician. Other presidents have sought re-election more openly, directly, and frankly, but none has quite equaled the political artistry of Abraham Lincoln.

In our American system of government statesmanship is coupled with politics, and the productive statesman must also be a successful politician. Tyler Dennett expressed this view well in an address on "Lincoln and the Campaign of 1864" before the Abraham Lincoln Association on Lincoln's birthday in 1935:

> When one describes Abraham Lincoln as a good politician, the adjective has the meaning of "successful," but it means more than that. The goodness of Lincoln's political skill was essentially the goodness of a good man. He was a magnanimous man, not because it was good politics, but rather because he could not be otherwise. That was his great characteristic. Magnanimity is good politics. The man of mean mind and spirit in politics, at least in national politics in the United States, defeats himself. This fact, of which American history affords abundant proof, is perhaps our best assurance of the essential soundness of our form of government.
>
> As for the importance of party government, party discipline, and party leadership, surely the campaign of 1864 is a good illustration. In being a good politician, Abraham Lincoln became a statesman. If he had not displayed his ability as a politician with so great success, it is doubtful whether we could now regard him as a statesman at all. And so it is likely always to be when great causes require corporate action.[70]

---

[70] Tyler Dennett, *Lincoln and the Campaign of 1864*, Abraham Lincoln Association Papers, 1935, pp. 57–58.

The upward swing of public opinion in his favor beginning after the nomination of McClellan did not make Lincoln overconfident. On October 13, less than five weeks before election day, in discussing the presidential election with the staff in the War Department telegraph office, he wrote down on a telegraph blank his estimate of the electoral vote. The following memorandum, except the items in brackets, was written in Lincoln's hand. The bracketed items are in the handwriting of Major Thomas F. Eckert, chief of the staff.[71]

Office U. S. Military Telegraph
War Department
Washington, D.C. [October 13th], 1864

[Supposed Copperhead Vote]		[Union Vote for President]	
New York	33	*New England States*	39
Penn	26	*Michigan*	8
New Jersey	7	*Wisconsin*	8
Delaware	3	*Minnesota*	4
Maryland	7	*Iowa*	8
Missouri	11	*Oregon*	3
Kentucky	11	*California*	5
Illinois	16	*Kansas*	3
	114	*Indiana*	13
		Ohio	21
		West Virginia	5
			117
		[*Nevada*	3]
			[120]

A few days after setting down his estimate of the electoral vote, Lincoln made one of his few public references to the campaign. The occasion was in response to a serenade by Marylanders in celebration of the adoption of a new constitution. A misinterpretation of a speech made by Seward in his home town of Auburn had led to the story that if Lincoln were defeated in the election he would do what he could to ruin the government before his successor was inaugurated. Coupled with this rumor was the equally preposterous intimation that if McClellan was elected he would immediately seize the government. Lincoln remarked that he hoped "the good people will permit themselves no uneasiness on either point." He then said:

---

[71] Paul M. Angle, *New Letters and Papers of Lincoln*, pp. 362–63.

I am struggling to maintain the government, not to overthrow it. I am struggling, especially, to prevent others from overthrowing it. I therefore say that if I live I shall remain President until the 4th of next March; and that, whoever shall be constitutionally elected therefor, in November, shall be duly installed as President on the 4th of March; and that, in the interval, I shall do my utmost that whoever is to hold the helm for the next voyage shall start with the best possible chance to save the ship.

This is due to the people both in principle and under the Constitution. Their will, constitutionally expressed, is the ultimate law of all. If they should deliberately resolve to have immediate peace, even at the loss of their country and their liberty, I know not the power or the right to resist them. It is their own business, and they must do as they please with their own. I believe, however, that they are still resolved to preserve their country and their liberty; and in this, in office or out of it, I am resolved to stand by them.[72]

Here was the *statesman* speaking effectively as a *politician*. He was moved by events and was at the same time endeavoring to move future events in the direction his honest judgment as well as his personal inclinations deemed that they should go. Perhaps it can be said that the statesman and the politician here spoke in unison.

As election day approached, Greeley urged the Unionists to do their full duty. On election morning, November 8, 1864, he poured out his pent-up feelings in a characteristic and impassioned adjuration to his readers. It was Greeley the unrivaled editor, Greeley the patriotic and devoted friend and defender of the Union, Greeley the honest and forthright American citizen, voicing anew in unmistakable language the convictions on principle he had consistently held throughout the war. He was a man of moods and of many changing fronts; but he here stuck to the basic text of his life.

NOW FREEMEN:

By your love of Liberty and hate of Wrong and Oppression—

By your love of country and detestation of those who would disrupt and destroy her—

By your recollection of the insults and indignities heaped on your loyal fellow-citizens through the long series of unprovoked, stinging, unresisted Rebel insults and outrages that culminated in the bombardment and reduction of Fort Sumter—

By your reverent, grateful affection and admiration for your brothers who

---

[72] Nicolay and Hay, *Complete Works*, X, 243–45.

have nobly died to avenge those insults and prevent the partition of your native land—

By your detestation of the assassins of Fort Pillow and the more deliberate, cold-blooded murder of thousands of your compatriots in the Rebel prison-camps at Andersonville and elsewhere—

By your faith in Humanity, in Justice, in God—

We adjure you to do your very utmost for the Union cause and candidates TO-DAY!

The verdict was not long in doubt. On the evening of election day, as was his frequent custom, Lincoln went over to the War Department to get the news. Before he left for the White House at two o'clock in the morning, the telegraphic dispatches clearly indicated that he had been triumphantly re-elected. He was met as he started for home by a party of serenaders with a band. Called upon for a speech, he said in part:

I earnestly believe that the consequences of this day's work, if it be as you assume, and as now seems probable, will be to the lasting advantage, if not to the very salvation, of the country. I cannot at this hour say what has been the result of the election. But, whatever it may be, I have no desire to modify this opinion, that all who have labored to-day in behalf of the Union have wrought for the best interests of the country and the world, not only for the present, but for all future ages.

I am thankful to God for this approval of the people; but, while deeply grateful for this mark of their confidence in me, if I know my heart, my gratitude is free from any taint of personal triumph. I do not impugn the motives of anyone opposed to me.[73]

The *Tribune* announced "The Grand Result" on November 9 in two very brief and restrained statements, but employing at the end the prayer "God Bless Abraham Lincoln!"

Lincoln carried every state except Delaware, Kentucky, and New Jersey. He received 212 electoral votes as against 21 for McClellan. Lincoln's popular vote was 2,300,532. McClellan's was 1,835,925. In the light of the result, one must conclude that Lincoln's estimate of the electoral vote had merely been a recording of his judgment of the worst possible contingency. And yet his apprehension about New York was not unfounded. He carried the state by a vote of only 6,749.

On the second day after the election Greeley tersely summed up the result in the words: "We hold that the People have just decided in the

---

[73] Nicolay and Hay, *Abraham Lincoln*, IX, 378.

election of Lincoln and Johnson, that the NATION SHALL LIVE AND THAT SLAVERY SHALL DIE—so much and no more."[74]

On December 6 and 7, the electors for the state of New York met in the Senate Chamber in the state capitol.[75] Organization was perfected on the first day, and Horace Greeley, elector-at-large, was chosen president of the college of electors by acclamation. He expressed the hope that the action of the college would be blessed by the perpetuity of free institutions throughout the world. On the second day the thirty-three votes of the college were recorded for Abraham Lincoln for President and for Andrew Johnson for Vice-President.

At the conclusion of the deliberations, Mr. Greeley thanked the college for the honor it had conferred upon him and spoke briefly. He felt great hope that the dark days of the republic were passing away. He referred to the President's message to Congress, submitted the day the college had assembled, and said that his hope for the future was strengthened by the message "as well from its firmness as its kindness of tone." He felt that the whole people—South as well as North—rebels as well as loyal men—would so regard it. He commented upon the appointment of Chase as Chief Justice of the Supreme Court, which Lincoln had announced the day before, and said that it gave evidence of the magnanimity of the President and added assurance that brighter days were ahead.

Greeley was frankly not for Lincoln, but he was unmistakably—and with telling effect throughout the nation—for free men and for the "perpetuity of free institutions." Lincoln most earnestly wanted re-election, but he accepted it humbly without any sense of personal victory and with the reaffirmation to Congress of the view he had long held "that the war will cease on the part of the government whenever it shall have ceased on the part of those who began it."[76] Thus again on a historic occasion, all personalities and whimsicalities aside, Lincoln the President and Greeley the editor were one in their hopes and purposes for the future.

---

[74] *Tribune*, November 10, 1864.
[75] *Albany Evening Journal*, December 6, 7, 1864.
[76] Nicolay and Hay, *Complete Works*, X, 310.

A call for a national thanksgiving is being prepared, and will
be duly promulgated.

Lincoln[1]

Never before had nation so much cause for devout Thanksgiving; never before had a people so much reason for unrestrained congratulation and the very extravagance of joy.

Greeley[2]

11 The dawn of peace

Lincoln's re-election in November, 1864, pointed the way to the
restoration of the Union, the abandonment of slavery, and the establishment of peace. Greeley approached the advent of the new Administration in a hopeful mood. It appeared to be no longer necessary to
exercise his self-appointed function of goading the President into
action. Viewing the possibilities of an early peace, he found the scales
tipping in favor of the cause for which he had earnestly labored for four
years. The destructive force of warfare was terrific. At the end of 1864
half of Virginia was a desert; Tennessee was a barren waste; the young
men of the South were in their graves; the old men were reduced to
poverty; the industrial system of all the slave states was destroyed; from
Mason and Dixon's line to the Rio Grande, desolation covered the
land. The Confederacy had nothing left but a single, sorely beleaguered
army that could not fight much longer. The rebels were near the end
of their resources.[3]

The North, on the other hand, was stronger than ever. The war had
actually developed its strength, wealth, and resources; and it was
stronger, infinitely stronger, and more capable of beginning an exhaus-
tive war after four years of effort than it had been when the first shot

---

[1] John G. Nicolay and John Hay, eds., *Complete Works of Abraham Lincoln*, XI, 84.
[2] *Tribune*, April 14, 1865.
[3] *Ibid.*, January 24, 1865.

362

was fired at Fort Sumter. The North had grown strong as the South had grown weak.

Peace was imminent. The North wanted peace, provided the terms and conditions were satisfactory. There was, to be sure, a "last ditch" group in the South; but there was also a steadily increasing group that demanded peace at any price. Impoverished, weary, bereaved, and hopeless, they cared little for the terms; they were ready to accede to anything the North demanded; they asked only that they might come back to the Union.

Greeley could not refrain from taking a hand. Convinced that his judgment of the Niagara episode had been sound and still smarting under his sense of failure, he looked about for some way of promoting peace negotiations. In December, 1864, he conceived the idea that Francis P. Blair, Sr., might be a fit instrument. He wrote Blair, gently baiting him with the thought that as "the counsellor and trusted adviser of men high in authority" he might make a move toward peace.[4]

Blair swallowed the bait, for the Blair dynasty was at low ebb. His eldest son Montgomery was out of the Cabinet and his youngest son Francis P., Jr., was having his troubles. It was an opportune time for "Old Man Blair," as he was known in political circles, to recoup in some way the prestige of the clan. He was well known and well regarded through family connections in the South. All aglow with the prospect, Blair went to Lincoln. But Lincoln, wary now of self-appointed peace-makers, gave him short shrift and merely said: "Come to me after Savannah falls."[5]

On December 26 Lincoln wrote General Sherman: "Many, many thanks for your Christmas gift, the capture of Savannah."[6] Blair wasted not a moment, and on December 28 he had received from Lincoln a safeguard which read: "Allow the bearer, F. P. Blair, Sr., to pass our lines, go South, and return."[7] Lincoln accepted no responsibility for whatever mission Blair had in mind. Blair proceeded at once to General Grant's headquarters and sent a brief note to Jefferson Davis[8] saying that he wished to visit Richmond to make inquiry about some title papers which he assumed had been taken from his house in Maryland

[4] Carl Sandburg, *Abraham Lincoln: The War Years,* IV, 28.
[5] John G. Nicolay and John Hay, *Abraham Lincoln—A History,* X, 94.
[6] Nicolay and Hay, *Complete Works,* X, 325.
[7] *Ibid.,* p. 327.
[8] Nicolay and Hay, *Abraham Lincoln,* X, 94–95.

at the time of General Early's raid. In a longer letter to Davis, which he enclosed with the note, he revealed his main purpose, to explain his views "in reference to the state of affairs of our country" and to submit ideas which Davis might "turn to good." He explained that while he had permission to pass the lines he was wholly unaccredited and that such suggestions as he wished to make had not been submitted to anyone in authority. One wonders if he had discussed his proposals with Greeley. They were fantastic enough to have come from that fertile source.

There was some delay in the reply from Davis, and Blair went back to Washington. Shortly after his return, he received a favorable response from Davis and he set out again for Richmond. On January 12, 1865, he was received by the President of the Confederacy. After discussing the desires of both North and South for peace, Blair made the amazing proposal that an armistice be sought and that Jefferson Davis head a force made up of troops from both sides to invade Mexico and drive Maximilian from his American throne, thus uniting North and South in support of the Monroe Doctrine. "Old Man Blair," eager as a youth for notice and acclaim, was surely growing senile; and the worries of office had apparently driven Jefferson Davis to distraction, for he was willing to consider this wild scheme of military conquest as a means of bringing to an end the war at home. He gave Blair a letter to show to Lincoln.

Richmond, Virginia, 12 Jany., '65

F. P. Blair, Esq.

Sir: I have deemed it proper, and probably desirable to you, to give you, in this form, the substance of remarks made by me, to be repeated by you to President Lincoln, etc. etc. I have no disposition to find obstacles in forms, and am willing now, as heretofore, to enter into negotiations for the restoration of peace; and am ready to send a commission whenever I have reason to suppose it will be received, or to receive a commission, if the United States Government should choose to send one. That, notwithstanding the rejection of our former offers, I would, if you could promise that a commissioner, minister, or other agent would be received, appoint one immediately, and renew the effort to enter into conference, with a view to secure peace to the two countries.

Yours, etc.,
Jefferson Davis[9]

---

[9] *Ibid.*, pp. 97–107, Jefferson Davis to F. P. Blair, Sr., January 12, 1865.

The whole world could have told by this time, with the possible exception of "Old Man Blair," the Confederate President, and a certain irrepressible editor, what the answer of the level-headed lawyer in the White House would be. His sole interest in giving an instant's further consideration to Blair was his hope that the despondency now revealed by the rebel leaders might lead to an abandonment of their resistance. He promptly gave Blair this reply:

Washington, January 18, 1865

F. P. Blair, Esq.

Sir: You having shown me Mr. Davis's letter to you of the 12th instant, you may say to him that I have constantly been, am now, and shall continue, ready to receive any agent whom he or any other influential person now resisting the National authority may informally send to me with the view of securing peace to the people of our one common country.

Yours, etc.
A. Lincoln[10]

The phrase with which Davis concluded his letter to Blair, "to secure peace to the two countries," did not escape the President. The phrase with which Lincoln concluded his answer to Blair, "to the people of our one common country" carried unmistakably the basis upon which the North would negotiate for peace. Blair went back to Richmond with trumped up excuses for Lincoln's refusal to consider a military alliance with the Confederacy in support of the Monroe Doctrine in Mexico. In order to cover his own discomfiture and retreat, he now proposed to Davis, entirely on his own responsibility, that effort be made to bring about negotiations between Grant and Lee looking to peace.

Davis called his Cabinet together and appointed a peace commission consisting of Alexander H. Stephens, Vice-President, R. M. T. Hunter, senator and former Secretary of State, and Judge John A. Campbell, Assistant Secretary of War. Although they all knew their cause was lost, there was some discussion in the Cabinet meeting about the phrasing of the instructions; Davis held out for "securing peace to the two countries." The commissioners were furnished with a copy of Lincoln's letter to Blair and with the following instructions:

Richmond, January 28, 1865

In conformity with the letter of Mr. Lincoln of which the foregoing is a copy, you are requested to proceed to Washington City for informal con-

---

[10] Nicolay and Hay, *Complete Works*, X, 342, Lincoln to F. P. Blair, Sr., January 18, 1865.

ference with him upon the issues involved in the existing war, and for the purpose of securing peace to the two countries.

> *Your obedient servant,*
> *Jefferson Davis*[11]

The instructions were not at all "in conformity with the letter of Mr. Lincoln." Davis fatuously persisted in speaking of "securing peace to the two countries" in the face of Lincoln's injunction that a conference might be held "with the view of securing peace to the people of our one common country." With these contradicting instructions the commissioners presented themselves at the Union lines near Richmond on the evening of January 29. They did not present their formal credentials, however, but asked admission "in accordance with an understanding claimed to exist with Lieutenant General Grant, on their way to Washington as peace commissioners."[12] Their application was telegraphed to Secretary Stanton who replied, after consulting Lincoln, that no one should be admitted until the President's instructions were received. Lincoln dispatched Major Thomas T. Eckert with written directions that the commissioners should be admitted if they would say in writing that they came in accordance with his letter of January 18 to Blair "with the view of securing peace to our one common country."[13]

Before Major Eckert arrived, the commissioners again took the matter into their own hands and addressed a new application to General Grant, asking permission "to proceed to Washington to hold a conference with President Lincoln upon the subject of the existing war, and with a view of ascertaining upon what terms it may be terminated, in pursuance of the course indicated by him in his letter to Mr. Blair of January 18, 1865."[14] This satisfied Lincoln, and he sent Secretary Seward to meet the commissioners at Fortress Monroe. Mr. Seward bore these instructions:

> *Executive Mansion, January 31, 1865.*

Hon. William H. Seward: *You will proceed to Fortress Monroe, Virginia, there to meet and informally confer with Messrs. Stephens, Hunter, and Campbell, on the basis of my letter to F. P. Blair, Esq., on January 18, 1865, a copy of which you have. You will make known to them that three things are indispensable—to wit:*

---

[11] *Southern Historical Society Papers*, IV, 214.
[12] Nicolay and Hay, *Complete Works*, XI, 13–14.
[13] *Ibid.*, pp. 14–17.
[14] *Ibid.*, pp. 17–18.

1. *The restoration of the national authority throughout all the States.*

2. *No receding by the executive of the United States on the slavery question from the position assumed thereon in the late annual message to Congress, and in preceding documents.*

3. *No cessation of hostilities short of an end of the war, and the disbanding of all forces hostile to the government.*

You will inform them that all propositions of theirs, not inconsistent with the above, will be considered and passed upon in a spirit of sincere liberality. You will hear all they may choose to say and report it to me. You will not assume to definitely consummate anything.

Yours, etc.,
Abraham Lincoln.[15]

Mr. Seward started on the morning of February 1. In the meantime Major Eckert had arrived at the front. The bewildered commissioners changed their approach again and produced the instructions Davis had given them. General Grant and Major Eckert had some differences of judgment as to procedure. Major Eckert promptly notified the commissioners that they could not proceed further, and General Grant telegraphed Secretary Stanton:

City Point, Va., February 1, 1865.
10:30 P.M.

Hon. Edwin M. Stanton: *Now that the interview between Major Eckert, under his written instructions, and Mr. Stephens and party has ended, I will state confidentially, but not officially—to become a matter of record—that I am convinced, upon conversation with Messrs. Stephens and Hunter, that their intentions are good and their desire sincere to restore peace and union. I have not felt myself at liberty to express even views of my own, or to account for my reticency. This has placed me in an awkward position, which I could have avoided by not seeing them in the first instance. I fear now their going back without any expression from any one in authority will have a bad influence. At the same time, I recognize the difficulties in the way of receiving these informal commissioners at this time, and do not know what to recommend. I am sorry, however, that Mr. Lincoln cannot have an interview with the two named in this dispatch, if not all three now within our lines. Their letter to me was all that the President's instructions contemplated to secure their safe-conduct, if they had used the same language to Major Eckert.*

U. S. Grant, Lieutenant-General.[16]

---

[15] *Ibid.*, X, 351–52, Lincoln to Seward, January 31, 1865.
[16] *Ibid.*, XI, 23.

On the morning of February 2, after having read Major Eckert's report at the War Department, the President was about to telegraph Mr. Seward to return when General Grant's telegram was brought to his attention. He immediately telegraphed General Grant that he would meet the commissioners at Fortress Monroe as soon as he could get there. Before Lincoln's arrival the commissioners went into another huddle and notified both General Grant and Major Eckert in writing that they would accept the President's terms as a basis for the conference. The historic Hampton Roads Conference was held on board the "River Queen" lying at anchor near Fortress Monroe where President Lincoln and Secretary Seward met the commissioners on the morning of February 3, 1865.

The conferees were not strangers to one another. Lincoln and Stephens especially could go back to the days when they had been in Congress together. The conference proceeded amiably for more than four hours. Lincoln stood firmly on the basis of his letter to Blair and his instructions to Seward. The commissioners were not fully in accord in their representations, they appeared to be seeking a cessation of hostilities with a postponement of the consideration of fundamental issues. Stephens even raised anew the absurd proposal of Blair. Lincoln stuck to his ground that the disbandment of the insurgent forces and the restoration of the national authority were the primary conditions of peace, and the conference ended.

Jefferson Davis was more vocal than his disappointed commissioners who returned to Richmond to acknowledge that their mission had failed. At a public meeting of protest on February 6 he reaffirmed the purpose of the Confederacy to continue its fight for independence and in his wrath branded Lincoln as "His Majesty Abraham the First."

Lincoln was apparently deeply impressed by his conference with the rebel commissioners. His sympathies were aroused and, his mind filled with the discussion which had taken place at Hampton Roads, he called his Cabinet together on the evening of February 5 and sought their opinion and advice upon a proposed message to Congress, which read:

Fellow-Citizens of the Senate and House of Representatives: *I respectfully recommend that a joint resolution, substantially as follows, be adopted as soon as practicable by your honorable bodies:*

"Resolved by the Senate and House of Representatives of the United States of America, in Congress assembled, That the President of the United States is hereby empowered, in his discretion, to pay $400,000,000 to the

States of Alabama, Arkansas, Delaware, Florida, Georgia, Kentucky, Louisi-
ana, Maryland, Mississippi, Missouri, North Carolina, South Carolina,
Tennessee, Texas, Virginia, and West Virginia, in the manner and on the
conditions following to wit: The payment to be made in six per cent govern-
ment bonds, and to be distributed among said States pro rata on their re-
spective slave populations as shown by the census of 1860, and no part of
said sum to be paid unless all resistance to the national authority shall be
abandoned and cease, on or before the first day of April next; and upon such
abandonment and ceasing of resistance one half of said sum to be paid in
manner aforesaid, and the remaining half to be paid only upon the amend-
ment of the National Constitution recently proposed by Congress becoming
valid law, on or before the first day of July next, by the action therein of
the required number of States."

The adoption of such resolution is sought with a view to embody it, with
other propositions, in a proclamation looking to peace and reunion.

Whereas, a joint resolution has been adopted by Congress, in the words
following, to wit:

Now, therefore, I, Abraham Lincoln, President of the United States, do
proclaim, declare, and make known, that on the conditions therein stated,
the power conferred on the executive in and by said joint resolution will be
fully exercised; that war will cease and armies be reduced to a basis of peace;
that all political offenses will be pardoned; that all property, except slaves,
liable to confiscation or forfeiture, will be released therefrom, except in
cases of intervening interests of third parties; and that liberality will be
recommended to Congress upon all points not lying within executive con-
trol.[17]

Gideon Welles was always suspicious of any undertaking upon
which he had not been consulted. He was disturbed by the rumors
about Blair's visits to Richmond and undoubtedly had some inkling
of the plans under way for the Hampton Roads Conference on January
30 when he revealed his irritation in his diary. "The President, with
much shrewdness and much good sense," he recorded, "has often
strange and incomprehensible whims; takes sometimes singular and
unaccountable freaks. It would hardly surprise me were he to undertake to arrange terms of peace without consulting anyone."[18] And
again on February 2 he made this memorandum: "The President and
Mr. Seward have gone to Hampton Roads to have an interview with
the Rebel commissioners. . . . None of the Cabinet were advised
of this move, and without exception, I think, it struck them unfavor-

---

[17] *Ibid.*, pp. 1–3.
[18] Edgar T. Welles, ed., *The Diary of Gideon Welles*, II, 231–32.

ably that the Chief Magistrate should have gone on such a mission."[19]

When Lincoln presented his proposed message to Congress on February 5, the entire Cabinet must have shared the view of Welles that the President was capable of "strange and incomprehensible whims," if not indeed of "singular and unaccountable freaks." Not a member of the Cabinet favored the President's resolution. Welles committed himself thus: "In the present temper of Congress the proposed measure, if a wise one, could not be carried through successfully. I do not think the scheme could accomplish any good results. The Rebels would misconstrue it if the offer was made. If attempted and defeated it would do harm."[20]

Lincoln was disappointed. He wrote the following endorsement on the draft of his proposed message: "February 5, 1865. To-day these papers, which explain themselves, were drawn up and submitted to the cabinet and unanimously disapproved by them. A. Lincoln."[21] Another peace effort had failed.[22]

On February 10, in response to a request, Lincoln sent a special message to the House of Representatives including copies of all the letters and telegrams with reference to the conference. His concluding statement in this message gives a terse account of what happened:

On the morning of the 3d [February], the three gentlemen, Messrs. Stephens, Hunter, and Campbell, came aboard our steamer, and had an interview with the Secretary of State and myself, of several hours' duration. No question of preliminaries to the meeting was then and there made or mentioned. No other person was present; no papers were exchanged or produced; and it was, in advance, agreed that the conversation was to be informal and verbal merely.

On our part the whole substance of the instructions to the Secretary of State, hereinbefore recited, was stated and insisted upon, and nothing was said inconsistent therewith; while, by the other party, it was not said that in any event or on any condition, they would ever consent to reunion; and yet they equally omitted to declare that they never would so consent. They seemed to desire a postponement of that question, and the adoption of some other course first which, as some of them seemed to argue, might or might not lead to reunion; but which course, we thought, would amount to an indefinite postponement. The conference ended without result.[23]

---

[19] *Ibid.*, p. 235.

[20] *Ibid.*, p. 237.

[21] Nicolay and Hay, *Complete Works*, XI, 3.

[22] Edward Chase Kirkland, *The Peacemakers of 1864*, pp. 206–58. See also, for further detailed account, Nicolay and Hay, *Abraham Lincoln*, X, 113–31.

[23] Nicolay and Hay, *Complete Works*, XI, 27–28.

There was one more gesture toward negotiation; it came from Robert E. Lee, the gallant Commander-in-Chief of the Army of the Confederacy. As the year 1865 opened, Lee was desperate. "No food, no horses, no reinforcement," says Freeman. "As that dread spectre of ultimate defeat shaped itself, Lee did not content himself with reorganizing his army."[24] On March 2, with the permission of Jefferson Davis, Lee sent a letter to Grant proposing an interview. "Sincerely desiring to leave nothing untried which may put an end to the calamities of war," he wrote, "I propose to meet you at such convenient time and place as you may designate, with the hope that upon an exchange of views it may be found practicable to submit subjects of controversy between the belligerents to a (*military*) convention."[25]

On the receipt of Lee's letter, Grant immediately telegraphed the proposal to the War Department. Secretary Stanton found Lincoln at the Capitol signing bills at the closing session of Congress, the night before his second inauguration. Lincoln read Grant's telegram, and calmly wrote out a reply to be sent by Stanton:

The President directs me to say that he wishes you to have no conference with General Lee unless it be for the capitulation of General Lee's army, or on some minor purely military matter. He instructs me to say that you are not to decide, discuss, or confer upon any political questions. Such questions the President holds in his own hands, and will submit them to no military conferences or conventions. Meanwhile you are to press to the utmost your military advantage.[26]

Grant wrote Lee promptly on the day Lincoln was being inaugurated. The substance of his reply was couched in two sentences: "In regard to meeting you on the 6th instant, I would state that I have no authority to accede to your proposition for a conference on the subject proposed. Such authority is vested in the President of the United States alone."[27] Peace was to come through military action, not military conventions.

Throughout January and February, 1865, the newspapers, both North and South, were filled with peace talk. Blair's visits to Richmond, at first mysterious, were discussed, approved, disapproved, and guessed at. The Hampton Roads Conference excited even greater

---

[24] Douglas Southall Freeman, *R. E. Lee*, IV, 1.
[25] *War of the Rebellion, Official Records of the Union and Confederate Armies*, Series I, XLVI, Pt. 2, 824.
[26] Nicolay and Hay, *Abraham Lincoln*, X, 158.
[27] *War of the Rebellion, op. cit.*, p. 825.

comment. The New York City papers, with the exception of the *Tribune*, were mainly critical of Blair's mission. Even Raymond of the *Times* "saw nothing to approve in the volunteer mission of Mr. Blair to Richmond." Taking a sly fling at Greeley, Raymond continued: "We objected to that on precisely the grounds which have led us to object to all the volunteer diplomacy which meddlesome busybodies have, from time to time, set on foot. All such negotiations, carried on without authority and involving no responsibility, are simply mischievous and discreditable."[28]

The *Tribune* printed conspicuous columns of news items about Blair's going and coming and about the conference at Hampton Roads. Almost every other day Greeley had something to say in the editorial columns.[29] He thoroughly approved of Blair's undertaking, held it to have "profound significance," and apparently knew more about it from day to day than he was willing to admit. He did not anticipate "immediate pacification" but felt that there could be no possible harm in ascertaining precisely what the rebels were ready to do. In the meantime, hoping for peace, he prayed that the "Loyal Millions" would "not flag nor pause" in their efforts to raise their respective quotas under the President's call. Mr. Blair's first visit to Richmond was "neither fruitless nor useless" or it would not have been repeated. After Blair's second visit Greeley said: "We did and *do* expect much from Mr. Blair's efforts, though we never supposed that our country would be pacified quite so easily or so promptly as two boys might swap jack-knives. And we say again that we believe Peace to be not far off."

After the results of the Hampton Roads Conference were known, Greeley still held the view that it would lead to peace. He took occasion to reaffirm his position at the time of his Niagara expedition. He held that the government could not conceivably hold a peace conference with the rebels without helping the national cause. Either the Confederates would agree to some reasonable terms which would lead to peace or they would evince a spirit which would rally thousands to the national standard.[30]

Greeley kept an even temper during January and February, while these peace maneuvers were before the public, and he was never more

---

[28] *New York Times*, February 7, 1865.

[29] *Tribune*, January 2, 4, 10, 24, 1865.

[30] *Ibid.*, February 8, 1865.

considerate of the man in the White House. The *Tribune* rested in "the confident trust that the Executive is equal to the high trust reposed in him by the People." Greeley counseled that the Executive should be left "wholly unembarrassed" as the negotiations proceeded, and contented himself with the ardent wish and hope that the overtures would result in a speedy and honorable peace. "Let us, for the present," he said, "fully trust our Government, prepared to aid it with our best efforts should a recurrence to arms become necessary."[31]

Hopeful that the Hampton Roads Conference might have "ultimate fruits," Greeley was obliged to record the immediate result as one of "futility and disappointment." In an editorial entitled "Peace Through War" on February 7, he praised the President for "eagerly" seeking peace, deplored the attitude of the "Confederate chiefs at Richmond," and reluctantly came to the conclusion that there must be more fighting "not to subjugate but to liberate the Southern people." He called for a prompt filling of "the thinned ranks of our gallant armies." Again, as he had done many times in the past, he fixed a deadline for the end of the struggle and predicted that sixty days would "suffice to stamp out the last embers of the Rebellion and secure us a country shielded evermore from the perils of Disunion and Treason." In this prediction Greeley was remarkably accurate. Sixty-one days later Lee surrendered to Grant at Appomattox.

The President must have been cheered, as he pondered over what to say in his Second Inaugural address, when he found the editor of the *Tribune* saying:

> *The Congress is soon to disperse; and we trust the President may not be required to re-assemble the next till Autumn at the earliest. Meantime he and his official counselors must deal with the momentous issues of Peace and War as circumstances shall dictate. The country confides in the President, and would to-morrow decide unhesitatingly to leave the matter to his uncontrolled discretion. If it were put to a general vote—"Will you uphold and prosecute the War 'till Abraham Lincoln says its end on your part has been attained, and then agree to such terms of pacification as he shall subscribe or accede to?"—we are confident that the Yeas would be a very large majority.*[32]

In this extraordinary mood of confidence in the President, Greeley looked forward to the Second Inaugural address for indirect overtures

---

[31] *Ibid.*, January 21, 1865.
[32] *Ibid.*, February 23, 1865.

toward peace. "Only let the Inaugural conform in tenor and spirit to its illustrious predecessor," he said, "and we shall have little further use for ball-cartridge."

Greeley was in high spirits on Inauguration Day as the President of the United States assumed once more the responsibilities of his high office.

As he advances to fresh duties [the now apparently devoted editor declared], all good omens attend him, and his inauguration is illustrated by recent victories over faction and treachery. The rejoicings of a hundred cities are the anthems which welcome him to this toil. From sea-board and from prairie, from the farm, the workshop and the pier, from old men in their wisdom, from young men in their strength, from mothers and from wives and from children, come the glad cries of encouragement and gratitude. The cloud which lowered upon the Republic has been lifted, and we see once more the glorious Summer of peace and prosperity advancing.[33]

It will be recalled that Greeley was lavish in his praise of the First Inaugural address. On March 6 the *Tribune* printed both the First and Second Inaugural addresses. Discerning critic that he was, he seemed not to catch the full import of the second address. He held that it was evidently inspired by hope of an early peace, but that it did not appeal to the rebels for a cessation of hostilities as "pleadingly" as its proto-type urged "forbearance" from beginning them. This view was strange coming from one who had watched minutely every turn of events from March 4, 1861, to March 4, 1865. In the First Inaugural the preserva-tion of the Union was Lincoln's theme; in the Second Inaugural, his theme was the preservation of the Union and the abandonment of slavery. A thousand times Greeley had urged that consummation. Continuing his analysis of the Second Inaugural, he said: "Now is the fittest time for putting forth manifestations of generosity, magna-nimity, clemency, which, however they may be spurned by the Rebel chiefs, are certain to exert a great and salutary influence among their duped, disgusted, despairing followers." Did Greeley think that Lincoln had failed in this? For eighty-seven years the whole world has found the living spirit of generosity, magnanimity, and clemency in the famous and familiar words with which the President closed his Second Inaugural address:

With malice toward none; with charity for all; with firmness in the right, as God gives us to see the right, let us strive on to finish the work we are

---

[33] *Ibid.*, March 4, 1865.

in; to bind up the nation's wounds; to care for him who shall have borne the battle, and for his widow, and his orphan—to do all which may achieve and cherish a just and lasting peace among ourselves, and with all nations.[34]

Greeley changed his tactics once more; he ceased his admonitions that the President should be left to his own decisions in dealing with the immediate issues of war and peace, and resumed his old habit of advising and exhorting. The President should now "lucidly" and "briefly" announce terms to the rebels on which he would have them lay down their arms and submit to the national authority. He should deliver an "ultimatum" on the following points:

> I. *Union—Disunion*
> II. *Amnesty—Treason*
> III. *Confiscation—Property*
> IV. *Emancipation—Slavery*
> V. *Reconstruction—State Subversion*
> VI. *Representation in Congress*

He insisted that if the President would now make a "specific, circumstantial, magnanimous public overture," the great body of the Southern whites, independent of their leaders, would insist on its acceptance. Having given the President the subjects to be considered in his ultimatum, Greeley proceeded to say that he did not mean to suggest or hint at any basis of pacification, since he desired that the conditions proffered should be emphatically the President's own. "We know," he said, "that his heart is right, and we are confident that the terms it will prompt him to offer are such as the insurgents ought to accept— such as a large majority of them will choose to accept."[35]

When Lincoln visited Grant at his City Point headquarters during the last week of March and the first week in April, Greeley surmised that peace negotiations might be under way. Although confessing that he was uninformed, he expressed confidence that Lincoln would not return to Washington without having satisfied himself that the "master-spirits" at Richmond were or were not ready to accept peace on the basis of reunion. If the President should return to Washington "without having achieved any approximation to Peace," then, the editor, still desirous of formulating the peace himself, would renew with increased vigor his earlier proposed overture and appeal to the Southern people. "We cannot realize," he said, "that the dignity of

---

[34] Nicolay and Hay, *Complete Works*, XI, 46–47.
[35] *Tribune*, March 22, 1865.

the Government would be lowered by such an appeal, while we are sure that its position would be strengthened and the power of its enemies weakened. If the result should be the shortening of the War by but a week and the saving of a bare thousand of human lives, who would say that it had been issued in vain?"[36]

The day before Greeley's last attempt to promote a negotiated peace, Grant began his last great offensive movement, and from his field headquarters at Gravelly Creek on March 29 he wrote to General Sheridan: "I now feel like ending the matter, if it is possible to do so, before going back."[37] Lincoln went to City Point, but with no plan for negotiating with the "master-minds" at Richmond—he had abundant evidence that such an effort would be fruitless. Before he returned to Washington, Petersburg and Richmond had been evacuated. When Lincoln entered Richmond, Jefferson Davis had been in flight for two days.

As it turned out Lincoln did have an unexpected and quite informal peace talk at Richmond and at City Point with Judge John A. Campbell, one of the rebel commissioners at the Hampton Roads Conference.[38] Judge Campbell had stayed behind when Davis and other members of his Cabinet fled from Richmond, and as soon as opportunity offered he gave himself up to the Union military authorities. He was granted a brief interview with Lincoln at Richmond, and the following day by appointment visited him at City Point. They both knew the war would soon be over, and they talked calmly of terms of peace and reconstruction. Lincoln gave Judge Campbell a fresh statement of terms of peace which in substance repeated the terms he had outlined at Hampton Roads:

> As to peace, I have said before, and now repeat, that three things are indispensable:
>
> 1. The restoration of the national authority throughout the United States.
>
> 2. No receding by the Executive of the United States on the slavery question from the position assumed thereon in the late annual message, and in preceding documents.
>
> 3. No cessation of hostilities short of an end of the war, and the disbanding of all forces hostile to the Government. That all propositions coming from those now in hostility to the Government, not inconsistent with

---

[36] *Ibid.*, March 30, 1865.

[37] Ulysses Simpson Grant, *Personal Memoirs of U. S. Grant*, II, 621.

[38] Nicolay and Hay, *Abraham Lincoln*, X, 220.

*the foregoing, will be respectfully considered and passed upon in a spirit of
sincere liberality.*

*I now add that it seems useless for me to be more specific with those who
will not say that they are ready for the indispensable terms, even on conditions to be named by themselves. If there be any who are ready for these
indispensable terms, on any conditions whatever, let them say so, and state
their conditions, so that the conditions can be known and considered. . . .*[39]

Lincoln and Judge Campbell discussed steps which might be taken
to withdraw the Virginia troops. Campbell assured Lincoln that the
Virginia Legislature was ready to repeal the ordinance of secession.
Lincoln therefore gave General Weitzel, Union commander at Richmond, authority to permit "the gentlemen who have acted as the
legislature of Virginia in support of the rebellion" to assemble and to
give them protection if they undertook no hostile action.[40] He informed
Grant of what he had done, and added this comment: "I do not think
it very probable that anything will come of this, but I have thought
best to notify you so that if you should see signs you may understand
them. From your recent despatches it seems that you are pretty effectually withdrawing the Virginia troops from opposition to the government. Nothing that I have done, or probably shall do, is to delay,
hinder, or interfere with your work."[41] Judge Campbell misinterpreted
Lincoln's instructions, called together a committee, and took steps to
bring together the "gentlemen who [had] acted" as if they constituted
the rightful legislature of the state. Lincoln was indignant and
promptly advised General Weitzel not to allow the insurgents to
assemble. Thus his last effort to end the war by political action came
to an end.[42] In the meantime he had sent this telegram to Grant.

> *Headquarters Armies of the U.S.*
> *City Point, April 7, 1865, 11 A.M.*

> *Lieutenant-General Grant: Gen. Sheridan says "If the thing is pressed I
> think that Lee will surrender." Let the thing be pressed.*

> *A. Lincoln*[43]

On the same day, six hours later, Grant sent the following note to Lee:

---

[39] Nicolay and Hay, *Complete Works*, XI, 71–73.
[40] *Ibid.*, p. 75.
[41] *Ibid.*, p. 74.
[42] Nicolay and Hay, *Abraham Lincoln*, X, 227–28.
[43] Nicolay and Hay, *Complete Works*, XI, 77.

Headquarters Armies of the U.S.
5 P.M., April 7, 1865

General R. E. Lee
    Commanding C.S.A.

The results of the last week must convince you of the hopelessness of further resistance on the part of the Army of Northern Virginia in this struggle. I feel that it is so, and regard it as my duty to shift from myself the responsibility of any further effusion of blood, by asking of you the surrender of that portion of the Confederate States army known as the Army of Northern Virginia.

                    U. S. Grant
                       Lieut.-General[44]

Lincoln returned from City Point on Sunday evening, April 9, to find that Secretary Stanton had received this telegram from Grant:

Headquarters Appomattox C.H., Va.,
April 9th, 1865, 4.30 P.M.

Hon. E. M. Stanton, Secretary of War,
    Washington

General Lee surrendered the Army of Northern Virginia this afternoon on terms proposed by myself. The accompanying additional correspondence will show the conditions fully.

                    U. S. Grant
                       Lieut.-General[45]

Lee's surrender meant the end of the war. The North went wild. Carl Sandburg has graphically portrayed the rejoicing in Washington and throughout the North, but he found no evidence of elation on the part of the President. Sandburg could only say that Lincoln's heart *probably* ran with that of his friend Professor James Russell Lowell writing that day to Professor Charles Eliot Norton: "The news, my dear Charles, is from Heaven. I felt a strange and tender exaltation. I wanted to laugh and I wanted to cry, and ended by holding my peace and feeling devoutly thankful. There is something magnificent in having a country to love."[46]

This was indeed Lincoln's day. He had been moving toward it, sometimes consciously, sometimes only in his dreams, for the entire twenty-eight years since he had joined with Dan Stone in the Illinois

---

[44] Grant, *op. cit.*, pp. 478–79.
[45] *Ibid.*, p. 495.
[46] Sandburg, *op. cit.*, IV, 207–14.

Legislature in the declaration of their belief that "the institution of slavery is founded on both injustice and bad policy."[47] There is no evidence that he laughed or cried, and God alone knows what "strange and tender exaltation" filled his soul. He seemed almost stunned into silence. On April 10, the day of the great celebration, serenaders flocked to the White House and called for the President. He uttered a few commonplaces about the "great good news" and told the crowd to come back the next evening when he hoped to be ready to say something.[48] Welles called on the President and found him "looking well and feeling well," and recorded in his diary: "The nation seems delirious with joy." The "cotton question" was the chief topic at the Cabinet meeting on April 11.[49] Under what appeared as "business as usual," Lincoln issued one proclamation closing designated Southern ports and another barring from all United States ports the war vessels of countries whose ports had refused equal privileges and immunities to war vessels of the United States.[50] The President gave his chief attention to writing out the speech that he was to deliver in the evening.

At the appointed time a vast throng with bands and banners assembled in front of the White House. Lincoln spoke from the second-floor balcony and started out by holding his manuscript in his right hand and a candle in his left hand. Noah Brooks came to his rescue and held the candle for him. His sole reference to the historic occasion which brought the great crowd to greet him was contained in the first paragraph of his address which read:

We meet this evening not in sorrow, but in gladness of heart. The evacuation of Petersburg and Richmond, and the surrender of the principal insurgent army, give hope of a righteous and speedy peace, whose joyous expression cannot be restrained. In the midst of this, however, He from whom all blessings flow must not be forgotten. A call for a national thanksgiving is being prepared, and will be duly promulgated. Nor must those whose harder part give us the cause of rejoicing be overlooked. Their honors must not be parceled out with others. I myself was near the front, and had the high pleasure of transmitting much of the good news to you; but no part of the honor for plan or execution is mine. To General Grant, his skilful officers and brave men, all belongs. The gallant navy stood ready, but was not in reach to take active part.

---

[47] Nicolay and Hay, *Complete Works*, I, 51–52.
[48] *Ibid.*, XI, 77–78.
[49] Welles, *op. cit.*, II, 278.
[50] Nicolay and Hay, *Complete Works*, XI, 79–83.

And then he went on for about fifteen minutes, reading painfully from his manuscript a lawyer-like brief on the process of reconstruction then taking place in Louisiana, and closed this singular performance with the drab statement: "In the present situation, as the phrase goes, it may be my duty to make some new announcement to the people of the South. I am considering, and shall not fail to act when satisfied that action will be proper."[51]

This was the climax of his career. The "tenor and spirit" of this political paper, aimed not at the throng before him but at a wider audience, did not reveal the real Lincoln. There was no feeling, no sentiment, no olive branch. What possessed him not to let his great heart speak we shall never know. This was the time for the public revelation of the spirit of magnanimity which had characterized his life. This was the time to repeat to the defeated and stricken South the immortal words "with malice toward none; with charity for all." Lincoln, to be sure, was thinking of reconstruction, but in terms of law and governmental administration. This was the time when the nation wanted him to speak of reconstruction in terms of human brotherhood. This was the time to welcome the South back to loyalty to the Union, its constitution and laws. The "strange and tender exaltation" which we know must have been stirring in the great soul of him was not voiced. Who knows what the real Lincoln, rising to his own level, might not have done that night from the balcony of the White House to hasten the healing of the wounds of civil war? It was his last speech, and one of his few notable failures on the platform.

The Washington dispatch to the *Tribune* on the night of April 11 said: "It is no criticism of the speech to say that it fell dead, wholly without effect upon the audience," and "caused a great disappointment and left a painful impression."

Greeley was charitable. The speech would be regarded by some as "reserved and indecisive" and less "lucid and definite" than some may have expected and wished. "He [the President] is evidently determined to do whatever he deems fairly within his power," said Greeley, "to restore our country speedily to peace and to heal the wounds inevitably inflicted by years of gigantic and desolating civil war. We cannot doubt that further and more conclusive proofs of this will speedily be given, and that the progress of pacification and restoration will henceforth be rapid and unbroken."[52]

---

[51] *Ibid.*, pp. 84–92.
[52] *Tribune*, April 12, 1865.

The *Tribune* and the *Times* for once were almost in complete harmony in voicing the jubilation of the people in these victorious days. Greeley had leaders on "Richmond is Ours," "Victory!"—and "Magnanimity in Triumph."[53] What Greeley and Raymond wanted from the President when victory was assured may be noted from these utterances:

Greeley	Raymond
We do not ask that the President shall disregard any danger by which the Union is still menaced. We would not have the breast of the Republic bared to the assassins who so lately sought her life. But we do ask and trust that, so nearly as may be, every one still clinging to the tattered, trailing flag of Disunion shall be supplied with reasons for quitting that unholy service and casting himself unreservedly on the mercy of his aggrieved and lately imperiled but victorious and placable country.[54]	*Words of good will from him, assurances that his policy, so far as the body of the Southern people are concerned, will be to bury the past, to remove sectional distinctions, to secure the universal enjoyment of every national blessing, would challenge confidence at once, and we verily believe, it would be followed by an enthusiastic response. If this is ever to be done, now is the golden instant. The Southern mind is now in its most impressionable mood. The hour of victory is always the hour of clemency.*[55]

It remained for Raymond in a later editorial to put into words what Lincoln thought but did not say on the night of April 11: "We should now, therefore, welcome a Proclamation from the President to the Southern people as earnestly as we should have deprecated it a month ago. What we want of the Southern people is not simply obedience, acquiescence, submission to the power of our national government; we want their confidence in its justice, their pride in its flag, their faith and devotion to the republican principles on which it rests. We have convinced them of its strength; we want now to convince them of its beneficence."[56]

The historic events of Good Friday, April 14, 1865, have been told and retold. The celebration at Fort Sumter where Major General Anderson raised anew the self-same flag he had lowered four years before; the Cabinet meeting attended by General Grant; the President's strange dream in which he "was moving with great rapidity towards an

[53] *Ibid.*, April 4, 8, 11, 1865.
[54] *Ibid.*, April 6, 1865.
[55] *New York Times*, April 5, 1865.
[56] *Ibid.*, April 7, 1865.

indefinite shore"; the stream of hopeful callers at the White House seeking pardons, releases, discharges; visits of the Speaker of the House, senators, and representatives to pay their respects; the President's letter to General Van Alen who had urged him for the sake of his friends and the nation to guard his life, saying "I intend to adopt the advice of my friends and use due precaution"; the afternoon drive of the President and Mrs. Lincoln and their talk of where they should make their home at the end of his second term; appointments for the following day; the theater party in the evening and its tragic end; all the incidents of this Good Friday have become a part of our folklore.

An ugly story, which has never been substantiated conclusively, recounted by no less a personage than Edward Everett Hale, has it that on this day Horace Greeley sat sulking at his desk in the *Tribune* office and penned a "brutal, bitter, sarcastic personal attack on President Lincoln," intended for publication on April 15. The managing editor, Sydney Howard Gay, it is said, suppressed the editorial on the ground that its publication would not leave "one brick upon another" in the *Tribune* building.[57] The only possible explanation of such a tale, assuming it to be true, was Greeley's supposed pique at Lincoln's failure to name him Postmaster General. The voluble Hoskins, Speaker of the Assembly in the New York Legislature, allegedly called on Greeley on April 14; and in their discussion of Lincoln's intimation that he intended to appoint Greeley, the editor burst out: "Hoskins, didn't I tell you that was a lie?"[58]

Greeley was subject to strange outbursts, but the record indicates that they were usually preceded by milder utterances in which he appeared to be working himself up to an explosion. For weeks prior to this time, he had been unusually moderate in his references to the President. It is true he had favored peace undertakings and had earnestly desired that the President issue a manifesto to the South, but there had been no criticism of Lincoln in these importunities and there were frequent expressions of faith and confidence in him. On circumstantial evidence alone the memory of Horace Greeley ought to be freed from this charge, for on the morning of Good Friday, the day when it is alleged that Greeley wrote the scurrilous attack upon Lincoln, the leader in the *Tribune*, which the editor must have approved if he did not write, was entitled "The Dawn of Peace." It ended with the words: "A new world is born, and the Sun of Peace

[57] Edward Everett Hale, *James Russell Lowell and His Friends*, pp. 178–79.
[58] Don C. Seitz, *Horace Greeley*, p. 270.

rises in splendor to send abroad over the land its rays of warmth and light! Never before had nation so much cause for devout Thanksgiving; never before had a people so much reason for unrestrained congratulation and the very extravagance of joy."

The "cause for devout Thanksgiving," the reason for "unrestrained congratulation, and the very extravagance of joy" voiced by the *Tribune* were overnight turned into the period of the nation's greatest sorrow. A month later a day of prayer and humiliation was called by President Johnson in memory of Abraham Lincoln. It required a volume of a thousand pages to include the messages of appreciation and sympathy which poured in upon the government from foreign lands. Mrs. Lincoln was also overwhelmed by personal letters and telegrams. One of the tenderest messages came from Queen Victoria.

Osborne.
April 29, 1865

Dear Madam,

Though a stranger to you, I cannot remain silent when so terrible a calamity has fallen upon you and your country, and must personally express my deep and heartfelt sympathy with you under the shocking circumstances of your present dreadful misfortune.

No one can better appreciate than I can, who am myself utterly broken-hearted by the loss of my own beloved Husband, who was the light of my life,—my stay—my all,—what your sufferings must be; and I earnestly pray that you may be supported by Him to whom alone the sorely stricken can look for comfort, in this hour of heavy affliction.

With renewed expression of true sympathy, I remain dear Madam,

Your sincere friend
Victoria[59]

On Saturday, April 15, the *Tribune* columns were separated by black bands which were continued for thirty days. Under the heading "Highly Important—The President Shot" three columns of special dispatches from Washington were carried. The paper went to press before word came of the President's death. Assuming from the dispatches that the President would not survive, the editor said:

We give the above dispatches in the order in which they reached us, the first having been received a little before midnight, for we know that every line, every letter will be read with the intensest interest. In the sudden shock of a calamity so appalling we can do little else than give such details of the

---

[59] Katherine Helm, *The True Story of Mary, Wife of Lincoln*, pp. 261–62.

murder of the President as have reached us. Sudden death is always over-whelming; assassination of the humblest of men is always frightfully startling; when the head of thirty millions of people is hurried into eternity by the hand of a murderer—that head a man so good, so wise, so noble as ABRAHAM LINCOLN, *the Chief Magistrate of a nation in the condition of ours at this moment,—the sorrow and shock are too great for many words. There are none in this broad land to-day who love their country, who wish well their race, that will not bow down in profound grief at the event it has brought upon us. For once all party rancor will be forgotten, and no right-thinking man can hear of Mr. Lincoln's death without accepting it as a national calamity. We can give in these its first moments no thought of the future. God, in his inscrutable Providence, has thus visited the Nation; the future we must leave to Him.*

The *Tribune* followed the funeral train, with detailed news accounts and with frequent editorials, day by day from Washington to Spring-field. The principal editorials, which appeared during the ceremonies at Washington and as the train progressed from Washington to Baltimore to Harrisburg to Philadelphia to New York City, contained notable and discriminating appraisals of Lincoln which stand the test of time remarkably well. They are presented in the order in which they appeared.

THE NATION'S LOSS

April 17, 1865

The immediate presence of the horrible crime which has stricken the Republic to the heart, in the hour of its transcendent and long-awaited triumph, is unfavorable to a full and clear conception of its importance and its consequences. It must necessarily appear to different observers under dif-ferent aspects, and each will especially lament it for some reasons which will have less force and weight with others.

For our own part, it intensifies our regret, while it is nevertheless our abiding consolation, that the lamented Head of the Republic now sleeping in his bloody shroud was never provoked to the exhibition of one trace of hate or even wrath toward those against whom he was compelled to battle for the life of the Nation. From the hour, now eleven years past, when, in view of the treacherous repudiation of the Missouri compact, he enunciated the axiomatic yet startling truth: "The Union cannot permanently exist half slave and half free," down to that of his assassination, he uttered no syl-lable of retort to the hideous vomitings of abuse and slander wherewith he was incessantly covered by the partisans of the doomed but still vital and venomous "institution." Perpetually represented to the Southern people as a libel on Humanity and a tiger ravenous for blood, he not only put forth no speech, no paper, no manifesto, that gave the least countenance to these calumnies, but he never, in his most intimate and confidential moments, indicated a hope, a wish, that evil should befall one of these enemies, save as it should be necessary for the salvation of the country. And this fact, hitherto suppressed and distorted, will now make itself felt and respected. The blow that struck down Abraham Lincoln bereft the Union's misguided and criminal assailants of the firmest and most powerful opponent of all avoidable severity, all not indispensable harshness, in suppressing their Rebellion. His very last public utterance—the speech of the Tuesday night prior to his assassination—was conceived in this spirit, and had no other purpose than to reconcile the North to the most gentle and magnanimous treatment of the discomfited insurgents. If ever man made war in a Christian spirit, Mr. Lincoln was that man. His first Inaugural is the most affecting appeal ever made to a disaffected party against the madness and crime of plunging their country into an abyss of blood and horror. His last Inaugural, so solemn and religious in its tone, and now seeming to have been written under the shadow of impending death, is pervaded by the same spirit. His failings as a leader in such a crisis were prompted by a nature slow to anger and shrinking from any but the most indispensable shedding of blood. No portion of the American people have greater reason to deplore his murder than those in whose presumed interest or to glut whose malignity it was perpetrated.

President Lincoln fell a sacrifice to his country's salvation as absolutely, palpably, as though he had been struck down while leading an assault on the ramparts of Petersburg. The wretch who killed him was impelled by no private malice, but imagined himself an avenger of that downcast idol which, disliking to be known simply as Slavery, styles itself "the South." He was murdered, not that Slavery might live, but that it might bring down its most conspicuous enemy in its fall. His death sets the seal of Fate to the decree that dooms Slavery speedily to perish, not in this country only, but in all its remaining lurking-places throughout the civilized world.

The Republic is saved forever from its giant curse and shame. It will not be divided; it will all be Free. If there had been doubt of this last week, as there was not, there is doubt no longer. Our abiding and serious peril is a transfusion into the veins of the Loyal Millions of some portion of the blood of the monster they have slain. The public feeling aroused by the double assassination at Washington needs to be calmed and directed, not inflamed and aggravated. There is depravity but no danger in the babble of the mad fool who says he is glad Lincoln is killed; there is food for graver thought, there is a call for sterner reprobation, in the pious suggestion that our good President has been Providentially called hence in order that the leading Rebels may receive that condign punishment which his kindness of heart would have averted.

For nothing can be further from the truth than the current notion that Mr. Lincoln was a man easily deflected from his course. He was slow to reach conclusions; but, once attained, they were immovable. He was among the last to perceive that the struggle into which we have been plunged could only be fought to a successful issue by openly recognizing the fact that Slavery had challenged the Union to mortal encounter and that the gage must be taken up as it was thrown down; but, once convinced of that fact, he was convinced forever. There was not in all America one man more inflexible in his resolve that Slavery should die and the Union be restored than was Abraham Lincoln. And whoever imagines that he could have been duped, or cajoled, or wheedled, out of his purpose on this head, does gross injustice to his memory. We venture to add that no man perceived more readily or repelled more sternly than he the error of Gen. Weitzel in consenting to the convocation under our flag at Richmond of Extra Billy Smith and presumptively impenitent confederates on the assumption that they are today the Governor and Legislature of Virginia.

To human vision, it would seem that Mr. Lincoln has fallen at the very moment when his loss would be most keenly and justly felt. The soldier had done his work: the hour of the statesman had fully struck: and the President was ready and eager for the task. Had he lived a very few days longer, we believe he would have issued a Proclamation of Amnesty which would have dissolved all that remains of the Rebellion, leaving its leaders no choice but between flight and unconditional surrender. We have no special knowledge of the purposes of his successor, but we will not doubt that the good Providence which has borne our country so nobly through her past trials will continue her guide and guardian through whatever may be still before her, and that the storm and gloom of the present will speedily be effaced by the sunshine of Peace, Union and Impartial Freedom.

MR. LINCOLN'S FAME

April 19, 1865

Without the least desire to join in the race of heaping extravagant and preposterous laudations on our dead President as the wisest and greatest man who ever lived, we feel sure that the discerning and considerate of all parties will concur in our judgment that Mr. Lincoln's reputation will stand higher with posterity than with the mass of his cotemporaries— that distance, whether in time or space, while dwarfing and obscuring so many, must place him in a fairer light—that future generations will deem him undervalued by those for and with whom he labored, and be puzzled by the bitter fierceness of the personal assaults by which his temper was tested.

One reason for this doubtless is to be found in the external, superficial, non-essential tests by which we are accustomed to gauge cotemporary

merit. A king without his crown and purple robes is, to the vulgar apprehension, a solecism, an impossibility. A coarsely clad, travel-stained, bare-
foot Jesus, could get no hearing in our fashionable synagogues, though his
every discourse were a Sermon on the Mount. And Mr. Lincoln was so
essentially, unchangeably a commoner—among embassadors and grandees
in the White House the identical "Old Abe" that many of us had shaken
by both hands at Western barbecues—his homely, pungent anecdotes so
like those we had heard him relate from political stumps and by log-cabin
firesides—that the masses thought of him but as one with whom they had
been splitting rails on a pleasant Spring day or making a prosperous voyage
down the Mississippi on an Illinois flat-boat, and had found him a downright good fellow. We had had Presidents before him sprung from the loins
of poverty and obscurity, but never one who remained to the last so simply,
absolutely, alike in heart and manner, one of the People. No one who
approached him, whether as minister or messenger, felt impelled either to
stoop or to strut in his presence. He was neither awed by assumption nor
disgusted by vulgarity. He was never constrained nor uneasy in whatever
presence, and he imposed no constraint nor ceremony on others. Every
one found him easy of access, yet no one felt encouraged to take undue
liberties. Mr. Everett, one of the best bred, most refined and fastidious of
our countrymen, after observing his bearing among the cabinet and foreign
ministers, the governors, senators, generals, and other notables, collected at
the Gettysburg celebration, pronounced him the peer in deportment of any
one present. Presuming that to be the fact, it is probably due to the circumstance that he alone never thought of manners, nor how he nor any
one else was appearing to others. His mind was intent on matters of wider
and more enduring consequence.

Mr. Lincoln has suffered in the judgment of his immediate cotemporaries from the fact that, of all things that he might have been required to
do, the conduct of a great war was that for which he was least fitted. For
War requires the utmost celerity of comprehension, decision, action; and
Mr. Lincoln's mind was essentially of the "slow and sure" order. It was
pretty certain to be right in the end; but in War to be right a little too late
is equivalent to being wrong altogether. Besides, War sometimes requires
sternness; and he was at heart tender and merciful as a woman. He might
have saved many lives by prompt severity toward a few of the active traitors
who thronged Baltimore and Washington directly after the fall of Sumter,
and openly, ostentatiously exulted over our disaster at Bull Run. That
extreme lenity which befits the close of a civil war was most unluckily
evinced by him at the beginning of ours, giving every coward to understand
that, while there was peril in steadfast loyalty, it was perfectly safe to be
a Rebel. To human apprehension, Andrew Johnson should have been the
man to grapple with and crush the Rebellion, with Abraham Lincoln to

pacify the country at its close and heal the gaping wounds opened by four years of desperate, bloody conflict: but it was otherwise decreed.

There was never an hour when the strength, the resources of the Republic were not ample for the direct and signal overthrow of Slaveholding Treason; but the imbecility, incapacity, and lack of purpose, so common among our high Military officers in the early stages of our struggle—disqualifications which our Commander-in-Chief should have promptly overcome, even though it had been requisite to shoot a General daily for two or three months—long rendered our success at best doubtful. Hence, foreigners, who noted the effect without knowledge of the cause—confidently, and not unreasonably, predicted our ultimate failure. It was a perfectly natural, though happily ill-grounded, deduction that a Government that could lose such a battle as that of Bull Run, when it had superabundant means to win it, would never put down a gigantic Rebellion. But our President was like our horse Eclipse, in the great Northern and Southern match race of 1824, wherein the North was badly beaten on the first heat, but won the second and third. . . .

—"I have not assumed to control events—events have controlled me," said Mr. Lincoln, in answer to a Kentucky complaint that he was more radical in 1864-5 than he had been in 1861-2. That was the simple truth, naively and tersely expressed; and in that truth is exhibited both the weakness and the strength of the utterer. He was not the man of transcendent genius, of rare insight, of resistless force of character, who bends everything to his will: On the contrary, he was one of those who have awaited opportunity, and thought long and patiently, before venturing on an important step, hearkening intently for that "voice of the people" which was to him, in most cases, "the voice of God." He hesitated to put down his foot, feeling the ground carefully, deliberately; but, once down, it was hard to make him take it up again. A striking and honored exemplar of some of the best points in our National character, he sleeps the sleep of the honored and just, and there are few graves which will be more extensively, persistently visited, or bedewed with the tears of a people's prouder, fonder affection, than that of Abraham Lincoln.

THE PEOPLE'S LAMENT

April 21, 1865

The draped streets, the drooping flags, the open churches, the closed stores, prove inadequate to symbol the solemnity of the grief which this city feels, bearing its share of the burden which the death of the President lays on the national heart. It was supposed the feeling would be the deepest and its expression most universal on the sad Wednesday when the funeral ceremonies at Washington accompanied the body from the White House to the Capitol, and when the sun looked down on the far more impressive spectacle of twenty millions of people, covering a continent, whose hearts beat time to the tread of that funeral cortege on Pennsylvania Avenue. But yesterday was if possible a more solemn day than Wednesday. The fasting and prayer which are seldom more than conventional were real and sincere. The procession which makes its mournful way northward casts a long shadow forward, and the approach of the remains of our murdered President was listened for in the hush of all business on two successive days, and the great city mutely reached out its myriad hands to receive the sacred ashes that for thirty-six hours will be intrusted to New-York.

Chastened indeed is this people by the affliction which was decreed to fall upon them, but purified also, uplifted, and strengthened. New-York has been the center of all that was merely mercantile, of devotion to a solely material prosperity, of disregard of the highest purposes of individual and national existence. By a revulsion that seems to be as durable as it was sudden, the city casts aside its baser gods, and walking day by day in a fiery furnace, day by day finds the dross and scum and slag of its poor previous life melted out of it, and its inner thought and faith refined, and brought to the surface gleaming with an unknown splendor. . . .

WHAT HE DID NOT SAY

April 24, 1865

The earthly remains of our late President will this morning reach our City on their way to their final rest, and will remain with us till to-morrow afternoon. It seems, then, a fit moment for recalling attention to the wisdom and patriotism evinced by our loved and lost leader in his reserve and silence—in what he took care not to say or do during his occupancy of the Presidential chair. For many a fool has the credit of clever or smart sayings—perhaps justly; but to refrain from follies that are current and popular, steadfastly to lend them any countenance whatever, evinces a profound and invincible sagacity rare among even the ablest of public men.

I. Mr. Lincoln, throughout his arduous term of service as President—in fact, throughout his entire public career—utterly, stubbornly refused to utter a word calculated to embroil us in a contest with any foreign power. "ONE WAR AT A TIME"—the words with which he decided the Trent case—were the key-note of his entire official career. He never proposed the idea, once so popular, of getting out of our domestic struggle by plunging into one with a European power. None of the bogus "Monroe doctrine" bravado, which so tickles the ears of most groundlings, ever escaped his lips. He was of course annoyed and embarrassed by the French invasion of Mexico, and he never concealed his dislike to that Napoleonic blunder; but he felt that it ill became the chief of a great nation to indulge in warnings and menaces which he was notoriously unable, during our Civil War, to back by material persuasions. It would have been easy and popular to plunge the country *into a great foreign war; but that would have been to ensure its permanent disruption and overthrow. Mr. Lincoln saw the right from the outset, and had the courage and the patriotism to pursue it.*

II. He never talked vindictively, nor threatened to hang or shoot men who were not in his power. He probably had as clear and keen a perception of the wickedness of the Slaveholders' Rebellion as any other man could have; but he said little about it, and never barked at those who were not within reach of his bite. Mrs. Glass's initial direction for hare-cooking—"First, catch your hare"—he was never tempted to violate. And if wrath and bitterness, with a fearful looking-for of judgment, now pervade the Rebel breast, it was not incited by anything ever uttered by President Lincoln.

III. He always kept us clear as might be of the tangle of premature "Reconstruction." He instinctively saw from the start, in this as in other respects, the folly of quarreling over the disposition of the fox's skin while the fox was still uncaught. First, break the back of the Rebellion before you undertake to pass sentence on the Rebel chiefs; vanquish and disperse the Rebel armies before you quarrel about the terms of readmitting to our counsels States not yet ready to come back on any terms. To settle questions as they severally arise, and not to divide the loyal strength on topics not yet in order, were among the maxims by which President Lincoln's course was steadily guided. When "Reconstruction" became practical, he was ready to act on it, and not before. His refusal to approve the Wade-Davis bill of last year was based avowedly on this principle. And his successor will find his task lighter in consequence.

Our country has had greater statesmen, abler speakers or writers, more efficient administrators, than Abraham Lincoln; but which of them ever evinced such a talent for silence where speech was perilous and the events of to-morrow very likely to overset the wisest judgment of to-day? While his wise and noble acts are duly honored, let not his equally beneficent hesitations and reticences be forgotten.

These editorials read in connection with Greeley's lecture on Lincoln and the chapter on Abraham Lincoln in his *Recollections* amply demonstrate that "a tree is best measured when it's down" and give enduring substance to Greeley's "hope to make the real Lincoln, with his thoroughly human good and ill, his virtues and his imperfections, more instructive and more helpful to ordinary humanity, than his unnatural, celestial, apotheosized shadow ever was or could be."

Posterity subscribes in large measure to Greeley's estimate of Lincoln as a man and not a superman. Lincoln was for all his life an "earnest partisan." For many years he "espoused the Whig cause" unavailingly, and when the Republican party came into existence and power he stood faithful by its principles and platforms to the end of his career. He was a skilled politician, never averse to using political power to gain the ends he deemed for the welfare of the nation.

Partisan that he was, he never departed from his early convictions that the Union was indissoluble and therefore that it must be defended and preserved above all hazards; that slavery was wrong, and that the government could not "endure permanently, half slave and half free." Holding these views, as President he kept constantly before him his oath of office, employed emancipation as a war measure, and sought the final and complete abolition of slavery through constitutional amendment.

Hating the institution of slavery as he did, living in the wish "that all men everywhere could be free," involved in debate throughout his political career upon the delicate issues of his time, he "put forth no speech, no paper, no manifesto" which revealed "one trace of hate or even wrath toward those against whom he was compelled to battle for the life of the Nation." Perpetually represented to the Southern people "as a libel on Humanity," he maintained his temper and his poise and never in his most intimate and confidential moments indicated a hope, a wish, that evil might befall his enemies, "save as it should be necessary for the salvation of the country." It is not surprising that myths have grown up in the intervening years about a man who did, as is universally acknowledged, possess this singular detachment.

Free from hate, free from the ordinary human desire to punish his enemies, he was adamant upon the fundamental principles in which he believed. Slow to act, often waiting for time and anticipated events to solve issues, when his mind was finally made up on a course of action, he was immovable. Notwithstanding the certainty of Lincoln's convictions and the confidence which could be put in his final conclusions, Greeley was by no means alone in his belief that a more vigorous "prosecution of War and of Peace" would have been desirable.

Lincoln moved slowly because he believed profoundly in the force of reason and argument. A truth portrayed with logical exactness he believed would prevail. "His *forte* lay," said Greeley, "mainly in debate, or rather in the elucidation of profound truths, so that they can hardly evade the dullest apprehension." His capacity for "putting things" convincingly has hardly been excelled in the annals of American statesmanship.

Lincoln was, as Greeley said, "essentially, unchangeably a commoner." He remained to the last "simply, absolutely, alike in heart and manner, one of the People. . . . There never yet was man so lowly as to feel humbled in the presence of Abraham Lincoln; there was no honest man who feared or dreaded to meet him." It is interesting to find one of Greeley's successors in the editorial rooms of the *New York Herald-Tribune* eighty-four years after Lincoln's death discussing "The Shadow That Lasts" and saying of Lincoln that the people of America "read of him with love and understanding which disregards fancy or myth. They believe in him and receive him as one of their own. For with democracy's instinctive wisdom Americans have always known that Lincoln lived and died as the embodiment of a people's government. . . . For the shadow of a tall Lincoln lasts as the truest substance of America. Above the people of a people's government it stretches still from coast to coast, the eternal word and incarnation of the nation's faith."[60]

There was a certain consistency in Greeley's inconsistencies. He could never quite bring himself to believe his definition of greatness was fulfilled in Lincoln. Greeley said that Lincoln was not a man "of transcendent genius, of rare insight, of resistless force of character"; and yet he also said that there was not "in all America one man more inflexible in his resolve that Slavery should die and the Union be restored than was Abraham Lincoln." In Greeley's view, our country had had "greater statesmen, abler speakers or writers, more efficient administrators than Abraham Lincoln; but which of them ever evinced," he also asked, "such a talent for silence where speech was perilous and the events of to-morrow very likely to overset the wisest judgment of to-day? . . . Greater men our country has produced; but not another whom, humanly speaking, she could so ill spare, when she lost him."

Greeley was unwilling to join in the race of heaping "extravagant and preposterous laudations on our dead President as the wisest and greatest man who ever lived," but he did feel that Lincoln's reputation would "stand higher with posterity than with the mass of his cotemporaries" and that future generations would "deem him undervalued by those for and with whom he labored." Posterity has no quarrel with Greeley for not finding Lincoln a great man, for it has proof today of the force and truth of Greeley's utterance at the time the funeral procession started on the memorable journey from Washington to Springfield:

---

[60] *New York Herald-Tribune*, February 12, 1949.

"A striking and honored exemplar of some of the best points in our National Character, he sleeps the sleep of the honored and just, and there are few graves which will be more extensively, persistently visited, or bedewed with the tears of a people's prouder, fonder affection, than that of Abraham Lincoln."

> If God now wills the removal of a great wrong, and wills also that we of the North, as well as you of the South, shall pay fairly for our complicity in that wrong, impartial history will find therein new cause to attest and revere the justice and goodness of God.
>
> **Lincoln**[1]

> In God's good time this is to be a land of real freedom, where equal rights and equal laws shall banish rebellion, treason and riot, and all manner of kindred diabolisms. I hardly hope to live to see that day, but hope that those who may remember me when I am gone will believe that I earnestly tried to hasten its coming.
>
> **Greeley**[2]

12 Epilogue

The day after Lincoln's death, the *Tribune* paid its respects to the new President: "Johnson is emphatically a self-made man, with the energy, self-reliance and courage befitting that character. He believes in the Republic, venerates the Union, and has learned to hate Slavery and the Rebellion with his whole soul. . . . He has decided ability, earnest patriotism, and undoubting faith in our national destiny. If any Rebel ever thought it would be well for the clan to have Andrew Johnson in the White House rather than Abraham Lincoln he is bitterly mistaken."[3] When it became evident that President Johnson was disposed to follow the policies of Lincoln in dealing with the problems of reconstruction, Greeley started out by supporting Johnson.

It appears that Montgomery Blair had urged Johnson to reorganize the Cabinet and to strengthen it by the appointment of Greeley. What Johnson thought of Greeley at this time was later revealed in a letter

---

[1] John G. Nicolay and John Hay, eds., *Complete Works of Abraham Lincoln*, X, 68.
[2] Henry Luther Stoddard, *Horace Greeley, Printer, Editor, Crusader*, p. 224.
[3] *Tribune*, April 17, 1865.

he wrote his secretary, Major Benjamin Truman, after his retirement. "I told Blair that I would not have Greeley on any account. I always considered him a good enough editor before the war, although I never agreed with him; but in all other matters he seemed to me like a whale ashore. He nearly bothered the life out of Lincoln and it was difficult to tell whether he wanted union or separation, war or peace. Greeley is all heart and no head. He is the most vacillating man in the country. He runs to goodness of heart so much as to produce infirmity of mind. Blair reasoned with me as a friend but I could not see his point. I told him that Greeley was a sublime old child but would be of no service to me."[4]

All unmindful of Johnson's attitude, the "whale ashore" stood by Johnson faithfully at the beginning of his Administration. Johnson's first message to Congress, on December 4, 1865, said to have been written by Bancroft, the historian,[5] could have been written by Lincoln, so closely did it follow the policy he had contemplated. The new President was able to report notable progress in the restoration of "the rightful energy of the General Government and of the States." Provisional governors had been appointed in the states which had been in rebellion, conventions called, governors elected, legislatures assembled, and senators and representatives chosen to the Congress of the United States. The courts of the United States, so far as could be, had been reopened; the blockade had been removed; the customhouses re-established in the ports of entry; and the Post Office Department had renewed its activities throughout the country. The President had used his pardoning power freely but with "every precaution to connect it with the clearest recognition of the binding force of the laws of the United States and an unqualified acknowledgment of the great social change of condition" which had grown out of the war; and he looked forward to a general amnesty "at the earliest epoch consistent with public safety."

He had extended an invitation to the states to participate in the amendment of the Constitution which "provides for the abolition of slavery forever within our country." He held that it was not "competent for the General Government to extend the elective franchise in the several States" but insisted that good faith required "the security of the freedmen in their liberty and their property, their right to labor, and their right to claim the just return of their labor." He held that

---

[4] *Century Magazine*, January, 1913.
[5] Claude G. Bowers, *The Tragic Era*, p. 91.

the freedmen if they showed patience and manly virtues would "sooner obtain a participation in the elective franchise through the States than through the General Government." All of the steps he had taken looked to the discontinuance of military rule and the restoration of civil government.

To complete the work of restoration, it remained for the states whose powers had been so long in abeyance "to resume their places" in the two branches of the national legislature. "Here it is for you," the President said, "fellow-citizens of the Senate, and for you, fellow-citizens of the House of Representatives, to judge, each of you for yourselves, of the elections, returns, and qualifications of your own members."[6]

It is no part of our purpose to record the details of the refusal of the radicals in Congress to accept the President's program and of the deliberate steps which followed to remove him from office through impeachment. Grumpy old Thaddeus Stevens was the leader in the movement which resulted in the disgraceful impeachment proceedings and in the tragic era of the "carpet-baggers" and the "scalawags." If Congress had accepted and ratified the President's message in December, 1865, orderly reconstruction might promptly have been effected.

The *Tribune* was quick to voice the popular acclaim which Johnson's first message received outside of the radical circles: "We doubt whether any former message has, on the whole, contained so much that will be generally and justly approved, with so little that will or should provoke dissent. It is a State paper of signal ability and of unusual frankness, dealing unreservedly with every great question of internal or international policy and calculated to increase the hold of the author in the regard and confidence of the American People."[7] Johnson stood firmly against the radicals, employed his veto power unhesitatingly, and kept his poise and temper in all his public documents. His remark that Greeley was "the most vacillating man in the country" was to be graphically demonstrated.

Step by step the *Tribune* went over to the radicals and to the advocacy of the impeachment of the President. On June 3, 1865, Greeley ardently hoped that the President's proposal that "each state should wisely and justly settle the Suffrage question for itself" would prevail; on July 10 he thundered forth his program of "Universal Amnesty— Universal Suffrage." On September 9 he believed "Andrew Johnson to

[6] James Daniel Richardson, ed., *Messages and Papers of the Presidents*, VI, 353–71.
[7] *Tribune*, December 6, 1865.

be a pure, good man, and above the suspicion of tampering with his high and merciful prerogative"; on February 23, 1866, he found it "impossible not to see in the recent utterances of our President a determination to make war on the advocates of Human Equality before the Law."

By the time President Johnson had reiterated in his second annual message to Congress the position he had taken in his first message, Greeley had deserted him entirely: "Mr. Pierce could not have written a weaker Message. Congress would as readily have heard an essay upon the cause of thunder as this tame and harmless disquisition. . . . For any living fact, for any suggestion, for any helpful thought, we might as well turn to the last novel of Mr. Trollope as to this Message. . . . There is not one word for the negro—not one word for the loyal in the South—not one sentence which might not as well have been written a hundred years ago as to-day, for all the truth and comfort it brings. . . . We have no heart to dwell upon this dreary, lifeless document."[8]

This was the message in which the President said:

I know of no measure more imperatively demanded by every consideration of national interest, sound policy, and equal justice than the admission of loyal members from the now unrepresented States. This would consummate the work of restoration and exert a most salutary influence on the re-establishment of peace, harmony, and fraternal feeling. It would tend greatly to renew the confidence of the American people in the vigor and stability of their institutions. It would bind us more closely together as a nation and enable us to show to the world the inherent and recuperative power of a government founded upon the will of the people and established upon the principles of liberty, justice, and intelligence.[9]

In his third annual message the President said:

To me the process of restoration seems perfectly plain and simple. It consists merely in a faithful application of the Constitution and laws. The execution of the laws is not now obstructed or opposed by physical force. There is no military or other necessity, real or pretended, which can prevent obedience to the Constitution, either North or South. All the rights and all the obligations of States and individuals can be protected and enforced by means perfectly consistent with the fundamental law. The courts may be everywhere open, and if open their process would be unimpeded. Crimes against the United States can be prevented or punished by the proper judicial authorities in a manner entirely practicable and legal. There is therefore no reason why the Constitution should not be obeyed, unless those who exercise its powers

---

[8] *Ibid.*, December 4, 1866.

[9] Richardson, *op. cit.*, VI, 445–59.

have determined that it shall be disregarded and violated. The mere naked will of this government, or some one or more of its branches, is the only obstacle that can exist to a perfect union of all the states.[10]

One can almost hear Greeley, had he chosen to tack into the wind in this direction, employing almost the very words the President had used in this reasonable appeal. Instead, he abandoned reason in his bitter criticism of the message: "He summons into new activity and acrimony all the feuds and hates which good men had hoped were quieted, and challenged a renewal of the mischievous, perilous strife already protracted beyond reason and for which there is no longer a shadow of excuse. So untimely, so wantonly, wickedly baleful an appeal to outworn prejudices and dying factions has not been made in all our past history."[11]

These were words which "impartial history" finds might more appropriately have been applied to Thaddeus Stevens and his fellow conspirators than to Andrew Johnson. In the meantime the build-up for impeachment progressed with the vigorous support of the *Tribune*. Greeley found Johnson guilty before the trial began and before he had heard the charges. "Whatever public sentiment will acquit Andrew Johnson," he said, "will convict and condemn Congress, the Republican party, and the whole loyal twenty millions of the people of the United States."[12] And again: "We prefer the impeachment and removal of Andrew Johnson to the legitimate and thoroughly constitutional mode of bringing about that obedience to the law which alone is necessary to Reconstruction."[13]

The formalities of the trial before the Senate, with Chief Justice Chase presiding, began on March 4, and the final vote was taken on May 26, 1868. Throughout this period the *Tribune* printed profuse news dispatches from Washington, and Greeley discussed the progress of the trial in numerous lengthy editorials. With singular uniformity he criticized the speeches of Johnson's lawyers and praised the speeches of the prosecutors. He condemned roundly senators who publicly announced they were for acquittal as Johnson's trial progressed, and ignored the patent fact that senators for impeachment had committed the same offense. He warned the senators that any Republican vote but one of impeachment would be a lie and that no senator could be insensi-

---

[10] *Ibid.*, pp. 558–81.
[11] *Tribune*, December 4, 1867.
[12] *Ibid.*, March 19, 1868.
[13] *Ibid.*, March 23, 1868.

ble to the verdict of history. Setting himself up as both prosecutor and jury, in the midst of the trial, he vehemently declared:

It is written that a President of the United States disgraced his high office, profaned the law, brought massacre and anarchy into these States, and made the American name a scandal among the nations. It is written that for these crimes and misdemeanors he was brought to the bar of the Senate and duly tried. The case is closed, the evidence has been told, the arguments have been heard. The Senators who fail to add to this history that by their vote the great criminal is justly punished may well pray for oblivion. Especially those Republican Senators who have steadily championed the policy which culminated in this proceeding, may well pause, before by their votes, they write their names with the infamous and degraded men, who in times of national trial sought to betray their country.[14]

Greeley was a poor loser. When acquittal came he declared that the Republican party would be forever free from Johnson's "future misdeeds" and that "Messrs. Chase, Fessenden and Co.," had taken "the Old Man of the Sea" upon their shoulders. He thanked "Infinite Mercy" that there was an ordeal before the United States in which a concurrence of two-thirds was not required to insure a righteous verdict, and picked the next Republican candidate for the presidency by looking forward to the "joyful advent of Grant and Victory!"[15]

Came the time for the fourth and last annual message of the President to Congress. The President stood his ground. There is no word in the message about the impeachment proceedings. He then put the responsibility for the existing troubled state of affairs squarely upon Congress and again confirmed the policies he had outlined in his first message:

The Federal Constitution—the magna charta of American rights, under whose wise and salutary provisions we have successfully conducted all our domestic and foreign affairs, sustained ourselves in peace and in war, and became a great nation among the powers of the earth—must assuredly be now adequate to the settlement of questions growing out of the civil war, waged alone for its vindication. This great fact is made most manifest by the condition of the country when Congress assembled in the month of December, 1865. Civil strife had ceased, the spirit of rebellion had spent its entire force, in the Southern States the people had warmed into national life, and throughout the whole country a healthy reaction in public sentiment had taken place. By the application of the simple yet effective pro-

---

[14] *Ibid.*, May 11, 1868.
[15] *Ibid.*, May 18, 1868.

visions of the Constitution the executive department, with the voluntary aid of the States, had brought the work of restoration as near completion as was within the scope of its authority, and the nation was encouraged by the prospect of an early and satisfactory adjustment of all its difficulties. Congress, however, intervened, and, refusing to perfect the work so nearly consummated, declined to admit members from the unrepresented States, adopted a series of measures which arrested the progress of restoration, frustrated all that had been so successfully accomplished, and, after three years of agitation and strife, has left the country further from the attainment of union and fraternal feeling than at the inception of the Congressional plan of reconstruction. It needs no argument to show that legislation which has produced such baneful consequences should be abrogated, or else made to conform to the genuine principles of republican government.[16]

Three years before, in the judgment of the editor of the *Tribune*, Andrew Johnson was "a pure, good man" whose first annual message to Congress was a state paper of "signal ability" which contained much which would be "generally and justly approved" and little that should "provoke dissent." In these three years Johnson's fundamental policies and convictions had not changed an iota. What had happened to Horace Greeley? Here is his verdict on the last annual message: "This message is his worst, and fortunately his last, insult to the American people. As he goes out of the White House he stops to shake his fist at the Capitol. . . . Truth and falsehood are so unnaturally mingled that we really long for one, good, honest, unqualified lie that may be knocked in the head without hurting anything else."[17]

And still obsessed, the day after General Grant was inaugurated, Greeley took this venomous parting shot at Johnson:

It is a blessed consolation that Andrew Johnson has ceased to disgrace his country in a public station. He will continue to be the low, unscrupulous demagogue he has already so often proved himself, and he is still capable of considerable mischief. His power for evil can never again be a tittle of what it was. For three years he has done all that one bad man could do to keep the country in turmoil, to strengthen the spirit of Rebellion, and to excite a war of races. The most he can do henceforth is to defend as a local demagogue the wrongs which a national calamity so long enabled him to enact as President. Let us thank God that we are so easily and so happily rid of him, and that we can turn our faces with hope and trust to the glad auspices of future harmony and prosperity afforded by the accession and the inaugural of President Grant. . . .

---

[16] Richardson, *op. cit.*, VI, 672–91.
[17] *Tribune*, December 10, 1868.

What we hope to receive from Gen. Grant is a splendid administration. We have had so many picayune Presidents that it is refreshing to find a man entering into the Chief Magistracy with something more than a mere caucus and convention record. He takes into his new place a broader renown than any President since Washington.[18]

It is the unquestioned verdict of history that the "splendid administration" was never realized. Greeley started out with Grant hopefully and abandoned him reluctantly. While not concurring in every recommendation in Grant's first annual message to Congress, he regarded it as one of "the wisest and most judicious Messages ever transmitted to Congress."[19] The second annual message would "be read with hearty approval by the great majority of his countrymen and with interest and pride by them all." The climax of his support of Grant was reached at this time in the glowing declaration: "He is Abraham Lincoln's lineal successor, and the popular heart beats in unison with his aspirations and his efforts."[20] The cooling-off process had arrived when Greeley found in the third annual message "much more to approve than to condemn."[21] A few weeks later he was writing his old friend, Beman Brockway: "I have had as much of Grant as I can endure."[22]

Events now moved rapidly and surprisingly. The revolt against Grant was fostered by the prominent journalists of the country. Under their leadership the "Liberal Republican" party met in a convention at Cincinnati on May 1, 1872, and nominated Greeley for President and B. Gratz Brown for Vice-President. The distinguished editors who engineered the convention did not really want Greeley as their candidate, but they were out-maneuvered by Whitelaw Reid, Greeley's principal editorial assistant. The platform was largely anti-Grant, and the issue in Greeley's view was substantially "the question of honest men against thieves."[23] The Democratic National Convention, which assembled at Baltimore on July 9, accepted the Cincinnati candidates and endorsed the platform. In the meantime, the Republican National Convention, assembled at Philadelphia on June 5, had renominated Grant for President by acclamation and had substituted Henry Wilson of Massachusetts for Schuyler Colfax as the candidate for Vice-

---

[18] *Ibid.*, March 5, 1869.
[19] *Ibid.*, December 7, 1869.
[20] *Ibid.*, December 6, 1870.
[21] *Ibid.*, December 5, 1871.
[22] Stoddard, *op. cit.*, pp. 302–03.
[23] *Ibid.*, p. 304.

President. Thus in the ensuing campaign, Greeley, who had never before strayed from the Whig and Republican parties, carried the banner for the Democrats, and Grant, a Democrat, was the Republican candidate.

All accounts agree that Greeley made a valiant effort. During August and September he spoke in New England and traveled to the Middle West. He did not question Grant's integrity or make any personal attack upon him, but he did not hesitate to characterize the "thieves" who surrounded him. At Indianapolis, Greeley was introduced by Senator Daniel W. Voorhees, who did not at first favor his candidacy, but who voiced the prevailing judgment, which has endured: "The public utterances of Mr. Greeley in his letters, and in his speeches, lift him up to the highest plane of statesmanship. I hazard nothing in saying that for elevation of thought, for purity of sentiment, for broad philanthropy, for general benevolence, and for Christian statesmanship, the speeches of Mr. Greeley, delivered in his present western tour, have no parallel in American history, and but few in the better portions of the history of the ancients."[24]

Mr. Greeley was obliged to retire from active participation in the latter part of the campaign because of the illness of Mrs. Greeley and her death on October 30. His extraordinary labors and this great affliction left him a broken man. He anticipated the result of the election. Grant's popular vote was 3,597,132, with 286 electoral votes; Greeley's popular vote was 2,834,125, with 66 electoral votes which were never to be cast. On May 15, 1872, after his nomination by the Liberal Republicans, Greeley had published "A Card" in the *Tribune* announcing withdrawal from the conduct of the paper until further notice. On November 7, two days after the election, a similar "Card" announced his resumption of the editorship of the *Tribune*, and his purpose to make the paper "a thoroughly independent journal." The old spirit flared up, however, with the editor's statement: "If he can hereafter say anything that will tend to heartily unite the whole American people on the broad platform of Universal Amnesty and Impartial Suffrage, he will gladly do so." Twenty-two days later, in the same column in which his leaders had appeared for thirty-one years, an editorial headed HORACE GREELEY began with the words: "The melancholy announcement of the death of the editor of *The Tribune*, though for a few days his family and intimate friends have admitted to themselves its possibility, falls

[24] L. D. Ingersoll, *The Life and Times of Horace Greeley*, p. 567.

upon us with all the shock of a sudden calamity." Toward evening on November 29, 1872, the end came.[25]

Greeley's body lay in state in the City Hall, and the funeral services were held on December 4 in the Church of the Divine Paternity attended by the President, the Vice-President, the Chief Justice of the United States, and many other citizens distinguished in public life. The *Tribune* published a "Memorial" of 268 pages including tributes from the pulpit and the press and many resolutions of official bodies and private agencies. Forty-three years after Greeley's death the Division of Archives and History of the University of the State of New York, under a special legislative act, published a memorial of 263 pages to Horace Greeley, including the proceedings at the unveiling of his statue at Chappaqua, New York, on February 3, 1914, and reports of other Greeley celebrations related to the centennial of his birth on February 3, 1911.

A biography of Horace Greeley—*Printer-Editor-Crusader,* by Henry Luther Stoddard—published in 1946, concludes with a quotation from Bayard Taylor's tribute to Greeley at the unveiling of the statue at his grave in Greenwood Cemetery, in which this sentence occurs: "A life like his cannot be lost; something of him has been absorbed in other lives."

A volume on Horace Greeley and the Republican party, by Jeter A. Isely, published in 1947, concludes with the sentence: "Much of his career had been spent in vain."

Perhaps the true appraisal lies somewhere between these differing views. The most effective period of his career was the quarter century from April 10, 1841, the day the *Tribune* was born, and December 20, 1865, the day he announced "The Death of Slavery." During these years, he had often pursued tangents in vain; he had often been in despair; he had often dabbled where he did not belong; but in all this time he kept almost daily before his nation of readers his genuine love of the Union and his never-ending abhorrence of slavery. He always printed the word with a capital letter, not to honor it, but to hold it up to the light. Something of Horace Greeley was absorbed in other lives in that long period of devoted effort; and something of him is still vital in the lives of men today.

With the enactment of the Thirteenth Amendment to the Constitution, providing that "Neither slavery nor involuntary servitude, except

---

[25] *Tribune,* November 30, 1872.

as a punishment for crime whereof the party shall have been duly convicted, shall exist within the United States, or any place subject to their jurisdiction," Greeley might well have laid down his editorial pen. At the age of fifty-four he was an old man. He did not add to his fame after his great task was finished. There were no worlds left for this warrior to conquer after slavery was abolished.

The opportunity for leadership in the dreadful days of reconstruction was open to him: No other editor of his time had the acid words and the indelible ink with which to portray the diabolic manipulations of the radicals in the impeachment proceedings. No other editor could have brought to the bar of public opinion with more clarity and vehemence the narrow, petty, bitter, well-nigh treasonable conduct of Thaddeus Stevens, Ben Wade, Zachariah Chandler, and their ilk. No other editor could have pilloried with equal scorn the abuses of the carpetbaggers and the scalawags. That he did not rise to this challenge, that he was unequal to a second great crusade, and that he allowed himself to be lured into a hopeless effort to gain the highest office in the land, hardly warrants the intimation that much of his life was spent in vain.

Any appraisal of Greeley's enduring fame must take into account his colossal egoism. He believed profoundly in the soundness and wisdom of his own day-by-day editorial utterances. Not only that, he was tremendously eager to bend others to his way of thinking and was subconsciously irritated by those he could not convince or lead. Nor did he lack the courage to put his personal convictions into action, no matter how unpopular. This disposition to carry out his own will in the face of public condemnation is illustrated in his decision to sign the bail bond of Jefferson Davis on May 13, 1867. This action caused a great furore and provoked embarrassment to the *Tribune*, but Greeley went quietly on his way and never regretted his decision. It was this exalted belief in himself that often made him critical of others. He condemned often and praised rarely. Henry Clay was the only statesman who ever gained his unqualified approval. "I have admired and trusted many statesmen," he said: "I profoundly loved Henry Clay."[26]

At the age of twenty-one, when Greeley was able to cast his first presidential vote, for Clay as against Jackson, he was already beginning to chalk down his list of *picayune* Presidents; and thereafter he recorded himself unmistakably.

---

[26] Horace Greeley, *Recollections of a Busy Life*, p. 166.

Van Buren was "an adroit and subtle, rather than a great man."[27]

William Henry Harrison "was never a great man, but he had good sense, was moderate in his views, and tolerant of adverse convictions."[28]

Tyler was "never trusted" and was retired to "fitting obscurity."[29] No President could "hardly by possibility do worse."[30]

Polk "was a man of moderate ability, faultless private character, and undeviating Jacksonism,"[31] but he was "a small man for President."[32]

Taylor "was a wise and good ruler, if not even a great one."[33]

Fillmore grossly misapprehended "the grounds and motives of the Republican movement."[34]

Pierce's Administration was characterized by "imbecility"; its "lack of principle" was "far excelled by its lack of sense," resulting in "acts of wickedness and folly"; and the "executive career" of Pierce was "a record of shame and ridicule to such a degree that the Presidency of John Tyler shines with glory in comparison."[35]

Buchanan was characterized as an "old rat" and a "hoary-headed libeler."[36]

Lincoln, Greeley frequently insisted, was not what he deemed a great man. "He is not infallible—not a genius—not one of those rare great men who mold their age into the similitude of their own high character, massive abilities and lofty aims."[37] Some idea of Greeley's personal definition of greatness may be had from the fact that shortly after he made the above characterization of Lincoln, he declared that "Mr. Chase is one of the very few great men left in public life."[38]

Johnson made "the American name a scandal among the nations,"[39] and he was a "low, unscrupulous demagogue."[40]

Grant's first Administration, in the language of the address and platform adopted at Cincinnati by the Liberal Republicans on May 3, 1872, which Greeley had accepted and endorsed, was "guilty of wanton disre-

---

[27] *Ibid.*, p. 113.
[28] *Ibid.*, p. 135.
[29] *Ibid.*, p. 159.
[30] *Tribune*, March 4, 1845.
[31] Greeley, *op. cit.*, p. 161.
[32] *Tribune*, March 4, 1845.
[33] Greeley, *op. cit.*, p. 215.
[34] Horace Greeley, *The American Conflict*, I, 248.
[35] *Tribune*, August 5, 1854.
[36] *Ibid.*, September 20, 1856.
[37] *Ibid.*, February 23, 1864.
[38] *Ibid.*, July 1, 1864.
[39] *Ibid.*, May 11, 1868.
[40] *Ibid.*, March 5, 1869.

gard of the laws of the land"; and the President himself had "openly used the powers and opportunities of his high office for the promotion of personal ends"; had "kept notoriously corrupt and unworthy men in places of power"; and had "shown himself deplorably unequal to the tasks imposed upon him by the necessities of the country, and culpably careless of the responsibilities of his high office."[41]

Knowing Greeley's extraordinary confidence in his own views, one can hardly avoid reading between the lines in hundreds of his editorials his complacent belief that, given the opportunity, he could himself have handled the particular undertaking he criticized better than the picayune types the people had chosen to do it. Whitelaw Reid insisted that Greeley's alleged "itch for office" was a passion for recognition.[42] That may be; but there can be little doubt that he often visualized himself in the place of the public official he dragooned. As late as December, 1868, he blithely ranked himself with Webster, Chase, and Cass. The difference between him and them, he said, was that they wanted throughout their lives to be President, and he did not.[43] And yet the poor "old" man eagerly accepted the nomination in 1872, no doubt honestly convinced that he was the best qualified man in the nation to fill the high office of President. He was born to be a journalist, and his fame in the newspaper world will endure. Posterity is kind to his memory and, as the years go on, pauses more and more to reflect upon the possible truth in his final appraisal of the man with whom he hoped "to be always on terms of civility but not of cordiality."

There are those who say that Mr. Lincoln was fortunate in his death as in his life: I judge otherwise. I hold him most inapt for the leadership of a people involved in desperate, agonizing war; while I deem few men better fitted to guide a nation's destinies in time of peace. Especially do I deem him eminently fitted to soothe, to heal, and to reunite in bonds of true fraternal affection a people just lapsing into peace after years of distracting, devastating internal strife. His true career was just opening when an assassin's bullet quenched his light of life.[44]

Something of Abraham Lincoln and of Horace Greeley has been absorbed in other lives. Perhaps, with reverence for the memory of these two great Americans, it is not far from the truth to say: Lincoln died too soon, Greeley lived too long.

---

[41] Ingersoll, *op. cit.*, pp. 540–50.
[42] *Century Magazine*, January, 1913.
[43] Stoddard, *op. cit.*, p. 292.
[44] Greeley, *Recollections*, p. 404.

BIBLIOGRAPHY

ANGLE, PAUL M. *Lincoln Day by Day, 1854–1861.* (Springfield: The Abraham Lincoln Association, 1933.)

———. *New Letters and Papers of Lincoln.* (Boston: Houghton Mifflin Co., 1930.)

BANCROFT, FREDERIC. *The Life of William H. Seward.* (New York: Harper and Brothers, 1900.)

BARINGER, WILLIAM E. *Lincoln's Rise to Power.* (Boston: Little, Brown & Co., 1937.)

———. *A House Dividing.* (Springfield: The Abraham Lincoln Association, 1945.)

BARTON, WILLIAM E. *The Life of Abraham Lincoln.* 2 vols. (Indianapolis: The Bobbs-Merrill Co., 1925.)

———. *The Lineage of Lincoln.* (Indianapolis: The Bobbs-Merrill Co., 1929.)

BASLER, ROY P., ed. *Abraham Lincoln, His Speeches and Writings.* (Cleveland: World Publishing Co., 1946.)

———. *The Lincoln Legend, a Study in Changing Conceptions.* (Boston: Houghton Mifflin Co., 1935.)

BEALE, HOWARD K., ed. *The Diary of Edward Bates, 1859–1866.* (Washington: U. S. Government Printing Office, 1933.)

BENTON, JOEL, ed. *Greeley on Lincoln.* . . . (New York: Baker and Taylor Co., 1893.)

BEVERIDGE, ALBERT J. *Abraham Lincoln, 1809–1858.* 2 vols. (Boston: Houghton Mifflin Co., 1928.)

Biographical Directory of the American Congress. (Washington: U. S. Government Printing Office, 1950.)

BOWERS, CLAUDE G. *The Tragic Era: The Revolution after Lincoln.* (Boston: Houghton Mifflin Co., 1929.)

BROCKWAY, BEMAN. *Fifty Years in Journalism.* . . . (Watertown, N.Y.: Daily Times Printing & Publishing House, 1891.)

BROWN, FRANCIS. *Raymond of The Times.* (New York: W. W. Norton & Company, Inc., 1951.)

BULLARD, F. LAURISTON. "Lincoln's 'Conquest' of New England," *The Abraham Lincoln Quarterly.*

CARMAN, HARRY J. and REINHARD H. LUTHIN. *Lincoln and the Patronage.* (New York: Columbia University Press, 1943.)

CARPENTER, FRANCIS BICKNELL. *Inner Life of Abraham Lincoln.* (New York: Hurd & Houghton, 1870.)

———. *Six Months at the White House with Abraham Lincoln.* (New York: Hurd & Houghton, 1866.)

CHASE, SALMON PORTLAND. *Diary and Correspondence of Salmon P. Chase.* (Washington: American Historical Association, 1903.)

COMMAGER, HENRY STEELE. *The Blue and the Gray.* 2 vols. (Indianapolis: The Bobbs-Merrill Co., 1950.)

CONWAY, MONCURE DANIEL. *Memories and Experiences of Moncure Daniel Conway.* (Boston: Houghton Mifflin Co., 1904.)

CRANDALL, ANDREW WALLACE. *The Early History of the Republican Party, 1854–1856.* (Boston: R. G. Badger, 1930.)

CRAVEN, AVERY O. *The Coming of the Civil War.* (New York: Charles Scribner's Sons, 1942.)

CRIPPEN, LEE F. *Simon Cameron—Ante-Bellum Years.* (Oxford, Ohio: The Mississippi Valley Press, 1942.)

CURTIS, FRANCIS. *The Republican Party, a History . . . 1854–1904.* (New York: G. P. Putnam's Sons, 1904.)

DENNETT, TYLER. *John Hay—From Poetry to Politics.* (New York: Dodd, Mead and Co., Inc., 1933.)

———. *Lincoln and the Civil War—In the Diaries and Letters of John Hay.* (New York: Dodd, Mead and Co., Inc., 1939.)

DONALD, DAVID. *Lincoln's Herndon: A Biography.* (New York: Alfred A. Knopf, Inc., 1948.)

FAHRNEY, RALPH RAY. *Horace Greeley and the Tribune in the Civil War.* (Cedar Rapids, Iowa: The Torch Press, 1936.)

FERGUS, ROBERT, comp. *Chicago River-and-Harbor Convention. . . .* Fergus' Historical Series, Number Eighteen. (Chicago: Fergus Printing Co., 1882.)

FREEMAN, DOUGLAS SOUTHALL. *R. E. Lee.* 4 vols. (New York: Charles Scribner's Sons, 1934–35.)

GILMORE, JAMES R. (Edmund Kirke). *Personal Recollections of Abraham Lincoln and the Civil War.* (Boston: L. C. Page & Co., 1898.)

GRANT, ULYSSES SIMPSON. *Personal Memoirs of U. S. Grant.* 2 vols. (New York: C. L. Webster & Co., 1885–86.)

GREELEY, GEORGE HIRAM. *Genealogy of the Greely-Greeley Family.* (Boston: privately printed by F. Wood, 1905.)

GREELEY, HORACE. *The American Conflict, a History . . . 1860–'65. . . .* 2 vols. (Hartford: O. D. Case & Co., 1864–66.)

———. *Recollections of a Busy Life. . . .* (New York: J. B. Ford & Co., 1868.)

——— and JOHN F. CLEVELAND, eds. *A Political Text-book for 1860. . . .* (New York: Tribune Association, 1860.)

GUROWSKI, ADAM. *Diary.* 3 vols. (Boston: Lee & Shepard, 1862–66.)

HALE, EDWARD EVERETT. *James Russell Lowell and His Friends.* (Boston: Houghton Mifflin Co., 1899.)

HALE, WILLIAM HARLAN. *Horace Greeley, Voice of the People.* (New York: Harper and Brothers, 1950.)

HALSTEAD, MURAT. *Caucuses of 1860.* . . . (Columbus: Follett, Foster & Co., 1860.)

HARPER, ROBERT S. *Lincoln and the Press.* (New York: McGraw-Hill Book Co., Inc., 1951.)

HARRIS, WILMER C. *Public Life of Zachariah Chandler, 1851–1875.* (Lansing, Mich.: Historical Commission, 1917.)

HART, ALBERT BUSHNELL. *Salmon Portland Chase.* (Boston: Houghton Mifflin Co., 1899.)

HELM, KATHERINE. *The True Story of Mary, Wife of Lincoln.* . . . (New York: Harper and Brothers, 1928.)

HENDRICK, BURTON J. *Lincoln's War Cabinet.* (Boston: Little, Brown & Co., 1946.)

HERNDON, WILLIAM H. and JESSE WILLIAM WEIK. *The Life of Lincoln.* 3 vols. (Chicago: Belford Clarke and Co., 1890.)

HERTZ, EMANUEL. *Abraham Lincoln—A New Portrait.* 2 vols. (New York: Horace Liveright, Inc., 1931.)

———. *The Hidden Lincoln.* (New York: Viking Press, Inc., 1938.)

HESSELTINE, WILLIAM B. *Lincoln and the War Governors.* (New York: Alfred A. Knopf, Inc., 1948.)

HILL, FREDERICK TREVOR. *Lincoln, the Lawyer.* (New York: The Century Co., 1906.)

HITCHCOCK, CAROLINE HANKS. *Nancy Hanks, The Story of Abraham Lincoln's Mother.* (New York: Doubleday & McClure Co., 1899.)

HOLMES, FRED L. *Abraham Lincoln Traveled This Way.* (Boston: L. C. Page and Co., 1930.)

HORNER, HARLAN HOYT. *The Growth of Lincoln's Faith.* (New York: The Abingdon Press, 1939.)

HOUSER, MARTIN LUTHER. *Abraham Lincoln, Student—His Books.* (Peoria, Ill.: E. J. Jacob, 1932.)

KIRKLAND, EDWARD CHASE. *The Peacemakers of 1864.* (New York: The Macmillan Co., 1927.)

INGERSOLL, L. D. *The Life and Times of Horace Greeley.* (Chicago: Union Publishing Co.; San Francisco: A. L. Bancroft & Co., 1873.)

ISELY, JETER A. *Horace Greeley and the Republican Party.* (Princeton: Princeton University Press, 1947.)

JOHNSON, CHARLES W., comp. *Proceedings of the First Three Republican National Conventions of 1856, 1860 and 1864.* (Minneapolis, Minn.: Harrison and Smith, 1893.)

LEA, HENRY and J. R. HUTCHINSON. *The Ancestry of Abraham Lincoln.* (Boston: Houghton Mifflin Co., 1909.)

LINCOLN, WALDO. *History of the Lincoln Family . . . 1637–1920. . . .* (Worcester, Mass.: Commonwealth Press, 1923.)

LUTHIN, REINHARD H. *The First Lincoln Campaign.* (Cambridge: Harvard University Press, 1944.)

MACARTNEY, CLARENCE EDWARD. *Lincoln and His Cabinet.* (New York: Charles Scribner's Sons, 1931.)

MC CLURE, A. K. *Lincoln and Men of War-Times. . . .* (Philadelphia: The Times Publishing Co., 1892.)

MC INTYRE, DUNCAN T. "Lincoln and the Matson Slave Case," *Illinois Law Review.*

MEARNS, DAVID C., ed. *The Abraham Lincoln Papers.* 2 vols. (Garden City, N.Y.: Doubleday and Co., 1948.)

MENEELY, A. HOWARD. *The War Department—1861. . . .* (New York: Columbia University Press, 1928.)

MERRIAM, GEORGE S. *The Life and Times of Samuel Bowles.* 2 vols. (New York: The Century Co., 1885.)

MYERS, WILLIAM STARR. *The Republican Party—A History.* (New York: The Century Co., 1928.)

NEVINS, ALLAN. *The Emergence of Lincoln.* 2 vols. (New York: Charles Scribner's Sons, 1950.)

———. *Frémont, Pathmarker of the West.* (New York: Appleton-Century-Crofts, Inc., 1939.)

NEWTON, JOSEPH FORT. *Lincoln and Herndon.* (Cedar Rapids, Iowa: The Torch Press, 1910.)

NICOLAY, JOHN G. and JOHN HAY. *Abraham Lincoln—A History.* 10 vols. (New York: The Century Co., 1890.)

———, eds. *Complete Works of Abraham Lincoln.* 12 vols. (New York: Lamb Publishing Co., 1909.)

OLDROYD, OSBORN H. *Lincoln's Campaign or the Political Revolution of 1860.* (Chicago: Laird & Lee, 1896.)

PARTON, JAMES. *The Life of Horace Greeley, Editor of the New York Tribune.* (New York: Mason Brothers, 1855.)

PEASE, THEODORE CALVIN and JAMES G. RANDALL, eds. *The Diary of Orville Hickman Browning.* 2 vols. (Springfield: The Trustees of the Illinois State History Library, 1925.)

PERSINGER, CLARK E. *The Bargain of 1844.* (Washington: American Historical Association Annual Report, 1911.)

PIKE, JAMES S. *First Blows of the Civil War . . . 1850 to 1860. . . .* (New York: The American News Co., 1879.)

PILLSBURY, ALBERT E. *Address on the Centenary Observance of Horace Greeley at Amherst, New Hampshire, February 3, 1911.* (Boston: The Stetson Press, 1911.)

POTTER, DAVID M. *Lincoln and His Party in the Secession Crisis.* (New Haven: Yale University Press, 1942.)

PRATT, HARRY E. *The Personal Finances of Abraham Lincoln.* (New Brunswick: Rutgers University Press, 1943.)

PUTNAM, GEORGE HAVEN. *Abraham Lincoln, the Great Captain.* . . . (Oxford: Clarendon Press, 1928.)

———. *Abraham Lincoln, the People's Leader in the Struggle for National Existence.* (New York: G. P. Putnam's Sons, 1909.)

RANDALL, J. G. *Constitutional Problems Under Lincoln,* rev. ed. (Urbana: University of Illinois Press, 1951.)

———. *Lincoln the President: Springfield to Gettysburg.* 2 vols. (New York: Dodd, Mead & Co., Inc., 1945.)

RAYMOND, HENRY J. *History of the Administration of President Lincoln.* . . . (New York: J. C. Derby and N. C. Miller, 1864.)

———. *The Life and Public Services of Abraham Lincoln . . . together with His State Papers.* . . . (New York: J. C. Derby and N. C. Miller, 1865.)

RHODES, JAMES FORD. *History of the United States from the Compromise of 1850 to the end of the Roosevelt Administration.* 4 vols. (New York: The Macmillan Co., 1900–28.)

RICE, ALLEN THORNDIKE. *Reminiscences of Abraham Lincoln by Distinguished Men of His Time.* (New York: North American Publishing Co., 1886.)

RICHARDSON, JAMES DANIEL, ed. *Messages and Papers of the Presidents.* 10 vols. (Washington: U.S. Government Printing Office, 1898.)

RIDDLE, ALBERT G. *The Life, Character and Public Services of J. A. Garfield.* (Cleveland: W. W. Williams, 1883.)

RIDDLE, DONALD W. *Lincoln Runs for Congress.* (New Brunswick: Rutgers University Press, 1948.)

ROTHSCHILD, ALONZO. *Lincoln, Master of Men—A Study in Character.* (Boston: Houghton Mifflin Co., 1906.)

SANDBURG, CARL. *Abraham Lincoln: The Prairie Years.* 2 vols. (New York: Harcourt, Brace and Co., 1926.)

———. *Abraham Lincoln: The War Years.* 4 vols. (New York: Harcourt, Brace and Co., 1939.)

———. *Lincoln Collector: The Story of Oliver R. Barrett's Great Private Collection.* (New York: Harcourt, Brace and Co., 1949.)

SCHUCKERS, JACOB W. *The Life and Public Services of Salmon Portland Chase.* . . . (New York: D. Appleton and Co., 1874.)

SEITZ, DON C. *Horace Greeley, Founder of the New York Tribune.* (Indianapolis: The Bobbs-Merrill Co., 1926.)

———. *Lincoln the Politician—How the Rail-Splitter and Flatboatman*

Played the Great American Game. (New York: Coward-McCann, Inc., 1931.)

SEVERANCE, FRANK H. *Buffalo Historical Society Publications.* (Buffalo: Buffalo Historical Society, 1914.)

SHEAHAN, JAMES W. *The Life of Stephen A. Douglas.* (New York: Harper and Brothers, 1860.)

SHERWOOD, ROBERT EMMET. *Abe Lincoln in Illinois.* (New York: Charles Scribner's Sons, 1939.)

SNYDER, CHARLES E. "John Emerson, Owner of Dred Scott," *Annals of Iowa.* (Iowa City, 1938.)

SPARKS, EDWIN ERLE, ed. *Semi-centennial of the Lincoln-Douglas Debates in Illinois, 1858.* . . . (Springfield: Phillips Brothers, State Printers, 1908.)

SPEARS, ZAREL C. and ROBERT S. BARTON. *Berry and Lincoln—The Store That "Winked Out."* (Boston: Stratford House, Inc., 1947.)

STAMPP, KENNETH M. *And the War Came.* (Baton Rouge: Louisiana State University Press, 1950.)

STANTON, HENRY B. *Random Recollections.* (Johnstown, N.Y.: Blunck and Learning, 1885.)

STANWOOD, EDWARD. *A History of the Presidency.* (Boston: Houghton Mifflin Co., 1898.)

STARR, THOMAS I. *Lincoln's Kalamazoo Address.* (Detroit: Fine Book Co., 1941.)

STEPHENSON, NATHANIEL WRIGHT. *Lincoln, An Account of His Personal Life.* . . . (Indianapolis: The Bobbs-Merrill Co., 1922.)

STODDARD, HENRY LUTHER. *Horace Greeley, Printer, Editor, Crusader.* (New York: G. P. Putnam's Sons, 1946.)

TARBELL, IDA M. *The Life of Abraham Lincoln.* . . . 2 vols. (New York: McClure Phillips and Co., 1908.)

THAYER, WILLIAM ROSCOE. *The Life and Letters of John Hay.* (Boston: Houghton Mifflin Co., 1915.)

THOMAS, BENJAMIN P. *Lincoln, 1847–1853.* . . . (Springfield: The Abraham Lincoln Association, 1936.)

———. *Lincoln's New Salem.* (Springfield: The Abraham Lincoln Association, 1934.)

TRACY, GILBERT A. *Uncollected Letters of Abraham Lincoln.* (Boston: Houghton Mifflin Co., 1917.)

Transactions of McLean County Historical Society. (Bloomington, Ill.: McLean County Historical Society, 1900.)

TWEEDY, JOHN. *A History of the Republican National Conventions, from 1856 to 1908.* (Danbury, Conn.: J. Tweedy, 1910.)

VILLARD, OSWALD GARRISON. *John Brown 1800–1859, A Biography Fifty Years After.* (Boston: Houghton Mifflin Co., 1910.)

WAKEFIELD, SHERMAN DAY. *How Lincoln Became President.* . . . (New York: Wilson-Erickson, Inc., 1936.)

War Department. *War of the Rebellion, Official Records of the Union and Confederate Armies.* (Washington: U. S. Government Printing Office, 1895.)

WARREN, CHARLES. *The Supreme Court in United States History.* (Boston: Little, Brown & Co., 1922.)

WARREN, LOUIS AUSTIN. *Lincoln's Parentage and Childhood.* . . . (New York: The Century Co., 1926.)

WARREN, RAYMOND. *The Prairie President, Living Through the Years with Lincoln, 1809–1861.* (Chicago: The Reilly and Lee Co., 1930.)

WEED, HARRIET A. and THURLOW WEED BARNES, eds. *The Life of Thurlow Weed.* 2 vols. (Boston: Houghton Mifflin Co., 1883–84.)

WELLES, EDGAR T., ed. *The Diary of Gideon Welles.* 3 vols. (Boston: Houghton Mifflin Co., 1911.)

WHITE, HORACE. *The Life of Lyman Trumbull.* (Boston: Houghton Mifflin Co., 1913.)

———. "Abraham Lincoln in 1854," *Illinois State Historical Society.* (Springfield, 1908.)

WHITNEY, HENRY C. *Life on the Circuit with Lincoln.* (Boston: Estes and Lauriat, Publishers, 1892.)

WILLIAMS, KENNETH P. *Lincoln Finds a General.* 2 vols. (New York: The Macmillan Co., 1949.)

WILLIAMS, T. HARRY. *Lincoln and the Radicals.* (Madison: University of Wisconsin Press, 1941.)

WILSON, CHARLES R. "The Original Chase Organization Meeting and the Next Presidential Election," *Mississippi Valley Historical Review.* (Cedar Rapids, Iowa: Mississippi Valley Historical Association, 1936–37.)

WILSON, HENRY. *History of the Rise and Fall of the Slave Power in America.* 3 vols. (Boston: J. R. Osgood and Co., 1872–77.)

WILSON, RUFUS ROCKWELL. *Uncollected Works of Lincoln.* 2 vols. (Elmira, N.Y.: The Primavera Press, 1947–48.)

WOLDMAN, ALBERT A. *Lawyer Lincoln.* (Boston: Houghton Mifflin Co., 1936.)

WOODBURN, JAMES ALBERT. *American Politics. Political Parties and Party Problems in the United States.* . . . (New York: G. P. Putnam's Sons, 1903.)